RUSSIAN AND SOVIET VIEWS OF MODERN WESTERN ART

THE DOCUMENTS OF TWENTIETH-CENTURY ART

JACK FLAM, General Editor

ROBERT MOTHERWELL, Founding Editor

Volumes available from University of California Press:

Art as Art: The Selected Writings of Ad Reinhardt, edited by Barbara Rose

Memoirs of a Dada Drummer by Richard Huelsenbeck, edited by Hans J. Kleinschmidt

Matisse on Art, Revised Edition, edited by Jack Flam

German Expressionism: Documents from the End of the Wilhelmine Empire to the Rise of National Socialism, edited by Rose-Carol Washton Long

Robert Smithson: The Collected Writings, edited by Jack Flam

Flight Out of Time: A Dada Diary by Hugo Ball, edited by John Elderfield

Pop Art: A Critical History, edited by Steven Henry Madoff

The Collected Writings of Robert Motherwell, edited by Stephanie Terenzio

Conversations with Cézanne, edited by Michael Doran

Henry Moore: Writings and Conversations, edited by Alan Wilkinson

Primitivism and Twentieth-Century Art: A Documentary History, edited by Jack Flam with Miriam Deutch

The Cubist Painters, by Guillaume Apollinaire, translated, with commentary, by Peter Read

The Writings of Robert Motherwell, edited by Dore Ashton with Joan Banach

Russian and Soviet Views of Modern Western Art

1890s to Mid-1930s

EDITED BY **ILIA DORONTCHENKOV**

TRANSLATED BY **CHARLES ROUGLE**

CONSULTING EDITOR **NINA GURIANOVA**

UNIVERSITY OF CALIFORNIA PRESS

BERKELEY LOS ANGELES LONDON

University of California Press, one of the most distinguished university presses in the United States, enriches lives around the world by advancing scholarship in the humanities, social sciences, and natural sciences. Its activities are supported by the UC Press Foundation and by philanthropic contributions from individuals and institutions. For more information, visit www.ucpress.edu.

University of California Press
Berkeley and Los Angeles, California

University of California Press, Ltd.
London, England

Library of Congress Cataloging-in-Publication Data

Russian and Soviet views of modern Western art : 1890s to mid-1930s / edited by Ilia Dorontchenkov ; translated by Charles Rougle ; consulting editor, Nina Gurianova.
p. cm.—(The documents of twentieth-century art)
Includes bibliographical references and index.
ISBN 978-0-520-22103-1 (cloth : alk. paper)—ISBN 978-0-520-25372-8 (pbk. : alk. paper)
1. Art, Modern—19th century—Sources. 2. Art, Modern—20th century—Sources. 3. Art criticism—Russia—History—19th century. 4. Art criticism—Russia—History—20th century. 5. Art criticism—Soviet Union. I. Dorontchenkov, Ilia, 1961– II. Rougle, Charles, 1946– III. Gurianova, N. A.
N6447.R88 2009
709.04—dc22 2008054649

Manufactured in the United States of America

18 17 16 15 14 13 12 11 10 09
10 9 8 7 6 5 4 3 2 1

The paper used in this publication meets the minimum requirements of ANSI/NISO Z39.48-1992 (R 1997) *(Permanence of Paper).*

To my parents

CONTENTS

PREFACE AND ACKNOWLEDGMENTS

This book reconstructs the reception of modern Western art in Russia during a period of immense and varied development—ranging from the early initiatives of Sergei Diaghilev to the ascent of Socialist Realism. My goal is to make this diverse and complex discourse understandable to English-speaking readers by allowing its participants—artists, critics, and to some extent the general public—to speak in their own voices. As readers will see, this discourse was quite vivid and oftentimes extremely pointed, for it was animated by a major underlying issue: the cultural reidentification of Russia during the crucial period when it was trying to reinvent itself as a modern country.

My exploration of this subject began in the last years of the Soviet regime, when discussion of the Russian-Western cultural dialogue of the early twentieth century was unwanted, if not suspicious. The present book was conceived in the 1990s, just after political and cultural walls had broken down. And it is being published at a time when anti-Western sentiment has returned to Russian cultural life. The central issues—the application of Western models and criteria to Russian culture, and the fight against isolationism—remain topical, lively, and as controversial now as a century ago. The study of Russian culture oscillating between integration and autarchy gives me hope that eventually my country will turn its face to the world again and recall that openness to the great art of Europe once resulted in an enormous blossoming of Russian culture.

Naturally, it has been impossible to include in a single volume all of the intense discussions during the almost four decades covered here. In order to make this anthology coherent as well as representative, certain parameters were set. Little material was included on modern Western sculpture or pre–World War I German art, for example. To those who see Russian avant-garde art as central to Russian culture during the first third of the twentieth century, the abundance of writings by its opponents or the attention to figurative trends may be surprising. In making what were almost always difficult choices, I have tried to follow the actual discussions of the time rather than our own contemporary art historical conventions.

It took a long time to complete this book, and I would like to name the people whose help was most essential. First, as a Russian whose education was received under the Soviet system, I want to thank those who played important roles in my intellectual formation at a time when thinking independently was not so easy. I am greatly indebted to my teachers in the art history department of the Repin Institute of Painting, Sculpture, and Architecture in St. Petersburg, commonly known as the Academy of Fine Arts. Foremost among them is my Ph.D. dissertation advisor, Professor Vera Razdolskaia, to whom I owe much both for her contribution to my professional training and for her lessons of personal kindness and tolerance. I am happy and proud of the support and confidence offered by Professors Nikolai Nikulin and Cecillia Nesselstraus, who remain for me paragons of dignity and courage, even in very hard times. I was privileged to enjoy the favor and warmth of the late Irina Punina and Lidia Radlova, who helped me develop a deep feeling for the people and events I studied. And I want to commemorate other teachers who have passed away: Iurii Boitman, Irina Bozunova, Boris Fedorov, and Raisa Vlasova.

I also wish to pay tribute to Dmitrii Sarabianov, Grigorii Sternin, and Gleb Pospelov, art historians with whom I did not study but whose research illuminated the opportunity for scholarly freedom amid the Soviet scholasticism of late 1970s and 1980s. The pioneering works of John Bowlt were another source of inspiration to me, as were the lectures of Christopher Green and John House at the Courtauld Institute in 1994, which helped shape my approach to the way developments in Russian art paralleled those in the West.

I should mention here that the issues treated in this book have an intensely personal relevance. In 1983, when I was defending my M.A. thesis at the Repin Institute, my approach to the perception of contemporary Western art in post-1917 Russia, even though at the time necessarily prudent and limited, attracted the hostility of Vladimir Kemenov, vice president of the Soviet Academy of Fine Arts and chair of the examining committee. His biased criticism could have thwarted a young Soviet art historian, and I deeply appreciate the courage of the other members of the board, who insisted on giving my work a high grade. Recalling that attack, by a man who started his career in the early 1930s as one of Stalin's "red guards," underlines for me the unfinished nature of the debate on Russian-Western artistic relations and the need for the present book.

Many friends and colleagues have provided support for my project in various ways. Aimée Brown Price and Monroe Price in 1999 turned their hospitable New York home into a safe haven during a crucial period of my work on the manuscript—and of my life. I am also grateful for friendly help from Elena Basner, Anna Kaminskaia, Irina Karasik, Irina Khmelevskikh, Albert Kostenevich, and Margarita Pavlova in St. Petersburg; Svetlava Evdokimova, Abbott Gleason, Vladimir Golstein, and Alexander Levitsky in Providence, Rhode Island; Tania Chebotarev, Serge Hollerbach, Daniel Rishik, and Rose Carol Washton-Long in New York City; Gerda Panofsky-Soergel in Princeton, New Jersey; Jennifer Cahn and David C. Fisher in Brownsville, Texas; Carol Adlam in Exeter, England; and Galina Winhart in Bodenheim, Germany.

This book grew from research conducted in many libraries: the Russian National Library (formerly St. Petersburg Public Library) and its Manuscript Department; the Library of the Academy of Sciences; the Library and Manuscript Department of the Institute of Russian Literature (Pushkinskii Dom); the Anna Akhmatova Museum's library in St. Petersburg; the Russian State Library (former Lenin Library); the Russian Central Archive for Literature and Arts; the Manuscript Department of the Pushkin State Museum of Fine Arts, Moscow; the Rare Book and Manuscript Library, Butler Library, Columbia University; and the New York Public Library. But my very special thanks are addressed to the staff of the Research Library of the Russian Academy of Fine Arts in St. Petersburg, whose friendly help made my study fruitful and comfortable.

My research led to lecture courses given at the European University in St. Petersburg; Brown University in Providence, Rhode Island; and the *Hauptseminar* at the Kunsthistorisches Institut, Albert-Ludwigs Universität, Freiburg, Germany (I am especially grateful to the institute's director Hans Hubert), as well as guest lectures at Rutgers University and the Davis Center for Russian and Eurasian Studies at Harvard University.

I would also like to acknowledge the foundations that supported my other research projects, simultaneously providing opportunities to work on the issues presented in this book: the Getty Grant program, the Fulbright program, and the British Council.

Long ago Jack Flam suggested that I create this anthology, and since then his encouragement has remained indispensable and his friendship has become one of my greatest treasures. The book itself would not have come to life without the generosity and devotion to art history of my long-time friend Alla Rosenfeld, formerly the curator of the Russian and Soviet collections of the Jane Voorhees Zimmerli Art Museum at Rutgers University.

Declarations of gratitude and respect go to my consulting editor, Nina Gurianova, an outstanding connoisseur of Russian avant-garde art. Our years-long dialogue sometimes turned into keen argument, but her friendly fire made this book more distinct, wide-ranging, and dense. The remarkable talents of Charles Rougle, an experienced translator and scholar, made him the right man to translate the words of early twentieth-century Russians for a contemporary English-speaking audience. I am greatly indebted to his Herculean work on this book, and I particularly want to thank him for his patience and good temper throughout this long and sometimes arduous process.

I deeply appreciate the efforts of the University of California Press staff—first of all Stephanie Fay, for the enormous amount of thought and work she has invested in this project, and also Sue Heinemann and Marian Schwartz. The cooperation and input of Charlene Woodcock, the original sponsoring editor of this book, was very important during the early phase of my work on it, and I want once again to express my thanks for her professional engagement and human understanding.

Above all, I wish to thank my family—my wife, Elena Kozina, and my daughter, Masha—for truly happy years together and, especially, for the love and patience they showed as I wrestled with the intricacies of this anthology. I also want to thank my parents, Erna Gaintseva and Askold Dorontchenkov, for their love and care for me, and for their devotion to their own scholarly research, which made it possible for me to conceive and fulfill a project whose importance is deeply personal as well as scholarly. Nothing could be more natural than my dedicating this book to them.

INTRODUCTION

Although the precise date of any new period is difficult to fix, two events in 1898 marked a decisive breakthrough in the Russian art world's relationship to modern Western art. The first was public and programmatic. At the "Exhibition of Russian and Finnish Artists" organized by Sergei Diaghilev, the members of the future World of Art appeared for the first time as a group. At this 1898 exhibition, the new generation demonstrated its openness to foreign trends, thus announcing the emerging *Drang nach Westen,* or "drive toward the West," of Russian modernism. The second event was Moscow industrialist Sergei Shchukin's purchase of a landscape by Claude Monet from the French art dealer Paul Durand-Ruel. This painting marked the beginning of Shchukin's unique collection of French art, which by 1914 had grown to include radical works by Matisse and Picasso and allowed Moscow to see modern painting at the same time as Paris.

From the turn of the century, modern Western art was part of the Russian context, and the art of Russia, conscious now of belonging to Europe, redefined itself in terms of this interaction. The history of Russian art in the first third of the twentieth century cannot be discussed apart from its dialogue with the West. Yet at the same time, anti-modernist, anti-Western polemics persisted. Russian artistic life continued to be marked by various forms of isolationism. This book traces the course of this tense dialogue over some thirty-five years, as Russian artists discovered, understood, and assimilated Western art, only to abandon it with the establishment of Soviet ideological control and the triumph of state-sponsored Socialist Realism in the 1930s.

After liberalization of the regime in the mid-1950s, international contacts in art once again widened, but until the late 1980s, when the Soviet system underwent major changes and eventually collapsed in 1991, these relations were mostly state-controlled and highly selective and never led to achievements comparable to those of the first two decades of the century.

The Russian intellectual tradition directly links local questions about culture with general problems of national existence, such as the relationship to the European tradition and the "West" as a whole. Over the centuries, various models of this relationship developed and then were periodically resurrected. Even if these models did not directly influence art, they inevitably determined its ideological context. In the early twentieth century, the problem of "choosing" a model became acute: after the 1917 Revolution, Russia, which Peter the Great had propelled toward the European path of development, defined itself in contrast to the West.

In the Russian discourse, the "West" has been not so much a political or geographical reality ("there is no 'West' in the West," Andrei Belyi wrote)[1] as an abstraction—a

1. Andrei Belyi, "Vostok ili zapad?" (East or West?), *Epokha* (Epoch) (Moscow) 1 (1918): 165.

positive or negative model embodying "not-Russia." The recurring question of the "death of the West" and the exhaustion of Western culture was raised in order to compel Russia to choose a path for itself. Each significant artistic movement in Russia had to create or "invent" its own "West" in relation to which it defined its own positions. This applies to the "Men-of-the-Soil" isolationism of the late Wanderers [11, 12], the Europeanism of the World of Art and the modernists of the *Apollon* (Apollo) circle [8, 59], as well as the provocative "Slavophilism" of the avant-garde [56, 63, 67] and the "proletarian chauvinism" of Soviet critics after 1929 [117].[2]

Russian art in the 1890s was a complex amalgam of Pleinairism, variants of Impressionism, Symbolist trends, the search for a "national style," and the first attempts at creating a *Gesamtkuntswerk* in the theater. The most influential group in the latter half of the century was the Society of Traveling Art Exhibitions (the "Wanderers," or "Itinerants," founded in 1870), and by the turn of the century it was with this group that society at large associated its conception of the Russian tradition in painting. It was from the Wanderers that a number of tenacious stereotypes of the new art of the West derived. The Wanderers gave Russian art a social and moral mission that rejected "aestheticism" of any kind. Ivan Kramskoi, the "brain" of the movement, declared, "Ideas and ideas alone create technique and elevate it; if content is impoverished, the level of execution declines." He was forced to admit, however, that this axiom was directly contradicted by Western art: "But what does this mean? Why do things in the West seem to be inside out?"[3] Thus the Wanderers' key opposition of Truth and Beauty was projected onto the art of Europe. French art embodied an "artistic" principle that to them seemed inappropriate or at least untimely in Russia, masterly but hedonistic and often superficial.

The initial reactions to the Neo-Romantic, modernist trends that in Russia became known as "decadence" established a model that would be reproduced for decades. From the outset, "decadent" art was received as Western and as challenging the Russian national tradition. The "decadents" regarded art as a sphere independent of social interests, and they freed the artist from traditional moral obligations and fidelity to nature. They broke with the qualities that, through the literature of "critical realism" and the Wanderers' painting, had begun to be regarded as specific features of Russian art. The "native–alien" opposition in the debate over modernism corresponded to the "old–young" opposition. His opponents' "panicky fear of the West" and related dread "of everything young and talented" was the source of Sergei Diaghilev's disagreement with them.[4]

2. Numbers in brackets refer to selections in this volume.

3. *Perepiska I. N. Kramskogo* (Correspondence of I. N. Kramskoi), vol. 2 (Moscow, 1954), p. 296. See also David Jackson, "Western Art and Russian Ethics," *Russian Review* (July 1998): 394–409; Elizabeth Kridl Valkenier, "Opening Up to Europe. The *Peredvizhniki* and the *Miriskusniki* Respond to the West," in *Russian Art and the West: A Century of Dialogue in Painting, Architecture, and the Decorative Arts,* edited by Rosalind P. Blakesley and Susane Reid (De Kalb: Northern Illinois University Press, 2006), pp. 45–60.

4. S. D. [Sergei Diaghilev], "Po povodu dvukh akvarel'nykh vystavok," *Novosti i birzhevaia gazeta* (News and Stock Exchange Gazette), February 9, 1897.

Accusations of foreignness, often quite rude, were a commonplace in anti-modernist polemics [11, 12]. A similar pattern was being reproduced in the debate between "conservatives" and "modernists" in other Western countries as well, including France and Germany, but it is telling that *Ein Protest russischer Künstler* never did appear in Russia. Despite the topicality of national problems there, the artistic community did not launch chauvinistic public campaigns.

The new trends were ostracized not so much because they were nationally "alien" but because their appearance in Russia at that moment seemed inherently to lack the proper social foundation. Such reasoning dated back to 1893, when the influential Populist Nikolai Mikhailovskii criticized a programmatic article by Dmitrii Merezhkovskii, the future leader of the "decadents," saying that owing to the peculiarities of its social development Russia was a "young country" that lacked the soil for trends such as French Symbolism. He regarded Russian "decadence" as a mechanical, morally flawed borrowing of a Western fad: "I think that we are still too young to lose faith in life to such a degree and to fear life to such a degree."[5] The Populists' opponents, the Marxists, considered modernist and avant-garde trends alien, too, but on different grounds. The Marxists regarded the West's development as a model that Russian capitalism had not even begun to approach. Russian modernists were thus presented as being doubly deficient. Whereas Western decadents were simply a harmful but natural product of decaying capitalism, in Russia such phenomena were not only morbid but premature [46].

THE DISCOVERY OF EUROPE: THE ARTISTIC POLICIES OF THE WORLD OF ART

The decade between the first exhibitions of the World of Art (1898–99) and those of the *Golden Fleece* (1908–9) saw the emergence of a sense of participation in the artistic development of the West. The World of Art group applied European criteria to Russian art and overcame the isolationist tendency generated by its artistic inferiority complex.[6]

In 1897 Diaghilev organized in the Russian capital the largest exhibition of Scandinavian art in Europe, and the next year Russian and Finnish artists held a joint exhibition [10], so it was no coincidence that the World of Art began its crusade to the West with Scandinavia and Finland [9]. The Russians observed how the Scandinavians gained a recognition in Europe that overcame their isolation and archaic artistic language. The art of the Northern Europeans, a moderate variant of modernism, was an essential phase through which not only the Russian public but also the members of the early World of

5. Nikolai Mikhailovskii, "Russkoe otrazhenie frantsuzskogo simvolizma" (Russian Reflection of French Symbolism), *Russkoe bogatstvo* (Russian Riches) 2 (1893): 57, 68.

6. On the cultural context of early World of Art projects, see Janet Kennedy, "Pride and Prejudice: Serge Diaghilev, the Ballet Russes, and the French Public—Art, Culture, and National Identity," in *Fin-de-Siècle Europe*, edited by Michelle Facos and Sharon L. Hirsh (New York: Cambridge University Press, 2003), pp. 90–118.

Art themselves had to pass before they could accept Parisian art.[7] Munich played a similar role at the turn of the century. A significant number of Russian artists who wanted to inject new life into painting (Vasily Kandinsky, Aleksei von Jawlensky, Igor' Grabar', and others) preferred that center of Secessionism to the capital of France.

Russia began to "discover" contemporary Western art right when the *juste milieu* that had followed Impressionism was being reevaluated and the linear conception of the development of modern painting that began with Edouard Manet was taking shape.[8] Russian artists adopted Impressionist devices gradually and generally at second hand, and Impressionism was not recognized in Russia as the central phenomenon of the previous century until the 1900 "Centennial Exhibition" in Paris. Most of the World of Art artists remained beyond its direct influence, but their journal played an important role in Russian art's final reorientation toward Paris. Two essays by Julius Meier-Graefe in 1903 marked a milestone. The numerous articles by German and Austrian critics that the *World of Art* had carried before had dealt mainly with the social issues of the new art. But Meier-Graefe shifted the emphasis to contemporary artistic language, saying that French art of recent decades had established a connection between the classical periods and contemporaneity through its *painterly* evolution. This tradition was seen as the only one possible for the new art outside France as well: "It must be firmly established that Manet is painting, whereas Böcklin is something else again."[9] Beginning in the middle of the first decade, this principle influenced the development of progressive Russian trends more and more clearly, as newly "discovered" Scandinavian, Belgian, and English art receded to the periphery and an initially lively interest in German art diminished [13]. By contrast, French painting's extraordinary significance became increasingly apparent. The first reproductions from Sergei Shchukin's collection, including canvases by Gauguin, Van Gogh, and Cézanne—who were then unknown in Russia—appeared in March 1905 amid a political crisis that was rapidly growing into revolution. Igor' Grabar' nonetheless declared that their publication was "more important than all the recent political events."[10]

THE AVANT-GARDE'S TROJAN HORSE: *GOLDEN FLEECE*

Russia's assimilation of modern Western painting in the first decade of the twentieth century was connected with the activity of modernist associations close to Symbolism.

7. See T. D. Mukhina, *Russko-skandinavskie khodozhestvennye sviazi kontsa XIX—nachala XX v.* (Moscow, 1984), p. 63.

8. See also Robert Jensen, *Marketing Modernism in Fin-de-Siècle Europe* (Princeton: Princeton University Press, 1994), pp. 201 ff.

9. Julius Meier-Grefe, "Sovremennoe frantsuzskoe iskusstvo: Impressionizm v zhivopisi i skul'pture," *Mir iskusstva* 9 (1903): 88. Originally: "Impressionismus in Malerei und Sculptur," *Neue Freie Presse* (Vienna), January 19, 1903.

10. Letter to Mstislav Dobuzhinskii dated February 20, 1905, in Igor' Grabar', *Pis'ma: 1891–1917* (Moscow, 1974), p. 158.

These associations, however, also brought art that ultimately repudiated their own aesthetics. This was also the case with the *Golden Fleece* (Moscow, 1906–9), a journal that played an extraordinarily important role in the development of the visual arts as a vehicle for a group of young artists who extended the principles of Symbolism to painting (the "Blue Rose" exhibition in 1907; Pavel Kuznetsov, Nikolai Sapunov, Martiros Saryan, and others) and who combined the influence of modern French painting with an interest in archaic imagery. The *Golden Fleece* is connected with the birth of Primitivism and with the first significant works by Natal'ia Goncharova and Mikhail Larionov, who in January 1908 became a co-editor of the journal's art section.

With the *Golden Fleece,* French art's Post-Impressionist tendency became synonymous in Russia with "new painting" and "modern art." Seeing in Impressionism an expression of the mechanistic "reproductive" view of the world that was hateful to the Symbolists, the journal propagated the art of Gauguin, Van Gogh, and Matisse as an alternative. Russian (Maksimilian Voloshin) and French (Charles Morice, Maurice Denis) contributors tried to present Post-Impressionism as the prologue to "realistic Symbolism" and a new religious worldview: "the new currents in French art insistently call for poets to take the initiative. It is the Word that always must rule over chaos."[11] In 1908 and 1909, the *Golden Fleece* organized two exhibitions that included works by young Moscow painters as well as the most prominent Post-Impressionists and the Parisian avant-garde, thus ending the period of discovery and selection for those artists begun around 1898. The first exhibition introduced the Russian visitor to the Neo-Impressionists, Symbolists, Nabis, and Fauves and asserted the heritage of Gauguin, Van Gogh, and Cézanne as the basis of the new art. The second singled out Fauvism as the main trend in contemporary painting and demonstrated how it had been surpassed in Braque's early Cubist canvases. Together with Shchukin's collection, these exhibitions had an immediate impact on the evolution of the Russian avant-garde, especially by providing the impetus to Larionov's primitivism. Even before Sergei Shchukin's collection was opened to the public, however, observers began insisting on the young Moscow artists' dependence on "fashionable French" painters. Running through reviews was a motif that became central during the following decade: overdependence on the French. "It is a question here not of interest in the French modernists, but of imitating them, *counterfeiting* them."[12] But the artists themselves initially felt no need to conceal the kinship. The participants in the "Link" exhibition in November 1908, for example, openly declared that the influence of the new French painting was crucial to the rebirth of Russian art: "Russian Impressionists raised on Western models—those who quivered when they beheld Gauguin, Van Gogh, Cézanne . . . here is the hope for regenerated Russian painting!"[13]

11. Charles Morice, "Novye tendentsii frantsuzskogo iskusstva," *Zolotoe runo* 11–12 (1908): viii.

12. Sergei Glagol', "Moi dnevnik," *Stolichnaia molva* (January 2, 1909): 2.

13. Quoted in Iv[an] Chuzhanov, "Vystavka I. 'Zveno,'" *V mire iskusstv* (Kiev) 14–16 (1908): 20. John Bowlt ascribes this passage to David Burliuk. See *Russian Art of the Avant-Garde: Theory and Criticism, 1902–1934,* edited and translated by John E. Bowlt (New York: Viking, 1976), pp. 8–11.

A CONSTANT PRESENCE: WESTERN ART IN RUSSIA, 1910–17

By the 1910s the Russians had caught up with Western art and were engaged in a full-fledged dialogue with it. An interested if not very broad audience had taken shape. In one way or another, virtually all the professional critics touched upon the problem of contemporary foreign art, especially its relationship to Russian painting. The writings of Western artists were published widely, and the declarations of new movements and writings of their propagandists were translated.[14]

Exhibitions in the 1910s, however, remained rather conservative. Little in them could compare with the audacity of Diaghilev's 1898–99 projects or with the 1908 and 1909 exhibitions financed by Nikolai Riabushinskii, the patron of the *Golden Fleece.* The most significant foreign exhibition of this period, "One Hundred Years of French Painting" (St. Petersburg, 1912), included masterpieces of the Impressionists and Post-Impressionists such as Manet's *A Bar at the Folies-Bergère,* but there were no contemporary artists more prominent than Bonnard or Marquet, and no one to the left of Manguin.

The most recent Western art was shown mainly at the exhibitions of the avant-garde, such as the 1912 "Jack of Diamonds" exhibition (Braque, Gleizes, Delaunay, Kirchner, Marc, and others—a total of twenty-one artists from France and Germany). Canvases by Matisse and Le Fauconnier folded into the motley Izdebsky exhibition were capable of causing a stir [32–34], but their immediate impact on painting was hardly substantial. The Petersburg avant-garde's Union of Youth aspired to establish a museum of contemporary art that would feature works by Western artists, but the project failed owing to lack of funds. As for the radical Moscow exhibitions, these took place with no foreign contributions whatever. "Donkey's Tail" (1912) and "Target" (1913) were avowedly anti-Western, and after August 1914 joint projects became impossible. If the 1908 *Golden Fleece* exhibition was analogous in character to the first London "Post-Impressionist Exhibition" (1910), there was nothing in Russia resembling the "Second Post-Impressionist Exhibition" (London, 1912) or the Cologne "Sonderbund" (1912). By comparison, the 1913 exhibition of contemporary French painting in Moscow was far inferior, despite an impressive list of participants.[15] In contrast to Germany, for example, there was still no

14. Several publications of Van Gogh's correspondence and Gauguin's Tahitian essays were available to the Russian public, as were Emile Bernard's memoirs about Cézanne (1912), Paul Signac's "From Eugène Delacroix to Neo-Impressionism" (1913), and two translations of Gleizes and Metzinger's *Du Cubisme* (1913). Also worthy of mention are essays included in avant-garde collections: Henri Le Fauconnier's "Contemporary Receptivity and the Picture," and Apollinaire's "Fernand Léger," both in *Sbornik statei po iskusstvu* (Moscow: Obshchestvo khudozhnikov "Bubnovyi valet," 1913), pp. 41–45, 53; and Le Fauconnier's "Works of Art," in *Obshchestvo khudozhnikov "Soiuz molodezhi"* 2 (1912): 36–37. Manifestos of the Italian Futurists were also widely known. The "First Futurist Manifesto" was published as early as March 8, 1909, in the St. Petersburg newspaper *Vecher.* There were also several publications related to Marinetti's 1914 visit to Russia: Genrikh Tasteven, *Futurizm (Na puti k novomu simvolizmu)* (Moscow, 1914); *Manifesty italianskogo futurizma,* translated by V. Shershenevich (Moscow, 1914); and F. T. Marinetti, *Futurizm* (Moscow, 1914).

15. *Frantsuzskaia vystavka kartin "Sovremennoe iskusstvo,"* art exhibit, Moscow, 1913. Among the participants were Picasso, Léger, Metzinger, and Gris.

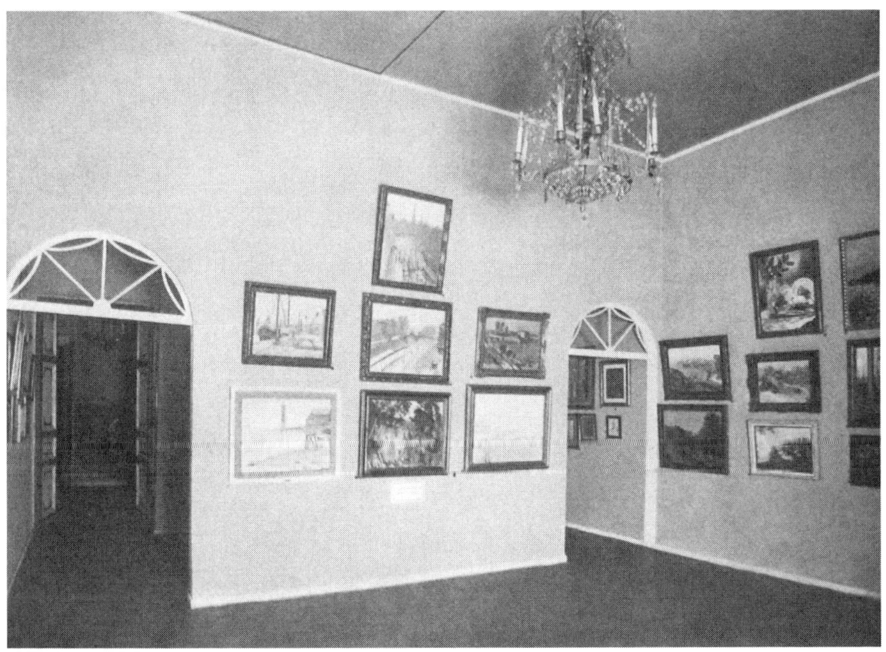

"One Hundred Years of French Painting" (exhibition), St. Petersburg, 1912. Published in *Vystavka "Sto let frantsuzskoi zhivopisi'* (St. Petersburg, 1912).

market for contemporary Western art; Shchukin and Morozov went directly to Paris to buy their Cézannes and Picassos. The Russian avant-garde had no Cassirer brothers, Herwarth Walden, or Roger Fry. The patrons of avant-garde groups were of relatively modest means, their propagandists were not very influential, and international contacts were maintained by the artists themselves rather than galleries.

Study in Paris and exposure to the painting "laboratories" were mandatory components in the avant-garde artist's training. In the years 1911–13, for example, Alexandra Exter, Aristarkh Lentulov, Liubov' Popova, and Nadezhda Udal'tsova [48] worked at the La Palette academy with Henri Le Fauconnier and Jean Metzinger, and in 1914 the impecunious Tatlin showed remarkable resourcefulness in getting to Paris to meet with Picasso.[16]

What determined Russian ideas about the new art more than anything else, however, were the Moscow collections of Sergei Shchukin and Ivan Morozov, which offered very different images of French art. Shchukin's collection, open to the general public beginning in 1909 (artists had been admitted earlier), presented its history as a rocket shedding its stages in flight: Monet was succeeded by Gauguin; after him came Matisse, and then Picasso [27, 28, 37, 40]. Although by the outbreak of World War I the Parisian avant-garde's latest experiments had taken up the central position in Shchukin's col-

16. See A. Strigalev, "O poezdke Tatlina v Berlin i Parizh," *Iskusstvo* 3 (1989): 29.

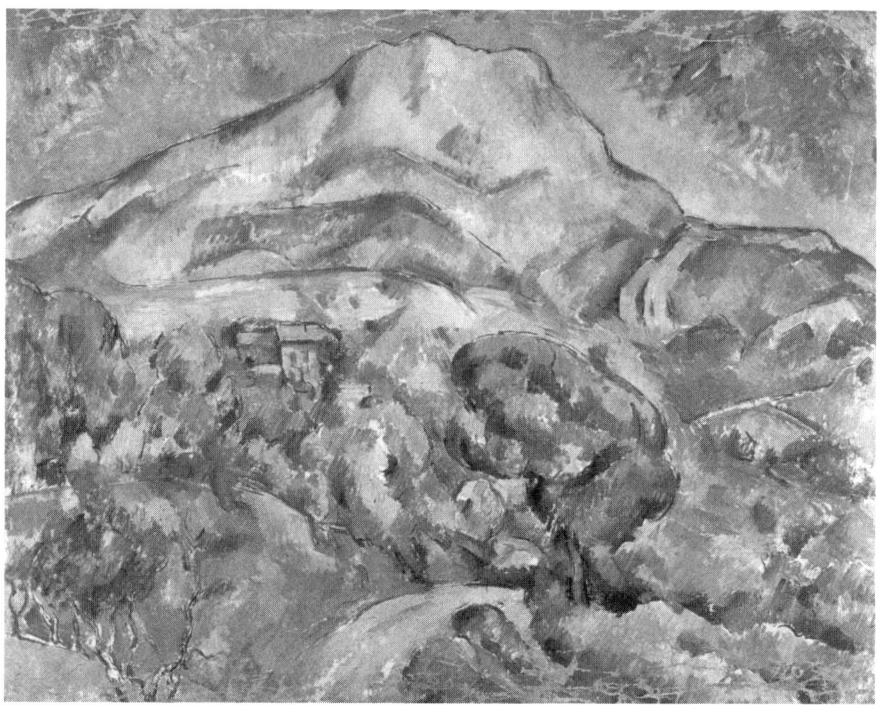

Paul Cézanne, *Mont Sainte-Victoire*, c. 1896–98, formerly in Morozov's collection, now in the Hermitage, St. Petersburg

lection, he was not collecting movements but artists: he did not acquire a single example of Futurism or virtually any "Salon" Cubism. Matisse and Picasso, on the other hand, were represented—unevenly, but more completely than ever before—by works from various stages in their evolution (see pp. 102, 113). Especially important was the way Shchukin's selection of pictures directly influenced viewers' perceptions [see 42, 43]. Visitors saw the rapid sweep in Picasso's work from figurative painting to Cubism as the model for contemporary art.

This image of French painting as a permanent revolution was balanced by Ivan Morozov's collection [30, 31], in which works by the same artists but in different proportions suggested a gradual, harmonious development. Morozov, moreover, limited access to his collection; as a result, it was Shchukin's radical version of French art that was in full public view.

The connections between Russian avant-garde works, the Shchukin and Morozov collections, and the exhibitions of the 1900s and 1910s have been analyzed more than once.[17] The many echoes of motifs and devices are obvious. This "conversation" often

17. See *Morozov, Shchukin, the Collectors, Monet to Picasso,* exhibition catalogue (Cologne, 1993), especially the articles by Marina Bessonova and Albert Kostenevich; Vladimir Poliakov, *Knigi russkogo kubofuturizma* (Moscow, 1998), pp. 23–26 ff.; A. G. Kostenivich, ed., *Pol' Sezann i russkii avangard nachala XX veka,* exhibition catalogue (St. Petersburg, 1998); among others.

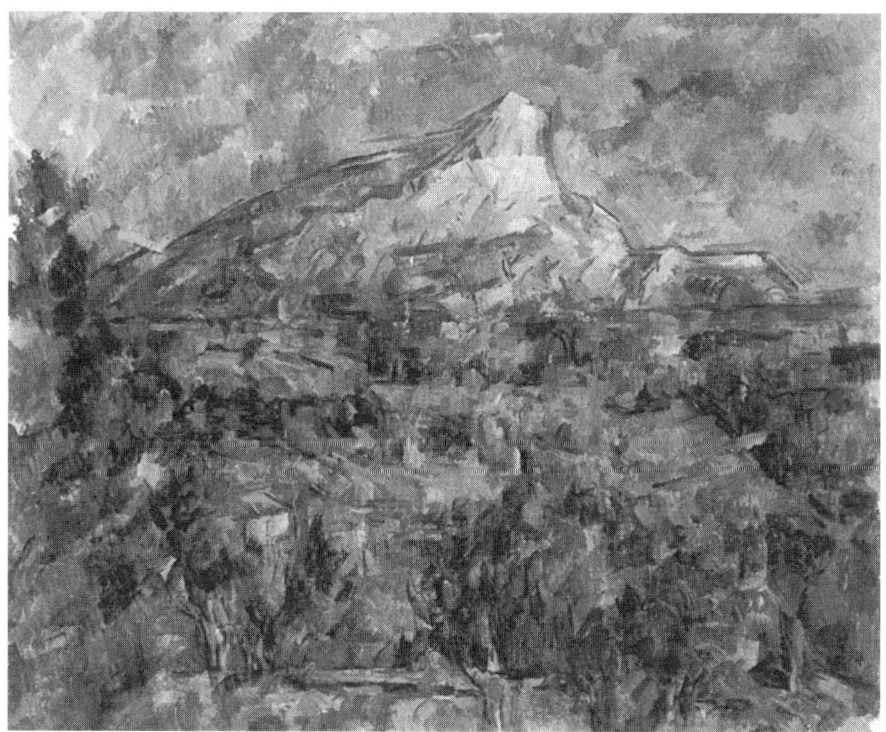

Paul Cézanne, *Mont Sainte-Victoire*, c. 1906, formerly in Shchukin's collection, now in the Pushkin Museum, Moscow

began with an imitation that was readily noted by the critics, but it was a necessary stage in the assimilation of a new poetics and soon developed into an ironic attitude toward the French models (see p. 10).

By the early 1910s the split between radicals and traditionalists within Russian modernism was complete. The fundamental conflict in Russian art was between modernists, who wanted to restructure a national tradition on a retrospective basis, and the avant-garde, which in just a few years had made the journey from Fauvism to nonobjective art. If at the turn of the century the World of Art had been the indisputable leader in the struggle, now its successors—grouped around the Petersburg journal *Apollon* (Apollo, 1909–17)—asserted their claim as the mainstream national school [59]. Whereas at the end of the nineteenth century the conservative "national" art of the Wanderers clashed with innovative "Western" painting, now both adversaries had a Western genealogy and acknowledged the authority of French painting. Interpreting Western art, therefore, became one of the central problems of Russian art. Monopolizing its interpretation meant in fact controlling the artistic discourse as a whole.

In the traditionalists' view, the Russian school could only achieve full stature by creating a "Grand Style"—heretofore absent in Russian art—which they believed was

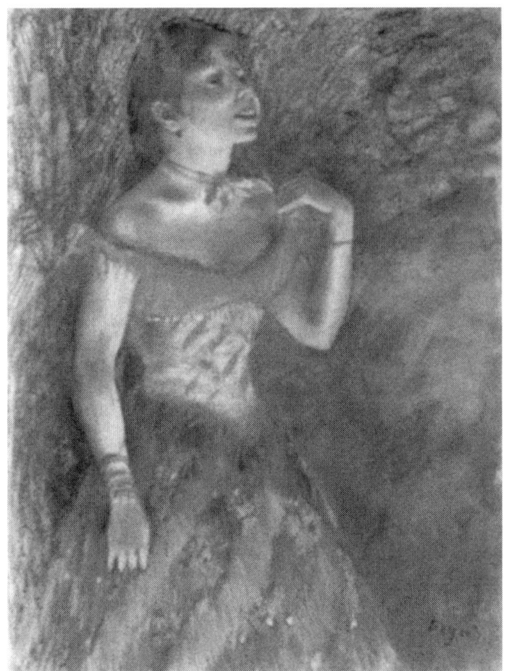

Edgar Degas, *The Singer in Green,* c. 1884, formerly in Dmitrii Riabushinskii's collection, now in the Metropolitan Museum of Art, New York. Compare the figure's gesture to that of Larionov's singer, almost thirty years later.

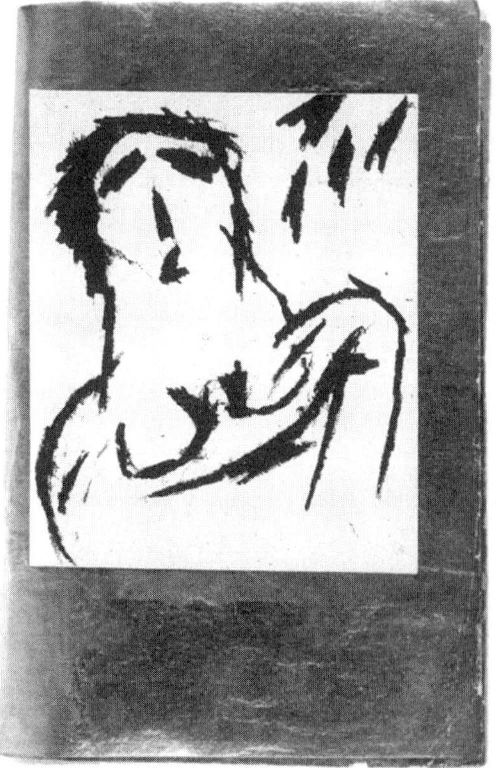

Mikhail Larionov, *Songstress,* lithograph for Aleksei Kruchenykh's *Pomada* (1913).

essential if the national artistic culture was to acquire integrity and stability. The performances connected with the Ballets Russes were the prototype. The guarantee for a strong and promising contemporary Russian art was continuity, a convincing example of which was to be had in contemporary French painting, in which the main road ran from Manet to the Nabis and Fauves by way of Gauguin and Cézanne. Influential modernist critics insisted on the equality of Impressionist and Post-Impressionist painting and the classical art of the museums, emphasizing its decorative qualities [60], which promised the restoration of an integral style. It was no coincidence that this circle, following Gustave Geffroy, should compare Cézanne to the old masters. For Benois and Muratov, such contemporary classics as Gauguin and Cézanne marked the conclusion of a great tradition rather than the beginning of a new art: "They are not models but a boundary; a door that has closed on what has gone before."[18]

The unusual language of "pure painting" used by the new French artists—even Matisse—seemed natural, for it followed from the logic of a consistent, successive development. From the point of view of the modernist *Apollon* circle, however, planting the new poetics in Russia bore with it dangerous and at the same time wretched fruit, since in their opinion a significant number of Russian innovators behaved like provincials with a weakness for sensational fads in their efforts to ape Paris [37, 59]. It was useless to try to become French but proper to express oneself like the French. Becoming European meant embodying the national by uniting modernity and tradition.

In the final analysis, the Russian traditionalist modernists did not achieve the *Apollon* critics' ideal. The traditionalist modernists themselves were little influenced by the new French painting, but in the 1910s the modernist interpretation of French art became predominant. The critics of the *Apollon* circle were trying to win over a public that was educated but still not well versed in the new painting, and they therefore brought out the traditional values in contemporary art (the "classical" quality in the new painting, the "museum," the "hero artist") [27, 30]. The enthusiastic discovery and defense of novelty was succeeded by the enthusiastic assertion of tradition.

IMPORTING REVOLUTION: THE AVANT-GARDE AND WESTERN ART

After 1910 the avant-garde, now united, ceased looking for a haven at exhibitions with programs alien to them. The first Jack of Diamonds exhibition, which opened in late 1910, marked the arrival of a new artistic force that openly declared its ties with archaic traditions, "low" folk art, and modern French painting. The event's manifesto was a huge self-portrait of Il'ia Mashkov with Petr Konchalovskii (see p. 72), both in the guise of carnival strongmen—a pugilistic blow aimed at the aesthetics of the World of Art and Symbolism. The weighty tomes on the piano made the canvas's message clear. Rearranged, the books' titles say, "Giotto and Cézanne are the Bible of Art."

18. A. Benois, "Sezann i Gogen," *Rech'*, January 27, 1912.

The unity attained in 1910 was short-lived, for the dynamic avant-garde was differentiating. Nonetheless, in both their heated internal polemics and their debates with the common enemy, the new Western art remained a critical problem. For the avant-garde, modern French art meant revolution, not tradition. It had generated pure painting, paving the way for a fundamentally new worldview. As if in response to Benois, Ol'ga Rozanova wrote, "But Van Gogh and Cézanne are only the estuaries of those broad and impetuous currents that are best-defined in our time: Futurism and Cubism."[19] The Futurists' task, however, was also to establish roots and continuity for the new art, but now in relation to nonclassical or non-European traditions [50, 61–64]. The radical trends had an ambivalent attitude toward Western art. The avant-garde not only propagated and analyzed foreign art but also demonstratively rejected it [56, 63, 65]. Significantly, they struggled less with France than with an abstract "West," to which they contrasted Russian artists assuming the role of champions of the "East" [63, 66]. The anti-Western attitude was directly tied to the Russian avant-garde's growing messianic spirit.

In this context, the problem of contemporary art's national roots remained significant to the avant-garde.[20] In about 1910 the Western avant-garde was exploring the possibilities of Primitivism as related to Fauvism and Expressionism. For Russian artists, however, the primitive was domestic, not African or Polynesian. Gauguin, known in Russia before the other Post-Impressionists (because his posthumous exhibition coincided with the Russian show at the 1906 "Salon d'Automne"), helped to foster a new way of seeing in painting.[21] At the same time, his art was perceived as a call not "away from" but rather "down into" the soil—to peasant art, the icon, shop signs, and the *lubok,* or folk woodcut.

The young Russians first greeted the art of Gauguin, Van Gogh, and Matisse more as liberation than as order or discipline—so acute was their need to break with the emasculated traditions of Realism and Art Nouveau. Without rejecting the traditional view of easel painting, in the latter half of the 1910s the Jack of Diamonds combined the Fauves' freedom of style with the disciplining influence of Cézanne. As for the radical avant-garde, it received a decisive boost when Cubism became known in Russia, liberating artists from the prison of nature, teaching them to view the picture as a self-sufficient structure, and paving the way for the new approaches partially based on the Cubist school—alogism (defined by Malevich as an artistic movement aimed at debunking conventional logic).

The avant-garde received most of its public attention through scandals, parody, and provocation, such as Mashkov's double-portrait and David Burliuk's lectures [47]. Many

19. Ol'ga Rozanova, "Osnovy Novogo Tvorchestva i prichiny ego neponimaniia," *"Soiuz Molodezhi" pri uchastii poetov "Gileia"* 3 (March 1913): 20–21.

20. These issues are thoroughly discussed in a broad cultural context with special emphasis on early modernist polemics and Russian–Western relations in Jane Ashton Sharp, *Russian Modernism Between East and West: Natal'ia Goncharova and the Moscow Avant-Garde* (New York: Cambridge University Press, 2006).

21. See also *Gauguin, Vzgliad iz Rossii* (Moscow, 1989).

of the avant-garde's provocative gestures during this period were connected not coincidentally with Western artistic phenomena: Tatlin's request that Liubov' Popova "teach him Cubism for 20 rubles a month,"[22] the legends of his meeting with Picasso in March 1914, and Il'ia Zdanevich's lecture, in which Goncharova's artistic biography was transformed into an epic series of invented encounters with all the great French artists, one by one—collaboration with Van Gogh in Arles, a visit to Gauguin in Oceania, and face-to-face conversations and correspondence with Cézanne.[23]

THE CONSEQUENCES OF WORLD WAR I AND THE 1917 REVOLUTION

World War I cut Russia off from Europe, and with the beginning of the Civil War in 1918, Russia's isolation grew into a blockade. The interaction between Russian artists and Paris stopped just as it was most intense. Yet it was precisely in these years of isolation that the Russian avant-garde formulated the radical principles of Suprematism, Constructivism, and production art, which not only developed and went beyond the Cubist understanding of the picture as a self-sufficient construction but also led artists beyond the problems of painting proper. In many respects, the disappearance of the Parisian model predetermined the radicalism of the Russian solutions. For almost seven years, practically nothing was known in Russia about the evolution of foreign art, which seemingly ceased to exist in 1914. In any case, the information that did penetrate from abroad did not become widely known.[24] On the one hand, this situation stimulated utopian projects for uniting artists throughout the world; on the other, it intensified the sense of a boundary between the past and the present and forced artists to reevaluate the founders of contemporary art. Shchukin's and Morozov's collections, which had been transformed into the state-run Museums of Modern Western Art, offered an excellent opportunity for this reevaluation.[25]

Gauguin receded to the periphery in the views not only of the avant-garde but also of the modernists, who only five years earlier had regarded his painting as one source of the new style [27]. Nor is there evidence during the revolutionary period of any substantial interest in Van Gogh, although a considerable number of his masterpieces were in Moscow. Only toward the end of the 1920s, when a dramatic *Lebensgefühl* intensified in Russian painting, was his influence once again felt. This tendency, however, was doomed from the outset: "The artist who regards the era of proletarian revolution as

22. An entry from Rodchenko's 1919 diary, in Varvara Stepanova, *Chelovek ne mozhet zhit' bez chuda* (Moscow, 1994), p. 59.

23. See also Il'ia Zdanevich, "Natal'ia Goncharova i vsechestvo" [1913], in *N. S. Goncharova i M. F. Larionov. Issledovaniia, publikatsii* (Moscow, 2001), pp. 176–77. Text published by Elena Basner.

24. A rare exception is Zinaida Vengerova's detailed essay, "Angliiskie futuristy," *Strelets* (Petrograd) 1 (1915), which deals with Imagism and Vorticism and contains a reproduction of a work by Wyndham Lewis.

25. Shchukin's collection became the First Museum of Modern Western Art and Morozov's became the Second. They were merged administratively in 1923 and brought under one roof in Morozov's former mansion in 1928.

a tragic time is alien to the proletariat."[26] Van Gogh's impact throughout the postrevolutionary period was unapparent and hidden.

During the revolutionary years, by contrast, Cézanne underwent a genuine renaissance, and his influence spread epidemically. In 1918, the Master of Aix was inches away from canonization in the pantheon of revolutionary heroes when it was proposed that a monument be erected to him in Moscow as part of the "monumental propaganda" program.[27] (But Cézanne's name was absent from the final list approved by Lenin.)

At this moment diverse trends of artistic thought acknowledged Cézanne, who had earlier influenced the Russian avant-garde in various ways, as the fountainhead of the new art. They now regarded the work of this predecessor of the avant-garde as a source that could be tapped to renew art without falling into extremism. Cézanne became the embodiment of an art that violated conventions yet introduced an authoritative new order into the reconstructed world [122, 123].

The events of 1917 soon changed the balance of forces in the art world. For the traditionalists connected with the *World of Art* and *Apollon,* the social and artistic revolutions were a national catastrophe. After October 1917, these artists and critics lost their former influence and felt it crucial to restore contacts with Europe and defend tradition in contemporary art. Projects to establish a national museum based on the Moscow collections of French painting, for example, were related to these issues [72]. The leftists, by contrast, advocated a museum of painterly culture that would embrace Russian and French works on an equal footing [73], or even exclude contemporary Western art entirely [74]. This project, like the international policy of the avant-garde, was connected with the idea of "painterly culture" formulated in 1919 within the IZO (visual arts) department of Narkompros. The roots of this concept can be traced to the prerevolutionary period, when, unacknowledged inside Russia, the avant-garde developed an even keener sense than early modernism had of belonging to an international movement. The avant-garde regarded the "French"-"Russian" opposition as less relevant, ultimately, than the conflict between "old" and "new" art. With the transition from Primitivism to Cubism, this feeling intensified: "The new cubist body . . . has nothing national, geographic, patriotic or narrowly popular about it" [52]. In 1919 the avant-garde artist felt that "the notion of artistic culture was connected . . . with the experiments of the young schools and could be developed only by them."[28] Artists were united not by belonging to a national school but by being engaged in artistic trends with common aesthetic criteria and a common language. Political radicalism of the Russian "Left" was often extrapolated onto innovative art and the artists who produced it [76].

The aspiration to end Russian isolation was embodied in the idea of an International

26. L. Ia. Zivel'chinskaia, *Ekspressionizm* (Moscow-Leningrad, 1931), p. 84.

27. Leonid Badarov, "Revoliutsiia i vozrozhdenie skul'ptury v Rossii," *Vestnik zhizni* 1 (1918): 75. The project also included plans for monuments to Gustave Courbet and Constantin Meunier.

28. "Polozhenie Otdela izobrazitel'nykh iskusstv i khudozhestvennoi promyshlennosti po voprosu o khudozhestvennoi kul'ture," *Izobrazitel'noe iskusstvo* 1 (1919): 73.

of the Arts, which was drafted by IZO's International Bureau in 1919. This project took shape under the direct influence of the Comintern, which was founded in March of that year. The International of the Arts, however, was above all an aesthetic, "life-creating" utopia, a means of solving the problems of art that had been aggravated by the war [75, 77]. At the same time, it was an idea unique in the history of the relationship between Russia and the West, for it signified a refusal on principle to choose between the Western and Russian positions—though upon closer examination of its program, the messianism of the "leftists" who wanted to convert the West to their faith is evident.

THE POSTREVOLUTIONARY REDISCOVERY OF EUROPE

With the victory of the Bolsheviks in the Civil War, the West was forced to establish relations with Soviet Russia. Dismantling the blockade took several years, from peace with Estonia (February 2, 1920) to the treaty with Germany (April 16, 1922). In the years 1920–22, the Russian art community assessed the changes that had taken place in European art in the intervening years, gathering information at first through rumors, then from isolated German publications that arrived via Tallinn and Riga, and later by way of reports from Berlin and Paris. At first, information was second-hand—reviews and surveys—and necessarily approximate. The suddenness of discovery also played a role: phenomena were not seen in their developmental context but surfaced ready-made, often already labeled by Western critics.

The fresh "discovery" of Europe brought with it some sensations, in particular, the return to figuration, especially in Neo-Classicism and Expressionism. In the first half of 1921, evidently, Russia was shocked to learn that Picasso was drawing "in the manner of Ingres." This was treason on the part of the revolution's leader. Whether his new manner was a natural development raised questions about the development of art in general. Picasso's evolution served the arguments of various participants in the debate, but neither his Neo-Classicism nor his postwar Cubism directly influenced Russian painting. Despite continued interest in his work, his role in the development of Russian art steadily declined. Before the war, the pictures of the Blaue Reiter and Brücke groups had been shown at Russian exhibitions,[29] but Expressionism was not regarded as an integral and independent phenomenon. Russians were accustomed to thinking that significant painting was done in Paris and that contemporary Germans at best imitated the French. Now, after the war, a new interest in Expressionism revived interest in modern German art generally. The conviction that the new German art was an aesthetically derivative phenomenon, however, was shared by various Russian observers, almost regardless of their position, even before they saw the original works. Neither staunch interest in Expressionism's manifestations in poetry, theater,

29. The Izdebsky Salon included works by Kandinsky, Jawlensky, and von Werefkin; in 1911 in Odessa, Kandinsky exhibited 54 works. Participants in the Moscow Jack of Diamonds exhibition included Kandinsky, Gabriele Münter, Macke, Marc, Kirchner, Müller, Pechstein, and Heckel.

and cinema nor the periodically voiced opinion that "no other country needs the implementation of Expressionist slogans more than Russia"[30] could shake the conviction that Expressionism was ideologically alien and artistically imitative. Yet it remained attractive as an important if negative attempt to express relevant content in modern language, an attempt to return a "human" element to painting, and in this sense it served as an alternative to avant-garde rationalistic currents dating back to Cubism [98].

It was George Grosz who personified contemporary German art in Russia [100–103]. His works were regularly published in the Soviet press, and travelers viewed life in the West through the prism of his drawings. Above all, his evolution from the nihilism of Dada to Communist propaganda made Grosz the model of the contemporary artist. Russians, however, were repelled by the "individualism" and "eroticism" of Grosz's drawings and of contemporary German art in general. As before, the "socially indifferent" art of France remained the aesthetic and professional model.

In the 1920s Soviet interest in foreign art was lively. Critics were able to embrace practically all significant contemporary phenomena, including those that were completely new to Russia—Dadaism, Purism, Neo-Classicism, Surrealism, and Neue Sachlichkeit—and distinguish the Neo-Romantic tendency in French painting. If attention had previously been focused on France, now Germany and Italy were no less interesting.

Although artistic contacts were reactivated when Russia's isolation ended,[31] all major exhibitions were organized by state-controlled institutions. Official support imposed ideological obligations, but it also made possible quite a few important exhibitions abroad, including the "Erste Russische Kunstausstellung" in the Berlin Galerie van Diemen (1922), and the Soviet section at the 1924 Venice Biennale. Of special significance was Russian participation in the 1925 International Exhibition of Decorative Arts in Paris, where Mel'nikov's pavilion and Rodchenko's workers' club made the Soviet exposition an expressive contrast to the ascendant Art Deco.

Works by foreign artists came to the USSR relatively late. Only in 1924–25 was there an exhibition of contemporary German art, organized by Mezhrabpom (International Workers Relief), in Moscow, Leningrad, and Saratov [94, 99]. In 1926 the State Academy of Artistic Sciences (GAKhN) arranged the exposition "Revolutionary Art of the West" [105]. Finally, in 1928, for the first time in fifteen years, Moscow was host to an exhibition of contemporary French art [112, 113]. Government policy in the mid-1920s generally favored such events—both openly political ones, such as the 1926 exhibition, and demonstrably neutral ones, such as that of 1928.

The colonies of Russian artists in Paris and Berlin were growing. Besides those which dated from before the war, they now included artists who had left Russia after the Revolution. The distinguished names were predominantly traditionalists, since a signifi-

30. Boris Zemenkov, "Nemetskoe iskusstvo poslednego piatidesiatiletiia (Vystavka v morozovskom otdelenii Muzeia nov[ogo] zapadnogo iskusstva)," *Sovetskoe iskusstvo* 1 (1926): 72.

31. The most substantial publication on this question is L. S. Aleshina and N. V. Iavorskaia, eds., *Iz istorii khudozhestvennoi zhizni SSSR. Internatsional'nye sviazi v oblasti izobrazitel'nogo iskusstva. 1917–1940* (Moscow, 1987).

cant portion of the avant-garde leaders remained in Russia. Settling abroad was at first not a strongly marked political act, and communication between the Russian artistic communities in Europe and the USSR was relatively free. In the mid-1920s, leftist émigrés from the West, such as the Hungarian critic János Mácza (Ivan Matsa) and the artist Bela Uitz, began to play an appreciable role in the artistic life of the Soviet Union.[32] Visits by foreign artists, usually in connection with political events or projects, also became more frequent. Notable here were George Grosz (1922), Käthe Kollwitz (1927), Diego Rivera (1927), John Heartfield (1931) [111], and Albert Marquet (1934).[33]

Foreign artistic education also continued to attract Russians, but travel started to become limited fairly early on. After around 1929, young artists rarely got to the West, and those who did had already distinguished themselves as "Soviet" painters. By the early 1930s, the mere fact of having visited the West and exposed oneself to the influence of "decadent" art could provoke attacks, even against politically reliable artists who were Communist Party members [119].

FROM "RUSSIAN" TO "SOVIET"

The early 1920s were no less important than the early 1900s in the history of relations between Russian and foreign art. Western art had evolved considerably during the seven years of Russia's isolation. Russian art had also changed, but what had changed even more was its social context. The question of the self-determination of Russian art in relation to that of the West became crucial again. The years 1920–23 were especially significant: practically all the participants in artistic life forged their own solutions regarding Russian art's place in the European context [80–86]. The answer was generally affected by the increasingly well-established notion that contemporary Russian art was "Soviet" and that its social functions made it qualitatively distinct. (For obvious reasons, those who did not share this opinion emigrated or lost access to any real audience.)

From the outset of the 1920s, Soviet evaluations of foreign culture were influenced by the notion that Western civilization as a whole was in crisis. This idea was central to the Bolsheviks, who were counting on world revolution. For a significant segment of the intelligentsia, however, a more typical approach, a compromise that called for preserving the unity of Russian and Western culture, was enunciated by music critic Leonid Sabaneev: "The West is decaying and its ideology does not satisfy us, yet breaking with it is fatal to our musical psyche."[34] That compromise was a logical snare, how-

32. See John E. Bowlt, "Hungarian Activism and the Russian Avant-Garde," in *Standing in the Tempest: Painters of the Hungarian Avant-Garde,* edited by S. A. Mansbach (Santa Barbara Museum of Art; Cambridge, Mass.: MIT Press, 1991), pp. 143–67.

33. See William Richardson, "The Dilemmas of a Communist Artist: Diego Rivera in Moscow, 1927–1928," *Mexican Studies* 3, no. 1 (Winter 1987): 49–69; Hubertus Gassner, "Heartfield's Moscow Apprenticeship 1931–32," in *John Heartfield,* edited by Peter Pachnicke and Klaus Honnef (New York: Abrams, 1992), pp. 256–87.

34. Leonid Sabaneev, "Na putiakh muzyki," *Vestnik zhizni* 5 (1922): 9.

ever, as Marxist radicals pointed out in the late 1920s and early 1930s. They regarded an artist's French pedigree as synonymous with his bourgeois status.

Following the Revolution, slowly but surely, the polemics changed. The analysis of contemporary art came to be based on the axiom that culture depended on relations to the means of production. Practically all the participants in public debates now accepted the Marxist argument (or at least the Marxist rhetoric), particularly with respect to contemporary foreign art. Opposition to the West demanded emphasis on the social provenance of artistic phenomena, and the search for a class equivalent gradually became the norm in the new study of art. By the mid-1920s, an essentially uniform Soviet view of Western art had taken shape, and other interpretations had an increasingly difficult time being heard [86–88, 121].

PARTING OF THE WAYS: THE DISCUSSIONS IN THE MID-1920S

During the years of isolation there had been no new geological tremors in the West—not that Russia needed them, as the revolution in the visual arts had been imported before World War I and the foundation of the new language laid for both radical avant-garde and figurative artists. Western art had ceased to exert any direct influence on Soviet art, which was becoming increasingly selective. There was a substantive professional interest in contemporary Western art, but it presumed no revolution of views, let alone any subordination. Purism and Neo-Classicism did not generate new art but did suggest solutions to problems with which Russian art was also struggling.

Two exhibitions held in 1921 were almost the last occasions when the avant-garde demonstrated fundamentally new approaches: "ObMoKhu" (in March) and "5 × 5 = 25" (in December). Production art, which arose at the beginning of the decade, broke radically with representational art. Gradually, however, the leftists' sphere of immediate influence began to shrink. After the liquidation of the Leningrad-based State Institute of Artistic Culture (GINKhUK) in 1926, avant-garde ideas developed for the most part in the Moscow Higher Art and Technical Studios (VKhUTEMAS) and in informal circles around Malevich, Matiushin, and Filonov. The revolution in form that distinguished the avant-garde of the 1910s was now succeeded by the development of technological methods by the members of isolated circles. These groups wanted to propagate their own art, not open themselves to foreign phenomena.

Meanwhile, the concept of easel painting, which had been buried by the Suprematists and production artists, was resurrected in 1923 at the "Exhibition of Pictures," where such avant-gardists as Nadezhda Udal'tsova and Aleksandr Drevin proclaimed their return to painting. Figurative art spread rapidly and widely, based on more than a simple reaction against the avant-garde. Figurative easel art gradually became so popular during the 1920s as to become virtually mainstream.

Because almost all the realist groups developed their methods from the art of the preceding decades, these groups themselves were inevitably tied to contemporary

French painting (Four Arts, The Circle, etc.). The Society of Easel Painters (OST), founded in 1925, became the first enduring organization of young artists who had grown up after the Revolution and considered themselves Soviet painters. Their manifesto recognized the "formal achievements of recent years,"[35] but the society's members constituted themselves as an emphatically un-French group. Their painterly language revealed the influence of the poster, the photograph, and the cinema, as well as the Neue Sachlichkeit.

Early in the decade, a conservative conception of painting arose that harked back to nineteenth-century Russian realism. Representing this trend was the Association of Artists of Revolutionary Russia (AKhRR), which was founded in May 1923 and expanded rapidly.[36] Narrative realism both helped make art intelligible to the masses and satisfied political leaders' needs. This organization, which had monopolistic ambitions, contrasted itself to practically all other artistic associations, declaring the art of recent decades flawed from the outset because it was based on transplanting "the crisis forms of Western, mainly French, art . . . into economically and psychologically alien soil" [cf. 84].[37]

AKhRR's resurrection of the Wanderer "zombie" and the association's accusations that other groups imitated decadent Western art challenged avant-garde and traditionalist artists alike. Clashing in this discussion were not only two opposing artistic positions but also two fundamentally different polemical strategies. AKhRR's supporters, among them People's Commissar of Enlightenment Anatolii Lunacharskii [107], oversimplified the problem by declaring the values of contemporary art, which harked back to modern French painting, a fiction. The deliberate "archaism" of AKhRR's defenders also rendered meaningless the whole discussion of artistic culture: "Compared with genuinely great artists, leftist painters are quite simply ignorant."[38]

Another important debate was devoted to the basis of Soviet art. A number of young Marxist critics and artists close to the pro-Communist Left Front of Arts (Lef) were convinced that Soviet art must preserve continuity with the art of the most recent decades. If socialism naturally succeeds imperialism and its highly organized productive forces, then socialist art must continue contemporary tendencies, especially rationalist trends in architecture and industrial design. This position was most clearly expressed in the writings of Ivan Matsa [106] and Aleksei Fedorov-Davydov, who in the late 1920s defended production art and joined the October group (1928–32).[39]

Their opponents denied any connection with contemporary Western art, which for

35. *Sovetskoe iskusstvo za 15 let Materialy i dokumentatsia* (Moscow, Leningrad, 1933), p. 575.

36. Beginning in 1928, the Association of Revolutionary Artists (AKhR). See Brandon Taylor, "On AKhRR," in *Art of the Soviets: Painting, Sculpture and Architecture in a One-Party State, 1917–1932,* edited by Matthew Cullerne Brown and Brandon Taylor (Manchester: Manchester University Press, 1993), pp. 51–72.

37. May 1924 circular letter to all branches of AKhRR and an appeal to all artists of the USSR. Quoted in *Bor'ba za realizm v iskusstve 20-x godov. Materialy. Dokumenty. Vospominaniia* (Moscow, 1962), p. 121.

38. A. V. Lunacharskii, *Ob iskusstve* (Moscow, 1982), vol. 1, 360.

39. See also "Ob"edinenie 'Oktiabr''. Deklaratsiia," in *Klassovaia bor'ba na fronte izobrazitel'nykh iskusstv* (Moscow, 1928).

them demonstrated the decline of capitalism and the intellectuals who depended on it. A grand style analogous to the one that had emerged in the early history of the bourgeoisie became the basis for socialist culture. This traditionalist approach was typical of Party journalists [108]. Even before the Revolution, Russian Social Democrats had preferred traditional art and hoped that communism would introduce a new synthetic style. In the mid-1920s, with the discussion of socialist art, Plekhanov's prerevolutionary criticism of Western "decadence" [20, 46] was widely noted, and his writings were made the foundation of Marxist aesthetics.

THE FRENCH DISEASE: EARLY STALINIST CULTURAL POLICY AND WESTERN ART

When the Great Depression hit the West in 1929, the political situation in the USSR changed radically. Conflict in the Party leadership led to the ousting of Nikolai Bukharin and gave Stalin absolute control of the country. Bukharin had advocated the gradual development of industry and peasants' ownership of their own land. Stalin opposed both policies, ordering feverish industrialization, total collectivization, and elimination of what remained of cultural pluralism. The new course he set presumed the country's isolation from the rest of the world; this created an atmosphere in which the relationship to modern Western art again became a key problem.[40]

The language of contemporary art had to be learned because it was not transparent and therefore resisted straightforward use for ideological purposes. The French, that is, the contemporary progressive tradition in its various forms, united practically all groups against whom the struggle was now turned—from the politically neutral Four Arts to the communist October. Art came under the supervision of radicals from the youth faction of the Association of Revolutionary Artists (AKhR, the successor to AKhRR), who had seized power in the AKhR in 1928 and founded the Russian Association of Proletarian Artists (RAPKh) in 1931. Between 1929 and 1932 they policed artistic life—for example, by launching a powerful campaign to unmask the "French disease of non-Marxist aesthetes" [cf. 116].[41] They also attacked those Marxists who, like Ivan Matsa, perceived contemporary Western culture as a source of socialist art. Matsa's approach was branded a variant of the Bukharinist theory that the kulaks (rich peasants) could be peacefully integrated into the socialist system [118]. Intellectual opponents were turned into political enemies.

AKhR-RAPKh did not limit its criticism to recent phenomena such as Expressionism and Surrealism but extended it to Impressionism and Cézanne. In the late 1920s Impressionism had again become a focus in Russia, not only because of the development of post-avant-garde painting but also because it was recognized as a source of

40. See Ilia Dorontchenkov, "Against the Cult of the French: Modern Western Art and Cultural Politics in the Early Stalin Era," *Zimmerly Journal*, no. 4 (Spring 2006): 32–51.

41. Compare "Otkrytoe pis'mo v redaktsiiu 'Komsomol'skaia pravda,'" *Iskusstvo v massy* 3–4 (1929): 40.

the new art [125–28]. Thus, to discredit Impressionism and Cézanne meant repudiating painting's entire subsequent evolution, down to the present. If in 1918 the Soviet government had been prepared to raise a monument to the Master from Aix, in 1930 the secret police were taking a more suspicious interest in the propagation of Western art. During the three months he was held under arrest, Malevich was asked, "What Cézannism are you discussing? What Cubism are you preaching?"[42]

In April 1932 the Central Committee dissolved all groups, thus putting an end to RAPKh's control of art as well. The Party's mission had been accomplished. By terrorizing and disciplining the art community it had created an environment internally receptive to unification. In 1933 Leningrad and Moscow witnessed an unprecedented exhibition, "The Artists of the RSFSR during the Past Fifteen Years," which included more than 2,500 works by 423 participants, among them some leading avant-gardists. Its guiding document, however, contained a statement of principle: "The moving force . . . of development is the struggle between the Marxist-Leninist worldview and idealist bourgeois aesthetics in the form of survivals of prerevolutionary Russian art, on the one hand, and the influence of reactionary contemporary European art, on the other."[43] Thus the Scylla and Charybdis of official aesthetics—naturalism and formalism—were plotted out in terms that were ill suited to actual works of art and that changed according to political contingencies. In the 1930s, there was nothing these monsters could not crush, if necessary, and after the newspaper campaign of 1936 that began with the persecution of Dmitrii Shostakovich and spread from music to the other arts, the label "formalist Westernizer" was tantamount to a political accusation [129].

Even after the 1936 campaign against formalism and during the harshest years of Stalin's rule, modern Western art remained a topic of discussion and even appropriation by official artists. For example, Impressionism had a significant influence on the poetics of Socialist Realism.[44] However, Impressionism was now seen in a very different—and telling—way. During the 1930s and later on, Impressionism played a role in Soviet art that recalls the initial conflict between the Salon and the avant-garde of the 1870s, only now "Impressionism" was rather perversely either accepted by the resurrected "Salon" or scapegoated as the major enemy of realist art, thus reflecting Soviet art's isolation from the contemporary artistic world. Not only had Impressionism long since lost its topicality in the rest of Europe, but by the late 1930s the Soviet Union had no sense whatsoever of artistic unity, mutual concerns, or shared cultural values.

Over the five decades that modern Western art had made itself felt in Russia, it had become an inevitable participant in the Russian artistic discourse, both with regard to

42. Diary entry of November 12, 1932, in Pavel Filonov, *Dnevnik* (St. Petersburg, 2000), p. 165.

43. Quoted in A. I. Morozov, "K istorii vystavki 'Khudozhniki RSFSR za 15 let' (Leningrad-Moskva, 1932–1935)," *Sovetskoe iskusstvoznanie* 82, no. 1 (Moscow, 1983): 122.

44. See Alison Hilton, "Holiday on the Kolkhoz: Socialist Realism's Dialogue with Impressionism," in *Russian Art and the West: A Century of Dialogue in Painting, Architecture, and the Decorative Arts,* edited by Rosalind P. Blakesley and Susane Reid (De Kalb: Northern Illinois University Press, 2006), pp. 195–216.

particular painterly devices and, in a general way, in relation to issues of national identity. Even the unavoidable aberrations and distortions had been productive and fruitful. In the dialogue with Europe, Russian art had created phenomena that came to be independent of, and even had their own influence on, Western culture, from the Ballets Russes to Suprematism. The search for the new and foreign helped to shape Russia's unique identity in the arts, and with unprecedented intensity. For half a century, almost every important artistic trend had absorbed something from modern European art, and even deliberate rejections of any Western influence—demonstrated by Viktor Vasnetsov in the late nineteenth century—nonetheless kept Russian artists working within the same aesthetic paradigm. One could refuse to be Western, but one could not ignore or remain ignorant of European art.[45]

The new Soviet epoch was marked by extreme exclusivity. Under Stalin, the monopolistic, dominant ideology made the fear of both novelty and foreignness part of Marxist rhetoric, and the paradigm changed. It became an official monologue by a collective Big Brother set against different groups of artists, whether conformist or nonconformist. Any possible response that artists might now have to contemporary Western art was predetermined by the new situation, which combined a lack of freedom of choice with the absence of reliable relations with the West, and—what was perhaps even more important—with the loss of a common visual language and common aesthetic and ethical criteria. An invisible wall had been built between Soviet and Western cultures that was in a sense higher than the Berlin Wall. Some sense of the extremity of the situation can be conveyed by noting that while the present book, which covers the period from the 1890s to the mid-1930s, is based almost entirely on printed sources (that is, it reconstructs a public discourse), a similar book for the period from the mid-1930s to the 1980s would have to be very different. During that later period, the Soviet artistic and intellectual communities were so isolated and cut off from open debates that a similar anthology would consist mostly of unpublished materials—private notes and diaries and texts circulated in *samizdat.*

Why, one might ask, was the discussion about Western art in Russia so grave and passionate that it could lead to such tragic results as the suppression of political opponents on the pretext of their defense of Western art? In large measure, all the discussion's participants, whether avant-garde or reactionary, shared the overt or implicit opinion that art both reflects and structures human life and that art can shape the mentality of a class or nation. As a result, Russian relations to foreign ("Western") culture acquired special significance, since borrowing from a foreign culture was not simply a normal process whose importance was limited to a narrow professional community but rather something that potentially could affect the mentality of the nation as a whole and affect its future.

45. Compare Vladimir Stasov, "Viktor Mikhailovich Vasnetsov i ego raboty: Vospominaniia i zametki," *Iskusstvo i khudozhestvennaia promyshlennost'*, 1–2 (1898); and Sergei Diaghilev, "K vystavke V. M. Vasnetsova," *Mir iskusstva*, 7–8 (1899).

The situation reconstructed in the present volume was a result of the extremely intense but diverse and contradictory process of modernization in Russia, at a time when the country's future had not yet become a matter of national consensus—and in being unclear, remained open to different perspectives. Today, the Bolshevik Revolution, which started in October 1917 and continued into the mid-1930s, when the new system achieved its final form, looks like a conservative revolution undertaken not so much for the sake of the well-being of the majority as for the perpetuation of archaic and patriarchal stereotypes that were dear to the less developed—but extensive—strata of the Russian nation. The hectic industrialization of the 1930s and scientific and technological achievements of the 1950s and 1960s were consistent with such a situation. They demonstrated a purely instrumental approach to modernization, using and producing modern equipment, not a modern social network. On the contrary, Soviet society needed to be oversimplified in many senses, as it could function only in isolation. The aftermath of the 1917 Revolution eliminated old elites and lifted brainwashed people with a limited cultural background and an archaic mentality into positions of power and influence. For them, the visual language shared by modern artists in both Russia and the West remained largely incomprehensible. As a result, not only were political borders closed but the very soil on which international cultural dialogue might thrive disappeared altogether.

RUSSIAN CRITICISM BEFORE THE REVOLUTION

1890s–1917

I

FACING EUROPE

IMPRESSIONS, CONTACTS, AND CRITICISMS

Around the 1890s, the number of foreign cultural contacts and art exhibitions in Russia increased significantly. At this time, what the Russian artistic community lacked was not so much information as definite aesthetic criteria. Symbolism, Impressionism, and Post-Impressionism all demanded a new set of values and a different historical perspective. The basic positions of the artistic camps were clearly expressed in the essays in this section by Mark Antokol'skii, Vladimir Stasov, and Igor' Grabar', who tried to present a coherent picture of contemporary art. In discussing the groundbreaking quality of contemporary Western painting in relation to Russian art, Antokol'skii attempted a compromise, while Stasov was hostile and Grabar' quite positive.

At the turn of the century, as Russian art was changing, a debate arose on the national character of that art. To opponents of modernism like Stasov, Western influence robbed artists of their "Russianness" and rendered their work inferior. For the conservative cultural establishment, Western influence was strongly associated with decadence. The World of Art—a group of young artists from the cosmopolitan cultural elite of St. Petersburg—altered Russian society's attitude toward Western art decisively. World of Art members defined their art policies as international and regarded their group as a mediator. Outside Russia they attempted to ensure that ideas about Russian art were associated with their group; inside, they deliberately defined themselves as new Westernizers. This duality, which was the basis of the group's ideology, culminated in the major projects of Sergei Diaghilev: the Russian exhibition at the 1906 "Salon d'Automne" and the performances of the Ballets Russes, starting in 1909.

The World of Art's early projects were emphatically international and sought, in particular, to bring together Russian and foreign artists, on the model of the Champ de Mars Salon and the Munich Secession, as in the "Exhibition of Russian and Finnish Artists" (1898) and the "First International Exhibition" (1899); however, the newly ascendant artistic generation faced open resistance from champions of the socially and nationally charged narrative art of the late Wanderers, whose leader, Vladimir Stasov, made the issue of Western influence central to his aggressive reviews.

The struggle for a new paradigm of Russian art paralleled their new discoveries in contemporary European art: from the art of the Scandinavian countries, through disappointment in the "German vogue" of the 1900s, to the recognition of contemporary French painting as a paragon for Russian art. As Muratov's essay makes clear, by the 1900s the modernists had made Russian painting a legitimate part of European art and successfully reevaluated the Russian nineteenth-century painterly tradition in the Western context.

1

Mark Antokol'skii

"Notes on Art" (1897)

Mark Antokol'skii (1843–1902), a sculptor close to the Wanderers, received his training at the St. Petersburg Academy of Fine Arts. He lived in Europe from 1871 until his death. Antokol'skii's article was written in Paris and published in a liberal St. Petersburg journal, *Vestnik Evropy* (Messenger of Europe) 2 (1897).

. . . Say what you will about French art, but not to love it and respect its mighty technique, the elegance and concreteness of its drawing, its colors, the taste that flows so generously throughout, means not to be an artist, not to love the sky and the spring and to reject the truth. In contrast, to be able to say that the sun has no spots, the rose has no thorns, and French art is impeccable one must be a calculating writer, turn one's sails to the wind, and know how to straddle the fence. The French despise such writers, as do decent people around the world. Be that as it may, this gives me an occasion to have my say on French art once and for all—and I write about French art because it is extremely interesting and instructive: something new and unprecedented in the history of art is going on in it now. To speak about French art is to speak about European art in general. . . .

. . . One must always take into account the difference between two characters such as the French and the Russian. I know of nothing more contradictory than these two natures, but at the same time I know of no two extremes so capable of converging. What the one has in abundance the other lacks, and vice versa. I shall begin with the fact that the French are an old people and we are young; they are rich and we are poor; they are calculating and we are carefree; they are polite, while we are good-hearted; they are culturally disciplined—we are careless. . . . With the French you do not know where sincerity ends and civility begins; we are always sincere and are therefore always abusing one another. The French work their entire lives so as to rest in their old age; we are always resting, yet we not only spend all we have but also run up debts. . . . In art, the French are Epicureans and we are Puritans. For them form is predominant, for us content. For them, the main thing is *how* something is done, while for us it is *what* is done. . . .

Artists such as Delacroix and Millet have become universal idols; they have eclipsed everyone, and no one has noticed other artists with other merits. . . . They are without a doubt very important artists; Millet's works, for example, are unusually plastic, and Delacroix has unusual colors and an ardent tone, but these are purely outward merits, especially in Delacroix, like beautiful language, sonorous verse, and so on in literature. But, after all, God gave people beautiful language so that they could express their feelings and intimate thoughts, but the latter is what I have found so very little of, though hardly anyone was demanding it at the time.

Along with this one-sidedness, however, I also found another more serious and important trend—something resembling a new age in art—although again in the realm of pure virtuosity. I have in mind the Impressionist *plein air* movement headed by Manet. . . . As an artist Manet has been of little use to art. All that remains of his works is a historical reminiscence. As a prophet and innovator, however, he has undoubtedly been enormously significant. . . . His immediate followers understood him least of all. Among them were many talented artists, but unfortunately they became too enamored of novelty and were unable to distinguish the good from the bad in their teacher. What they thought good was impossible, what seemed beautiful was ugly, and they began painting faces with violet hair, assuring us that in a certain light things are like that in reality. . . .

Working at the same time as Manet, but in the opposite direction, was another artist. I am speaking of Puvis de Chavannes, an interior decorator and muralist. . . . I became acquainted with his works in a strange way. I was walking around an exhibition and as usual I was looking at everything with intense attention. After an hour my attention was beginning to wane, my feet were getting tired, and the rows of pictures with all possible subjects and colors were starting to make me dizzy. . . . Suddenly I found myself in a large corner room, and spread out before me across the entire wall was a picture that had nothing in common with what had gone before. It was a kind of elegy; I forget the title, but what I saw I shall never forget. . . . Puvis de Chavannes, however, has two substantial shortcomings that render his works short-lived. First, in his pursuit of simplicity he draws his figures all too simply, adhering to primitive art; he affects naiveté, like a child, and of course what we find charming in a child is abnormal in an adult, and vice versa. Second, he affects naiveté even when he is depicting contemporary people in contemporary dress, and this is a complete anachronism. . . .

It would, however, be quite erroneous to think that French art is presently in decline. But in our century it has always led the way, changing directions many times, and everyone has followed it. Classicism, Romanticism, Realism, Naturalism, and so on—it was in France that all of this was created. True, these rapid transitions from one movement to another demonstrate that art has yet to find its foundations, its true ideal; however, this is the fault not of art but of the force of circumstances; it makes no sense to blame French art. On the contrary, at a time when art in other countries was divorcing itself from reality, the French were drawing closer and closer to it; at a time when artists all over the world were falling asleep over their illusionary ideals, French artists were awake, searching for what was genuine. . . . Whether they will find it is another question. . . . I don't think they will, not until this ideal is created for society itself. . . .

Yet, living here in Paris for so many years, amid the colossal activity of French art and industry, which have given their country so much fame and fortune, at times I think about our reality as well, and about our art and industry. . . . And I am pained and irritated. Why do we have such poverty? Why is everything there wrong and different from everywhere else? . . . Lately one can even sense a certain duality: on the one hand, we yield the palm like an obedient vassal to foreign forces and regard everything foreign with respect and without the least envy or trace of shame for ourselves and our people; on the other hand, we have a kind of childish ardor that makes us ready to clamber to the top of the bell tower and "spit down on everyone." . . . In fact, we know that art and poetry are the purest language of the soul and the best interpreter of human suffering, that there is no place in it for the "evil of the day," for envy, quarrels, and discord. . . . On the contrary, art ennobles and elevates our spirit, makes our hearts beat stronger, and makes us rejoice and care not about ourselves alone . . . and, like the sky, it shines and warms everyone equally. But we must not forget that we, like all Europe, are going through the fin de siècle, an age of decadence, religion without faith, egotism elevated to a dogma, and a struggle for survival. . . . What remains for art to do in such an age of rupture between emotion and intellect, between moral duty and self-preservation? Science, steam, and electricity aspire to embrace the globe and unite humanity into a single family, while we are prepared to surround ourselves with a Chinese wall. In such an age everyone squints, looking at the truth as though it were the sun and ready to tell each other precisely what they themselves want to hear. In such an age, perhaps all that remains for art as well is to lie, amuse, or come to a standstill. . . .

2

Igor' Grabar'

"Decline or Renaissance? A Survey of Contemporary Trends in Art" (1897)

Painter and critic Igor' Grabar' (1871–1960) was born in Budapest and studied law and painting in St. Petersburg. Between 1896 and 1901 he lived in Munich. In 1913 he became a trustee of the Tretiakov Gallery. After the Revolution, Grabar' worked mostly on medieval Russian art.

This essay, written in Munich, presented the evolution of contemporary painting, beginning with Delacroix, for the first time in the Russian press. It was published in the Monthly Literary Supplements to *Niva* (Field), January–February 1897.

. . . Yes, this is a renaissance, not a decline. We are living through a renaissance in painting precisely akin to what Europe once did in all spheres of the human spirit's expression. That was when painting was born, only to reach the apogee of its development in the mid-seventeenth century and come to a standstill. Two centuries passed before it again showed signs of its former life, and we are the witnesses to its rebirth. Yet with scarcely a thought or care we toss everything strong or weak in the art of our time into one pile, dub it decadence, and laugh and ridicule it. . . . The great masters' art was an independent art that had no auxiliary role thrust upon it. It did not preach, fulminate against vices, or tell edifying stories; it was concerned only with itself and its artistic problems. . . . Yes, art is pleasure and joy for the artist, and although this may offend the vanity of its high priests, the philanthropic principle of "utility" will never kill its egoistic manifestations. . . .

The artist-champion always sacrifices the purely artistic aspect of his work to the service of an idea. One such fighter—Delacroix—a brilliant *artiste né*—realized this; the braggart Courbet, who did battle through his pictures, failed to sense that as he was preaching his great message he was trampling on painting. He failed to notice that as he snatched human types and scenes from life the truth of colors eluded him. . . .

Only now have we understood what Courbet and the Realists were lacking. The latter were objective, didactic, and documental; the Japanese opened our eyes to the *subjectivism* of a work of art. . . . It took an outstanding artist—a genius—to translate the marvelous book of Japanese art from their obscure, alien language into the language of the European. And such a person turned up. His name, written in gilt letters on the pages of the history of the latest painting and blessed by the art world of Europe, is Edouard Manet. . . . Courbet and the Realists said that things must be shown truthfully, that is, as they are. This was advocacy for the *truth of life.* Manet, who at first worked to achieve this truth of life, made great strides in this direction when he founded his own realist school, the *plein air* school, and not satisfied with this truth, he showed that alongside it there was another truth, the *truth of art,* . . . a subjective truth, the only basis for which is the inner world of the artist-contemplator, the truth of his feeling. "What is truthful is not what is," he said, "but the *impression* I get from what is." Impressionism is the transmission of the impression. . . .

The titanic figure of Puvis de Chavannes combines in a very special way the objectives of Manet's school and echoes of a reborn idealism. He paints allegorical pictures almost exclusively, decorative panels usually of enormous size. After Manet, he and Carrière are the two greatest artists of France, two naturalists of the purest water, although at first glance they have nothing in common. No matter how distant both of them, especially the latter, appear to be from nature, they have come closer to it than anyone else. . . . Puvis de Chavannes is unquestionably an imitator of Raphael. . . . At the same time, however, he took his manner of seeing and harmonizing colors from Velásquez, the Japanese, and Manet. His is a most whimsical and capricious combination of very different, sometimes even directly contradictory objectives. That Puvis de Chavannes succeeded in emerging the victor from such an originally conceived problem there can be no doubt. One need only see his frescoes at the Hôtel de Ville and the Sorbonne to realize that he is the genius of our era. . . .

. . . The most important Swedish artist is Zorn. He is not even a Swede but a Frenchman through and through, with all a Frenchman's refinement and taste. He is fortune's favorite whom nature has endowed with everything that makes a master artist. . . . His is a furious, elemental artistry that can be compared only with that of Hals. His talent is supple and capricious and therefore sometimes uneven: besides amazing paintings he also produces mediocrities. . . . As you look at this thirty-six-year-old master's best works, they seem to have been painted only at the whim of an artist who takes pleasure in tackling problems beyond others' grasp; and this pleasure and this joy cannot help but be conveyed to the viewer. . . . This is perhaps his only shortcoming: he thinks too little, settles too quickly on the first impression to come along, and because he lacks a rigorous artistic criterion, his work frequently loses the fascination it might have produced under other conditions.

Contemporary art does have one artist, however, who may be even better endowed by nature than Zorn. . . . His name is Whistler. He is as great a master as Zorn; perhaps his artistry is not as furious and energetic, and it may lack that ardent temperament, but it is rigorous, calm, majestic, conscious, and balanced. Nature has allotted him a divine gift for seeing colors, for harmonizing, and for understanding the beauty of form, lines, and the totality such as we have not seen since Velásquez. . . .

Whistler, this greatest of contemporary artists, is a consummate master, an artist whose works bear the stamp of genius; in his marvelous creations of beauty and harmony he has found the final link in the chain broken by the centuries that henceforth will connect the age of Velásquez to the art of our day. Our time is not an age of decline or petty artists' petty passions, but an age of brilliant rebirth, an age of hopes and expectations. . . . Now that we have arrived at this time of rebirth, when brothers of the great masters of the past are appearing, now the time must not be far off when people will emerge who can move forward and surpass their predecessors beyond the old. We cannot say who these welcome people will be or what direction they will take, but we have every reason to hope and expect.

3

Vladimir Stasov

Nineteenth-Century Art: Painting (1901)

Vladimir Stasov (1824–1906) was the most influential art critic of the latter half of the nineteenth century. A defender of Realism and an ideologist of the Wanderers, he allotted the chief role in art to content, demanding that artists serve social progress and express national feelings. This text was written after Stasov's visit to the 1900 Paris World Fair and published in St. Petersburg.

They are trying to persuade us that Courbet is no longer modern; on the contrary, the full triumph of his thought, his prophecy, seems to me still to come and more needed today than ever. For he demanded of art what is most precious of all, something of unvalued but eternal nature: expressed truth, Realism.

Realism, as he put it, is a democratic art, fair, perceptive, and sensitive art, art that is in accord with the present day's soul, emotion, and concept of an indivisible humanity.

. . . Delacroix cared nothing about the essence of the scenes and people he depicted. As long as the task was picturesque and striking, as long as he had an opportunity to show off his wonderful colors, like a peacock spreading its magnificent many-colored tail, he was satisfied and content, and he needed nothing more. It was all the same to him, as it was to the school of countless imitators he placed throughout Europe, whether to paint *Heliodorus Driven from the Temple* or utterly pointless (but colorful) Oriental harem wenches, a battle in the Greek struggle for independence or *Apollo Slays Python.* Was there anything like this in Regnault's pictures? . . . What comparison can there be between such a superficial man, mighty in thought and brush, and the virtuoso Delacroix, who held not a grain of the nineteenth century? The latter is like a man who happened to have been tossed to us from some other century. . . .

Impressionism concerned itself only with external forms, art's external means of manifestation and expression, and never with the content of art and either completely forgot this content and dispensed with it entirely or distorted and diminished it. As for Impressionism expanding the bounds of art, conquering new horizons, and extending its realm to new areas of emotion, thought, and poetry, though, as Impressionism's advocates and defenders try to assure us, nothing of the sort ever happened, and Impressionism never bothered about this. It is simply unpardonable to exaggerate its significance and attach to it a meaning and influence such as it never in fact had. . . .

What sort of a creator of modern art is Manet when, all his great contributions and merits notwithstanding, the chief goal of art, the content of a picture, that of which it should consist, the only reason it comes into the world, was constantly slipping through his fingers and was entirely alien to him? I was struck most of all by the frivolous comparison between Manet and Courbet. . . . What incommensurate figures! Courbet's technique and brushwork may be far from perfect, and the stiffness of his brush and woodenness of some of his figures may be obvious to everyone—all this is regrettable, but these shortcomings will never diminish the enormous significance of his thought and feeling, his sympathies or antipathies toward the life scenes and characters he portrays; in Manet, by contrast, at every step, in every stroke of his, you sense only a concern for the brush and the colors, light and air. What are all his *Fifers, Smokers,* and *Beer Drinkers,* his *Guitarists,* his *Boaters,* his *Nana,* and all his other characters if not excuses to display his singularly colorful and brilliant brushwork? His naked *Olympia* stretched out on a couch, feeble, ugly, disgusting, and insignificant—what is she compared to a similar Spanish *grisette,* also naked and lying on a couch, but interesting and graceful—by Goya? What is his famous picture *A Bar at the Folies-Bergère* if not a masterful depiction of bottles and glasses on a bar, a superbly rendered reflection of a crowd of customers in a mirror, and the total neglect of the two main characters, the barmaid and the gentleman in the tailcoat? What is his celebrated picture *Luncheon on the Grass* (1863) if not a muddle-headed, fantastic, ridiculous collection of naked women and clothed men painted merely for the sunlight effect? The play of light and color are for Manet *everything;* for Courbet, quite the contrary, the *everything* is people, their life, labor, faces, expression, and fate. . . .

But a multitude of their [Monet's and Pissarro's] Impressionist comrades have become downright enemies of art, its veritable "mutilators" and executioners. Absorbed in their task of observing and conveying to the world their precious "impressions," they have spat upon all real tasks and have concerned themselves only with their own "moods" and elusive, ephemeral feelings and sensations. All objectives—of history, life, and the soul—all human relationships and all the events of our existence they have declared to be archaic, boring, and unnecessary. The study of the forms of real nature and the human essence seemed idle and futile. It was declared that today only *one* art should exist in the world, "art for art's sake," an art that, first of all, should be *new* at all costs and, second, intended to arouse the viewer's admiration of its colors and forms, apart from any idea, any naturalness, nature, or reality. Here, it must be noted, the main object of all pictures and drawings was almost always woman, her body, external appearance, pose, movements, and gaze—and all of this from the most exaggerated, insignificant, petty, distorted, and trivial perspective. This attitude and way of thinking and acting have produced something extremely limited and at the same time monstrous, barbaric, and hideous, something repulsive and revolting. Most people became indignant and objected, dubbing these strange sectarians "decadents."

4

Vasily Kandinsky
"An Artist's Text" (1918)

The first Impressionist paintings exhibited in Russia, evidently, were works by Monet, Renoir, and Sisley at the French art exhibition in St. Petersburg and Moscow in 1896. Among them, Monet's *Haystack* (it is not clear which canvas from the 1890–91 series) stood out for its unconventional style. The great Russian painter Vasily Kandinsky later recalled the importance of his encounter with Monet's painting when he was a law student at Moscow University.

The text originally appeared in a 1918 book by Kandinsky, published in Moscow, which also included twenty-five paintings and the poems *Stupeni* (Steps). The translation here, by Peter Vergo, is reprinted from "Reminiscences/Three Pictures," in *Kandinsky: Complete Writings on Art,* edited by Kenneth C. Lindsay and Peter Vergo, vol. 1 (Boston: G. K. Hall, 1982), p. 363; text

. . . I was not, however, confident enough to consider myself entitled to renounce my other responsibilities and lead, as it seemed to me then, the boundlessly happy life of an artist. . . .

At the same time, I experienced two events that stamped my whole life and shook me to the depth of my being. These were an exhibition of French Impressionists in Moscow—first and foremost, *The Haystack,* by Claude Monet—and a performance of Wagner at the Court Theatre—*Lohengrin.*

Previously I had known only realistic art, in fact only the Russians. . . . And suddenly, for the first time, I saw a *picture.* That it was a haystack, the catalogue informed me. I didn't recognize it. I found this nonrecognition painful, and thought that the artist had no right to paint so indistinctly. I had a dull feeling that the object was lacking in this picture. And I noticed with surprise and confusion that the picture not only gripped me, but impressed itself ineradicably upon my memory, always hovering quite unexpectedly before my eyes, down to the last detail. It was all unclear to me, and I was not able to draw the simple conclusions from this experience. What was, however, quite clear to me was the unsuspected power of the palette, previously concealed from me, which exceeded all my dreams. Painting took on a fairy-tale power and splendor. And, albeit unconsciously, objects were discredited as an essential element within the picture. . . .

5

Andrei Belyi

On the Border of Two Centuries (1930)

Andrei Belyi (pseudonym of Boris Bugaev, 1880–1934), a major Russian novelist, poet, and critic, recalled his early encounter with Monet's painting but dates it back to 1891, when the French industrial exhibition was held in St. Petersburg and Moscow and he was eleven years old. No firm evidence exists for the presence of a Monet there, although it is quite possible that some of the 1891 exhibits demonstrated the Impressionist manner.

The excerpt is taken from Andrei Belyi, *Na rubezhe dvukh stoletii* (On the Border of Two Centuries) (Moscow and Leningrad: Zemlia i fabrika, 1930).

At that time the French exhibition had opened; my mother took Mademoiselle and me to it very often; we wandered around it a lot and ate delicious French waffles; I was amazed by the machine section (the belts whirling, the wheels turning, the crankshaft clicking); but I was even more amazed by a phenomenon Moscow was laughing at: the French Impressionists (Degas, Monet, etc.); our professors' wives were indignant:

"Have you seen them? . . . Horrid. . . . Such brazen mockery!"

I saw them, too; and when I had seen them, for some reason I fell to thinking; my artistic education was equal to zero; besides the painting in the Church of the Savior and reproductions of Makovskii and Vereshchagin,* I hadn't seen anything; I could not have any prejudices or views based on the traditions of one school or another; and stopping in front of a pleasant and colorful spot, the "disgrace" of [Monet's] scandalous *Haystack,* I was terribly sad that I didn't know how to share my mother's and Mademoiselle's indignation; to be perfectly honest, what I liked about the French Impressionists was that they were colorful and that the colors pleasantly ran together in my eyes; but I concealed my impression once I had memorized it; and many a time afterwards I would ponder that strange but not unpleasant experience; I emphasize—"strange but not unpleasant." This "strangeness" seemed familiar; it was as though it hinted at something that had once been known to me, and there at the turn of my third year of life emerged my very first experiences of consciousness (perhaps it was then I had seen these objects?).

*The cathedral of Christ the Savior was built in 1839–83 in a quasi-medieval style, with interior decoration in the academic manner. Vladimir Makovskii (1846–1920) and Vasilii Vereshchagin (1842–1904) were Russian Realist painters.

6

Pavel Muratov

"On Grand Art" (1907)

Pavel Muratov (1881–1950) was trained as a military engineer and participated in the Russo-Japanese war of 1904–5. During a trip to Europe in 1905–6, he became interested in modern French painting, and he later worked as an art critic and museum curator. After 1922 he lived in Western Europe. This essay was published in *Zolotoe runo* (Golden Fleece) 11–12 (1907).

. . . The sense of decline in "new art" is most akin to a sense of fatigue and can be partially attributed to the unprecedented and incredible quantitative growth of all the arts. Suffice it to point out that in Paris alone about twenty-five thousand new works that lay claim to being works of art are exhibited annually. . . .

The terrible inner emptiness of contemporary art cannot be explained by quantitative excess alone, of course. Here there must be a substantial, vital reason, and it can be seen in the *technicality* of the "new art," where concern with technique is predominant and the quest for new devices and a new outward manner takes precedence over all other, more genuine quests. This is especially applicable to French painting. Surely it is significant that the "schools" of contemporary painting in France have formed and branched out under appellations signifying various techniques or outward devices—Pleinairism, Impressionism, Pointillism, Cloisonnism, Divisionism, and so on. I do not mean that the founders and creators of these "schools" were thinking only of technique. . . . But what these artists experienced and merely refracted in a device or manner became in a ready-made form the ultimate goal of their imitators and followers. . . .

Impressionism's tension and great height dropped very quickly. The fateful and inartistic nature of the analytical principle in art took its toll here. Indirectly, in the decline of Impressionism, intuitive creation once again triumphed over scientific creation. Impressionism did not blaze any trails or open any vistas. What once was considered new painting and was asserted as an end in itself, as an epoch, proved to be merely a new means of expression, a new and admittedly very clever and valuable device. Impressionism spread unusually rapidly and even more rapidly outlived itself. . . .

The rejection of Impressionism is not something that has come from outside. It arose within painting itself and after Gauguin and Cézanne became an accomplished fact. Instead of analysis came *synthesis;* instead of refined and conscious creation, naive intuition; instead of the latest atmosphere of scientific knowledge, the spirit of ancient ignorance. This, in broad outline, is the difference between Impressionism and its detractors. In this sense Van Gogh, Cézanne, and Gauguin are very important; they signal a major revolution. Erected with great effort, enormous skill, and all sorts of contrivances, the edifice of scientific painting was toppled by the onslaught of these primitives, these contemporary savages. With amazing forgetfulness, those who only recently had seen the path of truth in Impressionism proclaimed Gauguin the king of the newest painting and Cézanne the teacher of the younger generations.

. . . The spark found in Van Gogh and Gauguin was not passed on to others. It proved to be purely individual and inimitable, so to speak. Cézanne's spontaneity and primordial sincerity proved to be utterly individual and nontransferable. All in all, these two amazing and powerful artists were unable to shoulder the entire epoch. They were understood superficially, and only their devices were mastered—again only the technique! Painting could not sustain itself on them and continued to decline!

A new wave of inert technicality surged toward painting from the superficially grasped devices of Gauguin and Cézanne. Instead of a refined and complex technique, artists began looking for a refined and simple one—that was the only difference. I do not doubt that the best representatives of the "young" artists—Henri Matisse, Manguin, Derain, Puy, and so on and so forth—are all very talented men. In his solo exhibition, Henri Matisse showed himself to be an artist of great temperament and great daring. But to what does he apply his talent, his spiritual power, and his daring? To a new technique, a bold technique, an audacious technique—call it what you will, but it is nevertheless most certainly technique. And so close behind it comes a terrible emptiness, cold, and deathly fatigue!

You can't help but ask yourself whether painting can in fact proceed from Gauguin and Cézanne. Do these artists *begin* a new cycle of development? They both emerged from Impressionism, both came to reject it, both turned out to be individual and inaccessible. Both went on, and the door closed behind them. Would it not be more correct to think of them as having completed the cycle of development known as "modern art"? . . .

. . . Despite the vapidity and technicality of the "new art," some artists have had enormous inner resources and rich, lofty souls. There was the epically powerful Segantini, the profound Carrière, and the majestic and wise Puvis de Chavannes. Our contemporaries include Renoir, the heir to Fragonard, the austere Degas, the sensitive and intimate Vuillard, and the rhythmical and ecstatic Maurice Denis.

All of these are artists who have previous epochs behind them, who have not forgotten *traditions,* who have felt the breath of the classical past. This is a very characteristic and important feature of every great talent in the contemporary West. Their works always hold a reminder and a behest; they always speak of continuity, tradition, and a great love for and vital tie to the old. Even Gauguin, that most daring of innovators, was truly classical and eternally old in his medieval sense of the whole. . . .

With each passing day, the ideal of a high art is acquiring increasingly distinct features. The idea of high art is becoming more familiar as art's watchword of the moment. It is practically our homework for tomorrow. . . . One of the present moment's tasks—to restore painting's inner *content*—may have arisen as a reaction to the vapid beauty of decorative art. When decorative painting began its struggle with scientifically realistic painting, we could perceive in all this a move toward high art. But this move proved only temporary and relative. Contemporary painting could not be sustained by decorativeness and so manifested even more rapidly a tendency toward technicality and inner emptiness. . . . We must seek the reason for this in the generally inartistic nature of contemporary life. All quests for *style* do and cannot but end in failure. But only style provides the final moment, the high point and complete justification of decorative art. An era that has no artistic countenance of its own, no style of its own, can have no great decorative painting. . . . But, of course, contemporary art . . . must find its own content and express itself in its own way. To that end it may be more important at this moment to renounce decorativeness, forget musicality, relegate to the background color harmony and even the rhythm of the line, to sacrifice this temporarily in order to find the artist's very soul and his relationship to the world. . . .

The other goal and vital task of our day is to assert artistic *choice* as the basic condition of high art. The artist must assume predominance over the material of his art; he must restore his lost primacy vis-à-vis the world. That is, he must completely surmount meekly analytical realism. . . . Docile, scientifically objective painting found its highest expression in Claude Monet's well-known *Poplars* and *Haystacks* series. Here the artist selected nothing. He recorded nature as it was at a given moment—in the morning, at dusk, in the rain, in bright sunlight. The synthetic image, the *picture,* remains imagined, merely conceivable out of all these elements. For this is not the way to approach a picture. Analytical art took on the quality of an étude; it broke painting down into individual pieces and did not know how to combine them. Now what art needs most is the picture, the result of the artist's choice, the crystallization of his will. He must once again show that he is the master and first architect of the world. . . . He must recover his sense of divine proportions, his knowledge of natural architecture, and his power over the chaos of matter. . . .

What has been said here about the disappointment in "modern art" and the dream of high art it has engendered concerns art in the West, especially the more sensitive and "progressive" French art. It remains to be said to what extent all this applies to art in Russia.

Russia and the West are two different worlds with respect to literature and social, cultural, and daily life. They represent almost two different psychologies, two special types of psyche. . . . As has often been the case in Russian intellectual life, we had ten or fifteen years to master what had taken the West over a century to create. Almost all Western currents and artistic tendencies had some impact on Russian art, only the time periods strangely failed to coincide. The intimate landscape associated in France with Corot flourished among us in the day of Levitan and Iakunchikova,* mingling with Impressionism and almost simultaneously with experiments inspired by Gauguin. If Russian art had been nourished only by foreign influences, only by a reflected life, the inevitable result would have been complete turmoil and confusion. In reality this did not happen, and the mere fact that Russian art was able to survive

*Isaak Levitan (1860–1900), a landscape artist, was a progenitor of the "landscape of mood" in Russian painting. Mariia Iakunchikova (1870–1902), a painter, engraver, and designer, combined Art Nouveau motifs and Russian folklore.

this huge Western wave *in its own way* and so harmoniously and easily indicates that it stands on a firm foundation.

This foundation was there because, for better or worse, Russian art continued to exist throughout its long separation from the West. Without any save perhaps the most superficial influences, Ivanov blossomed and died . . . having surpassed his and any other epoch.* There was the marvelous Fedotov, there were Perov and Ge;† this period of "separation" produced Vasnetsov, Repin, Nesterov, and Surikov. We cannot discard and forget this period in Russian art, for it is vital and essential. The painting of the Wanderers contains a great deal that is decadent, heavy, and unnecessary. But we cannot in all fairness reject it completely. For there is something very important and typical in the very nature of the decadence and in this superfluity and heaviness itself without which we cannot understand the soul of Russian art. . . . Particularly now, when there is a desire to get away from technicality and even forget decorative and "musical" art for a while, they [the Wanderers—Ge, Perov, Kramskoi] may be valuable. These significant artists possessed content . . . inner content, seriousness, a responsibility, a soulfulness and depth that can be detected even through their rigid, crude, and tasteless painting.

Thanks to the Western wave and the World of Art, Russian painting emerged from its decline. Its level rose immediately and significantly. . . .

In the soulfulness and special "profundity" that are constant in Russian art and expressed now in religious quests or pure lyricism, we can see our historical tradition, so to speak. It extends from the thoughtful, serious portraitists of the eighteenth century to the poetic Venetsianov,‡ the great Ivanov, the delicately observant Fedotov, the recklessly honest Perov, and the tragic Ge, and from them to the torments of Vrubel' and the alluring and harrowing depth of Somov. This tradition is fully in keeping with the meaning contemporaneity has given to the dream of high art.

Perhaps this is why the idea of high art is becoming congenial to Russian art as well. In what already seems to us a remote time, during the era of darkness and separation from the West, in the mid-1880s, there was one Russian artist who independently . . . approached this idea. Frescoes by Vrubel' in the Church of Saint Cyril in Kiev represent the first and very rare example of the Russian dream of high art in the new era. In his subsequent works this absolutely extraordinary and singular artist came closer to the essence of high art than anyone else in "modern art" in either Russia or the West. . . .

The art of Vrubel', Somov, and Borisov-Musatov expressed the best features of

*Alexander Ivanov (1806–58), while living in Italy, worked for twenty years on *The Appearance of Christ to the People* (1857, State Tretiakov Gallery), a painting he meant to serve the moral transformation of Russia. In the studies for this work he developed a painterly manner close to Impressionism.

†Pavel Fedotov (1815–52) was a genre painter whose early works represent an original amalgam of Hogarth and Gogol. Vasilii Perov (1833/34–82) and Nikolai Ge (1831–94), both Wanderers, shared the conviction that art had a moral obligation to society to portray nature and character.

‡Aleksei Venetsianov (1780–1847) painted idyllic images of Russian peasant life.

Russian art—its religiosity, depth, and lyricism. In the stability and constancy of these features one is inclined to perceive that "something" that comprises the originality of Russian art. In this sense those who find that we cannot and should not learn *the main thing* from the *contemporary* West are correct. *Perhaps* it may be better to beware of the technicality and emptiness that are prevalent there *now.* But if we decide to do so and shield our independence from the influences of the moment, we must keep one point in mind.

We will study the great masters of the past forever and tirelessly. We will always pray to that high art in which religiosity, depth, and lyricism have been brought to complete and consummate expression. The ideal of high art has remained one throughout an endless variety of eras, peoples, countries and cultures, and individual talents. Today Western art is returning to it. Therefore, when we turn to our best traditions and to the primary sources of Western art, we are moving not toward a new separation but toward the merging of all into a single Ideal through the single Spirit of high art.

7

Sergei Diaghilev [and Dmitrii Filosofov]

"The Bases of Artistic Judgment" (1899)

Sergei Diaghilev (1872–1929), impresario of the Ballets Russes, was the leading cultural influence and inspiration of his day. This text is taken from a programmatic article, "Complicated Questions," published under Diaghilev's name in *Mir iskusstva* (World of Art) 3–4 (1899); however, most of it was written by Dmitrii Filosofov (1872–1940), the journal's literary editor.

Nationalism is yet another touchy subject in contemporary and especially Russian art. Many think it our only salvation and support it artificially. But what can be more fatal for a creator than the desire to *become* national? The only possible nationalism is an unconscious ethnicity of the blood,* and this is a rare and most precious treasure. Human nature itself should be ethnic; it should unconsciously reflect the brilliance of indigenous nationalism. One must bear the national character within oneself, be its native progeny, so to speak, with the ancient, pure blood of the nation. In such a case it is valuable, even immeasurably so. Nationalism elevated to a principle, on the other hand, is a mask and shows a lack of respect for the nation; all the crudeness of our art in particular arises from such false quests, as though capturing and conveying the essence of the Russian spirit demanded only the desire to do so. Now such seekers come along and capture what superficially seems most typical yet most of all discredits our national singularity. This is our error, and until we see well-proportioned harmony, majestic simplicity, and rare beauty of color in Russian art, we will not have true art. . . . Here another question arises. Must we protect this Russian blood, and, if so, how?

*In Russian "national" and "ethnic" are often used synonymously.

Many say that we do not need the West, which kills just this cherished delicate aspect in us, that it intrudes too much into our life with its sweet, aromatic fruits. This is wrong, profoundly wrong. You cannot understand who you are until you see what others are like. You must absorb all human culture, if only to reject it later. True Russian culture is too elastic to break under the influence of the West. Take other examples, recall the art of Pushkin, Turgenev, Tolstoy, and Tchaikovsky, and you will notice that only a subtle knowledge and love of Europe helped them to express our peasant huts and our folk heroes and the genuine melancholy of our songs. Restraining yourself or tuning your inspiration to the nationalist clatter is as annoying a delusion as an unconditional demand for, say, nature or truth. We can demand that artists approach a work with wholehearted sincerity and truthfulness, but this does not mean that we should seek sincerity and truth as necessary prerequisites for the act of creation itself. . . . We are above all a generation that hungers for beauty, and we find it everywhere, both in good and in evil. We have no clear-cut formula: formulas are blinding and lead only to stagnation. . . . We must not search for a universally obligatory definition of beauty because that would be blasphemy.

8

Sergei Diaghilev

"European Exhibitions and Russian Painters" (1896)

This article—published in *Novosti i birzhevaia gazeta* (News and Stock Exchange Journal) on August 26, 1896—was written as a critique of Russian artists who participated in exhibitions in Berlin and the Munich Secession in the Glaspalast.

. . . If Europe really does need Russian art, what it needs is its youth and immediacy. This our artists did not understand. They seemed ashamed to present themselves as Russians before the court of Europe and merely tried to prove that we can paint as well as the Western Europeans. Not once did it occur to anyone to ask whether we might teach them something they do not yet know. Can we break new ground in European art, or is it our destiny merely not to fall behind? This question never occurred to anyone, and this is what has depersonalized our artists.

Which of the major schools of painting has gained the most influence recently? The Norwegian. And why? As soon as all these snows, lakes, fogs, and fir trees appeared and there was a smell of the north in the air, all doors opened for these artists, and the school entered into the life of Europe as it took its appointed place in its art.

The same was expected of Russia as well; people expected not those grayish landscapes that gloomily peer out of corners as if begging to be noticed. They expected Neo-Byzantine "mystical" painting,* a Byzantine Puvis de Chavannes, so to speak. In its landscapes they expected to find a broad, endless expanse, the Russian coun-

*In summer 1895 Alexandre Benois was asked to compile "a section of the Russian Mystical School" for the 1896 Munich Secession.

tryside, and the serene ringing of village church bells. They expected the dazzling golden Russian autumn, and they expected the bright stormy spring with torrents and melting snow. Good heavens, had Levitan's *Quiet Cloister* appeared, or his *Above Eternal Rest,* or Nesterov's *Sergei of Radonezh* and *Monks,** we would have forced them to reckon with us and agree that we still possess an untouched poetry of our own. What we must present is not the trivial, caricatured coarseness "reeking of raw vodka," in Hanslick's† phrase, that our artists so often exhibit in the belief that it conveys our immediacy and originality. This coarseness merely shocks and repulses the cultured person, and we must crush it with the great strength inherent in Russian talent.

Our artists have satisfied none of these expectations. . . . But to be the victors in this brilliant European tournament they need thorough preparation and self-confident daring. They must push right on through. They must shock and not be afraid of doing so, and they must step forward all at once and show themselves completely, with all the strengths and weaknesses of their nationality. Fearing these weaknesses means concealing their strengths. Once they have won a place for themselves, they must become not occasional but constant participants in the art of all humanity. This solidarity is essential and must be expressed both by actively participating in the life of Europe and by attracting this European art to us. We cannot get along without this—it is the sole pledge of progress and the sole rebuff to the humdrum that has paralyzed our painting for so long.

9

Sergei Diaghilev

"The Exhibition in Helsingfors" (1899)

Diaghilev's review of the 1898 annual exhibition of Finnish artists at the Atheneum Art Museum in Helsinki (Helsingfors) was published in *Mir iskusstva* (World of Art) 1–2 (1899).

. . . We could learn something from the Finns' solidarity and love for their national art. Although there are noticeable differences among them—independent currents of populists and artists of an aristocratic Western bent—all of them manifest a single spirit imbued with a consciousness of their combined power. Their art has this power, which consists of an inborn love for their rugged national type, a poignant attitude toward their bleak nature, and finally an ecstatic cult of Finnish legends. The same populist element that so long impeded our painting has helped them become strong and stand on their own. This has happened only because they have penetrated the spirit of their people instead of taking a crudely photographic view of its unat-

*These works by Isaak Levitan and Mikhail Nesterov all include religious motifs in landscapes: churches in Levitan's *Quiet Cloister* (1890, State Tretiakov Gallery) and *Above Eternal Rest* (1894, State Tretiakov Gallery), and the life of hermits in Nesterov's *Sergei of Radonezh* (1891–99, State Tretiakov Gallery) and *Monks* (1895, State Tretiakov Gallery).

†Evidently the Austrian music critic and theorist Eduard Hanslick (1825–1904).

tractive aspects. As in the illustrations of Edelfelt (who at times can be truly national), as well as in Gallen-Kallela's decorative panels and Halonen's intimate scenes,* they have discovered and conveyed the poetry of the people. Especially charming in their works is their enormous skill and original technique, which is very much on a par with that of the West. They have all studied in Paris, and for them drawing is not the stumbling block on which so many capable artists break their necks. The support of the government and commissions from museums and private collectors enable young artists to spend entire winters in Paris and Italy. They keep abreast of everything and know the museums of Florence as well as they do the studios of Paris. . . . I would merely like to say that although Finnish art is very young, it emerged suddenly and with unusual vividness and originality. Finnish painting does not resemble the Scandinavian: it has none of Norway's naiveté, Denmark's feigned simplicity, or Sweden's European gloss. Nor does it resemble Russian painting, but it seems to me that the union of these two arts might produce just the results that both we and they desire. One can also sense in our painting of the past few years a turn toward a consciousness of our national strength. It is no accident that Vasnetsov and the significance of his individuality are beginning to be understood. His appeal to the Russian spirit in our art will not go unanswered. If, now that we have experienced the full bitterness of what thus far has been called the Russian style, we have nonetheless returned to the search for an art of our own, this is highly significant and we are indebted to Vasnetsov's advocacy for it. By combining the power of our nationality with the high culture of our closest neighbors, we might be able to lay the foundation for a new golden age and soon march off together to the West.

10

Vladimir Stasov

"Exhibitions" (1898)

The "Exhibition of Russian and Finnish Artists" held in St. Petersburg in January and February 1898, which included works by twenty-one Russian and ten Finnish artists working in different styles, is considered the first appearance of the World of Art group. This review was published in *Novosti i birzhevaia gazeta* (News and Stock Exchange Journal), January 27, 1898.

The organizer of the exhibition [Diaghilev] . . . went out and with great ardor and zeal indiscriminately invited a great many newly discovered buffoonish artists, some Russian, some Finnish, all of them decadent. Standing out in particular among the latter is Mr. Gallen, with his artistically hideous scarecrows intended to illustrate scenes from the Finnish epic, *The Kalevala*. The drawings, brushwork, color scheme, and composition of this artist are outrages, worse than the worst *lubok* drawings, but

*Albert Edelfelt (1854–1903) was the leader of the Finnish school in the latter half of the nineteenth century. Akseli Gallen-Kallela (1865–1931) was the major artist of Finnish Art Nouveau. Pekka Halonen (1865–1933) was a genre painter and landscapist who worked for a time with Gauguin in France.

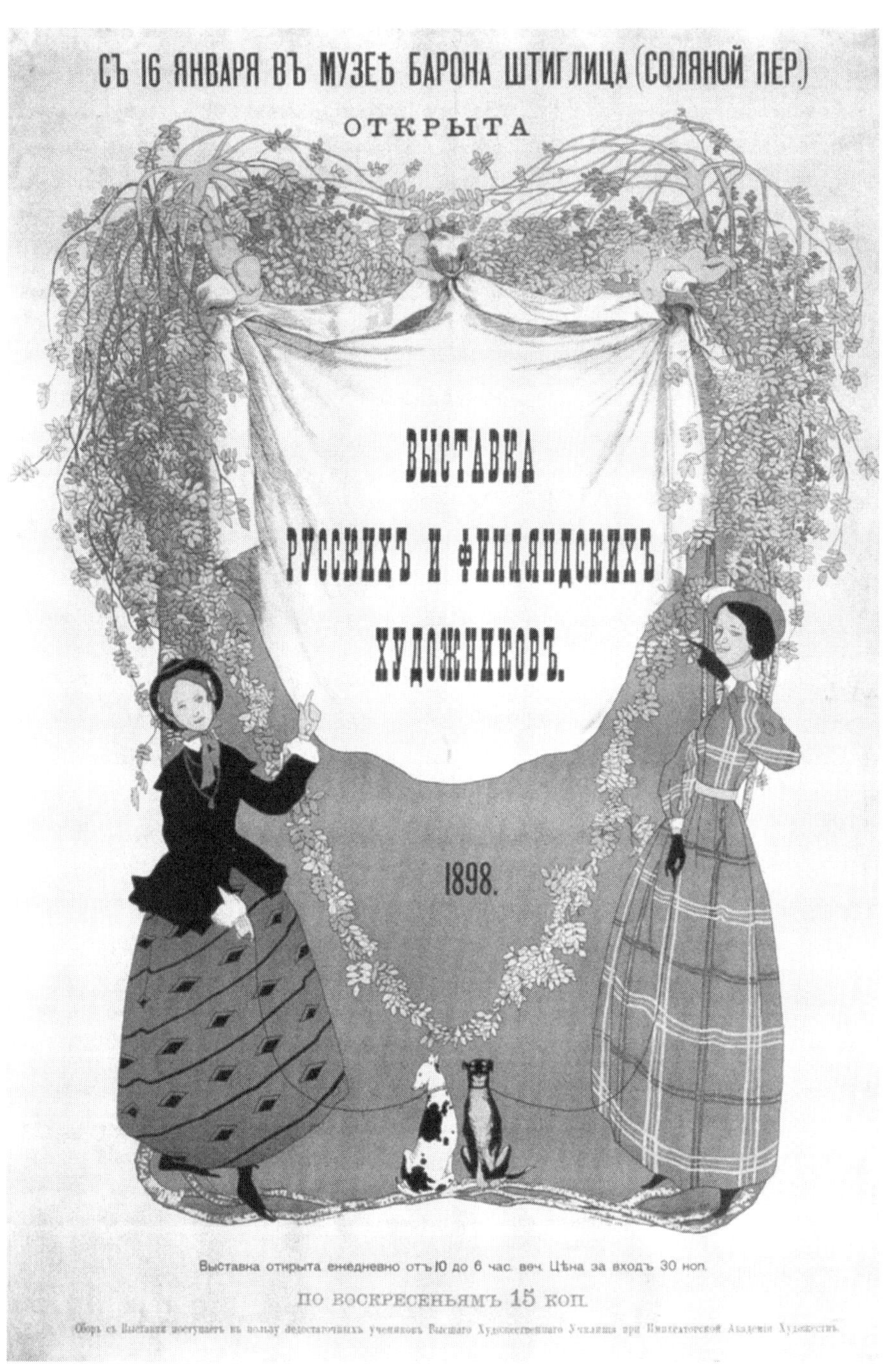

Constantine Somov, poster for "Exhibition of Russian and Finnish Artists," St. Petersburg, 1898

evidently Mr. Organizer likes them very much, since he has placed three of these pictures in the most honored spot, at the other end of the hall directly across from Mr. Vrubel' 's *Morning.* Strange tastes, amazing fantasies intended to introduce and propagandize this savage new art! Other pictures by the same artist (two portraits, *Brilliant Sunset,* and others) are specimens of the same monstrosity, and only the landscape *Imatra* bears a decent resemblance to the half-frozen, half-seething life of our famous waterfall. Besides Mr. Gallen, there is a platoon of deformities by Mssrs. Enckell (*Adam and Eve,* one entitled *Decorative Etude* of a boy twisted like a patient in an orthopedic clinic) and Järnefelt (*Noon Rest, Playing Children,* who are bowlegged and club-footed, and also *Green Islets,* in which the reflections of the sun on the water are painted simply as stripes of gold); finally, there is all of Vallgren's sculpture, which was done in Paris and therefore represents nothing but decadent French deformities in all these scraggly, worm-like figures. . . . The best of the Finns, of course, is Edelfelt, whose most remarkable picture, *Washerwomen,* is full of healthy, fresh realism and life; his *A Child's Funeral* and *Lake in Finland,* with their wonderful tones of water and sky are fairly good, but unfortunately during his long sojourn in Paris Edelfelt has become deeply Gallicized and has lost his individuality, as is unpleasantly evident in many of his pictures of the 1880s and 1890s. . . . Altogether, nearly all the works exhibited by the Finns at the current exhibition offer little comfort and bring little glory to the organizer's choice. What is new about the art here? What new accomplishments and new results are there?

The Russian part of the exhibition is much better. But here one must distinguish between the pictures by those of our artists who, following the present vogue, have rushed headlong to Paris, setting their hearts on its redeeming and ennobling power—like hundreds, almost thousands of our singers who have also run headlong to Milan, Rome, or Naples. They all end the same, bringing nothing home but various foreign banalities and routines without even touching upon what is important and good in Europe. . . .

11

Grigorii Miasoedov

Letter to Vladimir Stasov (1898)

The genre painter Grigorii Miasoedov (1834–1911) was one of the founders of the Wanderers. The occasion for his letter was probably the "Exhibition of Russian and Finnish Artists." The letter, dated March 6, 1898, is in the Manuscript Section of the Institute of Russian Literature (Pushkinskii dom), f. 294, op. 1, no. 398.

What are these foreign locusts who have swooped down upon the stunted field of Russian art? What manner of patriots are these who foist upon us primordial Finns, Swedes, Norwegians, Frenchmen, Englishmen, Poles, and Spaniards? . . . You might think that this is jingoism, that I am an enemy of everything foreign, and that, finally, we have nothing to learn from them. No, that's not what I think. . . . Our merchants and moneybags, who have so zealously championed protective tariffs, turn out to be the leading supporters and consumers of everything foreign. They are above what the Russian school has to offer; they need Decadents and Symbolists; they fancy French syphilis, English grace, German stiltedness, Finnish ugliness—anything but Russian life, which they find so disgusting because it reminds them too much of the lesser brethren who have crammed their fat purses. . . . Now, when most artists (except the Association) are reeling and rushing about like singed cats, don't you really think it appropriate to say something inspiring to them and remind them of their virtues and obligations[?]

12

Vladimir Stasov

"The Court of Miracles" (1899)

Forty-two Russian and Western artists participated in the "First International Art Exhibition," which opened on January 22, 1899. Mainly painters of the *Juste Milieu* and Symbolism were shown in the Western section. The Impressionists were represented by Monet (two works), Renoir (one), and Degas (eight). The title of this article, published in *Novosti i birzhevaia gazeta* (News and Stock Exchange Journal), February 8, 1899, was borrowed from Victor Hugo's *Hunchback of Notre Dame*.

. . . The "Decadent elder's" selection here was, as always, dismal. Suddenly we are being shown such unacceptable and insufferable works as Puvis de Chavannes sketches, Degas pictures, and Besnard portraits. And the prices displayed prove their great significance: for Puvis de Chavannes's works, 16,500 rubles and 10,200 rubles; for Degas's, 40,000 and 14,400; for Besnard's, 7,500. What a disgrace! . . . Why, Puvis de Chavannes's composition is pure academicism, utter carrion, a completely soulless work by Poussin of blessed memory! As for Degas's pictures, they consist entirely of ballerinas, ugly from head to toe, sitting and standing, with hideously spread and absurdly drawn legs, hands, and torsos, or else of absolutely meaningless, contemptible hordes of jockeys on glossy horses! (His *Return of Jockeys from the Race* is much better executed, although it costs a great deal less.) Besnard's buffoonish portraits are revolting figures of some women or other, disgustingly painted, whose faces and physiognomies and even every fold of their offensive clothing are repulsive. Evidently this impression is not ours alone, but is shared by everyone, since all these works—how long has it been now, and no one in Paris is buying?—have to be sent to us Russian fools. Maybe we'll be stupid enough to buy them, given their insane prices! . . .

To be fair, it has been a long time since the pictures of the deservedly well-known French painters L'hermitte, Dagnan-Bouveret, and Raffaelli have provided any idea

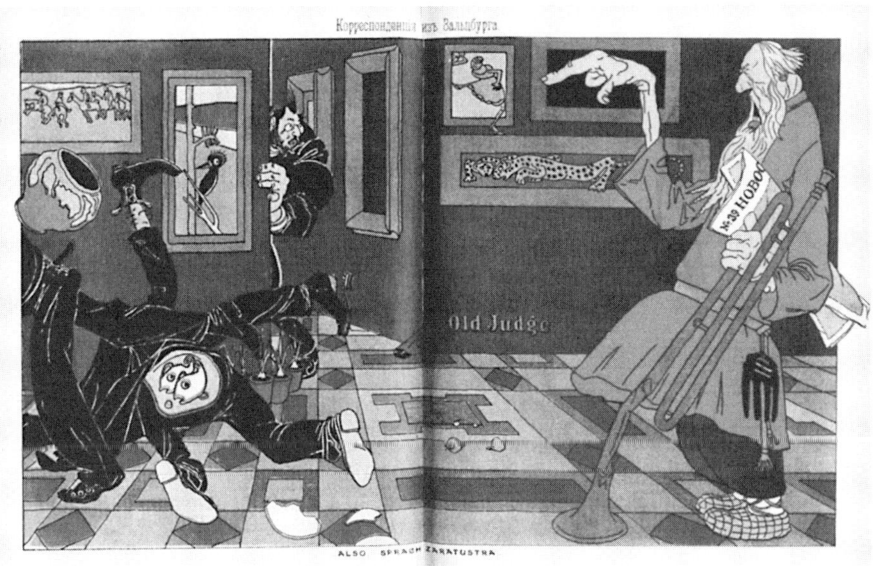

"Old Judge" (Pavel Shcherbov), "Also sprach Zaratustra," *Shut* (Jester) 8 (1899). On the right of this caricature Vladimir Stasov appears in ultra-Russian garb, carrying a trombone (a nod to his nickname) and a newspaper. Scrambling away from him are members of the World of Art, while a frightened critic, Nikolai Kravchenko (a scapegoat of Stasov's review), peers out from behind the corner. On the wall one can recognize two Degas paintings that Stasov mentions—a ballerina and a group of jockeys—as well as a gouache, *The Woodpecker* (1892–93), by Gallen-Kallela, who was also criticized by Stasov.

at all about the art and works of these remarkable and talented Realists. Some of them at this exhibition are weak, and others are mediocre. They were selected poorly. . . .

But here's what's sad. Supporters of the exhibition's foreign section and its unfortunate selections have turned up, supporters who try to defend everything there that is bad, weak, false, and licentious. One of our art critics of the "dauber" ilk is attempting to assure his readers that the exhibition is showing foreign works that are not only remarkable but good and even magnificent. How about that!

And who is he suddenly pushing into the foreground? Böcklin! . . .

After all, however, the daubers usually regard "realism" as something crude, improper, illicit, and inappropriate—something that should be hunted down and wiped from the face of the earth. . . . Together with the Decadents, the daubers can spit, if they wish, on that art of ours which has always sounded the same note of truth and realism as Pushkin, Griboedov, Gogol, Turgenev, Ostrovsky, Dostoevsky, and finally Lev Tolstoy. They can spit if they wish, but that will not change the matter one iota, and we Russians will still remain the faithful partisans and admirers of everything great and indestructible that Russian talent and genius have created—the pictures of Repin, Vereshchagin, Vladimir Makovskii, Surikov, and the best of their comrades.

13

Igor' Grabar'

"Around European Exhibitions" (1904)

In May 1904, Grabar' made a trip through Europe. This summary of his impressions, published in *Khronika 'Mira iskusstva'* (World of Art Chronicle) 7, is his last significant work on contemporary Western art. It is also a kind of postscript to the 1897 text by Grabar', "Decline or Renaissance?" [2], and thus not only illustrates his own evolution but also marks the line where most of the World of Art group halted in their acceptance of contemporary art.

. . . Significant talents appear so rarely in our day that, famished as we are, we greedily pounce upon them and endow them with qualities we ourselves have invented.

We too ardently desire to see our dreams come true as soon as possible. Afterwards we think we have been deceived. In fact, we were deceiving ourselves.

This is the source of all our disappointments.

WHISTLER

. . . Whistler's countless imitators have done him a perfidious disservice. They are the insufferable street-organs that can make you loathe even decent music if it is played beneath your window every morning and every evening. I cannot recall a single tolerable foreign exhibition at which "Whistlerism" was not represented in some form or other. The ones who most set my teeth on edge were the Scots. They have become positively unbearable. This so-called taste, which in reality is extraordinary tastelessness and vulgarity, is no longer to be tolerated. All this taste amounts to is setting a woman in a dashing pose, standing or seated, as far as possible *en trois quarts* and with only her eyes directed "interestingly" straight at the viewer; the painting itself should be in so-called pleasant tones, something light gray or brown with magnificently varnished blotches. The recipe for these "harmonies," "arrangements," and *"Stimmungbildness"* consists in letting one color dominate—the *"Leitfarbe"*—which must not be bright but rather slightly muted and a little dirty.

I recall that not so long ago in Moscow it was considered very *distingué* among rather good artists to admix a blackish tint "for harmony."

That was necessary, of course, after the horrible, truly barbaric colors that, thoroughly blackened, even today assault the eye from the Tretiakov Gallery's walls. The Germans, who had their own barbarians, needed it as well, as did the French. Whistler has done a great deal to ennoble the eye. He has done even more for the contemporary poster, whose large simplified blots come directly from *Miss Alexander.*

. . . It is now clear, however, that Whistler was not the giant he seemed just a short while ago. His talent is not free from what the French call *fumisterie.* At times something cheap and even downright vulgar has crept in. He has toyed with his talent too often and too long, and there is too much of the con man and performer in him. . . .

GERMANISM

The keenest disappointment is the specific Germanic spirit in art in which I once believed. Having lived a long time in Germany, I became accustomed to it. At that time it seemed to me that to appreciate specifically German art correctly one had to become accustomed to it and its language.

Nonsense! Nothing of the sort is necessary. I was gravely mistaken. Truly great works of art speak for themselves. Although we are not Spaniards we understand Velásquez no worse than they, and in our own day we appreciated and came to love the brilliant art of the Finns before Gallen and Järnefelt's contemporaries did. If we must enter the labyrinths of nationalism to savor a work of art properly, then quite frankly that work isn't worth a copper.

Dürer is great not because his "Germanism" is strong. This same Germanism did not save the fourteen works by Klinger (not the sculptures) exhibited in Munich. Everything of his here is somehow unbelievably pompous, and standoffish, and dreary. There is a pretension to genius throughout; the only thing lacking is talent. Klinger himself and all artists as well obviously regard these paltry drawings and boring *Studien* as masterpieces. . . .

CÉZANNE

In Berlin I managed to visit Cézanne's big exhibition. I had wanted to for some time, for up until then I had seen his works only at random and in snatches. . . . I still could not understand exactly what connected the latest French school and Cézanne. He could be not just the father, or even the grandfather of most of them, for he was a contemporary of Manet. Although much of what I had seen earlier pleased me very little, and some things seemed simply nonsense and not without their share of charlatanism, I had still not lost hope of seeing real masterpieces signed by this mysterious name. . . .

So there I was at last in three rooms packed full of his works at Cassirer's.* And I must say that awaiting me here was the bitterest of all the disappointments I experienced while knocking about Europe. . . . Cézanne will never stand side by side with not only giants such as Manet, Monet, and Degas, but even with great masters such as Renoir. . . . All of his art possesses one enormous, unusual virtue, and that is its sincerity. I insist that this is unusual, because in our day sincerity has been thoroughly cheapened. I think that sincerity is a far rarer guest in contemporary art than is generally accepted. I know many excellent works that contain not a drop of sincerity. This still does not make them bad. For example, in a certain sense everything that Maurice Denis does is insincere. . . . Cézanne is utterly sincere, as sincere as an unspoiled child or a medieval miniaturist. I am deeply convinced of this. I would have trouble nam-

*Cézanne exhibited at Paul Cassirer's gallery in May 1904.

ing any living artist who possesses this precious quality to such a degree. For that reason even in his most extravagant works I do not see a hint of charlatanism. Looking through all these many landscapes, portraits, *natures mortes,* and mythological scenes with naked women, you begin to understand that these works, dated not infrequently 1860, have something in common with the painting of the Impressionists. . . .

The difference between Cézanne and the first Impressionists is that the latter proceeded immediately from nature, whereas Cézanne began from the old masters. Curiously, Vollard simply cannot reconcile himself to the public's negative response to this artist. He allows that "one can fail to understand Claude Monet, but *parbleu,* not Cézanne, who has a place in the Salon Carré at the Louvre." . . . His black portraits of the 1860s do in fact seem to have been taken from some gallery or other. The beautiful black and silver tones and the psychology in some of them are superb. It is only their dislocated drawing that makes them unpleasant. Some of the mythological scenes are also very good, but best of all, of course, are the *natures mortes.* Yet together with the good things there are so many impossibly bad ones that it is simply maddening. Can't the man see? Among these in particular are a few large canvases, variations on some very commonplace genre scenes in the worst of taste. You don't want to believe that they were painted by the same person who did these energetic *natures mortes,* with their severe, almost metallic contours and their cheerful, uncompromising, and boldly assertive colors. They possess a kind of candid natural nakedness, a slightly cynical nakedness that is a thousand times more sweet and precious than the sanctimonious, hypocritical finery in which ordinary exhibition art struts about.

In spite of all the many good things I have said about Cézanne, nonetheless I left his exhibition completely disappointed. I did not find in it the main thing—the Grand Art venerated by so many people whose opinion I sincerely respect. He is an interesting, but not a great artist.

14

Vasily Kandinsky

"A Letter from Munich" (1909–10)

In 1902 Kandinsky began writing detailed surveys of German artistic life for *World of Art*. In the years 1909–10 he published these materials in *Apollon* (Apollo). The translation here, by Peter Vergo, is reprinted from *Kandinsky: Complete Writings on Art,* edited by Kenneth C. Lindsay and Peter Vergo, vol. 1 (Boston: G. K. Hall, 1982), 57–69;

APOLLON 1 (1909)

. . . Something of the utmost importance for artistic life in Bavaria happened: [Hugo] von Tschudi, who had left a similar position in Berlin "from force of circumstances," was invited by the government to take the place of the recently deceased director of the Bavarian galleries. Tschudi accepted this invitation, and arrived here this summer with his steely, quiet energy, to come to grips at once with the seemingly hopeless problem of our museums. As if by magic, the Alte Pinakothek was swept clean of a whole series of inferior pictures, while the important and powerful ones reappeared, hung in such away that their whole significance and profundity meets the eye at first glance. What will become of the Neue Pinakothek?

This same Geheimrat [Privy Counselor] von Tschudi immediately showed great interest in an association that had just been formed by the mutual efforts of a group of Russian and German artists, the Neue Künstler-Vereinigung München [New Artists' Association of Munich]. Thanks to his active involvement, the association has received serious support from several quarters and is now making its debut at the end of November at the Galerie Brakl, whence it will embark on a grand tour of Germany (more about this association in due course).

At the same time, another organization has sprung from the soil of the idea borrowed from the Parisian *Indépendants,* but alas, freely translated not into the language of the Germans, but of the Philistines! This—the Deutsche Künstler-Verband—is intended to organize exhibitions without a jury. To the shame of the Munich artists who took part in its constitutive assemblies, statutes were passed and adopted as part of the constitution denying the right of membership to both foreigners and women. (An interesting detail is that foreigners whose native tongue is German can become members, e.g., Austrians, Swiss—but not Austrian Slavs, Swiss-French, etc.!) . . .

Is there in truth a subterranean force to be found that is already preparing itself for a surprise attack on the enemy, that will succeed in banishing the "innovators" and temporarily shoring up the old walls, so that one will in conscience be able to say, "All's well"?

Or will we in fact soon feel a breath of fresh air? Will it reach the *"Kunststadt München"* [Munich, the city of art]?

Apart from the international exhibition in the Glaspalast, combined this year with that of the Secession (this meeting of the "old" and the "new" under one roof occurs from time to time as the result of a compromise between the latter and the government, where many laugh and few stand in wonder in front of the large canvas by Hodler—admittedly, almost the only serious and powerful work in an exhibition that habitually abounds in pictures—apart from this exhibition, there has now opened in the rooms of the so-called "Ausstellung München 1908" [Munich Exhibition 1908] a special exhibition of Far Eastern and Asiatic, predominantly Japanese art, "Japan und Ostasien in der *Kunst*" [Japan and East Asian Art]. . . . Again and again, so much that is part of Western art becomes clear when one sees the infinite variety of the works of the East, which are, nonetheless, subordinated to and united by the same fundamental "tone"! It is precisely this general "*inner* tone" that the West lacks. Indeed, it cannot be helped: we have turned, for reasons obscure to us, away from the internal toward the *external.* And yet, perhaps we Westerners shall not, after all, have to wait too long before the same inner sound, so strangely silenced, reawakens within us and, sounding forth from the innermost depths, involuntarily reveals its affinity with the East—just as in the very heart of all peoples, in the now darkest depth of depths of the spirit, there shall resound *one* universal sound, albeit at present inaudible to us—the sound of the spirit of *man.*

Munich, October 3, 1909

APOLLON 7 (1910)

Nowhere is so dreadful a caricature of art created with such assiduity, such conscientiousness, as in Germany. The German people (of which, naturally, the strong of mind and profound of spirit constitute only the better part) is unable, by its very nature, to discover just those forms, just those means of expression necessary for that as yet dimly perceived future content. Other nations, far more gifted from the formal point of view, do not entirely lose touch with the ground under their feet when the general state of culture oppresses and to all appearances banishes the spirit from life. The Germans, on the other hand, in this preeminently formal period, are found wanting and have no alternative but to seek foreign help. They have talent, but lack a firm basis; they have strength, but lack the material; they have ambition, but lack the goal. The result is dreary and abhorrent.

Here and there, one encounters some consciousness of this internal disorder, the search for a cure. Man is, however, inclined to mistake effects for causes, and thus not infrequently attacks the former, rather than the latter. This is what has happened in this case. It is made to seem as if those responsible for the dispirited state of German art are not those who have banished the spirit from our lives, i.e., for the most part the Germans themselves, but rather those at whom they clutched in their helplessness, i.e., the French. This strange logic has made rapid strides and has led to the facile conclusion: We must turn our backs on the French, and German art will be born anew. This is the root of the present patriotism and of the unpleasantly naive measures already taken by two artists' associations, aimed at the exclusion of foreigners. . . .

I could not free myself from the question: Why is it necessary to "paint" nature in different colors? If it is to derive pictorial *composition,* the *inner sound* of the picture, then why does this "composition," this "sound," extend only as far as the transformation of color? And why is drawing, that is to say, the nonpainterly, incidental aspect of art, so carefully avoided, thus, as it were, clipping the wings of the artist's *creative* imagination and power?

Strange how it appears necessary to find, discover, resurrect anew that principle of subordinating drawing, too, to internal aims that was so clearly, so definitely resurrected from the dead by Cézanne! In fact, if it were not for the presence of Matisse at this exhibition, one would suspect that this spirit had already departed again. That only one of the "younger" French artists exhibiting here has kept it alive may be explained by the fact that the others have not as yet impressed upon themselves the imperative necessity of creating pictorial composition, or indeed, developing the necessary language.

It is uncertain how far the spectator's imagination might have led him on looking at the above-mentioned Frenchmen, were it not for the fact that the Moderne Galerie recently took it upon itself to give over its large downstairs room (its native section) to two Berlin luminaries: Slevogt and Corinth. Here, one's imagination leads nowhere, or rather, if it leads anywhere, then it is not into artistic realms, but rather . . . anatomical or even gynecological. Into the latter, even the most modest spectator might well be led by, for example, Corinth's much-vaunted *Bathsheba.* A large, soft female is lying on her back. Naturally, with her legs apart. Naturally, naked. For some reason, around her waist a scrap of what appears to be black fur hangs down, disappearing between her large, soft thighs. In her right hand she holds a flower. A noble picture! . . .

Munich has never mastered painting, indeed, it seems as if in her naiveté she has never suspected its existence. There has, on the other hand, been an intensive study of organic form. It is linear form, in all its aspects, that has been the guiding principle in the schools (apart, of course, from the drawing classes of the Academy, where what is demanded is either simply fluency of technique, or else the careful annotation of every fold, boil, wart, and chance spot on face and body), and it has constituted the criterion of artistic production in the eyes of the liberal juries.

II

WESTERN INFLUENCES

SYMBOLISM, IMPRESSIONISM, POST-IMPRESSIONISM, AND THE *GOLDEN FLEECE* EXHIBITIONS

Around 1900 Art Nouveau and Symbolism rapidly acquired popularity in Russian modernist circles, and the first issue of *World of Art* provocatively declared the deceased Puvis de Chavannes a "great artist" (see p. 56). For modernist critics, Western Symbolism was an important alternative to pedestrian realism and an example of creative freedom [15]. But among artists, the direct impact of Art Nouveau and Symbolism often resulted in no more than the clichés of European "decadence."

Symbolism in Russia art had precursors in painting (Mikhail Vrubel' and Viktor Borisov-Musatov), but it became established primarily as a literary movement; thus it is no accident that it found passionate admirers among Symbolist writers, such as Ivan Konevskoi and Valerii Briusov, whose journal *Scales* popularized Aubrey Beardsley and James Ensor and presented Odilon Redon as the central figure in European art. In the early 1900s, Maurice Denis also became important as a potential re-creator of the Grand Style. He was the first modern foreign painter to produce a complete decorative ensemble for a Russian patron, *The Story of Psyche,* which was commissioned by Ivan Morozov (1907–9, presently at the Hermitage). Denis's articles were published in the *Golden Fleece,* and his approach to the picture as an autonomous organism was influential among the younger generations of Russian painters (Larionov, Goncharova). However, they rejected his Symbolist interpretation of the Post-Impressionists and instead took the painting of the Post-Impressionists themselves as the starting point for the avant-garde.

Russian exhibitions of the 1890s demonstrated a persistent Impressionist influence, assimilated secondhand. For Russian artists, Impressionism was mostly an aggregate of *plein air* painting techniques that produced a novel treatment of traditional landscape motifs. The works of the French Impressionist painters themselves, however, remained essentially unknown. The 1900 Paris World Fair was a turning point. After seeing it, Alexandre Benois declared, "The mere skirt on a ballet student [by Degas] . . . contains more art than hundreds and thousands of pictures by the official Realists."* For the most part, however, Russian texts on Impressionism are tinged with skepticism; because Pointillism was regarded as a natural outcome of Impressionism, the latter's rationalistic qualities were overemphasized. Such judgments, which proved tenacious, were expressed even when their context had changed. Consequently, the exemplary Impressionist for the Russians was Monet, whose works were most fully represented in Moscow. Many avant-gardists (Larionov, Burliuk, Popova, and others)

**Mir iskusstva* (World of Art) 21–22 (1900): 205.

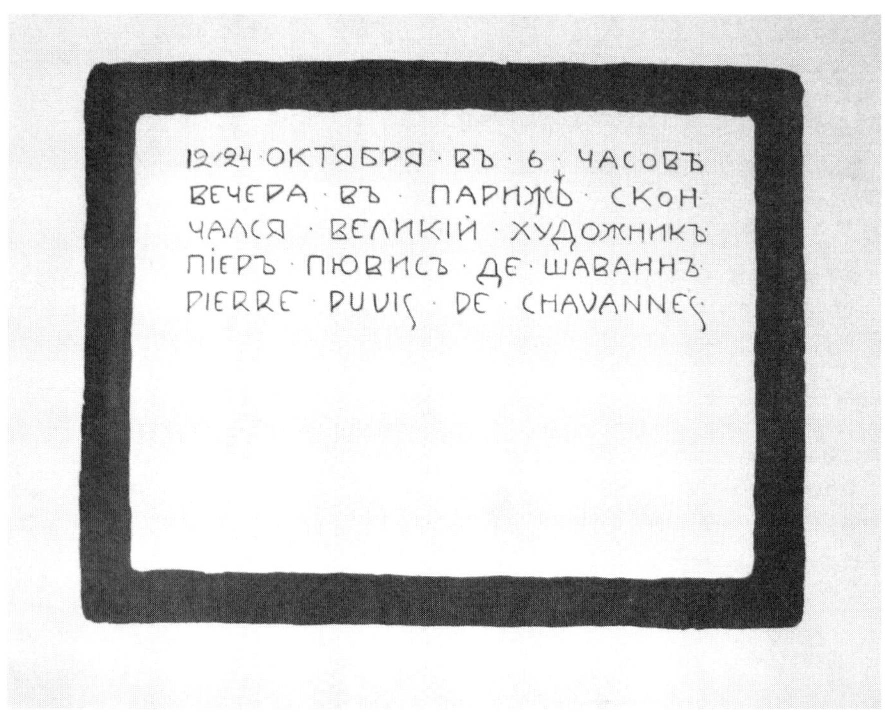

Notice of Pierre Puvis de Chavannes's death in *Mir iskusstva* (World of Art) 1 (1899)

went through a brief period of Impressionist influence and sometimes used the term "Impressionism" to label their movement (Burliuk, Kulbin).

The tradition of modern painting was radically reinterpreted in the mid-1900s, when Gauguin, Van Gogh, and Cézanne—previously known only to a small circle of artists and connoisseurs—moved to the center of attention. If the appearance of the Fauves passed almost unnoticed by the general public (in late 1905 Russia was in the critical phase of a revolution), the Post-Impressionists' exhibitions resonated in both Petersburg and Moscow [13, 21, 22]. The Post-Impressionists' discovery and recognition in Europe caused a split among Russian modernists, who had either to reconsider their ideas [23] or to reject the new art [21]. An important point in the new art's favor was how readily progressive Russian critics accepted the legend of the great Post-Impressionists as prophetic martyrs [cf. 22, 27].

Gauguin was the first to be appropriated in Russia. His retrospective exhibition at the 1906 Autumn Salon coincided with a Russian exhibition at that same salon, which many young artists visited. Russian texts on Gauguin were surprisingly few, but his influence on the pre-avant-garde is beyond question. He introduced a new approach to color and surface and directed younger artists to non-Classical and non-European cultures. (As early as 1910, however, his reception began to be "corrected" by an awareness of Matisse, who showed Gauguin's painting to be a forerunner of Fauvism and thereby exposed the limitations of Symbolist interpretations of it.)

Cézanne's influence on Russian painting was truly unprecedented in scope. In its early stage, Cézanne's reception was linked not so much to his method as to the liberation he brought from the conventions of Realism and Impressionism [24]. Russians adopted—and often exaggerated—the "sculpted" volumes, construction of perspective, and dissolution of line in his paintings. Early Larionov and Goncharova, and the Russian Cézannists—artists of the Jack of Diamonds (Konchalovskii, Mashkov, Fal'k, and others)—tended at this time to deny rather than demonstrate their devotion to Cézanne. They were deliberately rowdy, combining the French artist's manner with the techniques of the shop sign, the *lubok,* and so on. (Paradoxically, right when Cézanne's influence was particularly intense and fruitful, there were no monographic studies of him in Russian.)

The *Golden Fleece,* the Symbolists' magazine (1906–9), played a vital role in acquainting Russia with modern French art. Important articles came from foreign contributors such as Alexandre Mercereau (pen-name: Eshmer Valdor), Charles Morice, and Maurice Denis. Both French and Russian (Maksimilian Voloshin) critics on the *Golden Fleece* thought that contemporary painting's main task was to move beyond Impressionism and develop the poetics of Post-Impressionism, especially Gauguin, in a Symbolist direction [23]. The publication of Matisse's "Notes of a Painter" in 1909 was a landmark event. Two exhibitions organized by the *Golden Fleece* in Moscow, in 1908 and 1909, presented a wide range of artistic phenomena, from Impressionism to Matisse to early Cubist works by Georges Braque, and included young Russian artists who were rapidly moving toward Neo-Primitivism. These two exhibitions clearly demonstrated that Post-Impressionism had become a major source for radical developments in contemporary French art. They also forced Russian modernists [25, 26] into an ambivalent position. While accepting Gauguin, Cézanne, and Van Gogh as founders of modern painting, they criticized young Russian artists for an unwise and rootless "imitation" of contemporary French painters, particularly Matisse. This approach became a principal element in the modernist critique of the radical avant-garde in the 1910s [59].

15

Ivan Konevskoi

"Böcklin's Painting" (1900)

Ivan Konevskoi (pseudonym of Ivan Oreus, 1877–1901), poet and essayist, was a precursor of Russian literary Symbolism. In the 1900s the Swiss Symbolist painter Arnold Böcklin was remarkably popular among Russian modernists. Konstantin Fofanov's poem "Isle of the Dead" was written in 1902, and in 1909 Sergei Rakhmaninov composed a symphonic poem with the same title. Konevskoi's essay appeared in his book *Mechty i dumy* (Dreams and Reflections) (St. Petersburg, 1900).

. . . His painting opens up, and no matter where you look, it truly breathes the vastness of God's world. Fresh, unbound air sweeps from sea to sea. You can feel rippling life flowing in broad streams over the entire face of the earth, and all the ravishing joy of being speaks to the heart in this impetuous motion and overwhelming excitement. . . .

Böcklin revels and is lost in admiration for the world; he delights in it, blissfully, and never forgets himself or lets himself be befuddled by anyone's charms. He is always on the road, the eternal wanderer. All of his contemplations are like halting places, temporary crossroads on the great journey of life that rushes on and on and rushes him forward. In the most secluded grove of an ancient forest of broad-leaved oaks, the abode of the sleepy nymph or dryad, the throb and trembling of life pushes on. No matter what suffocating corner he hides in, the radiant and dismal expanse, the boundless expanse of the earth always enters his heart from somewhere, some corner. The day moves on; the trees and grasses grow; the wind flies in from across the sea. And the meditator always has the strength to arise, grasp his staff and bag, and bid his charming shelter farewell.

The artist has crossed the field of life from end to end without missing a single nook, and after experiencing everything, each time passing through the roaring fire, he and his lucid spirit have emerged whole and unscathed.

All his pictures' images are drawn into the same joyous torrent of universal, heart-stopping motion. . . .

In his *Play in the Waves,* Böcklin seizes upon images from all ages and ways of life. Thus, his pictures breathe freely not only because of the broad vistas that open in every direction, but also because he keeps alive the sense of the ancient breadth and infinity of historical existence. Along with this boundlessness of space, we are faced with the boundlessness of time. Throughout his painting, faces often of a pagan cast cross and collide with Christian or at least modern images. This is the same luxurious diversity of notions that holds such strange charms in the Shakespearean world or the art of the Italian Renaissance. You discover for yourself the simmering ferment of the seeds of different ages and cultures and see new, complex cycles of life begin to seethe.

And these human storms invariably arise out of the womb of the great ancestral elements, mute nature, whose life-giving depths hold sway throughout Böcklin's presentation of the world. . . .

[Vita somnium breve] Oh, how luxuriant and light it is there! How formidably do the easy air and clear light of the barely perceptible expanse there, beyond the knoll, in the mysterious rays, pour over this little corner beside a secluded spring pulsing with life. Something trembles in the hearts of the beings hiding here. How pleasant and sweet it is to be alive; passion is hot, rapture enthralls; yet sleep is as light as steam. It carries us like a cloud, and do we care? We love you, generous and untrammeled, kind and formidable life!

Here is the perfect symbol of Böcklin's thoughts about the unceasing flickering of life, the most complete view, *in breadth,* of its abundance and rippling surface. From here one's thoughts turn of their own accord to Böcklin's other most perfect contemplation of life *in depth,* his penetration of its eternal depths. . . .

It is difficult to believe that motion and change alone reign in the world. In these transformations the spirit hungers to feel perfect harmony and ultimate symmetry. The world of Böcklin's untrammeled emotion also holds this solemn moment. His *Sacred Grove* holds the promise of this mood, but here, in a way, the artist was still worshipping the great life that is latent and obvious in Nature . . . from the outside. Clearly seeing only its manifestations in the colorful universe, he distinguished nothing but twilight in its inner being. Yet in *Elysian Fields* (Gefilde der Seligen) he has managed to work a miracle. He has revealed the prototype of a fullness so complete that the longer you look at it the more clearly it tells your heart that fullness has been achieved and nothing more is needed. . . .

In Böcklin's rippling, wind-caressed pictures one feels the pure Goethean pantheism that suffuses the world in the continuous "Werden" (Becoming) of the single World Soul (Gott und Welt).* . . .

16

Alexandre Benois

"Maurice Denis" (1901)

Alexandre Benois (1870–1960) was an artist, art historian, and critic. After studying law and then, briefly, painting at the Academy of Fine Arts in St. Petersburg, he became known as a painter and illustrator, but especially as a stage designer for Diaghilev's Ballets Russes. After 1926 he settled in Paris.

Benois published this essay in *Mir iskusstva* (World of Art) 7 (1901), but became disappointed with Denis after seeing the artist's decorative panel series *The Story of Psyche* (1907–8) and readdressed his call, "Become as little children" (cf. Matthew 18:3), to Matisse.

Maurice Denis is one of the strangest talents in contemporary art. The first thought that comes to mind upon viewing his pictures is doubt. Is this truth or deception? Is his art sincere or a mystification? This is what I wondered when I first saw his pictures at the Paris Salon of 1897. Actually, at the time there was no question per se, since the works seemed obviously a joke, buffoonery, affectation, though not devoid of talent and wit. The genealogy of the component parts of his art, so to speak, was immediately clear to me. He borrowed the naiveté of his drawing from the Italian Pre-Raphaelites, his stylization from Puvis de Chavannes, his colors as well from Puvis and partly from the Gothic illuminators, and his human types from Botticelli and Filippino Lippi. Apparently nothing was his own; everything was but a clever compilation of others' work. Probably the only new and original elements were the eccentricity of the undertaking, the exaggerated naiveté, and the pursuit of extravagance. . . . Strange to say, however, Denis's pictures amused but did not disturb me. The *talent* of the imitations (I was sure they were imitations) was too obvious. . . .

*Konevskoi uses the German word *Werden* ("to become"), alluding to Goethe's poem "Selige Sehnsucht" (1814), from the collection *West-Östlicher Divan,* where the line reads: *Stirb und werde* ("die and become; die and be"). *Gott und Welt* refers to a cycle of poems by Goethe.

I visited the Champ de Mars Salon often that year and soon knew it by heart. Little by little, the marvelous works of Latouche, Simon, L. Frédéric, and Besnard, in front of which I sat for hours the first few days, lost their original charm. I tired of admiring them; I continued to appreciate them, but I was already feeling the indifference that is immediately followed by disillusionment. In contrast, Denis's "mad," "fraudulent" pictures attracted me with an irresistible power. I recall being even rather ashamed of this. . . .

Finally I surrendered—I *believed* in my enthusiasm. I became convinced that there was something more than clever charlatanism in Denis. Something similar happened to me in the early 1890s, when I first became acquainted with Maeterlinck's dramas.

. . . We have been so taken with realism and naturalism that we are somehow ashamed to look at an artistic technique that has not been borrowed directly from reality and is not concerned with photographic reality. Fantastic subjects are fine—banned for twenty years they are once again permissible—but they must be clothed in the same form as realistic depictions. Only then will people believe them. This is why Böcklin in particular has been trusted; he appears to have copied his monsters from nature with amazing zoological precision.

There is no denying the need for verisimilitude and persuasiveness in art. In contrast, fabrication is repugnant. What can be worse than Blake's strained, contrived fantasy? The compromise between realism and the fantastic in Félicien Rops and Gustave Moreau is equally unpleasant. . . . Despite meticulous technique and a flaunting of details from nature, helplessness and ignorance shine through everywhere. What is strange, however, is that works that are not entirely independent of reality are less verisimilar than others in which the artist has broken with it completely. This is what is most mysterious in art. . . . Artistic forms are a strange and mysterious thing. It is time to liberate them from the ill fate of naturalism and the Academy. Artistic truth depends on neither correct drawing nor a resemblance to reality. True art begins beyond this visible, photographic truth. . . . "Become as little children." We are constantly forgetting and, more important, misinterpreting these words. We should be not only as *innocent* but also as *wise* as children. We should constantly study our childhood and keep in mind what we did not yet know at that time.

Maurice Denis is just such a "child" in art. He could have drawn from nature as do thousands of his brethren, but he disdains to do so. He has disdained the decorous correctness of drawing and has boldly set forth in quest of that magic line, that fantastic art of which I have just spoken. This is an enormous labor. . . . I think that when persons such as Denis and Maeterlinck (what a pity that we have yet to find anyone of the kind in music) babble, when these poets babble like fools in Christ, it is a very serious sign of the times. . . .

At the beginning of my essay I referred to the "component parts of [Denis's] art." After a closer study of his works, however, I have concluded that there is not the shadow of plagiarism in this original, independent, and free artist. His resemblance to the masters mentioned above is much more easily explained by his poetic and thoroughly artistic nature's natural proximity to their art.

17

Igor' Grabar'

"Around Europe" (1902)

This review is a part of the survey by Grabar' published in *Mir iskusstva* (World of Art) 4 (1902).

The Secession this year is of quite exceptional interest; never has there been one like it in Berlin, nor do I remember anything like it in Munich. One of the most talented Norwegians of the youngest generation—Munch—has sent twenty-eight works that alone would make any exhibition interesting.

I have known him for a long time, have seen his strange, morbid drawings, and have always been amazed by his talent, but I could never reconcile myself with him completely. There have been moments when he seemed sincere, but there have also been others when I flatly refused to trust him. He has been both beautiful and ugly, brilliant and insipid, and he has seemed a mighty artist and a helpless child. I think that these twenty-eight canvases at the Secession should conquer everyone. At first the ugliness of his forms is repulsive; he seems to be trying intentionally to scoff at everything mankind has accumulated over so many centuries. He draws not at all like everyone else, will not hear of the laws of light refraction or perspective; he needs colors not to convey the colors of nature but to transmit as accurately as possible his own morbid sensations, his delirium, if you will. But this delirium is of an absolutely special character.

I don't know whether this happens to everyone, but I have at times experienced something resembling Munch's painting. . . . Sometimes a cheerful crowd will be coming toward you, all their faces joyful and all apparently extremely kind and sweet and trying to win your confidence; at other times you see only embittered faces, hatred peers out at you everywhere, and everyone seems frightening, diseased. At such moments you forget that you are in a crowd, that you yourself are a part of this crowd, and there really seems to be nothing around you, and all of this seems merely a morbid delirium, a savage, disgusting nightmare. This is the sort of crowd Munch has painted. It is moving straight at you down the street, strange and yellow-faced, with wide-open eyes; looking at it, you get an unpleasant, eerie feeling. . . .

Munch has also successfully avoided commonplaces in themes that lately have become very risky, namely, themes treating death. So many convenient clichés have been found in this tendency you cannot always distinguish the real from the counterfeit. Munch paints a room, deep within which a man who has just died lies on a bed. In the foreground a strange man who seems to have leapt out of a Hoffman tale opens the door and gestures to the gathered relatives to enter. The faces entering wear that special expression with which one enters a dead man's room. There is no pathos, but there is a kind of quiet horror, a suppressed terror.

. . . In everything Munch paints there is a clear desire to simplify the means of transmission, to reduce them to a *minimum,* here there must be nothing superfluous. He considers suitable only that which makes it easier for him to transmit his complex sensations.

I must stipulate, however, that although he has powerful and genuine works, this in no way blinds me to his shortcomings, which may be as energetic as his merits. His brushwork is extremely careless; everything is thrown onto the canvas with a feverish haste, as though he were afraid of losing the freshness and keenness of his sensations at any moment. Because of this, sometimes his works produce the impression of something that has merely been sketched out, something almost frivolous and unimportant. He is sometimes not averse to using quite cheap effects, too often, for example, resorting to wide-open eyes to express fright or surprise. On the whole I must state that although everything he has exhibited at the Secession possesses a tremendous amount of talent, you cannot agree with the form into which his conceptions have been poured. It is altogether too offensive.

18

Alexandre Benois

"An Artist's Conversations: 1. On Impressionism" (1899)

Written in October 1898 and published in *Mir iskusstva* (World of Art) 6 in 1899, this article was the first review of Impressionism to appear in the Russian press after Emile Zola's 1878 articles in *Vestnik Evropy* (Messenger of Europe).

Not that long ago the word "Impressionism" was an expletive; to say of an artist that he was an "Impressionist" was to undermine trust in him and make him out to be a charlatan and ignoramus. No sooner had the artists of this tendency finally, after long years of struggle, achieved recognition, assumed places of honor, and become classics of a sort than the younger generation began relegating them to the archive; what just recently was shocking novelty is now considered *vieux-jeu*—obsolete, unneeded, exhausted, and old. Such is the precariousness of contemporary taste, especially Parisian. Now that the bitterness of the struggle has abated, however, and we therefore can be more dispassionate, it is time to take a closer look at this tendency and consider whether the former hostile attitude toward the Impressionists was justified. . . .

The Impressionists taught that outside the impression there is no salvation . . . by which they meant exclusively the *first* impression, maintaining that the artist must not delve into the meaning of a subject—that should be left to the philosophers—or entertain the viewer with a story—which is the business of the novelist. Even the beauty of technique and colors, in their opinion, was not the artist's principal task, since nothing must impede the capturing of a fresh, immediate, and thereby powerful impression. They set the transmission of this first, fresh, and immediate impression as the main goal of artistic creation, and this is what distinguishes them so sharply from all their predecessors. . . . Thus the Impressionists seem to have been pursuing what can be provided by perfected color photography, and I think that the most consistent Impressionist theorists must have acknowledged that such an invention would mean an end to art. . . . Cognizant of their inevitable defeat in the struggle for an exact and faithful reproduction of the first impression in all its elusive immediacy, the Impressionists made concessions and decided that the first impression is not important in its own right but only to the extent that it registers in the artist's memory. They forgot that in this case "immediacy" is out of the question.

The clarity of these doctrines vanished, and little by little everything was reduced from the fundamental question of the significance of the *first impression* in art to the secondary, practical question of *the means of presenting the first impression*. . . .

The Impressionists' views are without a doubt very applicable to contemporary explorations in the area of color, and we can see that they are now universally accepted. . . . For art as a whole, however, their theories are not especially significant, as along with adherents of these theories there are people who disregard them entirely and nevertheless create works that are full of life and even the charm of color. Here I am by no means denying the Impressionists' *relative* significance in the struggle with obsolete and harmful theories in art. . . . The Impressionists smashed open the academic locks once and for all, to their enormous credit.

Standing quite alone at the head of the Impressionist school is the brilliant Degas. In studying him, of course, one must leave aside all of his latest works, which have clearly been affected by his eye disease and which so unsettle anyone expected to show the obligatory enthusiasm. Degas's striking and inimitable technical skill separates him completely from kindred artists; at the same time he is the most consistent and convincing of them, for he is truly the painter who has captured the swift rush of life. The suppleness and keen precision of his drawing very nearly surpass that of Menzel, who is the greatest of those artists who have portrayed life in our age, although, naturally, he does not penetrate as deeply and lacks Menzel's psychological subtlety and sweep. Like a true Impressionist, Degas has not produced whole pictures. His ballet, street, jockey, and intimate scenes are casual fragments that reveal the author's tremendous talent and rather superficial personality, yet after the great Berliner he alone has boldly and simply understood his age. . . .

The other pillar of Impressionism, Claude Monet, is not as convincing and may trouble those who do not wish to study him more intently and accustom themselves to his originality. His technique is so careless, and his drawing so muddled—rather, he ignores it to such an extent and so often limits himself to half-hints that many of his works are études rather than pictures. Yet he is rightfully considered a great master. . . .

Although the good pictures of this school abound in obvious talent and sincere enthusiasm for the school's principles, and they faithfully and precisely convey various elements of illumination or movement, they cannot be enjoyed as one enjoys the old masters—the Barbizon school, Menzel, Böcklin! These "drafts" (even those of Degas) have no substance, no presence of the artist himself, none of the main ingredient in art—poetry. In the best cases these pictures can serve, as does *trompe-l'oeil,* to recall, albeit superficially, certain phenomena or places, but more often they are merely chaotic and incoherent, more irritating than pleasurable. . . .

Thus, while recognizing the Impressionists' artistic significance, we must admit that they are a far cry from the great masters who revealed strong individualities and discovered new areas of beauty. The most successful works of this school can give pleasure only to the artist or specialist capable of appreciating the difficulty of the problem that has been solved, but they are unlikely to give much to the nonspecialist. They have no warmth or character and lack the capability to move or excite without which the work of art is dead.

19

Igor' Grabar'

"Around Europe: Letters on Contemporary Art" (1902)

By the early 1900s, Benois, Diaghilev, and Grabar' had registered their dissatisfaction with the state of European painting and looked forward to the emergence of a new art. This critique was published in *Mir iskusstva* (World of Art) 5–6 (1902).

. . . [The "Salon des Indépendants"] is dominated by Monet and his less prominent contemporaries Sisley and Pissarro. Some directly repeat what Monet has formulated so powerfully, but their rendition is infinitely weaker. Others truly attempt to find something in various currents to add to the formula for old Impressionism, giving us occasion to speak of Neo-Impressionism, whose representatives maintain that Monet did not exhaust the area of color impressions but was merely the first to begin to develop and outline it. To them he is not exactly obsolete but, just like Besnard, is simply not very refined. The latter merely hinted at the charm of Luminism and did not go beyond the rather crude effects that nowadays any bourgeois sees in nature.

When you exit the great Salon into the open air, your eyes aching from the blinding light, bright sun, luxuriant vegetation, and white paths, all your senses at once show you clearly the enormous difference between everything you've just seen in the Salon and this real nature. You realize what the best of the young Impressionists are seeking so avidly. They are willing to sacrifice everything if only they can somehow draw closer to this, thus far, so elusive light. Their exhibition really is brighter than the Salons. These artists stop at nothing to convey light. They have one room that seems to be entirely blue containing works by the well-known Signac and the now very fashionable Cross, Luce, and van Rysselberghe. . . . Signac, the most talented of them, has already turned the color scale he once discovered into a rather cheap template for turning out hundreds of copies. . . .

Simultaneously with the appearance of the Neo-Impressionists, other young artists have begun to react against the extremes of Impressionism. They seem to have given up on conveying the *intensity* of light and have instead turned to its *beauty.* Light is not always blinding, nor do your eyes always ache from it: it can be soothing, tender, and caressing. To get at its power the Neo-Impressionists have broken it down into its component parts, and this is why their works are so colorful. This is an *analysis* of painting. Reactionary youth have begun to long for tenderness in nature; they want once again to mix colors, leave variegation behind, and arrive at the calm silver-gray scales; they need simplification, generalization, and style. This is the *synthesis* of painting. While the Neo-Impressionists are racing each other in a feverish dash for brilliant colors, the Synthesists [Vuillard, Bonnard, Vallotton] are consciously muting these colors. Their gray painting, however, is much more subtle than the gray painting of the Pleinairists brought up on Manet. The color experiments of Claude Monet, Degas, Besnard, and even Latouche were not lost on them; they have merely reduced the intensity of their scales by several tones, often retaining the full beauty of this endless variety of subtle tints. . . .

To summarize what France has given us in the last few years that is new, from afar these results seem to favor the creative endeavors of the nation that has led all important movements in European art for an entire century. If a noticeable effort to seek out the new has been evident, and if we can recognize the precise direction in which the modernists are searching, nonetheless the lack of strong talents and energetic natures such as Manet, Monet, and Degas is all too obvious. Instead there is a sense of morbidity and overwrought nerves.

When you sit in a café on one of Paris's noisy boulevards and the streetlamps have just been lit beneath the marquees, and hundreds, thousands of people, men and women, are rushing constantly by amid yellow reflections from the electricity and the blue of the darkening sky, you seem to begin to understand the nervousness of this painting. . . . Life itself seems to have evolved here in a way that can be conveyed only in flight, rapidly, by vague hints. Degas himself begins to seem overly contemplative.

We need new titans to keep up with this life. There are none. Everything that has appeared to replace the old is endlessly pitiful and puny. France seems to have had her final say in the painting of Monet and Degas. Perhaps the time has come for other, younger nations.

20

Georgii Plekhanov

"The Proletarian Movement and Bourgeois Art" (1905)

Georgii Plekhanov (1856–1918) lived in exile in Europe from 1880 through 1917. As a leader of the Social Democratic movement he generally took an anti-Bolshevik position. This article, published by the Social Democratic periodical *Pravda* (no. 11, 1905) and the journal *Die Neue Zeit* (no. 28, 1906), discusses the Sixth Venetian Biennial.

[Symbolism] is artists' involuntary protest against the *lack of ideas.* However, this protest itself arose on a foundation devoid of ideas or any specific content and for this reason is lost in a fog of abstraction, as we see in literature in certain works by Ibsen and Hauptman, in the chaos of their vague, chaotic images, and as we can see in certain pictures by Toorop and Hodler. *Understand* this protest and you will inevitably return to those very *ideas* you were protesting. . . .

If the contemporary protest against the lack of ideas in art resulting in abstractness and chaos is to acquire definite content, certain social conditions must be present that are entirely absent today and that cannot be created by the wave of a magic wand. There was a time when the upper classes for which art in a "civilized" society mainly exists were moving forward; and at that time ideas attracted rather than frightened them. Now, however, these classes are at best standing still, and they don't need ideas at all, or only in minimal doses, and therefore their protest against the lack of ideas is inevitable for the simple reason that art without an idea cannot live and leads to nothing but abstract and chaotic Symbolism. It is not *being* that is determined by *consciousness,* but consciousness by *being!*

. . . Hermen Anglada [Camarasa] is content to defile his pictures for the glory of Impressionism. . . . The setting in these pictures is Paris, and the characters are the "flowers of evil," that is, demimondaines clad in fashionable dresses that in the nocturnal lights lend fantastic and sometimes astoundingly deformed shapes to their persons. It goes without saying that there can be no objections to the choice of such heroines. As for depicting them illuminated by the *nocturnal* lights, this too must be acknowledged as deserving approval. In today's large cities night often does in fact become day through new sources of light provided by modern technology such as ordinary lamp gas, acetylene, and electricity. Each of these new sources illuminates objects in its own way, and contemporary painting was bound to turn its attention to the light effects they produce. Unfortunately, however, Hermen Anglada has failed to solve the artistic problem he set himself. . . .

. . . This striving for paradox is Anglada's misfortune, an artist who is in any event not devoid of talent. When an artist concentrates his entire attention on *light effects* and these effects become the alpha and omega of his work, we cannot expect him to go beyond the *surface of phenomena,* and when he yields to the temptation to *startle the viewer with paradoxical effects,* we are forced to accept that he has started down the road straight to the ugly and ridiculous. . . .

It is of no use to say that Anglada is resurrecting the glorious tradition of old Spanish painting. Old Spanish painting did not shun effects, but it possessed a rich content; it had an entire world of ideas that gave it a "living soul." Today these ideas are obsolete even in Spain and do not correspond to the position of the social classes for which contemporary art exists. But these social classes have nothing to replace these obsolete ideas; they are themselves preparing to exit the historical stage and are therefore almost completely indifferent to ideas. This is why contemporary painters such as Anglada do nothing but strive for effects; this is why they pay attention only to the *surface, the husk of phenomena.* They want to say something new, but they have nothing to say, so they resort to artistic paradoxes: paradoxes, at least, can help them *épater les bourgeois.*

By this I do not mean that I see nothing good in Impressionism. Absolutely not! I consider many of Impressionism's results to be unsuccessful, but I think that the *questions of technique* it has raised are of considerable value. Its attentive treatment of light effects increases the pleasure nature affords man, and since in the "society of the future" nature will probably become much more precious to man than now, we must acknowledge that Impressionism as well is working, albeit not always successfully, for *that* society. As Camille Mauclair, who is very well disposed toward Impressionism, says, "It has brought us the caress of life illuminated by the sun."* We must thank Impressionism for that, although it has not always managed to convey this marvelous caress of nature. But Mauclair also admits that in the works of the French Impressionists, for example, the ideas are far less interesting than the *technique.* He considers this one of Impressionism's shortcomings. I think he has put it too mildly. Impressionism's lack of ideas constitutes the *original sin* that has brought it so close to caricature and has rendered it completely incapable of bringing about a profound revolution in painting.

21
Stepan Iaremich
"The Autumn Salon" (1904)

Stepan Iaremich (1869–1939) was an artist in the World of Art circle and a collector of old master drawings. This review was published in *Khronika "Mira iskusstva"* (Chronicle of the World of Art) 11–12 (1904).

The name "Autumn" given to the new Salon fully characterizes most of the works there. There is something raw, hard, cold, bleak, and senilely flaccid in this so-called young art. Most of the works bring to mind mushrooms cultivated in damp cellars. They have, of course, their own simple form, or rather a hint of form, but pasting garish labels on them does not render them more attractive and varied. Take Cézanne alone! Limited but stubborn, he methodically cultivates his mushrooms, which here and there contain hints of organic coherence, but that does not make them less repulsive and disgusting. What a terrible eye! As a portraitist he does not paint his subjects but spits on them and slaps their faces. These convulsively twisted faces with their squinting eyes and dislocated skulls are painful to look at. This is a collection

*Cf. Camille Mauclair, *The French Impressionists (1860–1900)* (London and New York, 1903; French ed. 1904).

of extraordinary monsters, filthy and lifeless, gathered and sealed up in jars by an equally inert and completely unviable lover of the impossible. As a landscapist he is not a bit more cheerful. But at least here he has his own special and original device: colors pasted on like strips of bandage. This mosaic of sticky plasters consists of four murderous shades—brick red, green, dark blue, and reddish gray. It is this crank whom the well-known local art critic Gustave Geffroy considers a "Venetian" by artistic temperament who should be ranked with such masters as Manet, Degas, and Renoir!

22
Alexandre Shervashidze
"Cézanne" (1905)

Prince Alexandre Shervashidze (Abkhazian name: Chachba, 1867–1968) was a stage designer and art critic. From 1894 through 1906 and again after 1917, he lived in France. Shervashidze's article in *Iskusstvo* (Art) 4 (April 1905) was the first in Russia devoted to Cézanne.

. . . We can take a long hard look around, but Cézanne has no connection to anyone, and we are completely ignorant of his *point de départ.* Cézanne is an Impressionist in the simplest form and most precise meaning of the word; perhaps unique in the history of contemporary painting, he is an example of a master who possesses the unusual courage, without traditions or knowledge, to stand face to face with the diversity of life. There is no Truth—there are many truths. There is no verisimilar depiction of life, but there is an impression of this life that has passed through the artist's temperament. There are no rules for selecting these impressions or rules for expressing them. A picture is a free, independent expression of the artist's personality and temperament, and only this personality and temperament have any value. Such is the remarkable formula of the Impressionists, which in our day has become almost an *idée courante.* Cézanne embodies this formula directly and powerfully, and if others have incorporated into their art more diverse quests and especially more picturesqueness, he has introduced a significant, magnificent simplification of form, a broad and noble interpretation of the simple and trivial aspects of life, and an unusual and unflagging desire to communicate his truth. His canvases, immediate impressions of nature in which his labor is so apparent, are like parts of a huge fresco, a huge canvas, for they are connected by a single common and profound feeling; they contain so much tranquility and nobility, and the smallest canvas is painted as though it were the spacious wall of a monumental edifice. . . .

None of this is real. The houses are cardboard, and the people are phantoms living a special life who cannot be soon forgotten and who haunt you for a long time. "*Ce sont des estropiés,*" someone near me once said in this dark room of Cézanne's. Well, yes, these are cripples, people broken by life with short arms and twisted faces, *les vaincus de la vie*—yes, of course. But why do you want art to duplicate nature—

the nature that you see and want to see? No, depicting what everyone sees is unnecessary and uninteresting; yet what the artist alone sees is invisible. Everything hideous and everything beautiful is important to the extent that it stirs the artist; only the forms of this agitation are dear and sacred to us, and to hold sway over us they must be significant and beautiful. . . .

To seek out and express the beautiful—yes, this is the highest art, and his most brilliant *chefs d'oeuvre* enchant us ineffably. But the beautiful is everything that is beautifully told, and only someone who lives and loves and hates can tell it that way. Indisputably and enormously gifted as a painter, Cézanne has put the problems of painting last. But despite this, there is another, remarkably painted self-portrait of him without a hat executed with a rich and delicate brush and in a dense, solid manner. In the main room next to a panel by Lautrec is a large, gray-blue, strange unfinished still life with a marvelous choir of colors, a high and mighty nobility, and a free, majestic manner. Beside it is a small, gray vase with blue-green combinations against an old dark rug, a work by Gauguin. It is probably these riches that led G. Geffroy to number Cézanne among the Venetians. Yet in both his falls and his grandiose ascents Cézanne *se suffit à lui-même:* he had no teachers; he is alone and unique, and fate has bestowed upon him the greatest blessing that any outstanding man could desire: solitude.

23

Maksimilian Voloshin

"Aspirations of the New French Painting" (1908)

Maksimilian Voloshin (born Kirienko-Voloshin, 1877–1932) was a poet, essayist, amateur artist, and passionate champion of French culture. He went to Europe in 1901 to continue his education, which had been interrupted by a brief period in prison following his participation in student protests. He worked in Colarossi's academy and visited Whistler's and Steinlen's studios, returning to Russia in 1905. He wrote this essay for issue 7–9 (1908) of *Zolotoe Runo* (Golden Fleece), which was devoted to the "Golden Fleece Salon."

. . . Cézanne is the Savonarola of contemporary painting. He burned everything superficially beautiful, all the masquerade costumes and masks and all the charms of this century on the redemptive bonfire of his art. He is an ascetic, a zealot, and an iconoclast. His painting is the naked truth. Not the truth of the blinding impression, as with the Impressionists, but the dreary and homely truth of persistent work that makes one's head spin, distorts figures, and turns colors tinny and dirty. His painting shows an invincible burst of creative will and profound vehemence. . . . Cézanne was appreciated earliest of all, back in the day of Huysmans's first heroic campaign, as an inventor of *natures mortes*—a blue tablecloth, porcelain plates, and red apples. This was what was most accessible in him.

Less pleasing to the eye are his dreary landscapes painted in heavy lumps like a crude mosaic of tarnished tin, acid-eaten zinc, and verdigris-covered copper. . . .

The power he has invested in his portraits is almost beyond the understanding of an eye unused to being sprawled out over the canvas. These portraits contain the terrible truth of a hallucinating eye saturated with work and blinded from intense gazing. Their figures are crooked, their faces twisted, their eyes in the wrong place; Cézanne the zealot rejects even the external correctness of the drawing, even fidelity to the anatomical skeleton, as impermissible luxuries, vulgar clichés of knowledge. . . . Lurking in Cézanne's portraits is abusiveness, unbridled rudeness, and the blazing purity and holiness of that kind of insult. They contain the spirit of a burnt offering, the flame of a magnificent asceticism. You can marvel at Cézanne—but can you love him? Yet at the same time the breadth and fullness of his palette suggest that, had he appeared in another age, when it was necessary not to destroy old clichés but to give splendid and beautiful speeches, he would have spoken in octaves no less sonorous than Veronese's and stanzas no less consummate than Titian's.

This is where he differs from Van Gogh. In whatever golden age Van Gogh might appear, he would always be the same epileptic of color, the same man with the bloodless, pale yellow face and pitiful colorless eyes wearing a blue hat trimmed in black fur and with a bloody bandage around his head, as in his famous self-portrait, where he painted himself with his severed ear. . . .

In Cézanne and Van Gogh, analytical painting has pushed psychology to its utmost limits. The spirit of contemporary man could no longer tolerate the ulcer, viewed by a defenseless eye exposed to the light. . . .

Alongside these martyrs of modern painting, these "vanquished ones whose hearts brim over with the ashes of sorrow," stands the heroic figure of the conqueror of empires—Gauguin. He alone comes from the mighty tribe of legendary demigods and heroes. . . . His thirst for gold could not be satisfied by Van Gogh's sunflowers on a turquoise background, nor could his yearning for purple and brilliance by Cézanne's red apples and porcelain plates on a blue tablecloth. His blood suffocated among these Impressionist trifles, these artificial trampolines of light in which Van Gogh and Cézanne searched for the philosopher's stone of painting.

Gauguin needed no philosopher's stone. He loved the simple, the real, the concrete, the human. He loved matter and its forms rather than ideas. He was not looking for new painting at all, but for new faces of life, and when he found them, he fell in love with and understood them, and in passing he also created a new kind of painting.

The profound truth is that art, contrary to philosophical thought, portrays only what is individual and thirsts only for what is exceptional. Rather than generalizing phenomena, it individualizes them.

The signs have been treacherously mixed up on the labyrinth's doors. Those who set out directly in search of abstract ideas, principles, and systems have fallen into the sticky nets of little things—Cézanne's gray and quotidian plates and apples . . . and

Van Gogh's smoked herring; but those who have ignored the general and fallen in love with things and have been willing to sacrifice all their immortality for the transient forms of this world have effortlessly found the philosopher's stone that turns all it touches to gold.

Gauguin left Europe in search of a new life, not painting.

24

Petr Konchalovskii

Letters from Paris to Il'ia Mashkov (1908)

Petr Konchalovskii (1876–1956) and Il'ia Mashkov (1881–1944) studied at the Moscow School of Painting, Sculpture, and Architecture. In 1910 they became leaders of the Jack of Diamonds group. In the spring and summer of 1908 Mashkov traveled around Europe, visiting Paris and Italy. These letters were published previously by Irina Bolotina in *Panorama iskusstv* (Panorama of the Arts) 78 (Moscow, 1979).

January 4, 1908

I've finally settled down in Paris and begun working. I wonder whether better conditions are to be found anywhere else. What is especially good is that there is beauty everywhere here, and to tell you the truth, I'm simply dazzled. So far I've only been to the Louvre, the Luxembourg, and Durand-Ruel's—that's the well-known dealer in the works of the famous Impressionists—Monet, Manet, Sisley, Pissarro, Renoir, and so on. But I still haven't seen the main thing—the Fayer gallery, where they say there is an amazing collection of Cézannes, Gauguins, Van Goghs, and others. A Van Gogh exhibition is opening on Monday; I'll write more about it later. I'm overwhelmed by impressions—everything is so fresh and so unusually earnest. Everything makes you want to work, to express yourself as profoundly as these people.

The difference from the Louvre, of course, is striking: there you have the luxury and beauty of the Italian Renaissance and you feel that art is only for the chosen; here, by contrast, there is the beauty of everyday moods and everyday surroundings, but the love of art is so deep that it completely conquers you. You are filled with reverence for these people, your soul is fortified, when you learn that all these people have endured poverty, that they have not known fame, and that they have all followed their own paths with fantastic energy, when you learn that they used soldiers as models to paint women, that they painted tables, oranges, and apples because they had nothing more luxurious around them, and you see that all these objects take on an enormous significance and beauty—but there's no telling all this in a letter. I'm not even trying and I don't want to compare the two impressions of the Louvre and the collections of modern art, although they have features in common, or perhaps one: both are beautiful. The difference in life itself is too great. Earlier I probably would have preferred the Louvre, but now I'm moved equally by both.

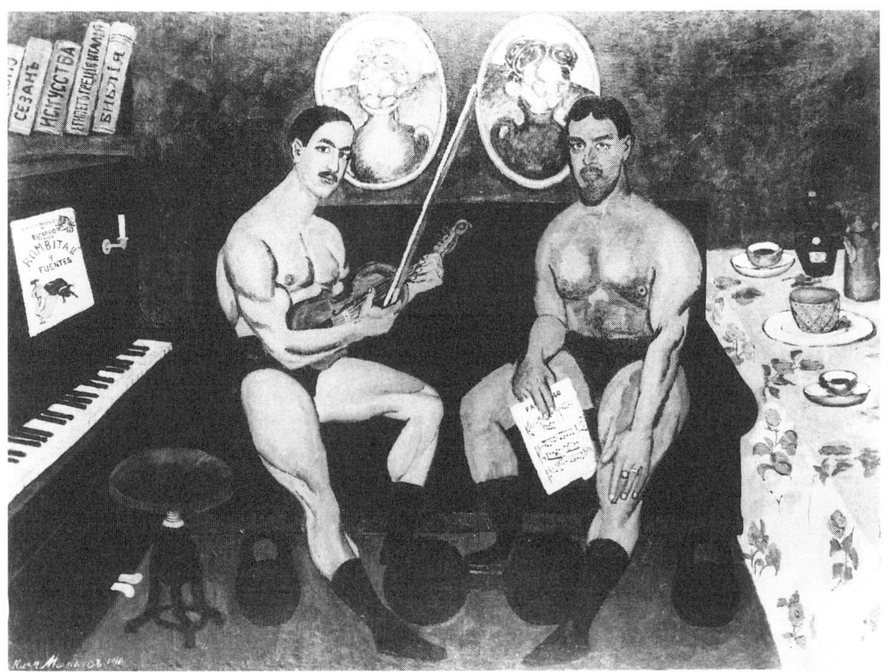

Il'ia Mashkov, *Self-Portrait with Petr Konchalovskii*, 1910, The State Russian Museum, St. Petersburg

July 1908
Here's what I found myself thinking about when I read your raptures over the [Italian] frescoists: it's good that before them you saw Van Gogh, Cézanne, and the other liberators of our day. If you had seen these frescoes first, I think you would have reacted to them quite differently. You would have admired them as historical works more than as great works of art. . . . Indeed, if Cézanne and Van Gogh have shown that what is most valuable in art is the preservation of childlike feeling unburdened by conventions created over long centuries, if they have shown that liberation from all these traditions is the true meaning of genuine art, by this alone they have opened up to us an entire world of models in those frescoes now before you.

[Latter half of September 1908]
Today I saw a marvelous work by Gauguin. My God! It is a kind of fairy tale—boundless and distant. After this majestic tranquillity of nature and savage humanity everything seems fussy and restless. And Gauguin's savage is so kind, so human, that our European faces seem harsh. I can't summarize my impressions: it's enchanting. The colors are pearls, emeralds, and sapphires, but these are vulgar in comparison with Gauguin's. It's divine. I also saw for the first time Cézanne's portrait, and his apples as well. The portrait is indescribable; his art is a breath of air. The face is

rapture. I hesitate before it, however, because it is too *nature morte,* yet at the same time this is its merit. If I acknowledge that it should be that way, it is delightful; if I don't, then something remains to be desired. As for everything around it, the hands, for instance, are too much! The apples are painted bulkily and are charming in tone, but I love Cézanne when he merely breathes on the canvas.

What will I find in Russia? I even want to go there; I dream of painting my life—the motifs outstrip each other in my head, and suddenly the cruel recollection of our universal slavery. . . .

Don't think that I'm referring to our political situation. We have already come a long way in this respect (or rather not we, but the people), but somewhere within there is this timid slavery. . . . Do you think you can love Cézanne or Gauguin in Russia? You're supposed to love what's native Russian, so stop all this romping around and hurry up and exhibit something. I won't upset you and myself any longer. I'll breathe in all that is bright and lofty here and try to arrive with a mask of disdain on my face—there's no alternative. The traveler entering Russia must have colossal endurance and colossal faith and love. You have to be made of granite.

[October 1908]
When I saw my works at the "Salon [d'Automne]" I realized that this is not yet within my power—it's much too early to return to Russia. To gather my strength I need at the very worst a winter in Paris. Oppressing everything I've been working on here is what remains of the lack of freedom I brought from Russia; only in my latest works is there a feeling of liberation. In the Salon I am still a slave. I say this only to you, with whom I am perfectly sincere.

. . . But Matisse is such a delight. He is a veritable tempest of harmonies. Not a single picture in the same register—all are different and all are magnificent. There are two works for Shchukin . . . both still lifes,* but absolutely special; you can't even call them still lifes. They are a kind of music, savage and civilized at the same time. They send shivers down your spine and give you the creeps. What a delight, if only you knew. I recall you remarking once that too much poetry is not good. You were right to say this about Musatov. The soul grows too soft, the firmness and fortitude of the spirit vanish, and here as well the Russians are rebelling against Matisse. He doesn't move them, you see, for he's not an aristocrat and curses like a cabman. I haven't even responded to this—it's all so very boring and familiar. Matisse, in my view, does not move you, he tears you to pieces—and this the Russian heart cannot bear. Maliavin† swears a blue streak and no one cares one way or the other, but Matisse is like the kite tearing out Prometheus's heart. All culture is

*One is *The Red Room* (1908, Hermitage); the second still life may be *Statuette and Vase on an Oriental Rug* (GMII).

†Philip Maliavin (1869–1940), Russian artist whose bold painting contemporaries felt conveyed the spontaneous sweep of the Russian soul.

reflected in him, and it has not corrupted him but, on the contrary, has made him hard as granite. I could have said all this to the Russians (and there are a lot of them here) who have been shouting out their trite ready-made Russian opinions in their squeaky voices. But I remained silent, dear friend, and found out for myself what Matisse is truly like. Ah, how highly art is regarded here. And you want it to be the same at home, where so much is still untouched—you just have to think and know how to think. Just now I can't work at all. I'm all mixed up inside. I need to experience and think through so much. But my faith is firm and there is joy in my heart. Yes, Matisse has already forged a promising link in the chain of art of which Gauguin speaks.

25

Pavel Muratov

"The Golden Fleece Salon" (1908)

The "Golden Fleece Salon" opened in Moscow in April 1908. In addition to Russian paintings and sculptures, it included works by fifty-one French artists ranging from the Impressionists and Pointillists to Symbolists and Nabis. It was the first public exhibition in Russia of paintings by Cézanne, Van Gogh, and Gauguin. There were also a significant number of works by the Fauves. Muratov's review was published in *Russkoe slovo* (Russian Word), April 6, 1908.

There are some excellent examples of Cézanne's painting at the exhibition—strong, powerful, strikingly beautiful, reminiscent of the old masters, communicating as they did the eternal life of matter. The now rare Gauguin is weakly represented, but among Van Gogh's works there are some very interesting examples such as his *Gardener* and especially *Night Café.* The very essence of Van Gogh's art can be grasped in this strange, morbidly harsh work—his keen, "poisoned" impressionability and the tortured tension of his lonely suffering. . . .

Especially numerous at the exhibition, however, are the representatives of the latest artistic formation, who tend to draw the most extreme conclusions from the premises preceding them and are inclined toward the most "daring" experiments and the most hopeless paradoxes. Typically, however, although they use the most unusual and bizarre devices, the vast majority of them remain realists with respect to themes. They begin throughout, or think they begin, with nature. All their "daring" and thirst for discovery is expended on the means of expression, on their allegedly individual manner, in short, that is, on technique.

A small group of Russian artists are exhibiting . . . their works with the French. The resulting contrast is extremely interesting and momentous. The French far surpass our young artists in all matters having to do with skill—in the subtlety or strength of their color combinations, in the precision of their image, and in their grasp of the rhythm of line. On the other hand, the poetic feeling, soulfulness, and genuine simplicity found only sparingly, rarely in the works of Western artists comprise the best

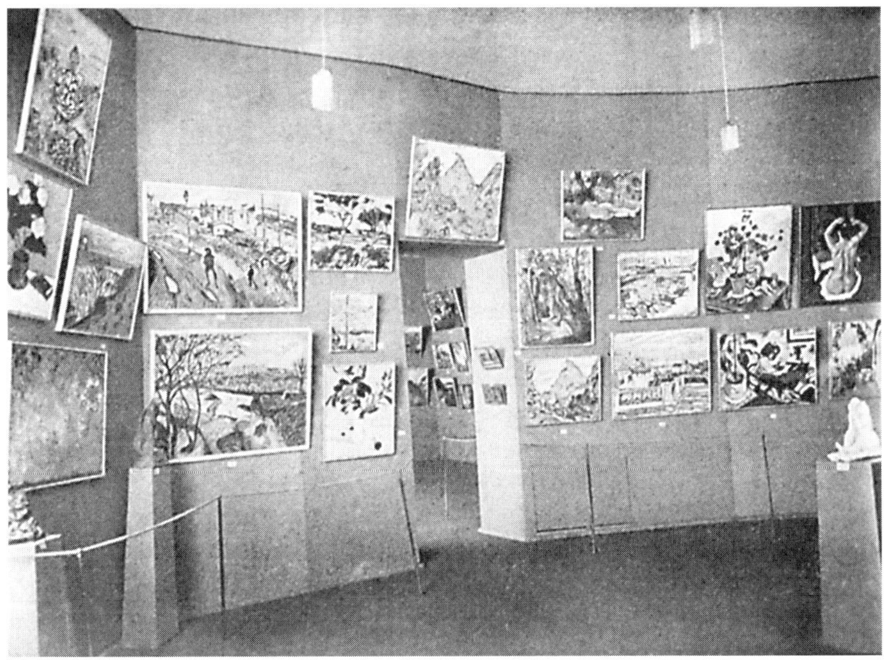

Room with Fauve paintings at the "Golden Fleece Salon," Moscow, 1908.
Published in *Zolotoe runo* (Golden Fleece) 7–9 (1908).

and distinctive property of Russian painting. Perhaps this is why, despite their obvious formal shortcomings, our young artists do pass muster alongside exemplars of brilliant French painting and produce a distinct and original impression.

26

Igor' Grabar'

"Moscow Exhibitions" (1909)

The second *Golden Fleece* exhibition ran from January 11 to February 15, 1909. The French section was limited to the Fauves. Especially important was the showing of four of Braque's early Cubist works. The Russian section consisted mainly of works by former Blue Rose participants Petrov-Vodkin, Goncharova, and Larionov. Grabar' published this review in *Vesy* (Scales) 2 (1909).

The French section is less muddled than at the first exhibition, which was an incredible mishmash mingling great masters with sharpers and vulgarians. True, not a one of these masters—Cézanne, Gauguin, Van Gogh—happens to be present at the exhibition, but a certain group of artists who have been the talk of Paris are given a showing—poorly and incompletely yet consistently and logically. These are the forces that have grouped around Matisse—the new Edouard Manet in the opinion of some, a brazen charlatan in the no less categorical opinion of others. That Matisse is not a charlatan is in my view beyond doubt, as is the fact that he lacks Manet's genius; however, he is an extremely important phenomenon, as should be clear to anyone who has followed the latest Paris exhibitions and knows their evolution since the "revolutionary" canvases of Matisse and his "school" began showing up. The vast majority of Paris youth has been infected by the most striking "Matissomania." Indeed, from a purely superficial point of view something is going on that resembles the famous scenes enacted in front of Edouard Manet's *Luncheon on the Grass.* At the exhibition, indignant bourgeois were already shaking their umbrellas in front of Matisse's pictures and shouting, *"Vous verrez que cela au Louvre, puisque cette vilaine 'Olympia' y est déjà!"* . . . the few tiny studies of his that have found their way here are too insignificant and casual to dwell upon. . . .

Albert Marquet is not quite a "Matissian" either, for although he has changed somewhat since joining the group he still gravitates much more toward Edouard Manet's legacy than toward their canon. His colors have become brighter and more defined and he copes with the complex problems of light better than before, but it is this obvious preference for the problems of *light* to those of *color* that distinguish him from Matisse's group. . . . Although Derain is closest to Marquet, he is far more decisive and is not daunted by the prospect of getting lost in a labyrinth of obvious absurdities, if that is where his logic leads him. His stubborn consistency has influenced Matisse himself, who before Derain could not bring himself to paint a tree trunk in pure red cinnabar straight from the tube. . . .

All of these artists, however, have adhered only to Matisse's first manner, or rather, his first two manners, and only two of them—Picasso and Braque—have been infected by his latest quest. Picasso has nothing at the exhibition, while Braque is represented by four canvases that both bewilder and often arouse indignation. If you saw only these works—rather indifferent ones, incidentally—you would be hard put to understand them, nor would you ever link them with the serious new trend that is marked by Matisse's new phase and might be called an awakened yearning for architectonics, the same yearning that twenty years ago tormented and perhaps led Seurat to his grave—a yearning for rigorous stability and a lost sense of structure coupled with a faith in a certain order, a certain mathematics of rhythmic sensibilities. Here Braque's *Woman Bather [Large Nude]* becomes almost an architectural blueprint, and his *Bridge,* and *Road,* and even the pears of his *Still Life* become the same sort of illuminated drawings. These are only hints, only a beginning, and Picasso expresses the same thing far more consistently and ruthlessly, but Braque's ill-fated pictures still do not deserve the consternation they evoked in Moscow.

III

MATISSE, PICASSO, AND THE SHCHUKIN AND MOROZOV COLLECTIONS

Educated Russians of the early twentieth century were not receptive on the whole to contemporary European art. No more than a dozen individuals in the entire country owned modern French paintings, and collecting unconventional Western painting was often considered extravagant behavior on the part of the notorious Moscow merchants *(kuptsy)*—not, tellingly, because it was speculation, but because it was a self-indulgent waste of money abroad [28, 34]. Mikhail Morozov (1870–1903) was the first in Russia to possess works by Gauguin, Van Gogh, Toulouse-Lautrec, and Munch. The works of the Impressionists made up only a small portion of Petr Shchukin's (1853–1912) motley collection, but it was in his museum, for the first time, that Muscovites could view works by the Impressionists (see p. 79).

The best and largest collections of contemporary French art in all Europe belonged to these two pioneers' brothers, Sergei Shchukin (1854–1936, see p. 78) and Ivan Morozov (1871–1921), whose Moscow collections concentrated many of the most important works of French painting, from Monet to Matisse and Picasso.

Both collectors declined to lend to exhibitions, and accessibility to their collections varied quite a bit. Ivan Morozov, for the most part, admitted only Russian artists he liked and whose works he bought. Beginning in 1909, by contrast, Shchukin's collection was open to the public on weekends, and a catalogue of the collection was published in 1913 (see p. 79). Shchukin collected the Impressionists until 1904, showing a particular predilection for Monet (thirteen pictures). Between 1904 and 1910, he turned mainly to the Post-Impressionists. In 1903 he bought from Durand-Ruel the first Cézanne in Russia, the still life *Fruits* (1879–80, Hermitage). Shchukin owned eight of Cézanne's canvases and four works by Van Gogh from the period 1888–89. Shchukin's hero at that time was Gauguin, sixteen of whose pictures he hung together in his main dining room as a decorative ensemble grouped around the large canvas *Gathering Fruit* (1899, GMII, p. 85) [see also 27]. Shchukin soon moved on to contemporary art, including the most radical and controversial recent works. As early as 1906 Shchukin bought his first Matisse (*Crockery on a Table,* 1900, Hermitage). All in all he owned thirty-seven of Matisse's paintings. By 1914 Picasso was represented in Shchukin's collection by more works than any other artist—fifty paintings and drawings.

These two Moscow collections differed strikingly. Shchukin focused on controversial works and presented French art as representing a state of permanent revolution. Morozov, on the other hand, wanted to show the artists he collected through works he considered at once typical and exemplary. He often returned to earlier works, carefully selecting them and filling gaps in his collection [cf. 30, 31]. Morozov began his French collection in 1903 with Sisley (*Frost in Louveciennes,* 1873, GMII), and by 1914 he owned

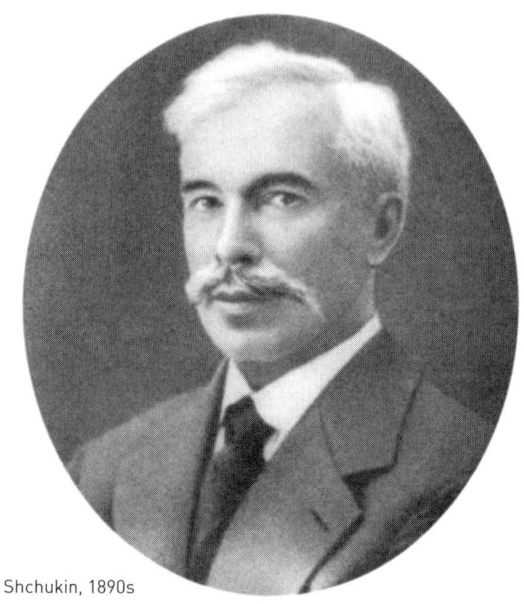

Sergei Shchukin, 1890s

eighteen Cézannes, which he had begun purchasing in 1907, and eleven Gauguins. Among the five pictures by Van Gogh were a number of the artist's greatest masterpieces, including *The Night Café* (1888, now at the Yale University Art Gallery, New Haven). Though Morozov owned eleven Matisses, he had only three Picassos, but they included two of his most celebrated works: *Young Acrobat on a Ball* (1905, Z.I.290, GMII), previously in Gertrude Stein's collection, and the now-famous Cubist portrait of Ambroise Vollard (1910, Z.II.214, GMII).

David Burliuk's letter to Mikhail Matiushin suggests how influential these Moscow collections were on young artists: "everything old is gone, and how hard and joyful it is to start over from the beginning" (April 1910).* Aleksei Grishchenko dedicated a book to Shchukin [64], while Vasilii Kamenskii created a paradoxical image of the collection *(Tango with Cows).* The avant-gardists' marginal position in the art world and odious reputation, however, prevented them from being the chief propagandists for the Moscow collections, which won recognition instead primarily through the efforts of the modernists grouped around *Apollon* (Tugendkhol'd, Muratov, Makovskii, Benois), who promoted them as being part of a mission vital to Russia's national culture [27, 30, 37, 40].

Around 1910, Matisse became the symbol of modern painting. For the first time, Russians could observe the evolution of a leading contemporary artist at firsthand. The *Golden Fleece* popularized Matisse and paved his way to the Russian public, and its sixth issue, in 1909, "the most complete single publication on Matisse in any language before 1920,"† carried an article by Alexandre Mercereau, reproductions of fourteen works, and a translation of "Notes of a Painter."

*Nikolai Khardzhiev, *Stat'i ob avangarde,* vol. 1 (Moscow, 1997), p. 33.

†Alfred H. Barr, Jr., *Matisse: His Art and His Public* (New York: Museum of Modern Art, 1951), p. 110.

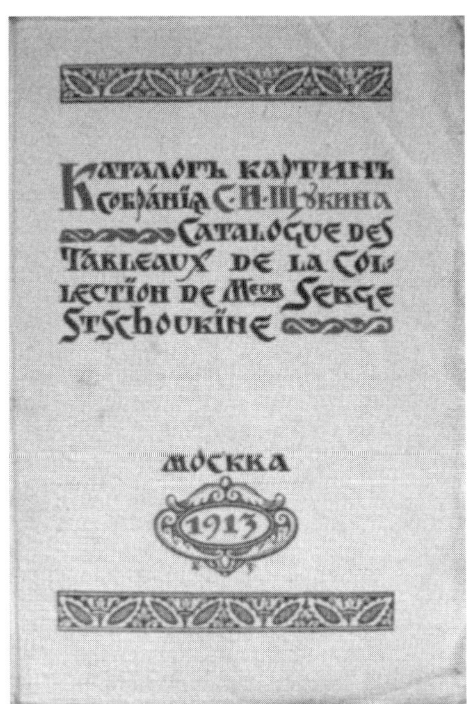

Cover of the catalogue of Sergei Shchukin's collection, Moscow, 1913

Camille Pissarro, *Place du Théâtre-Français,* 1898, originally in Petr Shchukin's collection, since 1912 in Sergei Shchukin's collection; now in the Hermitage, St. Petersburg

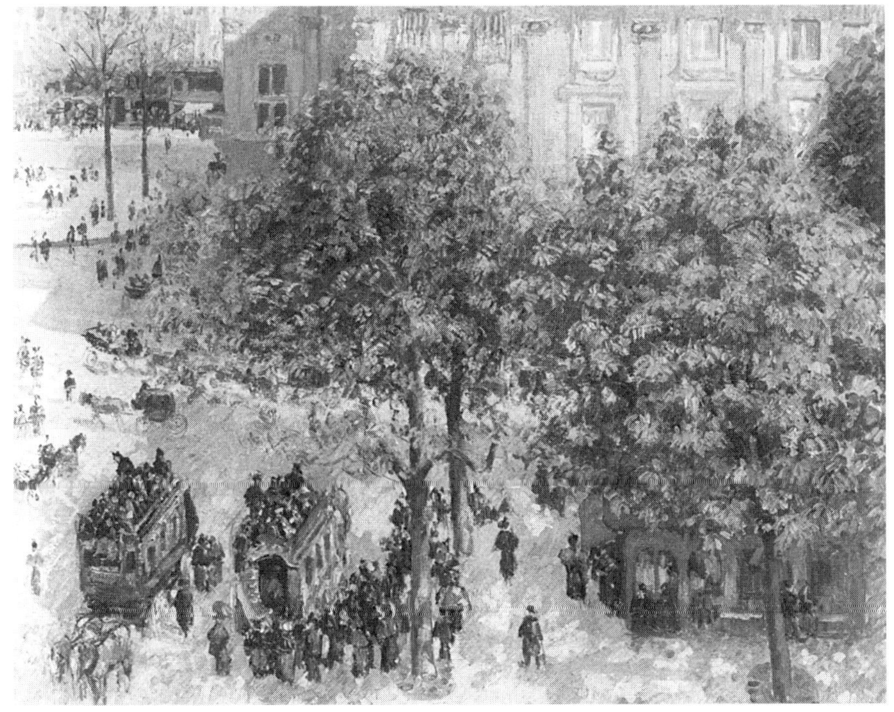

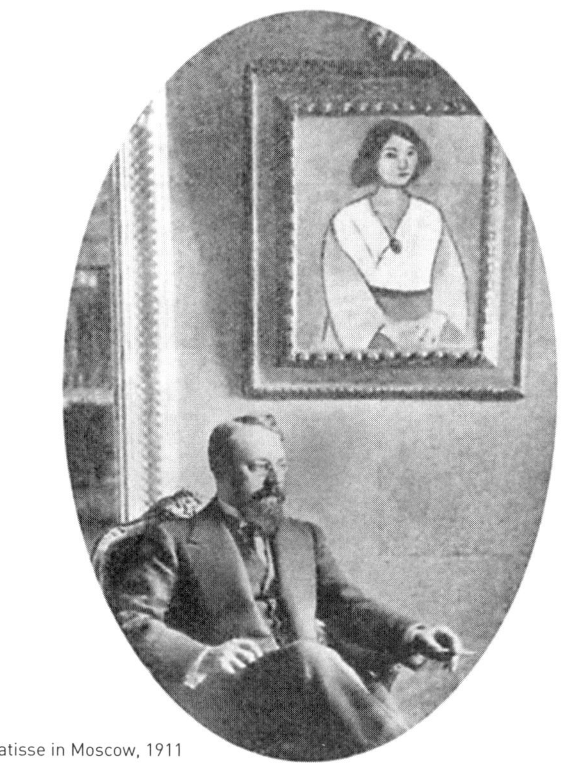
Henri Matisse in Moscow, 1911

In 1909, Shchukin commissioned the groundbreaking panels *Dance* (p. 102) and *Music* for 15,000 and 12,000 francs, respectively—some of the highest prices paid for prewar art. The novelty of Matisse's pictorial language took some getting used to, even for the panels' owner, but especially for the critics and the Moscow public [35–37]. Much more essential than any direct pictorial influence upon Russian painters was the panels' liberating impact. Their very presence prevented Moscow artists from seeing and painting as they had before. For many modernists, Matisse represented an artist whose progress was determined by the inner logic of French painting, and he was appreciated despite strong misapprehensions of him as alien, if not dangerous, to contemporary Russian art [33, 37, 59]. Greatly indebted to Matisse though the avant-gardists were, they wrote practically nothing about him in the 1910s, partly because of their desire to establish their independence. In addition, progressive Russian artists were beginning to feel the influence of Cubism, and Matisse quickly came to seem rather old-fashioned.

Although Picasso became known in Russia around 1910, and his 1908–9 paintings directly influenced the Primitivist canvases of Goncharova, Malevich, and many others, his art was seldom analyzed in the writings of the avant-garde. More often he appeared as the symbol of the new art, the model of the contemporary master. In this capacity he quickly became the object of criticism from within the avant-garde. Mikhail Le Dantiu, for example, asserted, "It is a serious mistake to consider Picasso a beginning—he is rather an ending, and it is probably impossible [to follow] his path" [cf. 65].* The most significant debate about Picasso, which involved a clash between Symbolist and avant-garde concepts of art, may have been influenced by the way Shchukin's paintings by the artist were concentrated in a small room, where they carpeted the walls all the way to the ceiling (see p. 88). Hung with no intervening spaces, these pictures demonstrated the paradoxical variety of Picasso's work in a way that seemed to intensify each one's expressiveness. The initiators of these polemics were the writers and philosophers Georgii Chulkov, Nikolai Berdiaev, and Sergei Bulgakov [42].† Although they acknowledged Picasso as the most significant contemporary artist, his painting became an occasion to create an apocalyptic picture of a dying Western culture.

The demonic images to which the authors of these essays resorted in order to express their understanding of the complete deformation of the visible world in Picasso's painting colored the debate about his work in a special way. Journalists quickly made Picasso's demonism a cliché. Even the young Aleksandr Rodchenko wrote to his future wife in the fall of 1915, as he was working on his own nonobjective compositions, "Today I created some monstrous things . . . I will rival Picasso in possessing the devil."‡ As a result of such interpretations, by around 1920 Picasso's name had become a symbol of deep cultural crisis. The avant-garde, evidently in connection with the outbreak of war, had entered the debate with the religious thinkers rather late. Their principal response was the first monograph in the world on Picasso, *Picasso and the Environs,* written by Ivan Aksenov in 1914 but not published until 1917. This book contrasted an emphatically "formal" understanding of art to the "mystical" conception of the artist [43].

27

Iakov Tugendkhol'd

"S. I. Shchukin's French Collection" (1914)

Iakov Tugendkhol'd (1882–1928) took part in the student unrest of 1902 and soon after went to Munich, where he studied art and law and was in contact with the Social Democratic emigration. In 1905 he settled in Paris and studied with Théophile Steinlen, and in 1910 he became a correspondent for *Apollon.* He returned to Russia in 1913. After the Revolution, Tugendkhol'd headed the Art Section of Glavpolitprosvet (from 1923) and the arts sections of the major newspapers *Izvestiia* (1922–26) and *Pravda* (1929) and wrote extensively on contemporary Western art.

Tugendkhol'd's article, published in *Apollon* (Apollo) 1–2 (1914), is not a guide to Shchukin's

*Mikhail Le Dantiu to O. I. Leshkova, 1917. Quoted in E. Kovtun, "Ochevidets nezrimogo. O tvorchestve Pavla Filonova," in *Pavel Filonov i ego shkola,* edited by Evgeniia Petrova and Iurgen Kharten (Cologne: DuMont Buchverlag, 1990), p. 16.

†Marilyn McCully, ed., *A Picasso Anthology: Documents. Criticism. Reminiscences* (Princeton: Princeton University Press, 1981), pp. 104–18.

‡Aleksandr Rodchenko, *Opyty dlia budushchego. Dnevniki. Stat'i. Pis'ma. Zapiski* (Moscow, 1996), p. 45.

collection. His description of the principal works does not follow Shchukin's generally arbitrary arrangement but instead reconstructs the evolution of modern painting.

. . . We can debate the timeliness or prematurity of such a "museum," but each acquisition bears the indisputable stamp of talent. Here we have Picasso's cell, but no monastic approach to painting. Here you are infected by the youthful enthusiasm and sage breadth of the proprietor, who never stands still, yet he does not renounce the old as he seeks out the new; respecting continuity, he does not burn yesterday's idols in favor of today's. Here a remark of Shchukin's should be inscribed on the doors as a motto: "Before I judge a picture it must hang in my home about a year so I can get used to it and understand it." . . .

Muscovites who knew the French only through Tretiakov's Barbizons* were as upset by the first Monet landscapes Shchukin brought to Russia as they are today by Picasso. . . . At that time even Serov saw in Cézanne's *Mardi Gras* only "wooden blockheads," but the years passed and he admitted with characteristic sincerity that he could not get those "wooden blockheads" out of his mind!† Shchukin won over his Sunday visitors. And it is not his fault if this victory was not only beneficial but also intoxicated Russian youth with modernism. On the contrary, what Shchukin's collection teaches is the value of *culture, consistency,* and *labor.*

Here is a suite of rooms containing works from the first Impressionists to Picasso. French painting developed very logically, and Shchukin himself evolved just as gradually. . . .

Cézanne's Romantic origins are beyond doubt. He took a keen interest in Delacroix and Baudelaire and began with literary topics. One of the last reflections of this interest is in fact the picture *Mardi Gras* owned by Shchukin—Harlequin in scarlet and black and a frigid Pierrot. This is, of course, not an illustration of the *commedia dell' arte* or a genre scene from Watteau or Lancret but, at first glance, inert marionettes, "two wooden blockheads." There is a categorical cogency to Pierrot's frozen clumsiness and Harlequin's exaggerated stride, though, as underscored by the lines of the drapery; the curtain on the right is as heavy as Pierrot's figure, the curtain on the left is tucked up as if to echo Harlequin's step. These bulky figures have an indestructible monumentality. Harlequin may not leap, but you also know he will *never* fall. This is life—not real life as in Degas's horse racing and ballet subjects, but fictitious life as expressed only in painting, that is, statically—not Harlequin and Pierrot but a monument to Pierrot and Harlequin. All of Cézanne's portraits are "monuments." . . . When you look at Edouard Manet's *Man with a Pipe,*‡ you have to feel

*Landscapes by the Barbizon artists were included in the collection Sergei Tretiakov willed to the Tretiakov Gallery.

†The anecdote about the painter Valentin Serov's (1865–1911) reaction was widespread in artistic circles. Grabar' dates it to 1904, the year the canvas was purchased. Cf. I. E. Grabar', *Moia zhizn'* (Moscow, 1936), p. 169.

‡Manet, *The Good Beer* (*Portrait of Emile Bellot,* 1873, Philadelphia Museum of Art). Shchukin owned Cézanne's *Man with a Pipe* (1890–92, R.790, GMII).

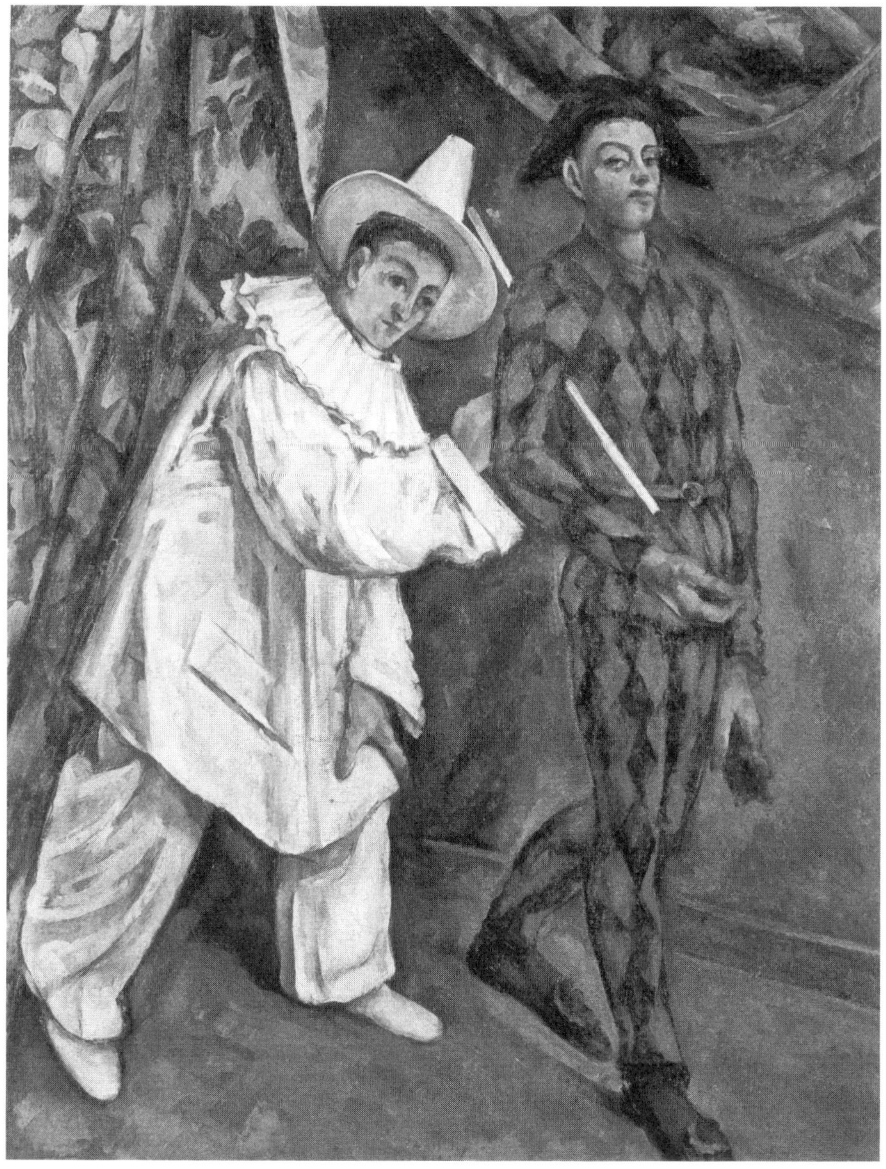

Paul Cézanne, *Mardi Gras,* 1888, formerly in Shchukin's collection, now in the Pushkin Museum, Moscow

Manet's temperament; when you look at Cézanne's painterly sculpture you sense the immutability of objective laws—the rhythm of gravity and complementary colors. Cézanne's classicism consists in this objectivism. . . .

You enter a Gothic cathedral and see painted glass, and you are so far away you cannot make it out—still you are captivated by its magic chord. This, as Gauguin once remarked *(Notes éparses),* is the picture's music.

I recall these words every time I cross the threshold of Shchukin's room, and my gaze—still ignorant of what it is seeing—falls upon Gauguin's painting. It is strange how little inclined he was to imagine his Tahitian pictures turning up in Moscow someday and how pertinent his remark is to Shchukin's wall and the Shchukin display itself. Here the full thrust of the owner's taste is in evidence. The pictures are crowded in, so at first you can't tell where one ends and another begins—as if you were standing in front of a single large fresco, a single *iconostasis.* All you see are magnificent, resonant colors, and all you hear is sonorous, solemn music—a hymn to the idle life. And you realize that the poet Aurier, whom no one heard at the time, was right when he demanded *walls* for Gauguin: "*des murs, des murs, donnez lui des murs.*"* . . .

Once you step closer you begin to understand where all this came from. It all came from that traditional china cup with the flowery pattern that Cézanne tucked into a corner of his *nature morte,*† from archaic art, from Breton wooden sculpture and folk art. True, Shchukin has no works typical of Gauguin at Pont-Aven, but he does have sixteen works from his most mature period. . . .

Cézanne went back from the light of the Impressionists to that of the Venetians, but his intellect and emotion were in too Olympian a balance. Although he loved color, he still considered it a function of form; although he loved form, he considered it a projection of reality. Even when he was young, Cézanne was too much the wise old man. Hence Gauguin's opposite inclination for the wisdom of childhood—the flowery pattern of the Breton cup and the brilliant East. . . .

Hence as well the watershed of subsequent French painting, which is so vividly represented in the next rooms of Shchukin's collection. Hence Matisse and Picasso.

. . . Only in Shchukin's collection can Matisse be studied and understood. Although I have had many opportunities to see his exhibitions in Paris and view his works in his own studio, I did not know Matisse until I visited Shchukin's home. Not only are there a great many of his pictures here (thirty-seven), but they are arranged in the most favorable surroundings. Like hothouse flowers, certain pictures need a suitable environment; this is a disadvantage of the museum, which lacks it, and an advantage of the private collection.

Shchukin's home is a hothouse and the apotheosis of Matisse's painting. Matisse and the owner hung his canvases here, combining agreeable neighbors. When you enter the living room that Matisse has decorated, you realize he has had a stroke of good luck, for rarely do artists in their lifetime see their works so successfully applied. After all, the practical inutility of painting, which in our day has become "art for art's sake," is one of the curses of contemporary art. . . .

I said just now that Matisse has *decorated* Shchukin's living room, and I want to emphasizc that word. You can't say that the large dining room is "decorated" by Gau-

*Albert Aurier, "Le Symbolisme en peinture: Paul Gauguin," *Mercure de France* (March 1891).

†In his still life *Fruits* (1879–80, R.427, Hermitage).

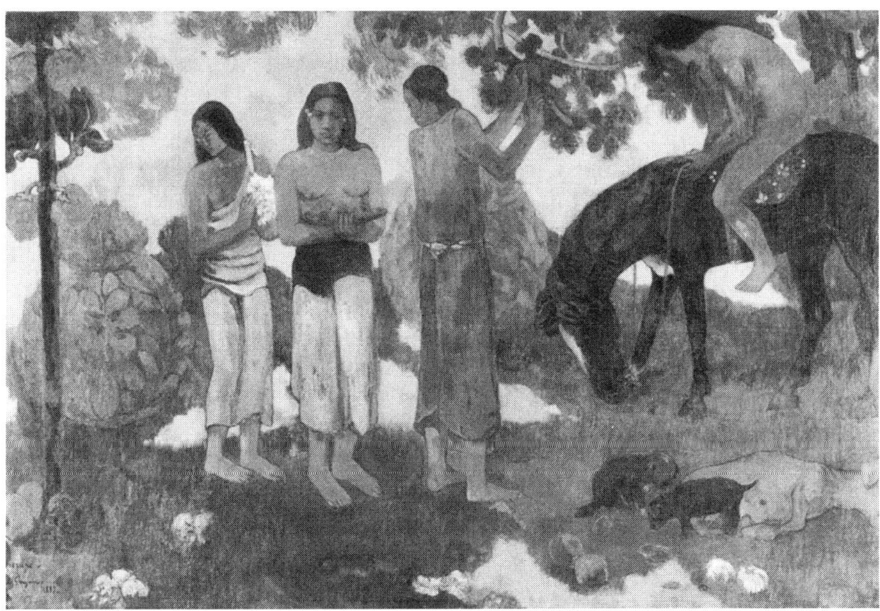

Paul Gauguin, *Gathering Fruit,* 1899, formerly in Shchukin's collection, now in the Pushkin Museum, Moscow

guin or that the small study is "decorated" by Picasso [see p. 88], because in both instances you forget the rooms in the name of Gauguin and Picasso. In Matisse's case, however, the expression is quite literal. This is not a reproach but simply a fact: Matisse's canvases possess an applied (in the highest sense of the word) *decorative* essence. They are apprehended *in conjunction with* their surroundings—the pale green "tapestry" on the walls, the pink ceiling, and the cherry-red rug—in the midst of which Matisse's azure, crimson, and emerald shine so vividly and joyfully. . . . The overall impression, however, is that all of it—the wallpaper, rug, ceiling, and pictures—is the work, the decorative dramatization, of Matisse himself. This is a false impression, of course, for all of it existed before Matisse; all that he or Shchukin did was to hang and combine the canvases skillfully. . . .

The genuine, metaphysical being of his painting, however, becomes apparent only in the living room ensemble. There he reigns alone, and his basic element—*decorativeness*—joyously asserts itself. He himself is aware of this chief feature of his talent. . . . In a famous article (cf. *Grande Revue,* 1908),* he expressed himself even more explicitly, comparing his ideal of art to "a good armchair where you can find peace." Well now—do not be too quick to smile ironically, reader—not all art can hold up to such a comparison; not all art can be enjoyed sitting in an "armchair": *it might be boring.* Say what you will about Matisse, he cannot bore you. You may not be able

*Henri Matisse, "Notes d'un peintre," *La Grande Revue* 52, no. 24 (December 25, 1908): 731–45.

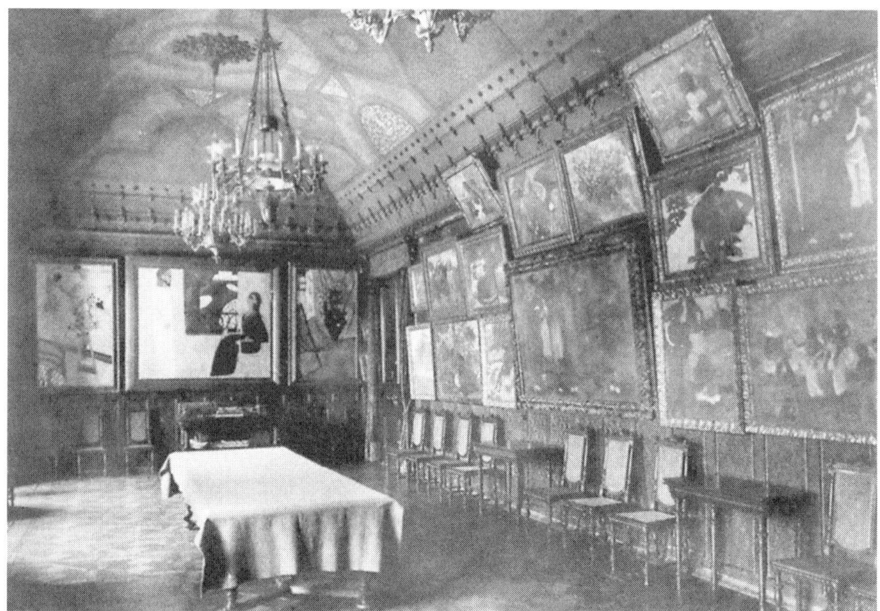

Dining room in Shchukin's house with paintings by Gauguin and Matisse.

to philosophize in Shchukin's pink living room, but you also cannot surrender to Chekhovian moods. This sonorous chiming of colors that rushes from the walls, these dissonances of sultry major and cold deep purples and blues . . . radiate a vital fullness. Here, without leaving your "armchair," you travel to the poles and tropics of emotion; here color is pure color abstracted from any representational function and contributes to our psychophysical "delectation." Although the artist selected them *rationally,* they are a purely *emotional* phenomenon.

. . . Boris Anrep has criticized Matisse for the blank spots in his works [see 39], but this is not quite right. These "voids" on the canvas are balanced by filled areas—areas of white by areas of color. Nonetheless, his composition does lack adequate organic closure. His canvases possess an ornamental harmony that can be extended and projected both vertically and horizontally. Take his *natures mortes,* which are interwoven arabesques: dark blue horn-shaped patterns on an azure-green field or yellow patterns alongside the dark blue back of a couch and a lilac tablecloth.* They flow over the canvas rhythmically, and this flow can be extended in space and repeated on the wall. Even *Harmony in Red,*† which blooms with the same dark blue patterns branching out like the antlers of a deer, seems to be not an enclosed room but a fragment of something larger. True, his large panel *Dance* does have a closed necklace of bodies, but *Music* again has a garland that could be extended. The fluidity of Matisse's

**Blue Tablecloth* (1909, Hermitage); *Spanish Still Life* (1910, Hermitage).

†*The Red Room* (*Harmonie en rouge,* 1908, Hermitage).

arabesques and their ability to extend hold a charm, of course, which may even be the secret reason why he is never boring—the secret of his delightful "armchair." These properties give his pictures a kind of life that rushes beyond the gilded frame and spreads across the wall. Here again, however, we are touching upon the Oriental quality of his decorative art. Matisse's pictures . . . do not appear to be "things in themselves" but pieces of some nonexistent frieze—an Oriental frieze. Such is the composition of Persian and Arabic glazed walls, rugs, and textiles—ornamental ligatures and patterns that flower unbounded by any spatial unity. Yes, Maurice Denis is right: Matisse's painting aspires to the *absolute,* but this absolute is limited by the relative, namely, the bounds of the easel painting or the gilded frame. Matisse's pictures are not an infinite frieze but "a thing in itself." . . .

Stained glass! Here at last we have found an appropriate term for Matisse's painting. Carrière once said that Rodin's tragedy was not having a cathedral he could adorn with his sculptures. If he had, they would not be so fragmentary. The same could be said of Matisse—although he is himself very modern, he should have been born in the age of stained glass, shining enamels, and glazed tiles. This becomes particularly obvious when you view his *Nasturtiums with "Dance"* and *Conversation** from the threshold of Shchukin's living room: the orange-pink bodies in *Nasturtiums* flicker against a dark blue background like window arabesques. Look at Gauguin's pictures and then again at *Nasturtiums:* the former will look like a matte fresco, the latter a stained-glass window.

Matisse's palette is richer, more complex, and more luxuriant than Gauguin's. He is *the most talented colorist of our day;* the most cultured as well, for he has absorbed all the luxury of the Orient and Byzantium. . . .

And here we are, finally, in the last room: a vaulted cell, a Stone Age museum, the kingdom of the Spaniard Picasso, that *enfant terrible* of modernity. But do not rush to judgment, reader. Let us arm ourselves with patience and for the time being follow the example of Shchukin, who even when he does not understand Picasso says, "He's probably right, not I." . . .

Picasso deserves this kind of *trust* because he is a sincerely inquisitive and diligent artist as well as a first-class talent. I cannot forget the impression I brought back from a visit to his studio.† I must say that the place was rather unusual for an artist. In the corner were black idols from the Congo and masks from Dahomey; on the table, a *nature morte* of bottles, scraps of wallpaper, and newspapers; on the walls, strange models of musical instruments that Picasso himself had cut from cardboard. Everything was stern, without a spot of bright saturated color. Yet I sensed in this cabinet of black magic a creative laboratory and an atmosphere of misguided yet serious labor filled with the intensity of boundless, tireless inquiry. *And there was nothing ridiculous about it!* . . .

**Capucines à "La Danse"* (1912, GMII); *Conversation* (1909–12, Hermitage).

†Tugendhol'd probably met Picasso in January or February 1913 (Anatoly Podoksik, *Picasso: The Eternal Quest: The Artist's Works in Soviet Museums* [Leningrad: Aurora, 1989], p. 66).

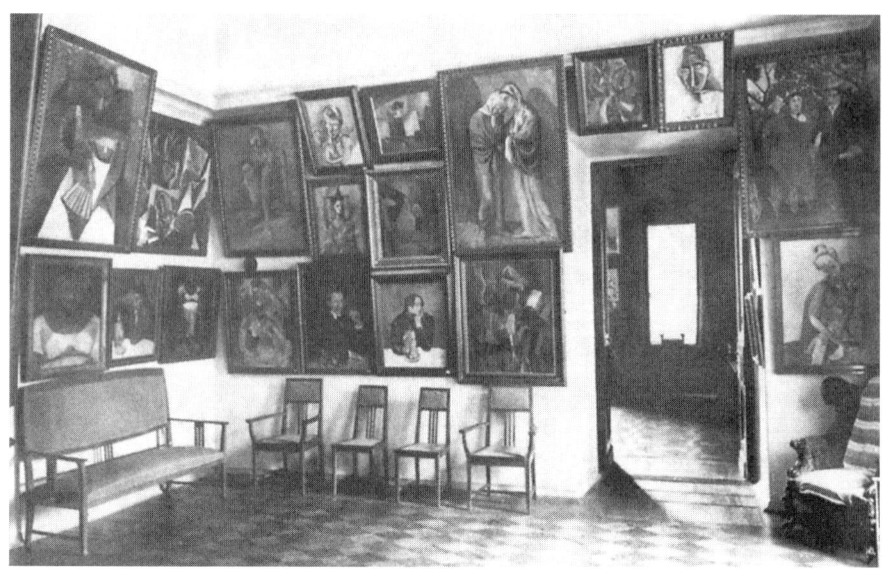

Picasso's room in Shchukin's house

. . . [Picasso] wants to represent objects not as they appear to the eye but as they exist in our *conception* of them; he wants to suggest above all their geometrical volume, their sculptural "solidity." He is obsessed by a mania to compress, a passion for hardness, a fetish for stone. Whereas in Claude Monet's works everything flows and liquefies, in Picasso's hands everything hardens. Monet transforms the Rouen Cathedral* into stone dust, whereas Picasso compresses clouds into piles of stone. Where Matisse has only a silhouette, he has only volume. Even his color scale has a stern mineral and "geological" quality. Take *House in a Garden*†—a stony yellow tree trunk, a gray fence and house, a solid mass of greenish foliage the color of ancient moss that sparkles like granite.

. . . When Picasso paints nudity he gives full rein to his love of earthy ochres and compressed, massive weight. His nude women seem to be made of stones held together by the black cement of their contours. Such are his brick-red *Three Women* [see p. 113],‡ who have the heaviness and relief of a monument. There is truly no way anyone could *react* any further to the nudes of Renoir and Degas and the picturesque sensuality of the Impressionists. Here is the self-assured triumph of the chisel over the brush, touch over sight! You can wax ironical over these three brick Graces, but you cannot deny that they are a peculiar monument to our age, which is in search

*Monet, *The Rouen Cathedral in the Evening; The Rouen Cathedral at Noon* (1893, dated 1894, GMII); Picasso, *Brick Factory at Tortosa* (1909, Z.II. 158, Hermitage), whose former title was *Factory at Horta de Ebro.*

†The reference is to one of two pictures titled *House at Rue-des-Bois* (1908, Z.II.80, 81, Hermitage and GMII).

‡*Three Women* (1908, Z.II.108, Hermitage). Until late 1913 or early 1914 it belonged to Gertrude Stein. Shchukin acquired it through Kahnweiler.

of the "organic" and the "statuary," an age of restive intellectuals infatuated by strength and sports but—alas—impotent. . . .

Despite the outward might of Picasso's women, they are feeble within: monumental beauty is not the mechanical sum of individual monumental boulders! His stone idols are not always intact monoliths! At first glance, of course, the schematic expressiveness of Picasso's women has a great deal in common with a mighty prehistoric Venus or the marvelous wooden sculptures from the Congo or Madagascar that Picasso loves so much and that adorn his room in Shchukin's collection. However, there is a profound difference between Picasso's abstraction and that of these primordial artists. When I was at Picasso's studio and saw the black idols from the Congo, I recalled what Benois said about the "cautionary analogy" between his art and the "religious art of the African savages," and I asked Picasso whether he was curious about the mystical aspect of these sculptures. "Not in the least," he replied. "What attracts me is their geometrical simplicity."* . . .

Although he is interested in the geometrical schematization in the African savages' art, Picasso essentially focuses only on the outward form, which he is unwilling and unable to fill with new content. In this sense, "what is frightening is not that Picasso's monsters resemble the religious art of savages" (Benois) but that they do not resemble it enough! The Union of Youth speaks in vain about creating a crooked and dark-haired Apollo:† Picasso himself cannot create any Apollo whatever; he has no standard, no idol, no ideal—not even in the area of pure form, for *Apollo is perfect order and Picasso's world is in a state of permanent disorder*. . . .

Faced with this tragedy of Picasso's, this triumph of quantity over quality, the many over the single, this terrible frigidity of inner emptiness, how pleasant it is to rest for a moment on Rousseau's serene and dovish lucidity—*Rousseau le Douanier*—who has not yet tasted of the tree of knowledge. It was clever of Shchukin to hang them side by side. Once you have rested, however, Rousseau's sacred "silliness" no longer satisfies after Picasso, and you need something more to surmount Picasso's tragedy. . . .

28

Natal'ia Severova (Nordman)

Intimate Pages (1910)

Writer and social activist Natal'ia Nordman (1863–1914; pseudonym "Severova") was the Realist painter Il'ia Repin's common-law wife. They made their visit to Shchukin's home, which Severova wrote about in *Intimate Pages* (St. Petersburg, 1910), in December 1909.

*Cf. Benois's "More on New Trends in Art" [40]. Avant-gardists frequently mentioned this episode. Cf. Vladimir Markov, "Negro Art" (1913), in *Primitivism and Twentieth-Century Art: A Documented History*, edited by Jack Flam with Miriam Deutch (Berkeley: University of California Press, 2003), pp. 63–64.

†Cf. August Ballier, "Apollon budnichnyi i Apollon cherniavyi" (Everyday Apollo and Dark-Haired Apollo), *Soiuz molodezhi* (Union of Youth) (March 1913): 11–13.

At the end of a spacious courtyard stands the beautiful manor house of Prince Trubetskoi, now owned by textiles manufacturer Sergei Ivanovich Shchukin.

Shchukin is a patron of the arts. He sponsors weekly concerts. He has a taste for the last word in music, and in art as well. But he collects only the French—*le dernier cri de la mode!* The latest fashions hang in his office but are moved into other rooms the moment new names begin to supplant them on the French market. Constant motion. Who knows what he has hanging in the bathroom? Unfortunately, Shchukin himself was not in Moscow but is being treated in Paris. We were given permission to visit the gallery. It was already four o'clock when we entered the vestibule. We were greeted by the "manager," a gray-haired woman in a velvet dress, who led us upstairs. As we stepped into each room it was flooded by a sea of electric light. The manager has a rather casual, naive attitude toward the pictures, as if she regarded them as an idle whim of their owner.

"Just a minute," she said, "I'll begin with the most passé and keep going until we reach the most fashionable."

The walls of all the beautiful old-fashioned rooms are entirely covered in pictures. The first—a kind of official waiting room—contains Cottet, Simon, and other wonderful painters of that period (about ten years ago). In the main room we saw many of Monet's landscapes, which have a certain charm of their own. . . .

There [in the living room] I was especially struck by the carpet. I thought that carpets like that appeared only in novels, in phrases such as "our feet sank into it," "our steps were noiseless," "the soft material enveloped our shoes." Yes, yes, it was just like that. We moved noiselessly through the deep living room and sank into the soft material, and the Cézannes gazed upon us from the walls!

The manager, having exhausted her entire reserve of bewilderment, confused the names, and suddenly sank into melancholy. She called on Shchukin's son for help.

There before us stood a young man about twenty-two years old, his hands thrust in his pockets in the Parisian manner. Why? Listen: he even speaks *Russian* with a Parisian burr. Why is that? He was educated abroad.

Later we learned that there were four brothers, all of whom were committed to and believed in nothing. One had already shot himself. *Shchukins* from a *French* lyceum with Russian millions—the strange jumble had robbed them of their roots.* I felt sorry for the young man the whole time—as we looked at the Cézannes and a series of Van Goghs in the main dining room, and finally, in the holy of holies, in Shchukin's own study—at Matisse's large canvases. Together there were three worldviews, three smiling faces. But these smiles were very different. One was the smile of the manager, whose soul had never been penetrated by a single ray of art but stood outside paradise's closed gates. The second smile was that of a cynic for whom fashion was God. *The new vogue.* Today a new carriage, automobile, woman, picture. To-

*There was no basis in fact for such accusations. Ivan, the youngest brother, studied at the Lyceum of Tsarevich Nikolai and then at Moscow University. He lived for a long time in Paris, collected paintings, and committed suicide in 1908. The three other brothers, including Sergei, had special training in business, and the fifth brother, Vladimir, graduated from Moscow University's medical school.

morrow everything would be old and boring. Shapeless, crude, insolent Matisse would fade into the background like the others. And there was a third smile, or rather a grimace of suffering, on the artist's face. His soul was filled with longing and pain. Paris's sneer at the Russians. These feeble Slavs, they allowed themselves to be hypnotized so willingly. They stuck out their noses—lead us wherever you like, just lead us.

"The Michelangelo of our time," said the young Shchukin of Matisse in that special tone of voice in which irony and truth are indistinguishable.

"And then there's Gauguin," I[l'ia] E[fimovich] said excitedly. "He has a deliberate formlessness, an affected naiveté, but a certain poetry nonetheless. Sometimes you do indeed think that by living on Tahiti with the savages he really did himself become wild. . . . But Matisse has nothing, absolutely nothing but impudence!"

As soon as I can I want to get out of this house, where there is no *harmony of life* and where "the Emperor's new clothes" reign supreme. . . .

. . . The scourge of capital, the twelve-hour workday, the lack of disability or old-age provisions for the ignorant, faceless workers who roll out cloth their entire lives for a crust of bread. . . . This magnificent house of the Shchukin family was once built by serfdom's slaves and is now nourished by the same juices of the oppressed people—all these thoughts throbbed inside me like a diseased tooth, and this large lisping man [Il'ia Ostroukhov] irritated me. The abnormality of private wealth was so clear to me. The galleries, the pictures, the luxury of art—all of this *should,* of course, be the property of the entire nation. Therein lies the gentle charm of the Tretiakov Gallery.

. . . After our visit to Shchukin's home we found the key to contemporary *Moscow* art, and nothing more could persuade us. The Union, the exhibition of Moscow artists, and finally the student exhibition at the School of Painting and Sculpture—all this was in the spirit of the times. The student exhibition was particularly symptomatic of our age.

. . . after reviewing it . . . I stood alone by the cashier's desk near a group of students.

"Well, what did Repin say?" their curious faces turned toward me.

I said nothing.

"Do you visit Shchukin's gallery often?" I suddenly asked.

They exchanged glances, looked at me, and we all burst into laughter. As usual, of course, we were laughing about *different things.*

"Often. Shchukin is constantly inviting groups of us. Why, do you see imitation here?"

Again I said nothing.

"Here's the thing"—and suddenly I actually felt a kind of hostility—"I don't want to go down in posterity colored green, or black, or blue. I want a portrait to immortalize *me* and nothing else. My skin and eyes, which express *my* temperament, *my* hair, everything, everything. I even want my dress to be *mine,* one I'm wearing today, not something from the time of the Marquise de Pompadour."

The students' faces expressed pity bordering on contempt.

"You're asking for the impossible. In the first place, we don't paint portraits anymore, and if we did, you would go down in posterity *only* as viewed by the artist. . . ."

When . . . we were sitting in the streetcar I asked Il'ia Efimovich, "Well, what do you think?"

"I think their demands are enormous. They want complete liberation from tradition. They're searching for immediacy, *super*-forms, *super*-colors. They want genius."

"No," I said, "that's not it. They want a *revolution.* All Russians without exception want to overturn and rip off something that stifles and crushes them. So they revolt."

29
Vasilii Kamenskii
"KARTINiia" (1914)

The most original avant-garde *hommage à Shchukine* came from the poet, aviator, and member of the Cubo-Futurist "Hylaea" group, Vasilii Kamenskii (1884–1961). In 1914 he authored a number of experimental texts that he called "ferroconcrete poems." The collocations of words and verbal "fragments" determined by the theme of the "poem" were printed in various typefaces and distributed across the page. The text created in this manner could be read in different directions with different combinations of words. Logical connections were broken, so that the construction resembled a kind of crossword puzzle in which the meaning of a word could change depending on which of the neighboring words (or fragments) was read after it. Such a text permits only an approximate interpretation and cannot be translated exactly.

Kamenskii first published "KARTINiia" in the brochure "A Naked Man among the Clothed" (Moscow, 1914), with another ferroconcrete poem, "Cabaret." The work became widely known when it was republished in the collection *Tango with Cows* (Moscow, 1914), a book printed on the reverse side of wallpaper, with the upper-right corner of the pages deliberately cut off.

The title points directly to the "theme" of the "poem," but it presupposes various readings.* Thus Iury Molok prefers to read it in two directions—down: *Kartiniia — dvorets S. I. Shchukin[a]* ("Kartiniia [is] S. I. Shchukin's mansion"), and up: *Shchukin S. I. Dvorets kartin i ia* ("S. I. Shchukin. The mansion of pictures and I"). Anatolii Strigalev sees in the title a resemblance to a street sign and the name *strana kartin* ("land of pictures"). Gerald Janecek notes that in contrast to similar texts marked off in enclosed "cells" most of the areas of "KARTINiia" are open toward the central area. In the center of the page is the "title" of the poem and the word *lestnitsa* ("staircase"), so that the composition of the work roughly corresponds to the layout of Shchukin's *dvorets* ("mansion"), the rooms of which surrounded the staircase with Matisse's panels in the entryway. The five open areas are filled mainly with the names of articles and titles of pictures (more than twenty can be determined on the basis of the catalogue). Most prominent here are Matisse (six pictures) and Picasso, whose name in various transcriptions is repeated four times (six of his works are also present). Individual words form statements and opinions—*Mone net . . . pri mne* ("No Monet . . . with me"), *Ostalsia poniatnym Sezann* ("Cézanne remained intelligible"), *Pikassosomnoi,* or *Pikasso so mnoi* ("Picasso is with me"). The closed triangles contain rhymed

*See Iu. Molok, "Tipografskie opyty poeta—futurista," in V. Kamenskii, *Tango s korvami* (Moscow, 1991); A. Strigalev, "Kartiny, 'stikhokartiny' i 'zhelezobetonnye poemy' Vasilia Kamenskugo," in *Voprosy iskusstvoznania* 1–2 (Moscow, 1995); G. Janecek, *The Look of Russian Literature* (Princeton: Princeton University Press, 1984).

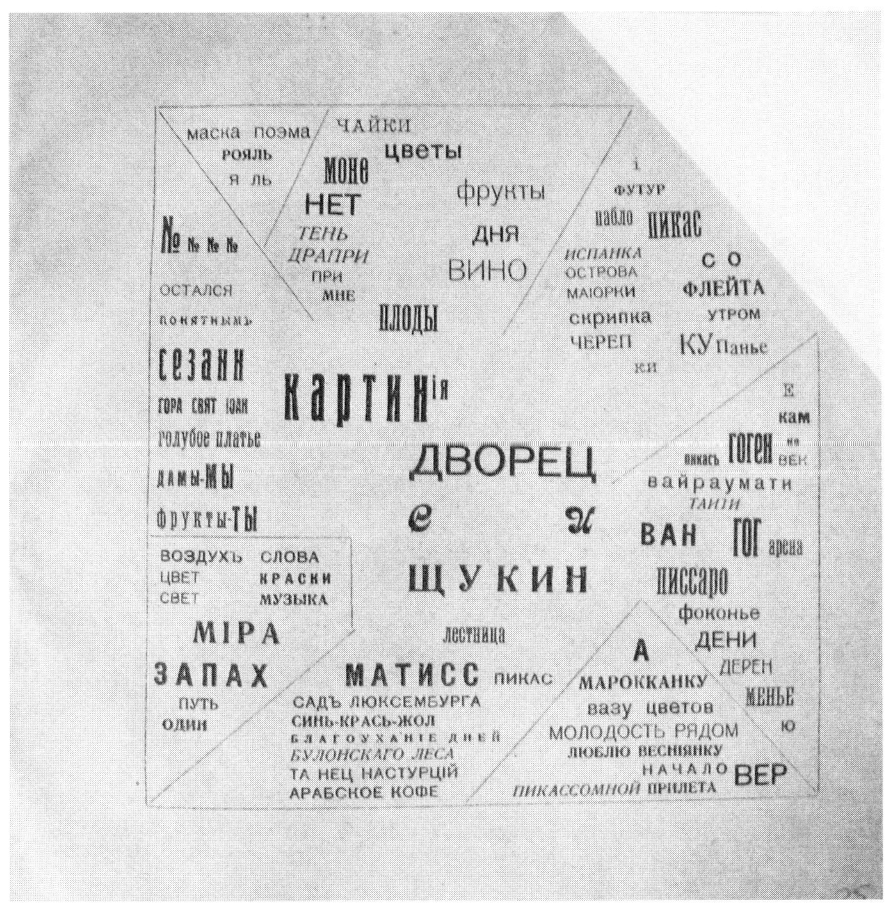

Vasilii Kamenskii, "KARTINiia," ferroconcrete poem dedicated to Sergei Shchukin, published in Kamenskii's *Tango with Cows* (Moscow, 1914)

lines, and, as Molok and Strigalev have both noted, the "trapezium" on the left contains the result of a "visit" to the museum—a declaration of the Futurist synthesis of the arts: *vozdukh* ("air"), *slova* ("words"), *tsvet* ("color"), *kraski* ("colors/paints"), *svet* ("light"), *muzyka* ("music")—*MIRA ZAPAKH* ("smell of the world")—*put' odin* ("[there is but] one way").

Some elements of the "poem" do not correspond to reality. The combination *i future* (evidently, *futuri* reversed) can be understood as a kind of "graffito"—a Futurist visitor's autograph on the wall of the museum (Shchukin did not own any Futurist pictures).

30

Sergei Makovskii
"French Artists in the Morozov Collection" (1912)

Sergei Makovskii (1877–1962) was an art critic, poet, and editor-in-chief of *Apollon.* After 1920 he lived in Paris and worked as a journalist. Because Morozov's collection was not generally

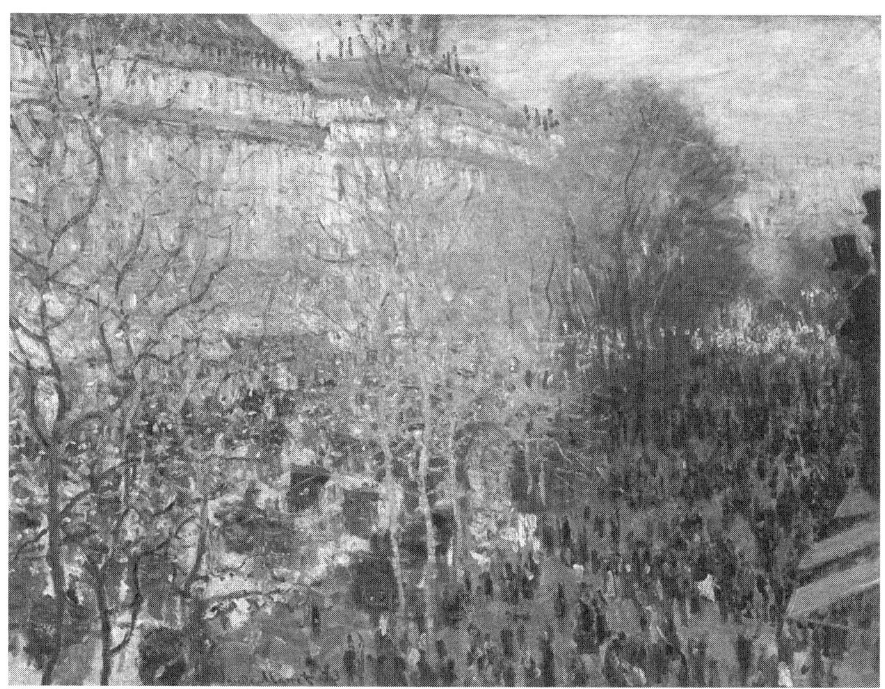

Claude Monet, *Boulevard des Capucines*, 1873, formerly in Morozov's collection, now in the Pushkin Museum, Moscow

accessible, Makovskii's article in *Apollon* (Apollo), nos. 3–4 (1912) and the accompanying catalogue and illustrations were a significant event.

Moscow can be rightfully proud of Ivan Abramovich Morozov's French gallery in his home on Prechistenka Street. There are few such collections—not only in Russia but even in the West. Here is a museum of painting that is infinitely valuable and necessary for anyone who understands contemporary art. . . .

A museum of personal taste, of course, is by no means an impartial museum. Here, if you will, the whole of French painting of even the past twenty-five to thirty years is not represented, and many excellent masters are absent; elegantly represented, on the other hand, are all the chosen, favorite, and glorified teachers of a generation that has already passed—Monet, Renoir, Sisley, Pissarro, Degas, Cézanne, Van Gogh, Gauguin, and their followers and heirs: Denis, Bonnard, Vuillard, Signac, Guérin, Marquet, Friesz, Valtat, right up to Matisse and the "wild" young artists inclined toward Cubism.

The museum's overall impression is unusually vivid. All of the elect are represented by masterpieces, and I emphasize that this exemplary quality is to the great and wholly personal credit of Ivan Morozov himself. He is one of those collectors who are absolutely independent and quite impervious to outside influence. He deems worthy of his gallery only what he likes and what agrees with his intuition and views on paint-

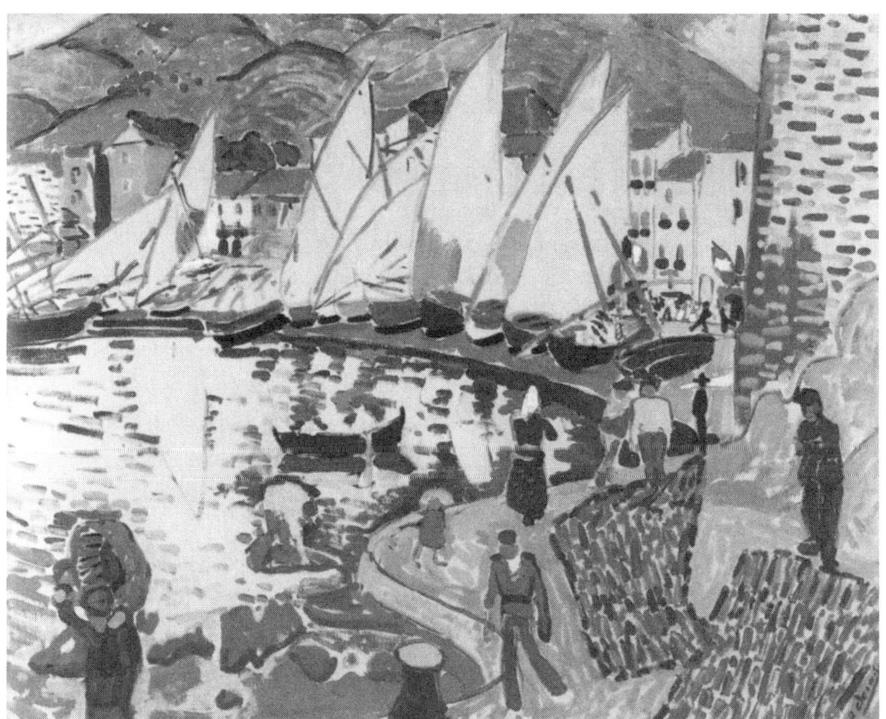

André Derain, *Drying Sails,* 1905, formerly in Morozov's collection, now in the Pushkin Museum, Moscow. © 2009 Artists Rights Society (ARS), New York/ADAGP, Paris.

ing; although he sometimes buys a picture more to encourage a beginning talent than out of any "infatuation," he never acquires anything out of snobbery or because the artist is a big name. For the most part, however, it is the connoisseur's "infatuation," together with his subtle taste and rare restraint, that influences his choice of works. Morozov truly knows how to acquire an artist's most vivid and *expressive* works (and this ability is so valuable!), and he can be uncommonly patient if he must, waiting for his chance to acquire a chosen picture and searching for years through artists' studios and the shops of *marchands de tableaux* for a "needed" canvas, some masterpiece of a favorite master he still lacks. . . . I recall that on one of my first visits to his gallery I was surprised to notice an empty space at the end of a solid wall of Cézannes. "This spot is reserved for a 'blue Cézanne' (that is, a landscape from his final period)," Morozov explained to me. "I've had my eye out for one for a long time but just can't decide which to choose." . . . The spot remained vacant for over a year, and only recently was a magnificent new "blue" landscape,* chosen from among dozens of others, enthroned next to the earlier elect.

**Blue Landscape* (c. 1904–6, R. 882, Hermitage).

This conscious and systematic "good taste" gives Morozov's collection the noble determinacy and integrity that collections of contemporary pictures, including public museums, so often lack.

Museums, however, and French museums in particular, cannot boast an abundance of works by the masters mentioned above, although these painters undoubtedly express an entire epoch in the history of art—a momentous epoch of painting's intense struggle for painting and for the painter's sacred right to be himself. For some incomprehensible reason the museums still cannot bring themselves to "recognize" Cézanne! Soon, when Pellerin's and Vollard's collections have all been sold, to judge the art of the great citizen of Aix you will be obliged to travel from Paris to Moscow. . . .

31
Boris Ternovets
"The Museum of Modern Western Art in Moscow (The Morozov Section)" (1922–23)

Boris Ternovets (1884–1941) studied economics and philosophy in Moscow and Berlin and went on to pursue art in Munich. In the years 1913–14 he studied with Emile-Antoine Bourdelle. After 1918 Ternovets worked with the nationalized Morozov collection. From 1922 to 1937 he served as the director of the State Museum of Modern Western Art (GMNZI).

This excerpt is from Ternovets's longer work on the Morozov section of the museum. Written in the years 1922–23, it remained unpublished until much later (see B. N. Ternovets, *Pis'ma. Dnevniki. Stat'i* [Letters. Diaries. Essays] [Moscow, 1977], 114–19).

Ivan Morozov's approach to his collection was truly that of a museum curator; the basic evolution of French art in the latter half of the nineteenth century is accurately delineated, and this period, which has already become classical, is represented by first-rate works. Objectivity, museum-like thoroughness, and balance were Morozov's guiding principles; we should not forget, however, that the magnificent edifice he erected is not complete. There are glaring omissions: no Edouard Manet, Seurat, Toulouse-Lautrec, or late Renoir; Degas is weakly represented; and the sculpture and drawing sections are by no means as complete and representative as the basic painting collection. Morozov was quite aware of this "incompleteness"; his planned acquisitions included not only the artists mentioned above but also earlier ones such as Daumier and Guys. We must always remember, however, that the gallery's rapid growth did not conflict with the mature caution and careful planning that informed every step he took. Severe in his judgments and striving with each purchase to acquire something valuable that would enhance the overall level of the collection, he thought of it as a collection of works, not a collection of names. He was not tempted by prominent names on casual and uncharacteristic paintings. He might wait years for truly major works by his favorite artists to appear on the market, and when they did he was decisive and dogged. This caution is very apparent in the history of his attempts to acquire Edouard Manet's pictures. Although he had always wanted to own works by this master, Morozov rejected a number of offers because he felt that those paintings inadequately reflected Manet's role and significance in the development of contemporary art. . . .

Morozov, however, had already firmly decided what kind of Manet he would bring to his gallery: he wanted Manet the landscapist, whose works would bring out and emphasize his ties to the Impressionists. *The Lion Hunter** did not satisfy these requirements; Morozov was also put off by the artificiality of the overall composition. For analogous reasons he was not interested in *The Bar at the Folies-Bergères,* one of Manet's most consummate works from his mature period, which was offered to Morozov at the "One Hundred Years of French Painting" exhibition in Petersburg. . . .

. . . He would rather wait than rush and make a mistake. He never hesitated to correct what he thought were errors, for he was not afraid of "amending" his collecting. Sometimes the works of the most prominent painters would be returned to the sellers because they did not harmonize with the collection and were insufficiently characteristic of the artists; such exchanges or returns, however, were rare. These traits of the collector explain the precious unity and wholeness you feel the first time you visit the collection.

With each passing year, Morozov became increasingly engrossed in collecting. He devoted himself to it with a passion one would not expect from such an outwardly phlegmatic, bulky man; when he went to Paris he did nothing but study the exhibitions and examine the holdings of the major dealers. Not infrequently he had the good fortune of fishing out of Vollard's "secret" storerooms a Cézanne masterpiece that had been tucked away for the time being, or of securing for himself a work intended for one of the best European galleries. Morozov was in his element in the Paris art world; he corresponded with artists and dealers, followed the auctions, and sometimes risked a purchase sight unseen. . . .

Shchukin had an amazing ability to sum up in his annual purchases all the most vivid phenomena and valuable achievements. His collection is a potent distillation of French art; these works make a more vivid and convincing impression than even in Paris, where they are eclipsed by the numerous secondary phenomena. This is why Shchukin's collection, which is far from an objectively designed museum, possesses such attractive and infectious power.

Morozov was different. His was not the glory of the pioneer. When he began collecting in the early 1890s,† the art of the Impressionists was already widely recognized. A stranger to Shchukin's passions, always cautious and rigorous in his selection and wary of anything extreme, not yet established, and struggling, Morozov preferred peaceful searches in Vollard's warehouses to the wandering temperament that lured Shchukin to unknown shores. Morozov brought a clear plan and objective design to his collecting, quietly threading one masterpiece after another, like a string

**M. Pertuiset, the Lion Hunter* (1880–81, Museu de Arte, São Paulo, Brazil).

†Ivan Morozov began collecting Russian art in 1901.

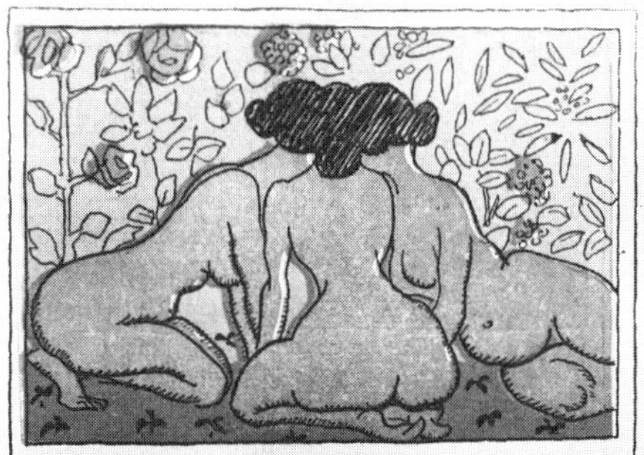

Портретъ трехъ очень бѣдныхъ женщинъ, купившихъ въ складчину одинъ парикъ.

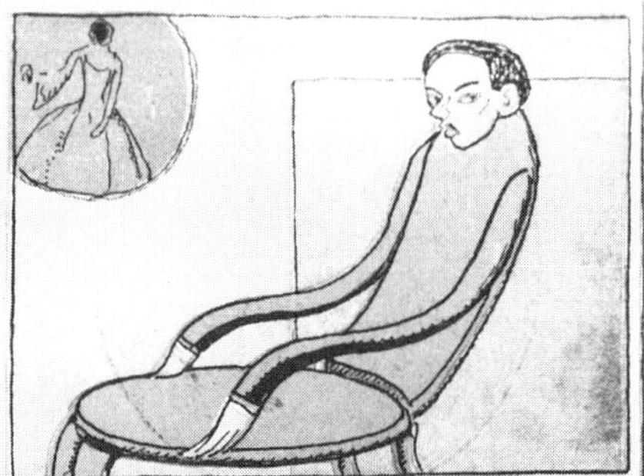

Ла-Фоконье.—Поэтъ или новая модель качалки.

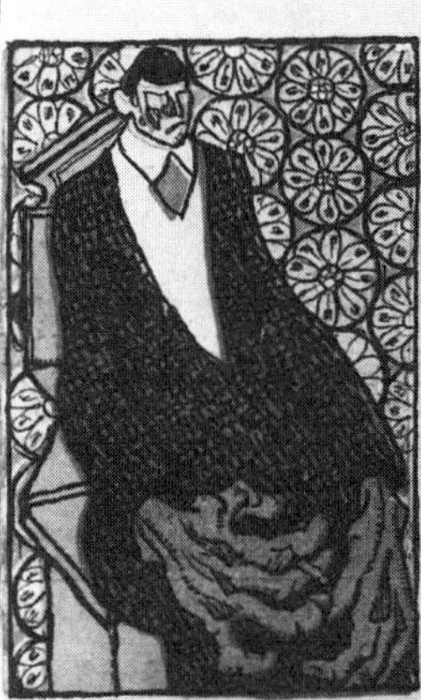

Машковъ.—Портретъ интенданта, желающаго дать работу сенатору Гарину.

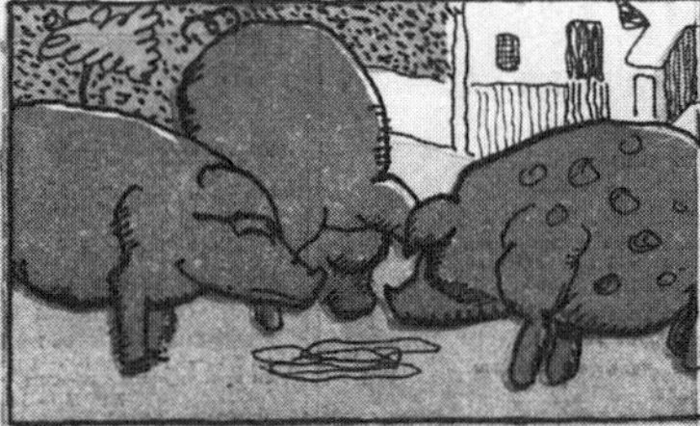

Кругликова.—Жестокая художница, подложившая сразу трехъ свиней г. Издебскому.

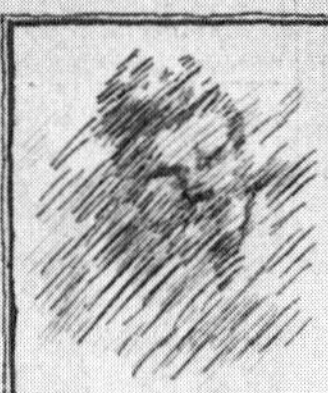

Роза Рюсъ — Портретъ Куприна въ ненастную погоду. Еще одна иллюстрація къ тексту: братья писатели! Въ вашей судьбѣ... и т. д.

Роза Рюсъ.—Портретъ г-жи Гриневской сто лѣтъ тому назадъ.

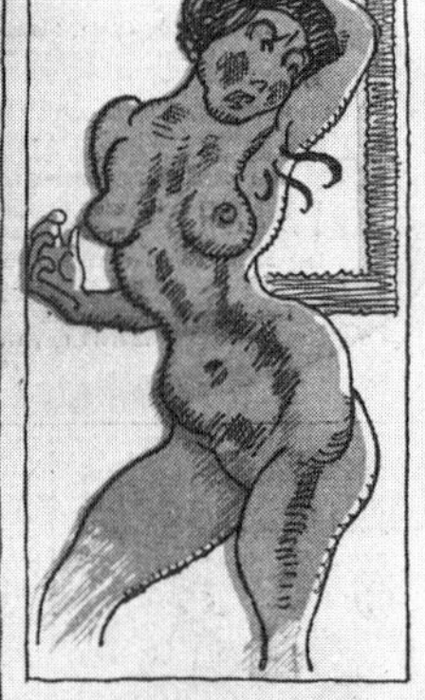

Машковъ.—Очень грязная женщина, поставивъ себѣ подъ мышку трехъ громадныхъ піявокъ, изучаетъ ихъ нравы. Зачѣмъ?

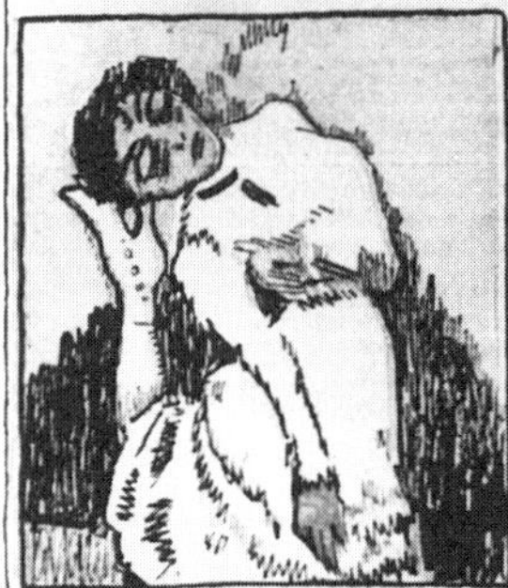

Ванъ-Донгенъ. — Отдыхающая испанка или разговоръ со своей душой, ушедшей со страху въ пятки...

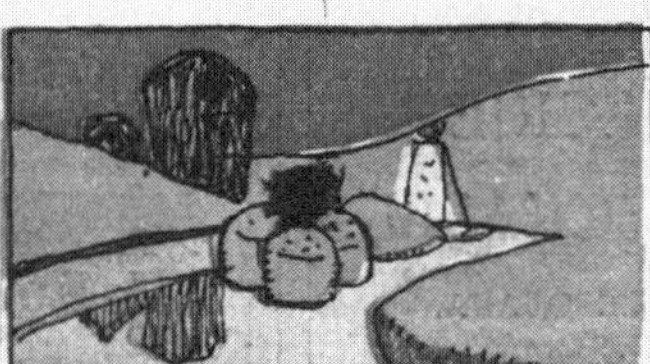

Ла-Фоконье.—Пасхальный столъ.

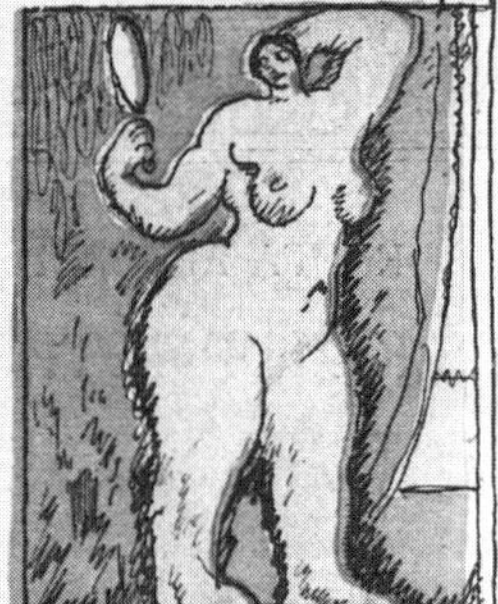

Ванъ-Донгенъ.—Глупая женщина, развившая себѣ низъ туловища въ ущербъ головѣ и лишившая себя, такимъ образомъ, возможности носить большія шляпки.

Arkadii Radakov, cartoon of Izdebsky's Salon, *Satirikon* 19 (1910)

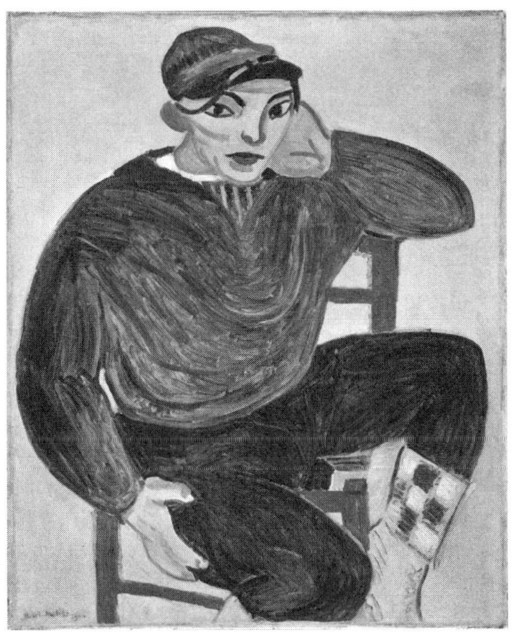

Henri Matisse, *The Young Sailor*, 1906, now in the Metropolitan Museum of Art, New York. Art © 2009 Succession H. Matisse, Paris/ Artists Rights Society (ARS), New York. Photo: Archives Matisse.

of pearls. His collection therefore more perfectly resembles a planned museum. If there are gaps, they are easy to explain; the European disaster prevented him from completing his beloved work.

IZDEBSKY'S SALON

The first important exhibition of contemporary French art was held in Petersburg from April 19 through May 25, 1910, as part of the traveling "First International Salon." The exhibition was organized by the sculptor Vladimir Izdebsky (1882–1965), who lived in Odessa and later in Munich (he was a founding member of the Neue Künstlervereinigung). During the pogroms, Izdebsky, an Orthodox noble of Polish extraction, organized an armed unit in defense of the Jews, for which he was imprisoned. He lived in Paris from 1913 until 1941, when he moved to New York.

In the years 1909–11, Izdebsky organized two extensive exhibitions—the only showings of contemporary Western artists outside Moscow and St. Petersburg. The first "Salon" went from Odessa to Kiev, Petersburg, and Riga and included over 800 works by 141 artists, including 43 foreigners. Only a few of the works can now be identified with certainty, but most of the French paintings were obtained from the Paris "Salon d'Automne." The linchpins of the exhibition were works by Matisse (*The Young Sailor,* 1906) and Henri Le Fauconnier (*Poet P. J. Jouve,* 1909). The second exhibition was held only in Odessa, in February 1911, and included 54 works by Kandinsky.

32
Nikolai Breshko-Breshkovskii
"The Salon" (1910)

Nikolai Breshko-Breshkovskii (1874–1943) was an extremely productive journalist and pulp fiction writer. This review was published on April 21, 1910, in *Birzhevye vedomosti* (Stock Exchange Gazette).

Every even slightly cultured Petersburger should visit the Salon, if only to take a quick look at the Matisse that caused such a fuss in Paris and indirectly became the bone of contention between Repin, on the one hand, and Bakst and Petrov-Vodkin, on the other.

Yes, yes, Mr. Izdebsky, the Salon's organizer, managed to get his hands on Matisse's *Sailor.* Half of Paris was mad about it; the other half stoned it.

You can reconcile yourself to the color scale—green combined with blue. But what form, what drawing! Mother Nature would not deform the most hideous cripple with the delirious zigzags of Matisse's unfortunate sailor.

As in a child's drawing, his eyes are circled by a line a good finger thick. Words cannot describe it—you have to go and see it.

. . . And here is another neighbor, the Frenchman Fauconnier, who has gone and "slandered" a Russian girl. Call her what you like, this foul deformed mug with a distorted torso and a face the color of a Nubian, but don't call her a Russian girl.

All of this gaudy roughness does not detract from the significance of the exhibition or even its overall level.

33
Alexandre Benois
"The 'Salon' and Bakst's School" (1910)

Published in *Rech'* (Speech), May 1, 1910.

I think that Matisse's two pictures at the Salon must puzzle even Russian art lovers who are well disposed toward him: "That's all?" Indeed, you cannot form an opinion of him on the basis of these excerpts, especially with regard to his most recent, strange, and controversial phase of development. . . .

Matisse is a despot who enslaves, and this elemental power is his *raison d'être.* Many artists probably hate him, for what he says and what they are used to saying are quite different. And he says it with such persistence and simplicity, it's hard not to trust him. Matisse not only paints different things in a different way, he also thinks about different things in a different way. The Impressionists' (even Cézanne's) approach was still traditional; they delighted in nature and tried to convey its charms. Matisse consciously *lies* and consciously *bypasses the truth,* and it is here that many quite rightly see the symptoms of his monumental decorative predisposition. Recently there was a rumor that he had been commissioned to paint the stairway in the home of a certain Moscow patron of the arts. These frescoes may not give me great pleasure personally, for my heart is in other systems and other tastes, but I think that this work of his could serve as the starting point for an entire movement that will in time produce much that is great and beautiful.

. . . Matisse elevates mistakes and failures to a system, or theory; in his works a grimace becomes a style. I still do not find any full achievements, and a great deal is halting and does not fit with the whole, but these faults cannot be corrected by the usual means. For him there can no longer be any return to "correct" drawing or "true" color. Such a return would be a compromise. . . .

34
Il'ia Repin
"The Izdebsky Salon" (1910)

Il'ia Repin (1844–1930) was a major Russian Realist painter. This essay was published in the evening edition of *Birzhevye vedomosti* (Stock Exchange Gazette) on May 20, 1910.

. . . Awaiting us there was a whole inferno of cynical *Western* daubers—hooligans, unbridled dobbins freely curveting paints onto the canvas.

I am thoroughly convinced that only untalented boors and madmen choose to be decadents. In the barbarian soul of the boor you can see the cold eunuch in art who will sell himself for sensational success. . . .

What would bring a true talent to paint such disgusting white dolls with typhus blotches on their bodies, holes instead of eyes, noses, and lips, with gaping red wounds and the decaying extremities of lepers? . . .

And the landscapes! . . .

"Cézanne!" The best explanation of this manner of painting is a snapshot of a donkey painting a picture with its tail. . . .

A brush was tied to the donkey's tail and a palette with paint and a canvas placed under it. It was given something tasty to eat; out of pleasure it swished its tail, and out from under its tail came a picture by Cézanne.*

"Wha-a-t?!" self-confidently declares the spirit of cynicism (the Devil), insolently rearing its head.

"I will force *the press—a great power*—to trumpet the glory of this art across the world. Billionaires will come from America and pay exorbitant sums for these easily and quickly manufactured wares. We will fill all the museums and private collections with them. We will toss out everything that is dear to you, and *you will worship my Daubsters of the Order of the Donkey's Tail!* . . . In Moscow some have already done so.

"In your backwardness you seem to imagine that those Muscovites are still dining on learned pigs and enchantingly warbling *nightingales? You are wrong. Now* they are collecting *Matisses.*" . . .

*Cézanne was not included in the exhibition.

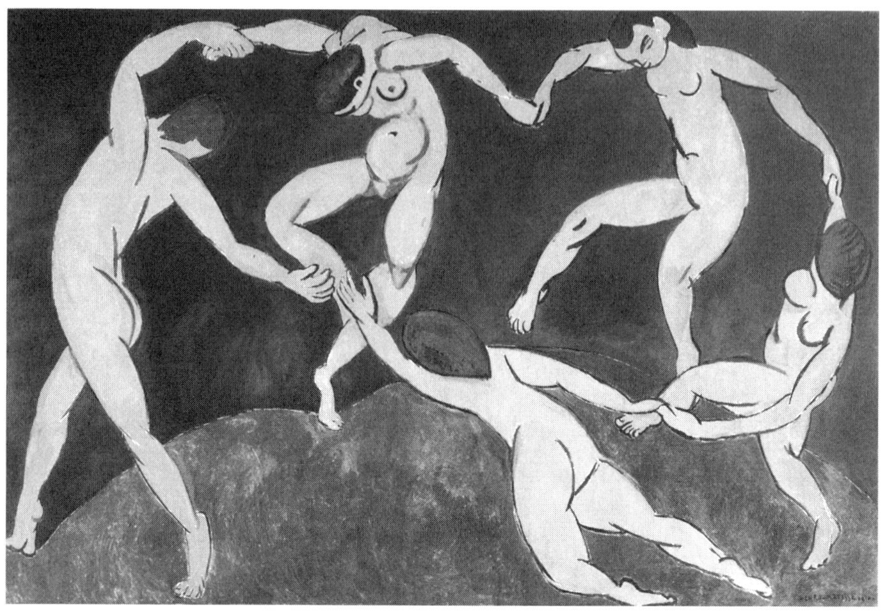

Henri Matisse, *Dance,* 1910, formerly in Shchukin's collection, now in the Hermitage, St. Petersburg. Art © 2009 Succession H. Matisse, Paris/Artists Rights Society (ARS), New York. Photo: Archives Matisse.

MATISSE'S *MUSIC* AND *DANCE*

In early 1909 Shchukin commissioned Matisse to paint two panels for his mansion: *Music* and *Dance*. Russians learned of this project from articles by Alexandre Mercereau (*Zolotoe runo* [Golden Fleece] 6 [1909]: ii) and Benois [37]. The panels were hung on the three-flight staircase. Shchukin said that *Dance* helped him ascend the stairs, in a sense bearing him upward with its swirling, airy movement.

35
Iakov Tugendkhol'd
"The Autumn Salon" (1910)

This review appeared in *Apollon* (Apollo) 12 (1910).

The "pure" art at the Autumn Salon this year demonstrates a very striking trend away from easel painting and toward monumental painting. It is so prominent that the earlier division into "pure" and "applied" is essentially meaningless. The decorative panels by Bonnard, Denis, Matisse, Girieud, and others are as "pure" as they are "utilitarian." The reign of the sketch and still life ended with the termination of Impressionism, and that of the panel and "theme" is approaching. Although all these artists are pursuing the same goals, however, the sources of their inspiration are so different that they can be listed in chronological order.

The works most deeply rooted in the past are *Music* and *Dance.* These two huge panels by Matisse done for Sergei Shchukin are both the highlight and the bugbear of the Autumn Salon. Their deliberately crude drawing and flashy colors may be unappealing, but they cannot be dismissed in the words of one well-known critic (Ch. Morice) as "nothing at all." Matisse's painting is not a soap bubble but a complex and natural phenomenon. Matisse is a great but split talent: one half of his being belongs to our nervous American modern world, while the other dreams of the naive monumentality of the primordial age and the lost harmony of the soul. Hence his voluntary descent into prehistoric depths; hence his decorative *ensemble,* the sharp silhouettes and brick-red bodies taken from ancient vases made of burned clay. Hence the Bacchanalian leaps of each member of the "ring dance" necklace . . . ; hence these boy werewolves hypnotized by the first sounds from the first instruments *(Music).* When he transfers these primordial patterns from vases to a contemporary panel, however, Matisse "Americanizes" the colors, transforming the work into a gaudy poster visible hundreds of yards away and forgetting that *the mural has its own traditions.* The modest Puvis de Chavannes remembered them; Matisse does not want, nor does he have the time, to understand them. Here again we see the characteristic contemporary *divorce of talent and material—a confusion of styles never witnessed by past ages.*

36
Boris Ternovets
Letter to Nadezhda Shamshina (1911)

Ternovets's cousin Nadezhda Shamshina (1888–1958) worked in the applied arts. This fragment, dated January 16, 1911, appears in B. N. Ternovets, *Pis'ma. Dnevniki. Stat'i* (Letters. Diaries. Essays) (Moscow, 1977), p. 10.

. . . But what especially astonished, gripped, and carried us away, the triumphant full and concluding chord, was Matisse's new fresco *Dance.* I was literally intoxicated by it: rushing by on a blue background is a ring of dancing women—it has just broken up—the movement is so powerful—but the circle will close once again and the dance will resume with new vigor; the figures are red, outlined here and there in black. I cannot possibly convey in words the completeness, inner closure, and wholeness of the composition; the dancers' crooked and dislocated limbs do not shock the eye for a moment: everything is so much in its place, so necessary as a whole, so imbued with inner naturalness. If you stand next to it in a dimly lit room and squint slightly, you see something fantastic, incredible: everything comes alive, moves, and rushes around in a wild, irrepressible outburst. This is the best thing Matisse has done, perhaps the best that the twentieth century has to offer thus far. It is not painting (for there is no form here), not a picture, but a different kind of decorative-monumental art, and it is a thousand times more powerful and staggering.

37

Alexandre Benois

"Moscow Impressions" (1911)

Published in *Rech'* (Speech), February 4, 1911.

. . . [Shchukin's] latest feat is the acquisition of two decorative panels by Matisse that stirred up all of Paris last fall and hang today in a staircase in his [Shchukin's] private home on Bol'shoi Znamenskii Lane. This feat caused Shchukin especially much suffering. He was on the verge of renouncing his purchase, but after returning to Moscow he suddenly began "missing" the pictures and hastened to order them. Now he no longer regrets his daring step, but friends and connoisseurs look askance at him more than ever, and even many of his usual defenders merely throw up their hands, perplexed.

I understand both him and them. Beyond all doubt, these pictures are "monstrous," and most importantly, poor. Particularly the panel depicting "music" (red, wooden boys sitting on a nondescript green hillock against the background of a dark blue calico sky) produces the impression of something deeply unhappy, a plunge into an abyss. But, I repeat, I also understand Shchukin. Now that he has believed in Matisse's "genuineness" in general (and how can he not believe in him, now that he can constantly admire the row of radiant pictures that takes up an entire room in his own home?), Shchukin could no longer allow any thought of charlatanism or lack of talent, and so attempted, as he has all his life, to find his way to the real meaning of these works, which the artist suffered so much to produce. . . .

I do not think that Matisse's panels have ever received recognition or found devotees outside, perhaps, a circle of snobs who are always prepared to play any fashionable tune. No, these are truly *unhappy* pictures, two truly awful *failures,* but I also believe in their honesty and am completely convinced of the extraordinary, first-rate talent of their author. . . . Matisse does not jeer at real traditions or the revelations of his predecessors, yet he wants to be considered worthy of creating his own new traditions, of starting anew. . . .

Matisse rejected [Maurice Denis's] sort of success, and he is as before engrossed in a problem that arose back in the works of Puvis and was further reflected in the pictures of Gauguin (and Denis) but is thus far unresolved: the problem of modern mural painting, the new decorative painting, but painting for sophisticated connoisseurs and curiosity shops; not virtuoso works, but art that is beautiful, whole, delightful, and uplifting and that works its effects just by the run and rhythm of interweaving lines and the resonance of its colors. Here Matisse shuns borrowing anything from his predecessors and moreover shuns realism, which is borrowing from nature. He refuses to compete with either the "salon masters" or the camera. If anyone is his lodestar, it is Giotto, but it is not forward from Giotto to a new renaissance of the same old formulae of Hellas that Matisse wants to go; instead, he aspires to go back from Giotto into the dark depths of barbarism, hoping to find there what contemporary art lacks: health, sincerity, immediacy, childlikeness. "Become as little children," he recalls the holiest of commandments.

Here is where the tragedy begins. One may perhaps "learn perfection" by imitating what is perfect, but "one cannot learn something in order to unlearn it." One can amass a great deal and collect it in the memory, but forgetting is far more difficult. Ultimately, it is even more difficult, once everything is forgotten, to discover it anew through your own experience. True, using what others have achieved and has served goals already passed is immoral, but one cannot replace all this with what one has just discovered. Matisse has reconciled himself, but in his own way. He teaches an enormous lesson in honesty. "I do not want anything that might not be mine," he says. "I do not want to be beholden, and I do not want schoolhouse rules or the traditional crutches." He has voluntarily arrived at what fate has had in store for him, the pillory to which he is tied, naked and pitiful, to be derided by one and all.

. . .

When you recall all the crudeness, provincialism, and absurdity there is in our art you can become frightened and begin to share in the general alarm that the Parisian example will muddle our very uncultured artistic youth. But now there is also hope. What if it is this crudeness and simplicity that Matisse wants to acquire by force and that we already have that will save us by creating in us that desirable "childlike disposition" out of which the new age of art is to emerge?

38

Boris Bugaev [Andrei Belyi]

"Stamped Culture" (1909)

Andrei Belyi published this article in *Vesy* (Scales), no. 9 (1909), under his real name. He saw the central conflict of modernity as the collision between organic national culture and faceless cosmopolitanism, and he interpreted this conflict as part of the global opposition between "Aryan" Europe and "Mongol" Asia. Belyi's article, which met a painful reception, is an exception in the Russian discourse on contemporary Western art, which was practically free of anti-Semitism.

Who is trying to use *"international culture"* and *"modern art"* to separate the flesh of the nation from its spirit so as to render the flesh of the national spirit soulless and the national spirit sterile? Who are these castrators? Who?

Strange and terrible though it is, we must say it.

These are alien people who are usually estranged from the life of the nation in whose bosom they live and who, unfortunately for culture, have limited civil rights and therefore no possibility to express themselves in any other arena . . . ; their number is growing, as is the influence of their criticism and cultural initiatives in society. The leaders of this culture are alien to this culture; they cannot understand the depths of the national spirit expressed in sound, color, and words. The pure streams of our native language are being polluted by a kind of faceless *Esperanto* of international catchwords, and furthermore, unconsciously (and sometimes consciously as well), a boycott has been declared on everything original outside this *Esperanto* channel. Instead of Gogol' we have Sholem Asch;* traditional life has been pronounced dead, and an international jargon has been created, just as Meyerbeer figures next to Beethoven and Matisse next to Vrubel'.

The strength of internationalism lies in the fact that (1) in all the countries of Europe, the areas in which individual culture is most powerfully expressed are being conquered one by one; that is, the arts are being conquered; and (2) the role of the critics and entrepreneurs is largely being performed by a homogeneous element, or rather a single nation, and the internationalists hint more and more at the veiled doctrine of a very narrow nationalism that is alien to Aryanism, namely, Judaism.

39

Boris Anrep

"Apropos of an Exhibition in London with Participating Russian Artists" (1913)

Boris Anrep (1883–1969) began studying art in 1908, traveling to Paris and studying Byzantine art in Greece and Turkey. He organized the Russian section of the 1912 "Second Post-Impressionist Exhibition" in London. In 1916 he took up permanent residence in England and became known for his mosaics. For an objection to Anrep's opinion on Matisse (published in *Apollon* [Apollo] 6 [1913]), see Tugendkhol'd's essay [27].

Here it would be appropriate to recall that, in the opinion of the English, Post-Impressionism is the "creation of visual music."† Although this principle was recognized earlier as well and was professed by absolutely every important artist, the "novelty" of the new doctrine is its quest for "*de la musique avant toute chose.*"‡ The hoisting of any banner is valuable in and of itself—especially a banner that reinvigorates the indispensable elements of art, which at present are barely surviving—yet I don't see anything desirable in the exclusivity with which the notion is being preached or the narrowness with which the principle—in itself very lofty—is understood. Artistic experiences are many-sided, and the loftiest are those which act most deeply and

*Sholem Asch (1880–1957), who wrote in Yiddish, emigrated to the United States in 1909. In a discussion of his plays in Moscow in February 1909, the writer Evgenii Chirikov criticized the popular idea of the "death of traditional everyday life" *(smert' byta)*. The debate that followed touched upon the "national face" of literature and caused a scandal in the press.

†Cf. Roger Fry, "The French Group: Catalogue of the Second Post-Impressionist Exhibition, 1912," in *Post-Impressionists in England*, edited by J. B. Bullen (London and New York: Routledge, 1988), p. 353.

‡A line from Paul Verlaine's poem "Ars poétique" (1874).

broadly upon the soul of the person experiencing them. Matisse's painting, although it has many virtues, does not satisfy all our artistic demands. There is no denying that his works—I mean the best of them—contain painterly "music"; with respect to freshness of color and originality, the best canvases I have seen in recent years are charming. The spell does not last long, however, for beyond the charming exterior there is nothing to nourish the spirit. The artist obviously had no intention of nourishing the spirit, but merely wanted to flatter it. One of the weakest aspects of Matisse's painting is what might be called its "saturation of space." It is bad when the eye begins to suffer from a picture's emptiness. . . . Imagine a canvas of several meters, sometimes even more, where the outer contours of various objects are outlined, usually human bodies, sometimes larger than life; the space inside and outside these contours is filled with a bright, monotone color, sometimes a rather flat one. . . . If every square meter of this picture could be reduced to a single square inch or less, if instead of flat and coarse colors with spots of bare dirty canvas we could see the same colors and lines on a beautiful glazed enamel no larger than the palm of the hand, these would be remarkable *objets d'art* for which even the ferocious enemies of Matisse's painting would pay thousands, especially if these enamels were sold in the elegant antiquarian shops in Old Bond Street. Contemporary critics would find in them all the most precious qualities of art. As they are, however, once you become accustomed to the brilliance of the colors, your eyes weary from his pictures' emptiness.

I think Matisse is remarkable, however, because better than anyone else he has preserved the picture's flattened appearance. This is a feature that has almost disappeared from painting, yet it is a basic requirement of painterly ornamentation, which is meant to adorn the plane, not disturb it. Matisse has also been a success because artists believe the time is ripe for an art that can liberate itself from Impressionism once and for all. Those for whom Matisse is a prophet have forgiven him all his shortcomings, assuming they even noticed them. In England, if he has not been recognized as a great master, his merits have not been passed over in silence, and both the public and the press have noted him as a significant painter. Some English artists were positively ecstatic over Matisse; perhaps they more than the French found the notion of painting that was "independent of nature" unusual, and Matisse's works seemed a revelation. He will at any rate be beneficial to England. For us Russians, who have been raised to revere the divine countenances created by the piety of our icon painters, for whom spiritual symbols had a single meaning and the objects of nature were merely evidence of the earthly and ephemeral, Matisse's art is neither a great revelation nor a great novelty.

. . . Two years ago, at the London exhibition, I saw a collection of the best of Picasso's works—drawings, etchings, oils—and was impressed by them. El Greco's spirit seemed to have entered this master, for his incarnations contained the same endless suffering and quiet pity. At that time, Picasso's art and school were intimately connected with earlier artists. Then suddenly a terrible change came about in his artistic personality that many have ascribed to mental illness: Picasso became the progenitor of the "Cubists."

These canvases, with their heaps of intersecting prisms, cones, various polyhedrons, broken and whole spirals, wires, wheels, spheres, and cubes, are already known in Russia. . . . All of this rubbish is painted reddish-gray on a grayish-red background, and across the entire "picture" is an inscription in block letters: "Kubelick," "Mozart."* This is "Cubism" in its extreme form. Less ardent Cubists, as we know, content themselves with faceting natural forms, arranging them into triangles and squares, and composing animal-like figures from these and similar geometric shapes. For some reason there is always something malevolent about these new formations.

. . . Their overall aspiration is the same as Matisse's—to create an art free from representation, to create their own language and graphic signs—and they unite around Picasso and set off on the road of "Cubism" to get as far away as possible from anything recognizable. I find it difficult to find any arguments for or against "Cubism" because none of its representatives, including Picasso, has produced anything beyond a boring reshuffling of geometrical bodies. Let's wait and see. Perhaps they, too, will stir our souls, but I don't think they will until the "Cubists" are over their illness and clear their heads with something balancing. . . .

. . . In his foreword to the exhibition catalogue, Roger Fry notes that one of the distinguishing characteristics of French art was and is its "classicism." French artists "do not rely for their effect upon associated ideas as I believe Romantic and Realistic artists invariably do."† . . . This to my mind wonderful quality of all good pictures by no means rules out "Romantic" and "Realistic" properties in pictures. . . .

40

Alexandre Benois

"More on New Trends in Art" (1912)

Benois's article from the December 29, 1912, issue of *Rech'* (Speech) was the first significant publication on Picasso in Russia.

. . . Indeed, the Picasso room makes a monstrous impression. Gazing at you from the walls are huge monsters, likenesses of stone idols—clumsy, squinting, and one-eyed, with stupid, gloomy, sagging faces that look like they were carved out of wood—or terrible landscapes, childishly drawn, dark and joyless. Some resemble unsuccessful prints of transfers that have slipped off center; others look like shop signs in a remote little town; others, wig-maker's dummies; still others, simply piles of stones or logs. In the midst of all this, the brown landscape of a moderate Cubist seems perfectly normal, almost saccharine, and one quite incomprehensible ultra Cubist picture

*Georges Braque, *L'affiche de Kubelick* (*Violin*, 1912, private collection, Basel).

†Fry, "The French Group," pp. 353, 355.

seems almost "comforting," for at least here there is no "picture" to tease you—what you see are some crossing lines and intersecting planes.* Evidently not even the author knew exactly what it was. Had we come across such a group of pictures five or six years ago, most of us would have walked on by what would have looked like an artistically uninteresting exhibition of works by inmates of a mental asylum. Two years ago we would have been angered and spoken of charlatanism. Even today you do not feel any "happy reaction" to this ugly art. But then what are we to do with the fact that Shchukin is in ecstasy over these works, spends enormous sums to acquire them, and assures us that he *will* love them more than everything else? Is he indeed ill, or is he simply trying to be original and is possessed of an insurmountable need to tease his guests and get the entire city talking about him? . . .

Some of the weightiest evidence supporting Shchukin's enthusiasm for Picasso and the Cubists, however, is right there in his gallery. Spend an hour in the Cubist "chapel," and your eyes will adapt to this frightening novelty and your attitude toward the rest will also undergo a change. Just a moment ago Matisse seemed cheerful and clear, so why do you now detect superficiality and emptiness, a cheapness in his art? You were ecstatic over Gauguin's radiant floridity, so why do you now detect sacharineness? The Impressionists seemed so alive, daring, and direct—so why is there now a touch of what we call academicism and the French brand "pompier"? Something in you has been poisoned, but something has also matured. At any rate, after you have studied the Picasso room, Shchukin's remarks can no longer seem insincere. Before you is the path he has been following, and he is inviting you to join him.

This path is not only his personal path but the path of perhaps our entire culture. No one is asking us whether to follow it—they will in any case and already are. Like it or not, they will drag us down it, and if anyone should manage to resist, a miserable loneliness awaits him. However, not only are they being frightened with such a prospect, they are also promised unprecedented delights if they join the movement. I am personally convinced that in any case many will be healthier, as will their entire attitude toward art, even the past art they liked the least. . . .

Now in the name of what will all this come to pass? In the same room where Shchukin hangs the Cubists led by Picasso are some ancient idols from central Africa—crude and strange sculptures whose candid animality is frightening. Especially striking is a statuette little more than a foot tall, yet executed with such power that you get an eerie feeling looking at it. This awkwardly squatting freak with its enormous head sculpted in layers and its strangely protuberant torso cannot be called a "godling"—it is a real, great, and terrible god into which terrible prayers have been poured and before which cruel sacrifices have been laid. Although it is small, you can sense its

*Benois is alluding to Le Fauconnier's *Village dans les roches* (1910, Hermitage) or Derain's *Montreuil-sur-Mer* (*Port,* 1910). The "ultra-Cubist picture" is probably Braque's *Le Château de La Roche-Guyon* (1909, GMII), which Shchukin purchased in 1910.

kinship with the Assyrian colossi. Yes, this god has probably not even died but is still alive, still waiting and demanding. Shchukin admires it as others admire Praxiteles' Hermes and assures us that the "beauty" of the statuette, which was made fifty years ago by savages in deepest Africa, helps him understand the contemporary beauty of Picasso.

There is undoubtedly a spiritual kinship among these works of art. But here some particularly importunate questions arise: What do these two arts serve? What exactly constitutes their spiritual kinship? When you stop to ponder these questions, the comforting answers to them begin to fade and your soul is filled with something resembling horror. . . . Only one thing is clear to me even now. What is frightening in the new art is not its "eccentric" behavior in creating monsters but the fact that it is penetrating secret and very dangerous places without knowing why and or even questioning its own ultimate meaning. . . .

41

S. Khudakov

"Literature, Art Criticism, Debates, and Lectures" (1913)

This excerpt from an extensive article—dated May 20, 1913, from Alupka (Crimea), and published in *Oslinyi khvost i Mishen'* (Donkey's Tail and Target) (Moscow, 1913)—is typical of the polemical manner of Larionov's circle. "Khudakov" is an unusual surname that could suggest indecent associations to the Russian reader. It is probably a pseudonym used by Larionov together with Il'ia Zdanevich (1894–1975).

. . . I think Picasso panders to bourgeois tastes and to artists of Matisse's ilk. Picasso is a great master, but he brings to his work the same corrupting principles that are really nothing but pure academicism. His beneficial and timely transition from Cubism to Futurism is to be welcomed, since Cubism is nothing but Neo-Classicism, and Futurism, despite all its purely romantic features, is certainly a timely and viable doctrine. Unfortunately, Picasso is also attempting in his scholastic labors to adapt and channel Futurism into academic forms, which puts him somewhere between Futurism and Cubism, between old tendencies and new. I'm not talking about a loss of traditions, but their complete adaptation to modern life; Picasso entirely lacks the Futurists' strengths. They love and praise contemporary life, and it is they who have created what Picasso is so powerfully making use of now, as previously he used the old art of the Negroes and Aztecs. His latest works have essentially been compiled from artistic problems addressed by two Futurists: Severini, who treats everything separately, in pieces (with individual brushstrokes); and Boccioni, with his constructions that unfold objects viewed from various angles and his introduction of numbers and letters. The latter artists may have fewer traditions and less talent, but their sense of contemporaneity and creative enthusiasm is none the weaker for that. Picasso has rearranged the tasks the Futurists set themselves in his own way and has begun using more reserved and harmonious light, but all this merely brings him closer to museum art. . . .

42

Sergei Bulgakov

"Beauty's Corpse (Apropos of Picasso's Paintings)" (1915)

In his philosophical evolution, Sergei Bulgakov (1871–1944) went from Marxism to Orthodox theology. Ordained in 1918, in 1922 he was deported by the Bolsheviks. In Paris he became a director of the Institute of Orthodox Theology and was active in the ecumenical movement. Bulgakov's article on Picasso, written in March 1914 and published in *Russkaia mysl'* (Russian Thought) 8 (1915), is a unique example of a religious approach to contemporary Western painting.

. . . When you enter the room devoted to the works of Pablo Picasso, you are gripped by a mystical unease bordering on horror. The veil of day, with its soothing brilliance and many colors, flies away, and you are embraced by the horrible, faceless night and surrounded by mute and vicious specters and shades. This is the suffocation of the grave. . . . Picasso's art is this night, moonless and starless, as mystical as that night. Moreover, it is a mysticism not of content or subject . . . but of the brush itself, the paints, the stroke; the very nature of his art is mystical through and through. His painting is, if not religious, then at least mysterial and rather iconographic, although in a very unusual sense. Despite the rapid evolution and radical change in Picasso's techniques, the spiritual content of his art is entirely monotone and imbued throughout with a single feeling—a growing anguish and horror of being. Picasso indisputably has power; he does not merely try to appear strong (as many do today, following Nietzsche's example), and his brush is genuinely powerful. . . . This young artist, a Spaniard by birth with an admixture of Moorish blood (very important!), has already made the long journey of artistic development, and all of its basic stages can be traced in this room. The works from his early period, painted with great skill and power but in ordinary, realistic tones (such as *The Drunkard,* two male portraits, *Old Jew and a Boy,* and *The Meeting*),* are distinguished by a keen, almost inhuman anguish in the eyes and a music of anguish in the figures. These are followed by works from his middle, Cubist, period, which make the strongest impression and are thus far the high point of Picasso's art. . . . Here are three women resembling nightmare visions in flaming scarlet tones, frozen in a dance. Here is the horrible *Farmer's Wife*† consisting of several geometrical cobblestones, all heaviness and inertness. Here the body has lost its warmth, life, and aroma, transformed into shapes, geometry, and masses; life has

**Absinthe Drinker* (1901, Z.I.98, Hermitage); *Portrait of Jaime Sabartès* (1901, Z.I.97, GMII); *Portrait of Francisco de Asís Soler* (1903, Z.I.99, Hermitage); *Old Jew* (1903, Z.I.175, GMII); *The Two Sisters* (1902, Z.I.163, Hermitage).

†*Farmer's Wife* (1908, Z.II.91, Hermitage).

lost its movement and frozen in a grimace; flesh has been desiccated and drained of blood by a demonic asceticism. This is spirituality, but the spirituality of a vampire or a demon; passions, even the basest of them, are rendered in their purely spiritual, incorporeal essence, their abstract bodies. Manifested here is a very special, inhuman manner of seeing and apprehending flesh, an evil spiritualism that despises and hates flesh and decomposes it, but at the same time inspires the artist, who, ironically, speaks only in images of flesh and through the flesh. From the standpoint of technical, artistic, and especially coloristic achievement, the works from this second period are probably quite significant. No less striking, however, is their mystical power and content, which is so significant that you soon forget the paradoxical, deliberate ugliness of the Cubist manner; you simply cease to notice it—a clear indication of the form's correspondence to its content and, in this sense, of the high artistic quality of the work. . . .

As I was looking at the pictures of this part-Spaniard, part-Moor, part-Parisian Picasso, my soul resounded with exclusively *Russian* thoughts and emotions. There is probably nothing coincidental about the fact that, through Sergei Shchukin, Russia has expropriated Picasso's painting from the French—if not for the sake of pleasure and amusement then as material for the agonizing religious labor that sanctifies the Russian soul. . . . As is especially clear in his second period, Picasso's art is the fruit of demonic possession. It expresses with great intensity the worldview of the evil spirit, who hates and reviles God's creation and at the same time is languishing in hellish torment. Picasso shows artistically what the world is like to the demon, how he perceives Femininity and how he experiences worldly flesh. . . . Every genuine artist is a knight of the Beautiful Lady. How can ice and flame, love and contempt be compatible? How is possession in art possible? Is not art protected from possession's vile encroachment by the veil of beauty? Picasso's answer to this question is an antinomy: yes and no. *Yes,* because although it is art, it is damaged, spiritually corrupt, sick, *vile*. . . . *No,* because despite its morbidity and corruption it is still art, even great art. This results in horrifying paradoxes: *vile art,* ugly beauty, untalented talent. Artists who possess this power and both mystical and artistic authenticity and persuasiveness truly are talented, and although they may be captive and bound, their deepest nature has not been affected and they have not been completely transformed by evil. Otherwise they would become hacks, for hacks—metaphysical hacks who can only produce a semblance of art by debauching other creative individualities in order to express themselves through their talent—are the Creator's self-appointed rivals. . . .

Inherent to Christianity is a sense of the flesh's individuality as well as its authenticity, that is, a sense of the body, my body, which in some respect is an inseparable aspect of my self. . . . Everything in Cubism, even that which is alive, becomes a thing, a component that grows numb and decays; sincere, unaffected Cubism has a special, certain sense of the flesh as merely "the physical dimension" rather than the body. This is why bodies are stripped of their warmth, color, and beauty and retain only their geometrical and mechanical nature. This is why the difference between living and inert nature, which geometry cannot capture, is felt so weakly, and the special Cubist predilection for the *nature morte* starts to make sense. . . . From this point we can begin to un-

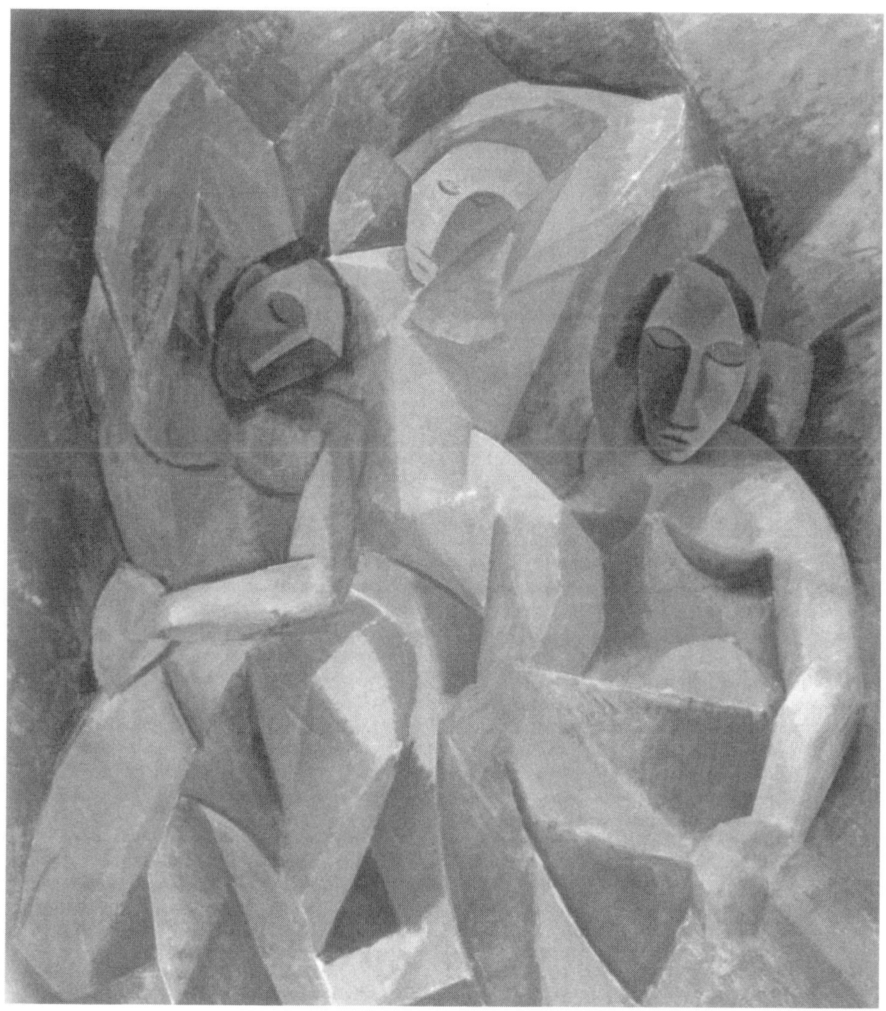

Pablo Picasso, *Three Women*, 1908, formerly in Shchukin's collection, now in the Hermitage, St. Petersburg. Art © 2009 Estate of Pablo Picasso/Artists Rights Society (ARS), New York.

derstand the most recent and darkest stage in Picasso's art. On the one hand, it is obviously only the latest step in the decomposition of the "physical dimension." The deeper the occult whirlwinds tear into Picasso's works, breaking down and desiccating his artistic individuality, the more the *nature morte* comes to dominate, moreover in dismantled form (there are several pictures from the most recent period in Shchukin's collection).* The picture becomes a notation of signs expressing emotions that are inexpressible in the language of the physical dimension because the images and colors of this world have been consumed by the occult world. In this most recent stage of Pi-

*The reference is to works such as *Violin* (1912, Z.II.358, GMII), *Guitar and Violin* (1912–13, Z.II.370, Hermitage), and *Tenora and Violin* (1912–13, Z.II.437, Hermitage).

casso's art, however, we seem to note signs of a return to health: there are no more deformed and formless astral monsters, although they have been succeeded by the icy, inert hush of a spiritual wasteland; furthermore, he seems to hear rhythms unknown to us, and perhaps this rhythmicality will ennoble, balance, and heal his muse. . . .

. . . Picasso's art is a mighty religious temptation, a test of faith. Demonism, of course, is the most intimate, subtle, and therefore dangerous form of Lucifer's contamination of art, for in comparison with, say, philosophy, and especially science, art is connected to the spirit's deepest strata. . . . It is not easy to get the better of him or candidly settle accounts with him. Picasso is frightening because his demonism is authentic. Demonic possession is becoming a widespread modern phenomenon; the struggle with it demands sobriety, spiritual health, and self-discipline, but above all the rock of faith—support not in subjectivity or isolation but in community and the Church. Only in the name of Christ, which is the Church, can demons be exorcized.

There is a mysterious rhythm, a musical correlation of light and shadow, to which the anonymous architect of the Notre Dame Cathedral yielded when he placed on its exterior balustrade his *Chimères*—demonic monsters of great artistic power and profound mystical authenticity. . . . But is Picasso's art the *Chimères* on the spiritual temple of contemporary humanity? . . .

And one extremely puzzling and mysterious question remains: Were the spiritual creator of the *Chimères* and the creator of the Paris cathedral's majestic portal one and the same person or not? History is silent. . . .

43

Ivan Aksenov

Picasso and the Environs (1917)

A regular officer in the Corps of Engineers, Ivan Aksenov (1884–1935) was persecuted for supporting his soldiers' insurrection in 1908. He began to write art criticism in the early 1910s, translated Elizabethan drama, and in 1915 joined the Moscow Futurist group Tsentrifuga (Centrifuge). During the Civil War he was a Red commissar. In the early 1920s he became friends with Meyerhold and wrote a great deal about theater.

Aksenov's book was the first monograph on Picasso. In the manner of Nietzsche or Rozanov, it consists of more than one hundred fragments organized into four chapters (the excerpt below includes principally the fragments dealing directly with painting). The circumstances surrounding the book's genesis are not entirely clear. In the spring of 1914 Aksenov was probably in Paris, where he became acquainted with Kahnweiler's collection and may have visited Picasso's studio. He also regularly received information on contemporary French art from his Kievan acquaintance Alexandra Exter, and, through her, from Ardengo Soffici.* The text here is dated June 1914 and was published by the Moscow Futurist publishing house Tsentrifuga in 1917 together with thirteen rare reproductions of Picasso's works in foreign collections.

*Daniela Rizzi, "Artisti e litterati russi negli scritti di Ardengo Soffici," *Archivio Italo-Russo* (Salerno) 2 (2000): 317–22.

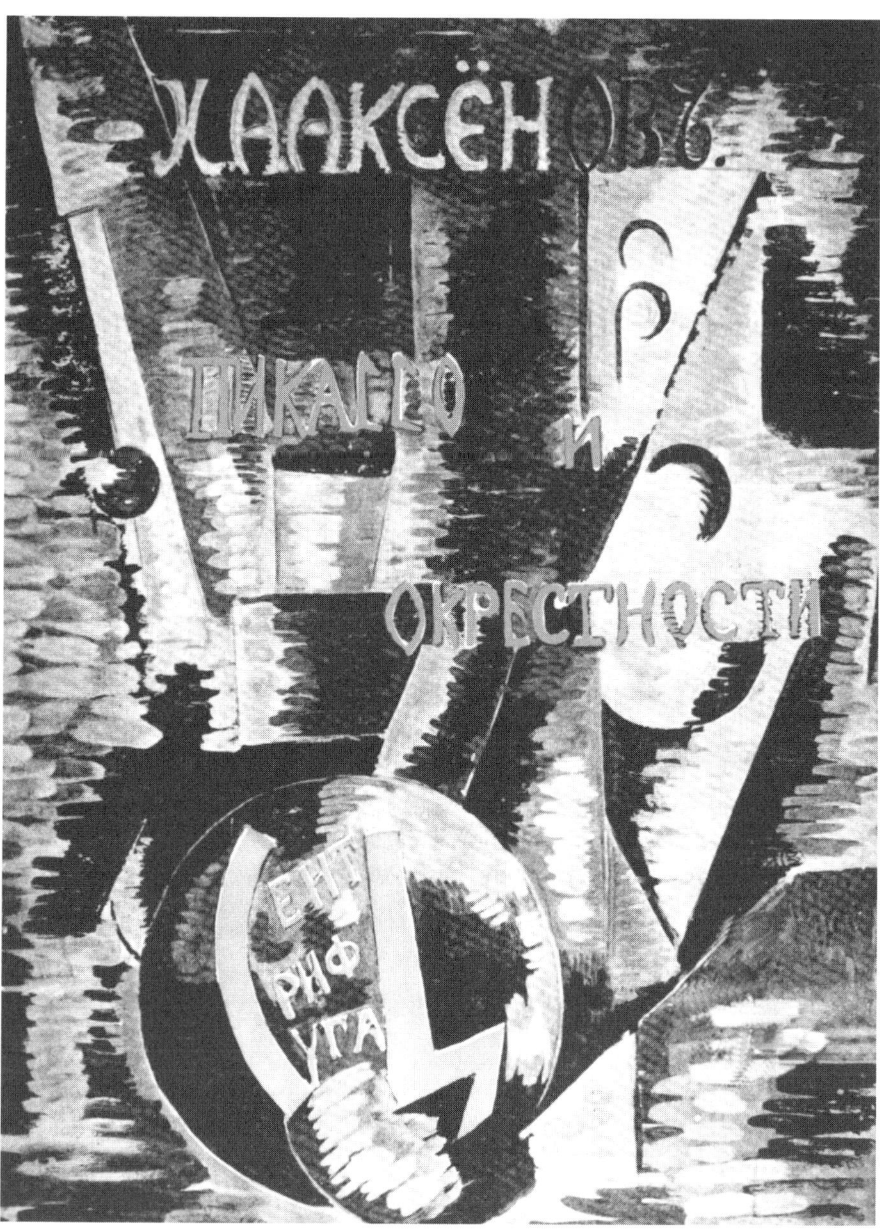

Alexandra Exter's cover for Ivan Aksenov's *Picasso and the Environs* (Moscow, 1917)

§1

My intention here is not to paraphrase Picasso's pictures in my own words. In view of the existing laws on defamation, one cannot even mention anything about a living person's biography. . . . More than likely, therefore, my intentions have assumed the form of defending Picasso the painter from certain accusations and shielding him from certain types of praise. . . .

§19

The counterfort plays as great a role in the Baroque as it does in the Gothic, but the eighteenth century reworked it ornamentally, treating it as a volute. The scroll did not replace the lion's head on the neck of the violin until the seventeenth century. This counterfort is essentially Baroque. Picasso is remarkably fond of this form and never breaks it down. It is easy to spot a violin in a composition by the presence of a scroll and sometimes also the sound holes.

§20

Regardless of how light is broken up in Picasso's pictures, the basic tendency toward the color diagonal is obvious. Anyone who wants to make absolutely sure of this should take a look at the Cubists' first works from their best period, when they openly plagiarized the Spanish artist. What the teacher had cunningly masked stood out brazenly in the works of his pupils. Everyone now knows that the color diagonal is as much a trademark of the Baroque as the color center is of the painting of the barbarous Renaissance.

§21

The Baroque is the angel of disaster. We are going through a Baroque age from which we cannot escape. What will the war give us?

§23

In *Bathers,** Gleizes put a violin scroll in the clouds—a Baroque counterfort, the vehicle of this style's dynamics. In his quest for dynamism Fernand Léger turns an entire picture into a template of this architectural detail. There they are—the crumbs from the master's table.

**Bathers,* "Salon des Indépendants," 1912. Reproduced in Albert Gleizes and Jean Metzinger, *Du Cubisme* (Paris: Eugène Figuière, 1912).

§25

Derain is a painter difficult to love but impossible to ignore. His influence on contemporary painters has been enormous. In due course this will become even clearer. If a new school of painters was born out of each of Picasso's periods, Derain's individual études provided sufficient material for some painters for their entire life. Derain himself changed very slowly and in contrast to Picasso was quicker to alter the correlation of colors in his works than the evolution of his line.

§37

Picasso is a genius of discovery. Nothing is more mistaken than this statement. Actually, it is nonsense, since a "genius" cannot be a discoverer. There is not a single technique of Picasso's that will not prove illusory when compared with earlier works by Derain or Braque. By and large, a list of the names of the artists who have influenced the art of the stubborn resident in building no. 13 would take up several pages—a silly undertaking. . . . A genius is a synthesis of the achievements of the preceding age. The span of his activity and the significance of his art are measured by how much he has absorbed and re-created.

§38

We must remember that it is Braque, not Picasso, who is the innovator, and that any mention of Picasso's discoveries should therefore read: Braque. A comment for idiots: by this I am by no means belittling the Spaniard in comparison with the Frenchman. Picasso's painting speaks for itself, and as a painter he is much stronger than his friend, which does not prevent the latter from being quicker off the mark with respect to invention.

§41

Briefly, the history of the first years of Cubism is as follows: a few artists began reproducing Picasso's and Braque's paintings in their own way. In order to keep this knowledge from the ill-informed but large public (Picasso was not exhibiting), they began raking the master they had robbed over the coals, denying that the Spaniard's canvases were of any significance to French painting. The only one who did not do so was Fernand Léger, but he was essentially not a Cubist.

§45

When people cease to understand a phenomenon, they resort to calling it "mystical," exploiting the notion's crudeness. Thus Cézanne (whose painting strikes no one as puzzling today) was at one time denounced as a mystic. The same thing happened to Picasso. There is no point in searching for any occult basis to his painterly manner. But wait! He lived in building no. 13!

§47

Like all conventional wisdom, the widespread opinion that a radical upheaval has occurred in Picasso's art is wrong. Picasso has not ceased to be what he was in the beginning—an artist who creates spontaneously. The impressions that generated the forms realized in his painting, however, did not always arise from directly perceived objects. Often, very often, they came from observing the pictures of others. But are not pictures objects of the external world? Those who blame a writer for bookishness or an artist for looking at too many pictures seem to want heredity eliminated altogether. Instinct tells them the proper course of action: their own heredity evidently includes some not entirely pleasant features.

§73 [–74]

It is sad to hear the malicious phrase "The Russians will not produce anything in painting," especially since, surveying the true state of this art within our borders, even healthy people would seek relief in a fit of hysterics. Some other comfort is to be had, however—historical comfort. France did not always legislate in painting. . . . As for us, why should we seek consolation for our own lack of talent by harking back to the distant times of the Novgorod school? Our stage designers have revolutionized French artists' approach to color, and Bakst is drawing costumes in the same Paris where Dufy modestly produces cloth prints and where the pictures by this same Bakst have simply not been noticed. If easel painting in France is on a level quite inaccessible to the artists of other countries, the explanation is to be found in the uniquely French way of marketing these paintings. There is a tendency in Paris to put money in paintings and to base artistic enterprises on this investment. The goal is to monopolize the work of promising artists through contracts that provide them a living and the possibility of a painting career. This convinces them that they must devote themselves wholly to their chosen task, while ruthless competition forces them to refine their technique as thoroughly as possible within a given time and with the available resources. As the professionals perfect their technique, the dilettantes are forced to adopt it, since they are disappointed if their pictures simply lie there like dust on a shelf. As for Russian artists, if they live by the work of their hands it is certainly not from easel painting, which for them is a pleasant relaxation and amusement after they are through painting stage sets, lining book illuminations, and designing costumes. They work till they drop drawing insertions for women's panties because they have to eat and a picture won't feed them anyway, so it will just have to wait. Thus if Russian coquettes wear elegantly sewn hems and you could die of shame at Russian painting exhibitions, it is not because our artists lack talent or are organically inept at the plastic arts but only because of the disorganized way the Russian talent for easel painting is exploited. That it has not perished altogether is amazing. What would Picasso be if he lived in Russia? A cabinetmaker, if not an acrobat.

§86

The way Picasso's painting treats objects can be described by considering the following: (1) his cultivation of the color plane; (2) his approach to the color plane's silhouette; (3) his treatment of the silhouette's volume; and (4) his approach to the planes that constitute the three-dimensional figure.

§87

Picasso's palette is amazingly monotonous. He changes colors periodically, but their relationship remains constant. In the spring of 1914 he repeated the color components of his acrobat period. His entire enormous evolution has ignored color. Without putting too fine a point on it, the palette plays no part at all in the development of his manner. Color is relegated to an auxiliary role, which is not to disturb the process. But in that case is this process not linear? Picasso has strenuously denied that it is. He is not necessarily aware of everything.

§88

"Matisse should paint palaces, Picasso cathedrals." I do not agree with the second half of Shchukin's remark. The decorativeness of some of Picasso's works comes not from him but from Matisse. He has dedicated all the vitality of his art to easel painting. But I think that Picasso could be a great architect if someone were to help him calculate the parts of the construction.

§91

His goal was to create depth in the picture by painting volumetric relations. First it was a matter of volume's formal properties; then, how to depict these properties in painting. In brief, first the object of Picasso's painting was nature; then, the painting of nature. If the first goal was achieved within the limits of the means commonly available to an artist, the second—the painterly rendering of the oil painting of heterogeneous objects—required introducing genuine fragments or symbolic fractions of the real things originally depicted.

§102

The first inscriptions in Picasso's paintings quite clearly quote their sources in everyday life. These are the enamel letters that the merchants in Paris use in shop windows instead of our signs. (Although there are some of these, they are hidden by tick marquees.) "Pale ale" and "Bass," which appeared later and acquired the persistent quality of captions, really exist on a glass screen partitioning the Boulevard Raspail next to the Café Rotonde, where Picasso walks his dog (a nice German shepherd) on his (almost) only stroll of the day. Serving as the background is usually an excerpt from the poster "Tous les soirs" or the label on a bottle of Vieux Mars(alla).

§104

The shop window suggested to the artist a new coulisse—the transparent plane. The plane itself was not to be depicted; what was depicted in the most naturalistic manner were the opaque inscriptions on the glass. This gave the picture depth, and it was achieved using a purely painterly device. The influence of graphics did not extend beyond the bounds of the contour. Naturalism, however, demanded the imposition of the letter on a stencil (note the mechanicalness) and the use of enamel paint, which produces a monotonous, mechanically homogeneous surface. Visual habit (habit kills more than passion) soon made the unvarying enamel unnoticeable. Thus a painterly undertaking became a graphic device and the original meaning of the inscription was lost, but the relative novelty of the effect obliged imitative observers to strew handfuls of letters and numbers over their pictures. The appearance of these new patterns was even given a moral interpretation, that is, no interpretation at all. The most sincere explanation was, "Just because I want to." To which one can ask, "Why exactly do you want to?"

§106

The introduction of real fragments of objects onto a surface painted in oils undoubtedly gives the composition a certain depth. We must not forget, however, that this technique is widely used in the construction of so-called panoramas, where it is common, has long ago lost its edge, and is therefore judged on its merits.

§108

"From whom and what are these blockheads independent?" L. Bloy wondered at the "Salon des Indépendants." They are free from the jury, and a picture's admission to the exhibition depends only on the timeliness of the entry fee, which is a pittance. Granting position according to rank is a powerful factor, however, and whether a picture hangs in front of the door in the first room depends on an administrative committee, that is, a secret jury. This is the physical aspect; as for moral dependence—the dependence of art on the authority of the day—it is amazingly obvious. The most recent Salon (1914) was essentially the "Salon Delaunay." Picasso's influence has been waning and dying.

§110

Picasso needs to die as soon as possible, but the war is in the way. Poor genius!

§111

Although . . . the life of a single individual, after all, is an abbreviated biography of the species; the structure of the tragic poet's verse echoes the composition of the entire play; and if "real works" do mediate most painting, won't the entire period be the intermediary in Picasso's *obras*? Isn't this portraitist of innumerable violins who has led his careless guides astray in thickets of paper and tin preparing on the sly to confront them with a candid synthesis of high-style realism? Be that as it may, now and forever, happy are they who have loved his art, who as they finish reading this page say, "No, this portrait doesn't look like her"—the usual remark of a lover as he gazes upon a picture of his beloved.

§112

But what, then, is this whole formal-analytical method? No bankruptcy here. It was not Picasso who created the aspiration of a race to plot garden paths as straight lines, circles, and ellipses or to clip trees in the shape of cubes, cones, and spheres. For some reason they call this artist Kant, who with respect to impact and influence resembles—if resemblance is possible—only Descartes. In the following quotation I substituted "painting" for "philosophy," touching not a letter more, but look at the result: *"Il porta cet esprit de géométrie et d'invention dans la peinture qui devint, entre ses mains, un Art tout nouveau, et s'il s'y trompa en quelque chose c'est qu'un homme qui découvre de nouvelles terres ne peut tout d'un coup en connaître toutes les propriétés. Ceux qui viennent après lui ont au moins l'obligation de la découverte"* (Voltaire, *Mélanges de littérature et de philosophie,* 4th ed., 1729, p. 249).

§113

As a woman surrenders to a lover, as the maenads surrendered to the spirit of music, thus did Picasso surrender to the spirit of painting. He devoted all the power of his talent to embodying the elemental demands of this external imperative and was flung beyond the boundaries of painting, because picture painting suffocates in the fetters of oil tempera, just as music is stifled in the cage of the twelve notes of the tempered scale. Picasso represents an attempt to go beyond outdated technique and use any kind of material to lay the foundations of painting. The moral of the story is that such art is possible only within the limits set by colored pastes and that the paints Picasso proposed to substitute for oils cannot replace them. *Un point c'est tout.* But Picasso is still young, and Lord willing he will live twice as long as he has up to now and will paint many more good pictures, and Vollard, who will probably again sell them *(on revient toujours à ses premièrs amours),* will not complain that business is slow. All's well that ends well, gentlemen; Job has many children and camels as before, so why are we dissatisfied? The innovative significance of Picasso's art is in the past, but the march to rejuvenate the materials of painting will not stop. New artists will appear, and as they fight for the life of their art they will discover new resources, new tools of the solar rhythms of which the diastole of the human heart is the echo and guarantee.

A POLEMICAL ADDENDUM: PABLO PICASSO AS A PAINTER

Some will approach God as fire, others as light.
St. Gregory of Nyssa

. . . Following the example of a certain acquaintance and many German reviewers, Picasso has been designated a mystic.

Graphic wanderings in the fourth dimension are ascribed to him; every evening foreigners thronging the Montparnasse taverns buttress their "latest and most subversive theories" with allusions to "the words of Picasso," and every year in late July somewhere between Munich and Darmstadt the news is that "Picasso has gone mad." The real legends, however, are yet to come, though not to the Germans, who are too positive, or to the Italians, who are too gullible. Only the Russians are promised the dubious honor of finally substituting the mystic for the artist. . . .

The creative process that led Picasso to the methods whose results are evident in the pictures of Shchukin's collection is unbroken and can be studied over its entire course. True, the Moscow gallery is inadequate for such a study, since a few periods in Picasso's evolution have been omitted, whereas one that is rather brief and essentially transitional [1908] is represented by so many canvases, its relative significance in the overall process is distorted.

. . . It was the young artist's individual approach to the heritage of the creator of *Mardi Gras* [see p. 83] that determined his subsequent position among the heterogeneous currents around him, an approach shaped by his latent gravitation toward sculpture and volumetric interpretation of visual impressions. This interpretation gave rise to the generic character of Picasso's painting and sharply distinguished him from the contemporary school of Matisse. With respect to Matisse, of course, the word "influence" is apropos, but strangely enough, at first Matisse influenced him in the area of line, not color. Picasso turned his attention to the silhouette in the pictures by the Fauves' leader, covertly arguing against Matisse's treatment of color as the content of large surfaces and the implied absence of depth. *Pierrot Seated* (in a harlequin's costume)* is a very delicate polemic, perhaps the only example of such a consistent rejection of an ostensibly accepted method. Concerns about new means for silhouetting objects forced Picasso to reject working with oil paint. The new materials—pastels, sanguine, watercolors—allowed considerable room for graphic exploration and simplified working with color, which was of only secondary significance, thus allowing him to shorten his experiments. The results of these studies were summarized in the "acrobat period," to which I take the liberty of adding the great "still life" period, the two being united by time (1906–7) and painterly technique. The graphic aspirations that had been slaked by his previous work occupied a fitting position in the linear composition and did not encroach upon the area of color, on which his intense work with nonplastic materials left a certain mark.

The stroke's limitations eliminated, Picasso begins working with the tip of the brush. The color layer becomes very thin and the layers multiply, but the differences between them are determined not so much by their degree of relative transparency as by the variety in their structure. The pictures of this period, which at first glance seem naturalistic thematically, are morphologically a sequence of color planes applied one upon the other and mechanically connected by the contour of a painterly silhouette. To Matisse's formula ("Apply the object's formal characteristics to the linear silhouette and apply color to the silhouette's surface") is added another postulate: "Apply volumetric characteristics to the color planes of the silhouette's surface." This demand stems from the structure of the color layer, that is, from the painterly material itself and so is inevitable, internally insurmountable, and therefore impossible not to implement. Shchukin has nothing at all from the years 1906–7 (or from the "blue" and "rose" periods),† which to some extent prevents anyone who knows Picasso only on the basis of the famous Moscow collection from understanding him correctly. . . .

A new way of expressing depth was also in preparation, and it would establish itself in Picasso's works beginning in 1911. The outline of objects was expanded, both to increase the expressiveness of each component's contours and to exploit their texture better. Volume is a sculptural concept, whereas easel painting concerns the plane of the canvas. The expression of volume on a plane, a picture's depth, was achieved primarily through graphic perspective. Painting was subordinated to graphics and helped create a visual illusion erroneously taken for resemblance. Artists who wanted to renounce the predominance of the graphic aspect of their art sacrificed depth in their works. Picasso set himself the goal of expressing volumetric perspective through primarily painterly means. To do so he refused to reduce the characteristic planes of objects to a closed relief. He now regarded each such plane as an independently valuable element, and its position in the space of the canvas was de-

**Harlequin* (1913, Z.II*.333, Gemeentemuseum, The Hague).

†Aksenov is wrong here.

termined not by a photographically obligatory reproduction of nature but by its compositional connection to the picture's other elements. The space enclosed within the picture's frame was a special world with its own obligatory laws whose ultimate goal was to endow the object with plastic characteristics through painterly means. Since the planes in the picture were component parts of a single object, that is, they consisted of a single material, and since we know about Picasso's love for material, they were colored the same and differed only with respect to the distribution of light. If Neo-Impressionism is the analysis of light, then in this period Picasso created an analysis of chiaroscuro. Not limiting himself to light, however, he introduced the so-called sliding plane, that is, a transparent plane which the picture's other elements showed through.

This device posed the new problem of the individual characteristic of each of the planes constituting the volume. The solution was expressed in two ways: one graphic, through complete freedom in selecting the location of the plane and in turning it to the angle that showed its features most clearly; and the other painterly, by individualizing the texture of each structural element. Thus the simplest object became a hierarchically ordered perspective, and the volume was ready to lose its characteristic, having become an indefinite alternation of a large number of elements in an unlimited space. The way out of this trap was suggested by some everyday observations of two extremely quotidian things—the shop window and the poster. The foreground of the picture comprises inscriptions on an invisible plate of glass framed by the window opening . . . and intersecting the formally disassembled object. The inscription on the poster peeking out from behind the object defines the background—the volume of the object is limited by a simple comparison of perfectly flat elements. It might seem that the discovery of this new perspective would end the quest; it might seem that everything has been found—yet in reality this achievement served as the impetus for new work on the plane.

We have seen that planes were individualized by individualizing their painterly texture, which had to be varied considerably within the picture. But at first glance it's a strange thing: no thickening of the paint layer or affected virtuosity seems to have occurred. The explanation of this oddity is to be found in Picasso's special treatment of multiple layers: several layers of paint are applied within a single component, but they overlap only partially; each layer's texture differs from that of the layer beneath it. Thus it becomes possible to combine not only layers but textures, which greatly increases the painter's technical resources without destroying their unity. For example, with 5 different layers we have 5! = 120 different planes. The graphic element has completely disappeared from Picasso's painterly resources. Only in *Girl from Arles** is it present in the form of intersecting black strokes in the background evidently applied with a pen, but this device is purely graphic and does not pretend to be painting, and the nature of the material makes it the opposite of the old technique.

**L'Arlésienne* (1912, Z.II.356, Thomas Ammann Fine Art, Zurich).

This is something of a confrontation between his old, semi-graphic and present, purely painterly technique. Although graphics were driven out of the plane, they continued to play an important role on its edge, linearly determining the components' convexity or concavity. When he decided to individualize the components, Picasso simultaneously complicated his task by rejecting linear relief. Now the components of the composition were differently outlined segments of a Euclidean plane. . . . He continued to increase the number of components, evidently assuming that an inadequately dismantled curvature of the object's surface would have a covert effect on the elements of the analysis. Multiplying planes resulted in multiplying layers of paint: in the most complex composition—*The Poet* (1912)*—the simplest segment has up to eight layers, each of which seems to be a volume. The solution was in the letters evidently introduced for purposes of perspective. By inserting them into his picture Picasso repeated the technique used in his Parisian studies, which was to create depth through the inclusion of something whose color and texture were alien to the picture's overall structure.

Picasso's reproductions of enamel shop-window signs were precise. He made them with a stencil using lacquer and enamel, another consequence of the demand for opacity. The technique for the new material differed substantially from that for oil paint, being a single-layered wash—a canonical painting device. These letters turned out absolutely flat. Thus, the multilayer technique produced depth; each sector was not a "surface" but a series of combined planes, which, because they absorbed light in different ways, produced the sensation of depth. The cause had been found, and so the struggle began.

Polygons that absorbed light were replaced by others that reflected it; lacquer and enamel washes no longer served as coulisses. As texture was being simplified, color needed to be more complex. The picture's overall tone was broken: pure white enamel was juxtaposed with black lacquer. The results obtained from structuring the paint layer demonstrated that rejecting a curved linear outline for the segments was untenable, and they reappeared. Actually, the texture's simplification was only apparent, and the techniques changed with the material. This new material introduced by the letters brought with it other properties of the letter itself, properties that define the notion of *canonism.* The letter is the most immutable visual impression. If the hieroglyph is the extreme generalization of the drawn object, then the letter—the surviving lines of the vanished hieroglyph—is the canon of graphics. Spontaneous generalization, however, is possible not only in drawing. Centuries of representing certain objects have organically synthesized them and established their color canon in applied painting. This is true mainly of wood and marble.

Picasso exploited these techniques. In *The Poet,* where thematic considerations prevented him from introducing the perspective of the letter, he used a comb to paint the hair and mustache of his model in "imitation wood." This produced a completely

**The Poet* (1912, Z.II.313, Kunstmuseum, Basel).

unexpected impression and was a revelation. The point was not the novelty of the technique (400 years before, Pierre de Maré had used a comb to paint the garments of Mary Magdalene in his *Crucifixion*) but the feeling of certitude generated by this most conventional means of representation. When we look at a cupboard done in "imitation oak," we know that it is made of anything but oak; a wall done in imitation marble can never be suspected of containing such a material. The "oak," "ash," and "marble" are only in the layer of paint applied by the house painter, and this layer must be completely opaque in order to mask the real material of the painted object. The house painter's "canonical" application of color produces an impression of pure surface, an absolute plane devoid of the third dimension—depth. Thus began the honeymoon of "canonism": "wood," "marble," "porcelain," and "imitation clay" became the basis for a new technique. To these devices were added an approach to the color gray and the use of pencil lines to rework white planes, which served as a transition from solid washes to ribbed surfaces. The abstractness of the manner, of course, made the entire composition abstract with respect to both line and color, and their interaction led Picasso to the new series of experiments that define his present stage of development. The eye, particularly the professionally trained eye, quickly adapts to recurrent impressions. The conventionality of the new devices no longer satisfied the artist, for it evidently left too much room for his personal whim and was not absolutely conventional.

Once again Picasso has set painting aside. On a picture he pastes pieces of "marbled" paper and rectangles of an "imitation wood" panel and substitutes newspaper clippings—absolute planes—for penciled lettering on white, sometimes joining them with a few lines of charcoal or chalk. He puts different household trash—pieces of boxes, ink bottles, visiting cards, pieces of cardboard, rules, violin fragments—on wooden panels, ties them all together with string, impales them on nails, and hangs it on the wall; sometimes he calls in a photographer. The simplicity of the outlines and the limited number of constructive elements and color combinations allow us to interpret this most recent stage in Picasso's art as a new form of the experiences from his mirror period. We have the same peering into the material structure of the plane and the same proximity to the natural elements of everyday perception. It remains to be seen what will come next, but one thing can be said: we will see nothing nonexistent in this exclusively plastic art. Neither mysticism, nor demonism, nor the fourth dimension has ever been or ever will be present in Picasso's works. We have surveyed his entire career here and have seen that it has been exclusively painterly tasks—tasks of the painting craft—that have determined its trajectory. These tasks are eternal: the eternal beauty in Picasso's art.

IV

CUBISM AND FUTURISM

Coming immediately after a basically Fauvist primitivism, Cubism made the Russian avant-garde more radical and consistent by introducing a new visual language, and it became the theoretical norm and quasi-scientific foundation for the avant-garde's methods and goals. The grafting of Cubism onto Russian art was a necessity, but the history of its reception in Russia consists to a large extent of accidents and aberrations and today would be difficult to reconstruct in its entirety.

Russian artists began actively studying Cubism in the years 1910–12, the high point of the process coming in 1913–14, following the exhibition of a number of significant Cubist works in Moscow in 1912–13. Some of the artists, such as Liubov' Popova and Nadezhda Udal'tsova, who had visited Paris, had learned directly from Metzinger and Le Fauconnier [48]. These Russian artists approached Cubism primarily as a system that prepared their transition to nonobjectiveness. In the spring of 1913, an analytical "Cubist circle," whose members included Popova and Udal'tsova as well as Aleksandr Vesnin and Grishchenko, formed in Vladimir Tatlin's studio in Moscow.

Gleizes's interview in the popular Petersburg press [44] was the first in a series of publications in which the principles of Cubism were explained by its Parisian popularizers. For the less radical modernists, Cubism marked the limit of their receptivity to contemporary art. If many of them acknowledged Matisse in one way or another, they rejected Cubism unanimously [45].

Great interest was aroused by Gleizes and Metzinger's *Du Cubisme,* which the press greeted with predictable contempt; the Marxists regarded it as new evidence of the crisis of art in bourgeois society [46]. In fact, in 1913 this book was published twice in Russian. The translation put out by the Moscow publishing house Sovremennye Problemy was signed "M.V." The translation published by Zhuravl' in St. Petersburg was done by Ekaterina Nizen and edited by Mikhail Matiushin [cf. 49]. Matiushin was not a Cubist, but the new trend awakened theoretical interest even in those avant-gardists who did not belong to the movement. In his 1912 attempts to explain Cubism, David Burliuk formulated his own understanding of contemporary painting, introducing a number of notions central to the Russian avant-garde ("shift," "texture," "dissonance") [47].

The Russian discourse on Cubism was marked by its attempt to emphasize archaic or national "wellsprings"—as if the "Gauguinesque" vector of the years around 1910 were still in force [50, 61]. References to Cubism's "African" provenance were in a similar vein. Symptomatic as well were attempts to perceive a Russian forerunner of Cubism in Mikhail Vrubel' [cf. 51].

Cubism influenced virtually every Russian avant-gardist, but it was not a long stage in the evolution of any significant artist. It provided Malevich with a number of key devices (cross-sectioning of form, collage, etc.), which he used not so much to construct a picture but as painterly phenomena reinterpreted to break down logic and gain entry to a new reality lying beyond the boundaries of representational painting. Malevich remained a passionate and attentive analyst of Cubism, but for him it was a "completed" stage "canceled" by Suprematism [52]. Others who criticized Cubism from different positions included Mikhail Le Dantiu [65].

Beginning in the spring of 1913 the notion of "Cubo-Futurism" gradually gained currency in Russia, initially with reference to the Hylaea group in literature and in relation to certain paintings by Malevich, Goncharova, and others. Subsequently, however, the name "Cubo-Futurism" was applied to nearly the entire Russian avant-garde of the mid-1910s.

In Russia, Italian Futurism achieved more notoriety than any other phenomena of contemporary Western art. Manifestos that became known immediately after their publication, critics' reports of Futurist exhibitions in Europe [54], and, finally, Tommaso Marinetti's visit to Moscow and Petersburg in early 1914 created a sensation. A significant part of society saw the Futurists as signaling a new worldview that broke with traditional culture. At the same time, "Futurism" became a brand name for radical currents in Russian literature and art. The label owed its persistence to journalists who emphasized the similarity between the Italian and Russian avant-gardes, but the innovators themselves accepted it as a name that expressed their aspirations (a number of Russian avant-gardists adopted names that were synonymous with the Italian "Futurists," i.e., "budetliane," "budushchniki"—"futuremen").

Using the identical name "Futurists" forced Russian avant-gardists to assert themselves constantly, especially in view of the predominant opinion among the public that Russian innovators were dependent on the West. This conflict came to a head at Marinetti's lecture in Petersburg on February 1, 1914 [56]. Ten days later, Benedikt Livshits and Artur Lourie hosted a gathering entitled "Our Response to Marinetti," at which they developed the points in the manifesto "We and the West" [66].*

In contrast to Cubism, the Italians' painting had relatively little immediate impact on Russian art, which merely borrowed certain means of representing motion. The Russian literature on Futurism, however, was extensive. Most of it regarded the phenomenon as a "malaise of the time," drawing no distinction between Russian and Italian Futurists. There were two separate tendencies in Russian criticism: interpretations of Futurism as an indicator of the state of culture; and analyses of its poetics [57]. A majority of critics regarded the new current as a symptom of the growing crisis (Genrikh Tasteven's book being a rare exception [55]).

*Cf. the recently published draft of Goncharova's letter to Marinetti, in John E. Bowlt and Matthew Drutt, *Amazons of the Avant-Garde: Alexandra Exter, Natalia Goncharova, Liubov Popova, Olga Rozanova, Varvara Stepanova, and Nadezhda Udaltsova* (New York: Guggenheim Museum; London: Thames and Hudson, 2000), p. 314; and Jane Ashton Sharp, *Russian Modernism between East and West: Natal'ia Goncharova and the Moscow Avant-Garde* (Cambridge: Cambridge University Press, 2006).

The Russians wrote relatively little, however, on Futurist painting and sculpture per se. With rare exceptions [54], writers opposed to the avant-garde did not attempt to analyze Futurist practice, and, remarkably, the avant-garde made almost no positive evaluations of Futurist painting (the exceptions were polemical in nature [41]). Russian critics turned their attention to the discrepancy between the Italians' radical theory and its implementation and to Futurism's dependency on Impressionism.

As early as 1920, Nikolai Punin summarized the significance of Italian Futurism: "The Futurists did not create positive artistic values so much as they made it possible to open minds and hearts that were waiting to be liberated from the old fetters."* It was at this time that Roman Jakobson wrote his essay [58], probably the most thoughtful analysis of Futurism in Russia.

44
E. Dmitriev
"What Is Cubism?" (1912)

This interview with Albert Gleizes for the St. Petersburg newspaper *Birzhevye vedomosti* (Stock Exchange Gazette), March 13, 1912 (evening edition), is a rare example in the popular press of an unbiased approach to a sensational artistic phenomenon.

. . . When I met Albert Gleizes, the founder of Cubism, I received in response to my questions an invitation to visit his studio. . . .

He opened up a huge folder of watercolor landscapes, domestic scenes, and village dwellers. Most were in the good "old" manner, and I rushed to acknowledge that all of them showed great talent and subtle execution and that prior to his evolution Gleizes had had every right to demand admittance to the Academy's official Salon. But his most recent watercolors were in his new style. One picture was an evening landscape of a copse on a riverbank, and everything in it—the trees, the water, the sky—was conscientiously recorded. On the other was a Cubist interpretation of the same landscape: instead of water and sky there were colored squares and rhombs; instead of trees, black stakes thrust into a mass of something or other. There were also drawings of an individual tree. In one of them all was as it should be: branches, bark, foliage, the play of light on the leaves. In the other was a naked pole with crossbeams.

"Why do you prefer this naked pole that looks like it was made of little cubes to a real tree with all its rounded details?" I asked.

"Because when I draw a tree I must show a synthesis of the tree. Copying details would distract the viewer's attention from the essence of the idea of the tree."

"But a tree isn't a pole, it's a complex being whose entire individuality and beauty lie in its details."

*N. N. Punin, *Pervyi kurs lektsii, chitannykh na kratkosrochnykh kursakh dlia uchitelei risovaniia. Sovremennoe iskusstvo* (Petrograd, 1920), pp. 65–66.

"There! That's exactly where we disagree!" Gleizes exclaimed. And he began explaining.

"When we see or imagine a tree, we first of all picture a more or less tall trunk with more or less broad branches rising out of the ground. How the rest appears to us—the bark, the leaves, how they are lit, as well as the atmosphere surrounding them—depends on the weather, the time of day, and our own mood. The artist's task is to portray the essence of a landscape, scene, or human face, and it is up to the viewer to supplement, embellish, and elucidate the picture according to his own impressions and emotions. His emotion must not be violated, as it has been up to now; we must not try to compel the viewer's emotion artificially but simply be in sympathy with his moods.

"I show them a forest landscape, a synthesis of such a landscape, and it is up to them to look at the forest in bright daylight and see the poetry of life or fill the forest with darkness and phantoms."

"So you want to provide only the outline, and leave it to the viewer to fill it mentally with patterns, shapes, and colors?"

That was not quite it, Gleizes objected, and he took exception to my remark that at best he was excessively reducing the artist's significance and role. On the contrary, in his opinion, Cubism greatly expanded the tasks of painting.

Some critics have almost tried to draw a parallel between Cubism and Impressionism. But the ambitions of the former are far greater. Cubism is not content to register a transient impression. It shows a face, thing, or view at once, "from all sides," and responds to all moods. "All-sidedness" is another goal. Take, for example, one of Gleizes's pictures showing a *nature morte*—a table and tablecloth, a dish of apples, a cup—in the middle of variously colored squares and triangles. On the plate is another, smaller plate, and there is a smaller cup in the cup. All this is supposed to represent only one plate and one cup, but "from different sides." It may be unintelligible to us, but Gleizes is convinced that it is artistic truth.

"I'm not about to argue," I answered, but pointed to another picture and asked, "Why do you paint this woman with rectangular shoulders and triangular breasts? Surely that's not the way you see a woman, whose entire beauty is in the roundedness of her lines?"

The founder of Cubism replied, "I make an effort. I force myself to see a woman that way in order to imagine the synthesis of her shapes."

"You mentally cut her up into squares and triangles?"

I did not add that, although his theories were worth discussing, his geometry could not be taken seriously. As we were saying goodbye, though, Gleizes readily acknowledged that geometry in the Cubists' works was a whimsical and minor detail. They might even reject the very name "Cubism," which has not yet taken final shape and is still in an exploratory phase. The only thing they will never abandon is their new understanding of artistic truth and the mission of art.

45

Iakov Tugendkhol'd

"A Letter from Paris" (1912)

Published in *Apollon* (Apollo) 6 (1912).

. . . One wonders whether the Cubists are not tossing out great spiritual values together with the literary bric-a-brac. Indeed, they devalue art and strip it of any philosophical or creative meaning, reducing it to a form of *cognition.* As I have often had occasion to hear from the Cubists, the sole goal of their art is *être vrai,* to convey what they see *truthfully.*

Truthfully! Here is where the muddle begins. Having finished with literature and narrative, the Cubists also want to be liberated from the laws of sensory experience. To express the "genuine essence of things" they want to portray things not as they are apprehended empirically but as they are *imagined* outside the accidents of light and perspective. This supersensory, purely intellectual apprehension of the world based not on immediate sensation but on ideas is in essence nothing new. This is how children and primitives perceive the world. They depict objects not as the objects seem in perspective distortion but as they *know* them abstractly. Geometrical volume plays an enormous role in miniatures, in the painting of Giotto and El Greco, and even more in that of Cézanne.

The Cubists, however, want to go further and so fall into an indubitable disarray of consciousness known as fragmented personality—the same illusionism of which they accuse the Impressionists. Out of the various forms that one and the same object assumes depending on the distortions of perspective, the primitives chose the one that seemed the most *important* and that corresponded to the object's *ideal and practical significance.* The Cubists have no subject, no inner content, and no ideational criterion. All sides of the object, all its angles and volumes, are of equal value to them. Moreover, they elevate this equivalence to a principle as the highest *objectivism* and obedience to nature. . . .

Cubism has one healthy element, namely, the volumetric analysis of form, which is a natural reaction against the Impressionists' amorphousness. The geometrical analysis of form, however, is merely a rough, preparatory technique that should not become an end in itself or cross the studio threshold. A picture at an exhibition is a *social* phenomenon, and humanity, to whose judgment the artist voluntarily submits his work, has the right to demand not a rough draft but the completed result of his labor. Picasso and Braque have evidently understood this, for they have ceased participating in exhibitions. They are behaving logically.

46

Georgii Plekhanov

"Art and Social Life" (1912)

Plekhanov attended the 1912 "Salon d'Automne." This article was based on a lecture he delivered in Paris on November 10, 1912. The passage on Cubism was written later, after he had read Gleizes and Metzinger's *Du Cubisme.*

Plekhanov's critique of Cubism has to be viewed in the context of the debate around 1910, when Lenin and Plekhanov were attacking "Machism" and its supporters (including Aleksandr Bogdanov and Anatolii Lunacharskii). This philosophical trend, named after the Austrian physicist Ernst Mach (1838–1916), regarded reality as a complex of sensations, questioned the objective nature of matter, and rejected the principle of causality.

The article, which was originally published in the Moscow Marxist journal *Sovremennik* (The Contemporary) 12 (1912), is reprinted here as translated in George V. Plekhanov, *Art and Society,* introduction by Granville Hicks (New York: Critics Group, 1936), pp. 78, 83–88.

. . . The idea that our ego is the sole reality has always been the basis of subjective idealism; but it required the unbounded individualism of the period of the decline of the bourgeoisie to convert this idea, not only into an egoistic rule of conduct, governing the relations between men, each of whom "loves himself like God" (the bourgeoisie has never been distinguished for excessive altruism), but also into a theoretical basis for the new esthetics.

The reader is undoubtedly acquainted with the Cubist school of painting. I think I do not err in assuming that those who have seen examples of the work of the Cubists were not moved by it in the least. In me, at any rate, Cubism produces nothing that resembles esthetic pleasure. "Stupidity cubed!"—this is what comes to mind when one is confronted with these attempts at art. But Cubism is nevertheless subject to definite laws, and to call it "stupidity cubed" is not to explain its origin. We cannot, of course, digress to trace the origin of Cubism in detail, but at least we can indicate the direction which such a search would have to take.

I have before me a most interesting book called *Du Cubisme* by Albert Gleizes and Jean Metzinger, both painters of the Cubist school. Following the maxim, *auditur et altera pars,* let us allow them to express their views themselves. How do these artists justify their disconcerting creative methods?

There is nothing real outside ourselves; there is nothing real except the coincidence of a sensation and an individual and mental tendency. Be it far from us to throw any doubts upon the existence of the objects which impress our senses; but, rationally speaking, we can only experience certitude in respect of the images which they produce in the mind.*

From this the authors deduce that one cannot know the form assumed by things in themselves, and there is therefore every justification for giving them whatever form one pleases. However, they make the interesting reservation that they do not wish to

*Albert Gleizes and Jean Metzinger, *Cubism* (London: Unwin, 1913), pp. 45–46.

confine themselves, like the Impressionists, to the realm of perception: We seek the essential, but we seek it in our personality and not in a sort of eternity, laboriously divided by mathematics and philosophers.*

In these arguments, as the reader can see, there predominates the familiar idea that the ego is the sole reality. It is true, of course, that here the idea has been modified somewhat. Gleizes and Metzinger say they do not doubt the existence of objects. But, immediately upon admitting the existence of the external world, they declare it to be unknowable. This means that for them, too, there is no reality except the ego.

If images of objects are produced in the mind by reason of the impingement of those objects upon the senses, then it is obviously impossible to speak for an unknowable external world. We know the external world precisely because of this impingement. Gleizes and Metzinger are mistaken; and their arguments about the form of things in themselves are extremely weak. We should not, however blame them too seriously for their errors; greater philosophers have made similar errors. But we must not overlook the fact that the supposed unknowability of the external world leads our authors to conclude that it is necessary to look for the essential in "our personality." Now this conclusion may be interpreted in two ways. "Personality" may refer to the human race in general; or it may refer only to each individual personality. The first interpretation leads to the transcendental idealism of Kant; the second to the sophistry that each individual is the "measure of all things." Our authors seem inclined to the sophist reasoning implied in the second interpretation. . . .

The extreme individualism of the epoch of bourgeois decadence shuts artists off from the sources of true inspiration. It sets up a barrier, screening tumultuous social events and condemning them to endless confusion over their petty personal experiences and morbid fantasies. The net result of such rumination is art which not only bears no relation to any kind of beauty—but which is obviously absurd, and justifiable only through a sophistic distortion of the idealist theory of knowledge. . . .

47

David Burliuk

"Cubism (Surface—Plane)" (1912)

Poet and painter David Burliuk (1882–1967) was the most enthusiastic promoter of the early avant-garde. His painting does not reveal strong Cubist influence, but because of a series of scandalous public lectures, for a time he almost monopolized the propaganda related to Cubism in Russia, despite his approach being criticized by avant-garde artists [65]. Burliuk left Russia in 1920 and after two years in Japan settled in the United States.

This essay was first published in *A Slap in the Face of Public Taste* (Moscow, 1912); the translation here is reprinted from *Russian Art of the Avant-Garde: Theory and Criticism, 1902–1934,* edited and translated by John E. Bowlt (New York: Viking Press, 1976), pp. 69–77.

*Ibid., pp. 47–48.

It would perhaps not be a paradox to say that painting became art only in the twentieth century.

Only in the twentieth century have we begun to have painting as art—before there used to be the art of painting, but there was no painting Art. This kind of painting (up to the twentieth century) is called conventionally—from a certain sense of compassion toward the endless sums spent on museums—Old Painting, as distinct from *New* Painting.

These definitions in themselves show that everyone, even the most Ignorant and those with no interest in the Spiritual, perceives the eternal gulf that has arisen between the painting of yesterday and the painting of today. An eternal gulf. Yesterday we did not have art.

Today we do have art. Yesterday it was the means, today it has become the end. Painting has begun to pursue only Painterly objectives. It has begun to live for itself. The fat bourgeois have shifted their shameful attention from the artist, and now this magician and sorcerer has the chance of escaping to the transcendental secrets of his art.

Joyous solitude. But woe unto him who scorns the pure springs of the highest revelations of our day. Woe unto them who reject their *eyes,* for the Artists of today are the prophetic eyes of mankind. Woe unto them who trust in their own abilities—which do not excel those of reverend moles! . . . Darkness has descended upon their souls!

Having become an end in itself, painting has found within itself endless horizons and aspirations. And before the astounded eyes of the casual spectators roaring with laughter at contemporary exhibitions (but already with caution and respect), Painting has developed such a large number of different trends that their enumeration alone would now be enough for a big article.

It can be said with confidence that the confines of This art of Free Paint have been expanded during the first decade of the twentieth century, as had never been imagined during all the years of its previous existence!

Amid these trends of the New Painting the one that Shocks the spectator's . . . eye most is the Direction defined by the word *Cubist.* . . .

In order to understand Painting, the art of the New Painting, it is essential to take the same standpoint vis-à-vis Nature as the artist takes. One must feel ashamed of the fatuous adolescent's elementary view of Nature—an extremely literary, narrative standpoint. One must remember that Nature, for the Artist and for painting, is Exclusively an object of visual Sensation. Indeed, a visual sensation refined and broadened immeasurably (compared with the past) by the associative capacity of the human spirit, but one that avoids ideas of the coarse, irrelevant kind. Painting now operates within a sphere of Painterly Ideas and Painterly Conceptions that is accessible only to it; they ensue and arise from those Elements of visual Nature that can be defined by the 4 points mentioned above.

The man deprived of a Painterly understanding of Nature will, when looking at

Cézanne's landscape *The House,* understand it purely narratively: (1) "house" (2) mountains (3) trees (4) sky. Whereas for the artist, there existed (I) linear construction (II) surface construction (not fully realized) and (III) color orchestration. For the artist, there were certain lines going up and down, right and left, but there wasn't a house or trees . . . there were areas of certain color strength, of certain character. And that's all.

Painting of the past, too, seemed at times to be not far from conceiving Nature as Line (of a certain character and of a certain intensity) and colors (Nature as a number of colored areas—this applies Only to the Impressionists at the end of the nineteenth century). But it never made up its mind to analyze visual Nature from the viewpoint of the essence of its surface. The conception of what we see as merely a number of certain definite sections of different surface Planes arose only in the twentieth century under the general name of *Cubism.* Like everything else, Cubism has its history. Briefly, we can indicate the sources of this remarkable movement.

I. If the Greeks and Holbein were, as it were, the first to whom *line* (in itself) was accessible

II. If Chiaroscuro (as color), texture, and surface appeared fleetingly to Rembrandt

III. then Cezanne is the first who can be credited with the conjecture that Nature can be observed as a Plane, as a surface (surface construction). If line, Chiaroscuro, and coloration were well known in the past, then *Plane* and surface were discovered only by the new painting. Just as the whole immeasurable significance of Texture in painting has only now been realized.

In passing on to a more detailed examination of examples of a surface analysis of Nature in the pictures of modem artists, and in passing on to certain constructions of a theoretical type that ensue from this view of Nature—as plane and surface—I would like to answer the question that should now be examined at the beginning of any article devoted to the Theory of the New Painting: "Tell me, what is the significance of establishing definite names for Definite Painterly Canons, of establishing the dimensions of all you call the Establishment of Painterly Counterpoint? Indeed, the pictures of modem artists don't become any better or more valuable because of this. . . ." And people like to add: "Oh, how I dislike talking about Painting" or "I like this art."

A few years ago artists wouldn't have forgiven themselves if they'd talked about the aims, tasks, and essence of Painting. Times have changed. Nowadays not to be a theoretician of painting means to reject an understanding of it. This art's center of gravity has been transferred. . . .

It has been known for a long time that what is important is not the *what,* but the *how,* i.e., which principles, which objectives, guided the artist's creation of this or that work! It is essential to establish on the basis of which canon it (the work) arose! It is essential to reveal its painterly nature! It must be indicated what the aim in Nature was that the artist of the given picture was So attracted by. And the analysis of painterly phenomena will then be a Scientific criticism of the subject. And the spectator will no longer be the confused enemy of the new art—this unhappy spectator who has only just broken out of the torture chamber of our newspapers' and magazines' cheap, presumptuous, and idiotic criticism, a criticism that believes that its duty is not to learn from the artist but to teach him. Without even studying art, many critics seriously believe that they can teach the artist What he must do and *how* he must do it! . . . I myself have personally encountered such blockheaded diehards.

Line is the result of the intersection of 2 planes. . . .

One plane can intersect another on a straight line or on a curve (surface).

Hence follow: I *Cubism* proper—and II *Rondism.*

The first is an analysis of Nature from the point of view of planes intersecting on straight lines, the second operates with surfaces of a ball-like character.

Disharmony is the opposite of harmony.
dissymmetry is the opposite of symmetry.
deconstruction is the opposite of construction.
a canon can be constructive.
a canon can be deconstructive.
construction can be shifted or displaced
The canon of displaced construction.

The existence in Nature of visual poetry—ancient, dilapidated towers and walls—points to the essential, tangible, and forceful supremacy of this kind of beauty.

Displacement can be linear.

Displacement can be planar.

Displacement can be in one particular place or it can be general.

Displacement can be coloristic—(a purely mechanical conception).

The canon of the Academy advocated: symmetry of proportion, fluency, or their equivalent harmony.

The New painting has indicated the existence of a second, parallel canon that does not destroy the first one—the canon of displaced construction.

1) disharmony (not fluency)
2) disproportion
4) coloristic dissonance
3) deconstruction

All these concepts follow from the examination of works of the New painting. Point 3) I placed out of sequence, and it has already been examined above. Both Cubism and Rondism can be based on all these four basic concepts of the Canon of Displaced Construction.

But Cubism and Rondism can also live and develop in the soil of the Academic Canon. . . .

Note. In the past there was also a counterbalance to the Academic Canon living on (fluency) harmony, proportion, symmetry: all barbaric Folk arts were based partly on the existence of this second canon (of displaced Construction). A definitive examination of our relation to these arts as raw material for the modem artist's creative soul would take us out of our depth.

48

Nadezhda Udal'tsova

Diary (1912–13)

The painter Nadezhda Udal'tsova (1886–1961) studied in Moscow and together with Liubov' Popova worked in Paris at the La Palette studio in 1912–13. She participated in the most radical exhibitions, including "Streetcar V," "0, 10" (both in 1915 in Petrograd), and "Store" (1916, Moscow), and was a member of the Supremus group. In 1923 Udal'tsova and her husband Aleksandr Drevin (1889–1938) turned to figurative painting.

The text here is from N. Udal'tsova, *Zhizn' russkoi kubistki. Dnevniki. Stat'i. Vospominaniia* (Life of a Russian Cubist. Diaries. Essays. Reminiscences), with commentary by E. A. Drevina, V. I. Rakitin, and A. D. Sarabianov (Moscow: RA Publishers, 1994), p. 104. Entries are dated according to the Old Style.

DECEMBER 12 [1912]

. . . I think constantly about Fauconnier, and I'm thinking of throwing myself at his mercy. I'm going to see him for the simple reason that his is the only studio where you can talk and work freely on form. . . .

I regard Cubism the same way I do Impressionism. Both are rather ugly. You have to move toward composition and the old masters—there's no way without them. Leonardo—he has everything—composition and form. You have to understand his composition and forms. There is mathematics here, but it's hidden from external observation; it's his secret. Cubism should be its artists' secret, too. The viewer should see beauty—painting and not a charade.

When the Impressionists said that viewers should be reared on their pictures and get used to chaos, it was nonsense—just like Cubism. You can accustom yourself to anything, but not everyone can understand Leonardo, and you have to train your eye considerably in order to penetrate the secret of Titian, Veronese, and Poussin.

It's bad enough when an artist says, "In our age of airplanes, factories, and so forth, you have to search for an appropriate form"; you might as well be reading the newspaper. You have to look, know how to look, and know what you want to do. . . .

I need a foundation in form, and I'm going to see Le Fauconnier to learn how to build man and nature out of cubes.

Cézanne built a monument out of the Impressionists and the old masters.

Cubism can be contrasted to Impressionism quite well. Only those who went their own way and still remain—Cézanne, Gauguin, Degas, Manet, Renoir—only they! All the rest are minor art, and there have been hundreds, thousands of them. If I had come two years ago—Matisse was everywhere. Now the Cubists' monstrosities are everywhere, and years from now, only three or four people will stand out among this garbage. . . .

DECEMBER 17

I'll get a foundation for everything from Le Fauconnier: the precise construction of figures, and from there of landscape and composition. I'll get a lot in any case, but I don't know whether I'll go as far as Cubism, I don't know whether that's the goal. As a means to an end, it's a great thing, and everything is becoming clear and disciplined. Especially landscape—I see such possibilities.

I think I'll exhibit something soon. All of this is no longer just something random, and that's the main thing for me. Yes, a new age is dawning. Leonardo is drawing closer, Poussin. You're entering the strict temple of the mathematics of construction. . . .

JANUARY 2 [1913]

. . . I've always been alone. What all these Kisses* have told me is alien to me, and I have coerced myself. But I will have everything here. I've come to believe in Metzinger; it is he rather than Le Fauconnier who will help me. Even though Le Fauconnier's works are much closer to me, he is a painter, whereas Metzinger is a graphic artist, and everything in his works is alien to me, Cubist absurdity. My ideal is Le Fauconnier's *L'Abondance;*† I must buy a photo of it and study it.

Still, Matisse did me a service. He taught me to see motion. So did Van Gogh, Gauguin less than the others, and as for Cézanne—Cézanne is everything. . . .

Well, I screwed up my courage, pulled through it, and did a drawing on my own, and Le Fauconnier himself said, "*Ce n'est pas mal,*" and ordered me to paint it. Very well, I feel the ground beneath my feet and I'll work, and *maîtres* like Le Fauconnier and Metzinger will comment on my work.

49

Mikhail Matiushin

"On *Du Cubisme* by Metzinger and Gleizes" (1913)

From 1881 to 1913 Mikhail Matiushin (1861–1934) was concertmaster of the Imperial Orchestra in St. Petersburg. He was among the founders of the Union of Youth and composed the music to the opera *Victory over the Sun* (1913). Together with his wife, the poet and painter Elena

*Karol Kiss (1878–?) was a Hungarian artist in whose Moscow studio Udal'tsova worked for a time.

†Henri Le Fauconnier, *Abundance* (1910, Gemeentemuseum, The Hague).

Guro (1877–1913), he developed the idea of organic art, which regarded the world—both inanimate and animate—as a single whole.

Dated March 10, 1913, Matiushin's essay was the first serious attempt to acquaint Russian readers with Gleizes and Metzinger's *Du Cubisme.* In his translation, Matiushin assembles fragments of *Du Cubisme* and Petr Ouspensky's *Tertium Organum* (1911) and *Fourth Dimension* (1909), along with quotations from Charles Howard Hinton (as cited by Ouspensky). He takes liberties with the order of the sentences and paragraphs in the fragments that he cites, and he introduces a reference to "unknown dimensions" (*plan* in the French text), and gives the notion *réel* a vague but all the more significant metaphysical meaning, translating the word as "the uniquely existing" *(edinoe sushchestvennoe).* Thus Matiushin in fact creates a text of his own.

Matiushin's text was originally published in *Soiuz molodezhi* (Union of Youth) 3 (1913); the translation reprinted here is from Linda Dalrymple Henderson, *The Fourth Dimension and Non-Euclidean Geometry in Modern Art* (Princeton: Princeton University Press, 1983), pp. 368–75. For a detailed account of Matiushin's creation of his text, see Henderson, pp. 265–69.

Despite its extreme youth, Cubism has given birth to a mass of definitions, investigations, a multitude of arguments, perplexities; it has summoned against itself extreme hatred as well as great admiration. But in essence no one yet has presented such important words about the process of world perception and the evolution of the human soul. Whereas, following the revelation of the universal human soul—blazing up with a wonderful fire of divinely creative thought now here and now there—we sense the advancing regal moment of the passage of our consciousness into a new phase of dimension, out of three-dimensional into four-dimensional. Artists have always been knights, poets, and prophets of space in all eras. Sacrificing to everyone, perishing, they opened eyes and taught the crowd to see the great beauty of the world which was hidden from it. Likewise, Cubism has raised the banner of the New Measure—of the new doctrine of the merging of time and space.

Before beginning with the account of some chapters of the excellent book of Metzinger and Gleizes, *Du Cubisme,* which explains with extraordinary objectivity and great force of youthful consciousness the principles and theory of the new creative work—I permit myself to turn in the form of a premise to some pages of the interesting book *Tertium Organum* of P. D. Ouspensky, which confirms in the highest measure many theses concerning the new phase of art, Cubism, and the attributes of the fourth dimension:

TERTIUM ORGANUM

In art we have already the first experiences of the *language of the future.* Art advances in the vanguard of psychic evolution. We still do not have a clear idea as to which forms the development of human abilities will follow. But we can say already that the forms of consciousness and the means of their expression evolve *continuously* and that, apart from the forms which we know, new ones must arise.

The common law of evolution tells us that if something has primary forms, then it must have higher ones. Consequently, if sensation is something primary in relation to perception—perception is something primary in relation to idea, then this means that there must exist or, with time, there must arise something which is higher in relation to concept or idea.

At the moment we have three units of psychic life: *sensation, perception, conception* (and idea), and a fourth unit is beginning to arise—higher *Intuition.*

Passing to the account of the book of Metzinger and Gleizes, we find that the word Cubism, as the conception of volume evoked by this word, cannot in itself define a movement that aspires to the integral realization of painting, and is in common use only in the sense of a definition for the reader of the book's contents. The evolution of painting from Gustave Courbet up to this so-called Cubism is very clearly and simply stated:

DU CUBISME

Courbet inaugurated the realistic aspiration towards which all contemporary efforts are directed. But he and his followers remained slaves to the very worst visual conventions, accepting without the control of intellect all that which was perceived by their retina. They did not even suspect that the whole visible world becomes real only with some operation of creative reason, and that objects, striking us by their force, do not always contain rich plastic truths (revelations). Courbet was the one who contemplates the ocean for the first time and, diverted by the play of the waves, thinks not of its depths.

Edouard Manet advanced further—scorned the way of composition and diminished the importance of anecdote, painting "no matter what."

We see in him our predecessor. We for whom beauty is in the work itself and not in a pretext.

For us Manet is a realist, not because he represented everyday life, but because he gave a radiant reality to some hidden possibilities imprisoned in the most ordinary objects.

After Manet the realistic movement divided into superficial realism: The Impressionists—Monet, Sisley, etc., and Profound realism—Cézanne.

The art of the Impressionists bears in itself one contradiction: by diversity of color it tries to create life, but it produces lifeless and hollow drawing. A dress shimmers, marvelous, but forms disappear, atrophied.

Here, even more than in Courbet, the retina predominates over the brain, but Impressionism is not a false direction. The only mistake possible in art is imitation, which encroaches on the law of time, which is Law.

The great realist Cézanne is accused of awkwardness and naiveté but he despised the superficial appearance of objects, penetrating to their unitary essence.

This unitary essence is in fact that area of the new consciousness where the ideas of Cubism come closely into contact with the ideas of the fourth dimension.

TERTIUM ORGANUM

We see in objects, apart from the external, something internal; we know that this internal constitutes an indissoluble part of objects and is their principal essence. On asking ourselves where this essence is located and what it represents, we can see that it does not lie within our spatiality. In this way, we form the idea of a higher spatiality, one that has a greater number of dimensions than ours.

DU CUBISME

If Cézanne did not attain those regions where profound realism imperceptibly becomes luminous spiritualism, then he left to us, who also seek this goal, a simple and wonderful method. He who understands Cézanne is close to Cubism. One may say that the difference between Cubism and previous manifestations is only one of intensity: it is sufficient to regard attentively the process of the passage of realism, moving away from the superficial realities of Courbet's realism and with Cézanne into profound essence, and overtaking the luminous unknowable, which has retreated. He teaches us to dominate the universal dynamism. He reveals to us the modifications which arise from the interaction among objects considered inanimate. From him we learn that to change or to intensify the color of a body is to violate its structure. He prophesies that the study of primordial volumes will open up infinite horizons. His work, a homogeneous block, stirs under our glance; it contracts, extends, melts, and flares up, proving beyond all doubt that painting is not—or is no longer—the art of portraying objects by means of lines and color, but must involve the revealing of the plastic consciousness of our instinct.

Ouspensky's position, as quoted below, perhaps best clarifies the significance of the work of such great artists as Cézanne and that evolution of understanding which he and others like him introduced into the world:

TERTIUM ORGANUM

At the present stage of our development we possess nothing so powerful, as an instrument of knowledge of the world of causes, as art.

The artist must be a *clairvoyant:* he must see that which others do not see; he must be a magician: must possess the power to make others see that which they do not themselves see, but which he does see.

To return to the account of the ideas of Metzinger and Gleizes, we come across a highly characteristic definition of the present moment in painting:

Many consider that decorative aspirations must direct the spirit of the new painters. They do not realize that decorative work is the exact antithesis of the picture in general. It exists only by virtue of its destination; it is animated only by the relations established between it and the given objects. Essentially dependent, necessarily a detail, it must in the first place satisfy the mind so that the mind does not become distracted in completing it. *It is an Organ.*

A painting carries within itself its *raison d'être.* You may take it with impunity from a church to a drawing room, from a museum to a study. Essentially independent, necessarily complete, it need not immediately satisfy the mind: on the contrary, it should lead it, little by little, toward imaginative depths where burns the primary light. It does not harmonize with that or another ensemble, but harmonizes with the totality of things, with the universe. *It is an Organism.*

Today oil painting allows us to express all the previously inexpressible signs of *depth, density,* and *duration,* and permits a veritable *fusion,* a *blending* of things, to be expressed with a corresponding rhythm within a very restricted space.

Dissociating, for convenience, things that we know to be an indissoluble whole, we study, by means of form and color, the integration of the plastic consciousness. The ability to discern a form implies, besides the ability to see and to move, a certain development of the mind.

For the majority, the external visible world has no form.

The artist, having discerned a form, which presents a certain intensity of analogy with his preexisting idea, prefers it to other forms, and gives it a symbol that is likely to affect others. If he succeeds in this, he forces the crowd to relate to his plastic consciousness exactly as he recognized it before nature. But while the artist, preoccupied with creation, rejects the natural image that has served him, the crowd remains the slave of the painted image and long continues to regard nature and the universe through the accepted sign. This is why every new form seems monstrous, and why there is such admiration for the most servile copies and repetitions.

Let the artist deepen his creative work and not repeat it. Let the forms which he discerns and the symbols in which he incorporates their quality be sufficiently remote from the commonplace so that their truth will not take on an ordinary character.

The painter has the power of rendering enormous that which we regard as minuscule, and as insignificant that which we know is important: he changes quantity to quality. This is understood by the Cubist painters, who tirelessly study pictorial form and the space that it engenders. This space we are accustomed to confuse negligently with visual space or Euclidean space.

If we wished to tie the painter's space to a particular geometry, we should have to refer not to the scientists of the Euclidean school; rather, we should have to consider seriously certain of Riemann's theorems.

TERTIUM ORGANUM

The noted mathematician Riemann understood that when higher dimensions of space are in question, time, by some means, translates itself into space, and he recognized the material atom as the entrance of the fourth dimension into three-dimensional space.

Everything lies for us in time and only the *section of the thing* lies in space. Transferring our consciousness from the section of the thing to those parts of it which lie in time, we receive the illusion of motion on the part of the *"thing itself."*

DU CUBISME

As far as visual space is concerned, we know, as the Cubists say, that it results from the sensation of accommodation and the convergence of lines in space.

For the picture, a flat surface, the accommodation is negative. The convergence of straight lines that perspective forces us to postulate cannot evoke the idea of depth. Moreover, we know that the most serious infraction of perspective does not compromise in any way the spatiality of a painting. Chinese painters evoke space in spite of the fact that they are strongly convinced of the idea of the divergence of lines.

To establish pictorial space, we must have recourse to the sensation of movement and of touch and to all our faculties. It is our whole personality which, contracting and expanding, modifies the picture. The basic forms appear with a dynamism that we must overcome.

The American scholar Hinton, whose thoughts on the fourth dimension are so full of significance and surprisingly coincide with the most extreme ideas of the innovator of painting, speaks as follows:

TERTIUM ORGANUM [AND *THE FOURTH DIMENSION*]

It is important to develop the space sense, for it is the means by which we think about real things.

The space sense, or the intuition of space, is the most fundamental power of the mind. But I do not find anywhere a systematic and thoroughgoing education of the space sense. We usually see objects as either above or below us, or on the same level with us, to the right or to the left, behind us or in front of us, and always from one side only—the one facing us—and in perspective. Our eye is an extremely imperfect instrument; it gives us an utterly incorrect picture of the world. What we call perspective is in reality a distortion of visible objects which is produced by a badly constructed optical instrument—the eye. We see all objects distorted. And we visualize them in the same way. But we visualize them in this way entirely owing to the habit of seeing them distorted, that is, owing to the habit created by our defective vision, which has weakened the capacity of visualization. But, according to Hinton, there is no necessity to *visualize* objects of the external world in a distorted form. The power of visualization is not limited by the power of vision. We see objects distorted, but we know them as they are. And we can free ourselves from the habit of visualizing objects as we see them, and we can learn to visualize them as we know they really are. Hinton's idea is precisely that before thinking of developing the capacity of seeing in the fourth dimension, we must learn to *visualize* objects *as they would be seen from the fourth dimension,* i.e., first of all, not in perspective, but from all sides at once, as they are known to our consciousness. It is just this power that should be developed by Hinton's exercises. The development of this power to visualize objects from all sides at once will be the casting out of the self-elements in mental images.

According to Hinton, casting out the self-elements in mental images must lead to casting out the self-elements in perceptions. In this way, the development of the power of visualizing objects from all sides will be the first step toward the development of the power of seeing objects as they are in geometrical sense, i.e., the development of what Hinton calls a *higher consciousness.*

[Matiushin here quotes at length passages from *Du Cubisme* in an arbitrary sequence.]

50

Aleksandr Shevchenko

The Principles of Cubism and Other Currents in Painting from All Ages and Nations (1913)

Aleksandr Shevchenko (1883–1948) studied painting first in Moscow and then, in 1905–6, at the Académie Julian in Paris. He participated in the "Donkey's Tail" (1912), "Target" (1913), and "No. 4" (1914) exhibitions. Although he was close to Larionov, his style gravitated mainly toward Cézanne. In this book (published in Moscow), Shevchenko applied vocabulary taken from Russian Cubists to the history of world art.

. . . All principles and theories of all currents of contemporary painting, up to and including Cubism and Futurism, have their origins deep in the ancient past. Thus contemporary currents are not something wild and unbridled; they are not, as some critics would have it, the product of a degenerate age, an age of decline; on the contrary, in everything going on in painting just now we see a new surge—a new renaissance for the higher sensibilities that awaken life, provide new forces, and open new roads to art. . . .

Above all, Cubism allows us to see and present objects in as much relief as possible and to facet them. This both simplifies their form and brings it out more fully, since when something is faceted—that is, when curved surfaces are laid out on a flat plane—all of the insignificant planes and details on the curve fall away; manifested most fully in this manner is not only the relief as form but its essence as well. We can move the planes around and see the object from several sides at once without circling it. This expresses its nature more completely, since each object has not one but several forms depending on its position. For example, a face that is round when viewed *en face* tends in profile to resemble a triangle or pyramid; in other words, Cubism permits objects to be viewed and presented from different points of view simultaneously. Furthermore, it enables us to turn a plane and effect shifts, allowing us to envisage objects not in a single form chained to a plane but in the constant, living, real form that existed at the moment of their re-creation. We see objects in motion. These same shifts and displacements of planes justify violating the tenets of linear perspective as a science in order to liberate painting from its constant yoke; they do not expel perspective completely, however, but only subordinate it to art by introducing not one but several horizons or points of linear coincidence to achieve a more beautiful and free construction of the whole composition. But that is not all. Cubism permits planes to be shifted not only by turning them but also by displacing them completely, putting them closer or farther away as needed; that is, we can represent objects not on the actual scale but on an arbitrary one chosen once again to suit not mathematical perspective but the demands of the given instance.

This refers only to form.

But we also have color. . . .

In Egyptian art, for example, we encounter the human torso shown *en face,* while the breast (particularly clearly in the case of female figures), head, and legs are always shown in profile.

Is this not a manifestation of Cubist principles? Is this not a shift? . . .

And the representation of kings on a large scale and ordinary mortals on a small scale—is this only to show worship?

No, undoubtedly this shows not only reverence for the king but also a sophisticated understanding of the pictorial plane and of composition. . . .

. . . All of the examples above run throughout the art of all ages. The only difference is that sometimes these principles appear clearly in all their primordial charm, whereas at other times they are skillfully masked; but no matter what, they are always there.

51

Nikolai Kulbin

"Cubism" (1915)

Nikolai Kulbin (1868–1917) was an amateur artist and *privatdozent* at the Academy of Military Medicine. In 1908 he founded the Triangle group and organized the "Exhibition of Contemporary Trends in Art," the first avant-garde exhibition in Petersburg. Kulbin's article is based on a number of his public lectures and includes long quotations from *Du Cubisme,* omitted here. It appeared in *Strelets* (Archer) 1 (1915).

For a definition of Cubism, let us turn to the trend's apostles, Gleizes and Metzinger. Both are genuine Cubists, *pur sang*. Both are competent artists who enjoy a good reputation in our ally France. Where Cubism became a passionate heresy. They say:

> The notion of volume evoked by the word "Cubism" does not define the corresponding movement in painting in its entirety. This movement (called Cubism) achieves the integral realization *(réalisation integrale)* of painting. The Cubists aspire to express all of infinite art within the bounds of the picture.

For the time being let us content ourselves with this self-definition of Cubism and its goals. . . .

Where did Cubism come from? China. All sorts of painting come from there.* Cubism was there, both in ancient times and now—mainly in sculpture—to which it is more closely related than it is to painting. The notion of Cubism is connected above all with form, and form is the essence of culture. True, the Cubists also advanced a theory of color recently, but color (the essence of painting) has not yet flourished in their works. In Europe there is Cubist painting; there is almost no Cubist sculpture (Duchamp-Villon does not count, and Arkhipenko began Cubist sculpture but is now going over to Futurism).

The founders of Cubism were Cézanne in France and Vrubel' in Russia. The Cubists trace their genealogy to Courbet and also acknowledge a certain connection between Cubism and the principles of Impressionism. This genealogy provided by Gleizes and Metzinger is inaccurate and incomplete. Courbet is related to Cubism as he is to all other realistic tendencies in painting.

There was no real Cubism at all in Courbet. If we acknowledge a link between his works and Cubism, then we are no less justified in acknowledging all other realistic painters, beginning with ancient times, as its progenitors. We are somewhat more justified in finding the embryo of Cubist ideas in the Impressionists, who violated the tradition of verisimilar naturalism.

The Japanese dulcified the harsh painting of China and passed it on in this delicate form to Paris in the mid-nineteenth century. This is how Impressionism came to pass. As Impressionism was being sown in the earth, some seeds of Cubism also fell, like weeds in a wheatfield. Manet and Degas were already good at form understood in the new way. Their works adumbrate the later achievements of Cézanne and Vrubel'.

For convenience, we can divide the history of Cubism artificially into two periods: the first, to 1908, when the Cubists appeared as a group for the first time and the word "Cubism" was invented; and the second, from 1908 to the present.

In the first, preparatory period, so to speak, the focus was almost exclusively on volume and form in general. At that time Cubism was defined by its aspiration to create simplified, geometrical, primary forms, so to speak.

*"And all sorts of wisdom" (Kulbin's note).

. . . Cubists manifested geometrism so vigorously in their works that the phenomenon seemed unprecedented, new, frightening, and illegitimate to viewers. The word "geometrism" does not cover the notions of volume expressed by the Cubists, however. Contrary to geometry, these ideas were aesthetic. The Cubists created volumetric properties—new conceptions. Their works contain artistic combinations of lines and surfaces—a painterly construction. . . .

Composition triumphs so completely in the works of Cézanne and his followers that anatomy, photographic similarity, and so forth are gladly sacrificed to it.

Moreover, these works raised the question of construction. They presented what was subsequently called "shifted construction." It was Cézanne who first resolutely produced the "shift," which was expressed not only in a change in the former "correct" construction but in various other paradoxes as well. The apparent incongruities in their pictures began to irritate the viewer's artistic imagination. . . .

In Russia, Vrubel' was working simultaneously with but independently of Cézanne. Vrubel' 's Cubism was first expressed openly in his studies for *The Demon,* the final pictures of which were a miserable failure.* Cubism appeared with the same brilliance in other works of his as well. Vrubel' 's painting brings out both the painterly surface and the role and interrelationship of straight and curved lines. Together with the harmonious crystallization of form we also see a complex harmony pouring forth in slaglike excrescences. . . .

The second period of Cubism aspired to broaden painting's framework through a new theory of color and a resolute desire to create new painterly properties not found in nature.

Since 1907 I have repeatedly spoken of the painter's right not to be limited to conveying the color and form of objects.†

Painters can represent anything in their works that stimulates their painting, including motion, sounds, and smells. This right has been recognized in recent years by the Futurists and Cubists and has generally become self-evident, so I shall not examine the matter in any detail here.

To what has already been said above on the Cubists' opinions, I shall add the rest of their statements.

Painting should not be decorative. The picture is self-sufficient and contains its own *raison d'être.* It can be carried with impunity from a church to a salon, a museum to a private home.

Inherently autonomous and whole, painting does not satisfy the intellect immediately or all at once. On the contrary, we are lured little by little into its fictitious depths. It conforms not to any particular ensemble but to all objects at once, to the universe: it is an organism.

*In the 1890s and 1900s Vrubel' produced a number of paintings based on Mikhail Lermontov's long poem *The Demon* (1837–39).

†An example of fictitious chronology, characteristic for Russian avant-gardists. Kulbin published his first essay on modern aesthetics in 1910.

The cognition of art lags behind its creative potential. The painter produces a symbol that expresses the correlation between a phenomenon's appearance and the aspiration of his mind, a symbol capable of expressing the property of form and moving the viewer's imagination. . . .

The Cubists strive for "plastic integration."

Simplification plays a very large role in their method (as in all contemporary painting).

They declare that painting is infinitely free and acknowledge the laws of taste as the only obligatory laws. However, they do not acknowledge the existence of good and bad taste. Taste is only developed or undeveloped.

In conclusion, they appeal to beauty, finding in it justification and support for their activity.

The feats of the latest art have filled viewers with a peculiar terror. They are prepared to recognize the necessity of new artistic devices, and the leading new artists have become rather widely known. Especially famous just now is Picasso. Viewers like his harlequins, Pierrots, drunks, and his "youthful works" in general. All of the Cubists' recent works fill the public with horror mixed with a keen curiosity; not wishing to appear backward, however, many conceal their feelings. . . .

Might those who shun Cubism be right? Of course not! There is joyful, bright art behind the mask of a harlequin cracking amusing and sometimes intimidating jokes to the jingling of bells and the exclamations of charlatans pulling their wagons loaded with the only true recipes for painting. Soon the screens of gloomy and clumsy yet precious idols smeared in a sallow ochre with greenish-gray and other temporary colors will be removed to the museums. People will recall Gauguin and his purist school, and soon the quintessence of painting—color—will shine forth once again. The Cubists' fascination with form has not been fruitless. They discovered new plastic qualities and improved painting technique. They even did something useful for color. They have a new theory of color whose implementation is still in the embryonic phase. Like all new theories, it will of necessity have to be supplemented gradually, at first only by a small number of colors, which to some degree explains the paucity of colors in the works of Picasso and most Cubists.

Cubism is essentially heading gradually into oblivion. The even more vociferous Futurism has come to take its place. The cards of Futurism and Cubism have already been shuffled in the latest feats of Picasso and his brethren. . . .

In our great age, when official physics has abolished absolute time and space,

When a new life is being built in new and higher dimensions,

The harlequins' heads are overfilled and dizzy with good cheer.

Experiments, one more motley than the next, stage sets, one scrappier than the next.

What remains of this idle bustle?

Each "ism" brings something beneficial to the technique of art.

Let everything be real.

To music—sound. To sculpture—form in the narrow sense.

To literature—the power of naming.

In the new synthesis of art, we know how to tell the wheat from the chaff.

Painterly painting—this is the painter's watchword.

Everything else is freedom.

52

Kazimir Malevich

"On New Systems in Art: Statics and Speed" (1919)

This brochure was written in the summer of 1919 (dated July 15), when Malevich was working on the "White on White" series of pictures. Compared with his 1915–16 texts, his strategy here has changed considerably. Now he underscores the evolutionary nature of modern art, singling out Cézanne, who is not even mentioned in the 1915–16 brochures, and defending Cubism against its Marxist critics.

"On New Systems in Art" was published as a lithograph in Vitebsk. The brochure included lithograph illustrations by the author, and the cover was designed by El Lissitzky. A significant portion of the text appeared in Malevich's *From Cézanne to Suprematism* (Petrograd, 1920). The translation by Christiana Bryan is reprinted from *Malevich on Suprematism: Six Essays, 1915–1926,* edited by Patricia Railing and Stephen Prokopoff (Iowa City: University of Iowa Museum of Art, 1999), pp. 47–81.

. . . Cubism and futurism were revolutionary movements in art, anticipating the revolution in economic and political life of 1917. . . .

Cézanne may be said to represent the combination of the treatment of the world according to the image and likeness of the world of classical attitudes and problems. With him ends the art that kept our will on the leash of objective, imitative art while we dragged ourselves along behind the creative forms of life. . . .

Cézanne also gave impetus to a new textural painterly surface as such, bringing painterly texture out of its impressionist state. By means of form, he gave the sensation of form moving towards contrast, as can be observed in Cézanne's work, where all straight horizontals strike a vertical line or a painterly plane near its center, and all the bent curved ones are grouped in contrast to the plane or volume, and the volume itself contrasts with the plane. These were especially important for the future development of cubism but were not immediately seized on by the cubists as something essential for development. Intuitively, in the depths of their consciousness, the cubists perceived this scheme of contrasts but could only realize it as an academic and seemingly rational undertaking, rendering the object in question exhaustively. As if leaving Cézanne aside, they began to deal with the object from all its aspects. They argued that, hitherto, artists had been conveying the object from only three sides using three-dimensional measurement when, as we know, an object has six, five, ten aspects, and to convey it more fully, as it is in reality, it is essential to portray all its sides. . . . It turned out that the power lay not in conveying the completeness of the thing but, on the contrary, in its breaking up and dissolution into component elements that were essential as painterly contrasts. The thing was regarded from the intuitive aspect as a collection of contrasts between painting and the graphic lines which were necessary as material for the building of a new painterly construction but not of a narrowly utilitarian or technical one. And therefore, in the first stage of cubism's development, the object was reduced to an abstraction, to the geometrical simplicity of volumes, and the model's face was drawn both frontally and in profile, as contrasting juxtapositions of different aspects of the descriptive form.

First having freed the object in its logical interpretation as displacement, the cubists (the second stage) said that if the artist were unable to find enough essential painterly, textural, graphic, volumetrical, linear, and other forms in the given object for his construction, then he would be free to take these from elsewhere, bringing together these essential elements until his composition achieved the necessary tension of harmonious and dynamic conditions. In view of these solutions, cubism's first undertaking regarding the complete handling of the object was abandoned in favor of a new logical solution: that the revelation of the object in space at various moments of time is simply aimed at constructing on the plane a variety of units into a new asymmetric cubist unity. . . .

Before cubism, the object was found interesting both as such and as the painterly expression of a definite textural content and color saturation. No way was known to convey painterly content other than by the complete rendering of the form of an object. This represented a pure, direct expression of painting. The object played the same supportive role for the impressionists in the resolution of their operations with light. The need to transfer objectivity onto the painterly canvas stems from the fact that the painter has no basis and lacks the initiative to build a purely painterly organism.

Despite his immense feeling for the painterly in an object, Cézanne made only small displacements of forms. He could not produce a purely painterly construction, despite his striving towards the cone, cube, and sphere, which he indicated as figures organizing painterly constructions.

His self-portrait (in the S. I. Shchukin collection in Moscow)* is his best painterly work. He did not so much see the face of the portrait as invest in its forms something painterly that he felt rather than saw. Whoever feels painting sees the object to a lesser degree. And whoever sees the object feels less what is painterly.

The main axis of cubist construction was the straight and curved line. The first category called forth other lines, forming angles, and from the second came reversed curves. On these axes were grouped different types of painterly texture: lacquered, granular, and matte. Collages were used for textural and graphic variety, plaster was introduced, and the bodily texture was always constructed in such a way as to achieve cubist textural and formal rhythm and constructive unity among the elements of painterly and graphic forms.

*Cézanne, *Self-Portrait* (circa 1885, R. 445, GMII).

It was the cubists who first began to consciously see, know, and build their constructions on the foundations of the general unity of nature. . . .

The cubists had no reason to deal with the object and to drag it onto the canvas with whatever pictorial content happened to be in it. The person who made the objects did not think of using them for painterly expression but, rather, thought about their technical purpose and the conquest of space by means of form: capturing contemporary culture is represented in the object. Similarly, the artist should think about what is painterly but not about the technical and should build up a painterly system as a living body.

Cubist construction strives for economy by rejecting the repetition of identical forms. Repetition in form and texture weakens the tension of the construction. By simplicity of expression, by the geometricality of volumes, planes, straight and curved lines, it is economical without indulging in the superficial combinations found in the academic nature of its treatment. . . .

Cubism is not, as the socialists think, bourgeois decadence. Cubism is a tool that breaks up the existing sums of the solutions and the bondage of the creative aspect of previous movements in painting. It marks the artist's emancipation from slavish imitation of the object and the beginning of his search for the direct discovery of creativity.

Cubism has emancipated the branches of painting, and painting has begun to grow according to the artist's will. Just as nature decomposes a corpse into its elements, so cubism breaks up the old assumptions about painting and builds new ones according to its own system. Nature acts in this way, excluding and dissolving its previous culture, coming to new solutions and producing a new sum of culture. . . . The new cubist body that has been built up is not opposed to life. It is a new solution, drawn from the previous ones, formed a painterly movement, and has nothing national, geographic, patriotic or narrowly popular about it.

. . . Society has never considered painting as such. It has regarded works from the point of view of likeness, skill, and decorative colors, with the thematic material taking pride of place. Only a few artists regarded painting as an end in itself. These artists see neither houses, mountains, sky, nor rivers as such. For them, they are painterly surfaces and therefore it is unimportant that there be a resemblance, that the water or plastered wall of a house be expressed, or that the painterly surface of the sky be painted above the roof of the house or from the side. All they see is painting growing on surfaces, which they transplant onto the canvas in a new harmonious system. . . .

In the art of painting there are two basic features: heaviness and lightness. Cézanne may be related to heavy-weighted growth,* Van Gogh to light growth. Cézanne's

*Cf. the opinion of Malevich's pupil Lev Iudin (1903–41): "Malevich approached Cézanne constructively. The main thing with him was weight, which caused us to make many mistakes. Much was sacrificed for the sake of weight" (quoted in I. N. Karasik, "Malevich v suzhdeniiakh sovremennikov," in *Kazimir Malevich. Khudozhnik i teoretik* [Moscow, 1990], p. 196).

weight is a slowing movement. Van Gogh also possesses heaviness but now without slowness and he is accordingly better equipped for extensive growth in space. The more strongly and firmly the artist wishes to build his body, the more the texture and forms will be saturated with the weight and monumentality of its construction.

Heaviness, statics, duration: these are what cubism is breaking up. Cubism develops movement in static inertia. But since it is by its very nature based on statics, its system is limited by a certain boundary beyond which cubism cannot develop its movement, since the boundaries are determined by the basis of the construction and the harmony of contrasts.

If cubism is based on the texture of painting, futurism has got rid of this dependence. Its texture is no longer painterly but dynamic. And aesthetic action, joining the proportions and tonalities of spots of paint, goes overboard, for dynamic dependence serves as the force that links them. If in a bustling town, people and things circulate like black, white, red, blue, and yellow spots, then they are united by movement, not by mutual color relationships. The very movement of the town, its millions of forms of human creation, is an attempt to unravel the tangled mass of human movement into one broad path that is both straight and clear. Futurism, with its various expressions, is in the center of movement and conveys speed in a concentrated form, crossing into the highest dynamic stage.

The attitude of futurism to objects, machines, to a world of exclusively urban creations, was the same as that of Monet to Rouen cathedral in the painterly sense. For futurism, objects and machines did not exist as such, but were the means or symbols for expressing speed and dynamics. The cubists, Academists, and the entire world of art before futurism regarded the object as the content of painting, but the futurists regarded mechanization as dynamic content. Going beyond the limits of the entire objective expression of the new iron world, futurism is the final stage of the objective expression of movement, having produced new systems for the building of this. . . .

Futurism has not yet developed its systems. It still contains a great deal that can be developed further but our consciousness makes incredible progress and develops new signs along the path towards the conquest of the infinite. It is also possible that the new suprematist solution will lead us to new systems going beyond the confusion of objectivity to a purely energic force of movement.

World energy is moving towards economy, and every step it takes towards the infinite is expressed in the new economic culture of signs. A revolution is simply a solution to new economic energy, rocked by world intuition. Revolution never occurs without special pretexts and that is why reason produces all sorts of proposals for which it would not mind doing a bit of work since nobody will come forward for the purpose of simple movement into infinity. Revolution always stands on the disintegration of all the economic conclusions of the past. Art goes on uninterruptedly since the same energy lives in it, with the same infinite aim. . . .

53

Nikolai Punin

"Escapes from Cubism" (1923)

Nikolai Punin (1888–1953) began publishing in *Apollon* (Apollo) in 1913 and soon became the first professional critic to support the avant-garde. As a member of the Narkompros IZO Department—the visual arts section of the People's Commissariat of Enlightenment—Punin held a number of administrative positions from 1918 to 1921 and then worked at the GINKhUK (State Institute of Artistic Culture) and the Russian Museum, where he established the Department of Most Recent Trends. He was arrested three times and finally died in the GULAG. This article, written in 1923, was first published in Nikolai Punin, *O Tatline* (On Tatlin), compiled by I. N. Punina and V. I. Rakitin (Moscow: RA Publishers, 1994), pp. 42–52.

I. FEATURES OF CUBISM

By "Cubism" I mean not only a "trend in art" but also a cultural phenomenon. Sooner or later all crafts may even pass through a latent "Cubism"—probably not only painting but also the other arts. The sciences are probably passing through it now, the basis of this process being our consciousness or "inner life." As a cultural phenomenon, Cubism is defined in the broad sense by a single overall feature, namely, a new sense of time. Up until our day, time was perceived as an unbroken continuum. . . .

There is another feature that covers a smaller number of phenomena but is typical of Cubism: "professionalism." Whenever work, no matter what kind, becomes so important in and of itself that the professional relationship to it eclipses everything else, then we are without question dealing with at least latent Cubism, that is, with a phenomenon that in pure Cubism was raised to a principle, on the one hand, and is latent in all ages and cultures, on the other. . . .

More often than not, students of Cubist painting define it as painting that analyzes (deforms) the object, or as nonrepresentational painting. This is correct, but deformation and abstraction are secondary rather than fundamental features of Cubism and are typical only of painting and not of Cubism as a cultural phenomenon. Deformation in painting results from a temporal shift (the new sense of time), whereas abstraction is a consequence of a profound professionalism whose aspiration to reveal and form the pure element of painting would only be hindered by an object.

A more independent third feature of Cubism both as painting and as a cultural phenomenon is something negative, namely, the absence of utilitarianism—its lack of purpose or utility. Because and only because of this feature, we think of Cubism as a transitional phenomenon. A segment of culture whose entire significance amounts to the rupture of forms, or at least the rupture of their outlines, cannot last. In Cubism we see and value humanity's heroic efforts to break through to new worlds; in and of itself, however, Cubism is not this process, but merely the blast furnace where elements of style and form with a new utilitarian meaning are smelted. . . .

. . . Picasso's entire oeuvre can be regarded as a struggle with Cubism. I consider Cézanne's influence on him to be relatively slight, and for that reason Cubism for Picasso is not an organic painterly worldview, as it is for Braque. Cubism does not grow out of Picasso like a tree but is merely a method. Jean Pougny [Ivan Puni] once made a remarkably apt comment on a work by Picasso: "he's integrated the object but hasn't integrated himself."* In none of Picasso's works do we find the whole of him together. None of his canvases and panels seem to be made by his hand; instead, he has emerged from them as would a snake, by molting. Picasso himself is elusive; nowhere is he completely identical to his works. I see inadequate creative synthesis here, but at the same time it is a strength, for he never elevates the method to a system. Cubism was never a goal in itself for him; rationalism has never dominated his consciousness, and reason has never taken over his spirit. All of "Picasso's Cubism" is therefore at the same time an escape from Cubism.

External evidence of this relationship between Picasso and Cubism can be seen in his constant returns to figurative art, which have become more intense of late. Uneducated people follow the German Grautoff† and speak of the "Ingres traditions" in Picasso's art. In a great many figurative works of his most recent period I detect no "Ingres" whatsoever. Picasso represents and includes in each new form the experience of his preceding analytical Cubist works; thus he runs, as it were, on alternating current—analysis and synthesis—combining what he has divided and dividing what he has combined. The realism of painting itself being at issue here, do we have the grounds to categorize art into representational and nonobjective? After all, both the object and its distorted form are nothing more than "occasions" for painting, because painting, Puni writes, is by and large the development and expression of rhythm, similar to music; deformation and the constructed object are equivalent, but when juxtaposed, they contrast, as "occasions." This apt observation, however, does not apply to Picasso, because he was not under pressure from Cézanne. Only he who perceives any system of painting merely as a method can segment painting, if only on the inadequate and indirect basis of the "occasion" (in Puni's sense). In Picasso's terminology, there can be "synthetic representational painting and analytical abstract painting." His entire significance lies precisely in the fact that he is outside the "natural element of painting," that in Cézanne's sense he is not a painter. Again in Cézanne's sense, for him painting does not mean drawing.

. . . All of humanity's age-old, agonizing need for art derives neither from the contemplative inclinations of a certain segment of viewers nor from educational motives but from something far more real and vital: the need to shape feelings and thoughts

*Cf. letter of Ivan Puni to Nikolai Punin, 1922, Berlin (N. Punin, *Mir svetel liubov'iu. Dnevniki. Pis'ma.* [Moscow: Artist, Rezhisser, Teatr, 2000], p. 151). Cf. Ivan Puni, *Sovremennaia zhivopis'* (Berlin, 1923), p. 29.

†Otto Grautoff, *Französische Malerei seit 1914* (Berlin, 1921), pp. 44–46. Cf. the Russian edition (Moscow, 1923), pp. 50–51.

and give them form as they arise out of elemental chaos. Old European art always served this need. The content of its age-old utilitarian form—representation—was what we now call the *consciousness-shaping force.*

Picasso's escape is traditional because it preserves form's old European utilitarian content. Whatever painterly riches Picasso may possess (thanks to Cubism), his synthetic representational art has no more utility of form than what was produced by the Renaissance tradition. Even if it has a new sign (thanks to Cubism), the image of concreteness that has been restored to painting through Picasso does not have a new utilitarian significance; as before, it serves as a support for humanity's quest to shape consciousness through art. Was it worth going through Cubism for that? For French art the question may even be fatal. . . .

V. TATLIN'S ESCAPE

. . . The singularity of Tatlin's Cubist constructions compared with those of French artists is that Tatlin sensed his materials not aesthetically and not as a painter but as a man who had to build something out of these materials. In his consciousness, Cubism was not an academic (abstract) experiment or a game in the tradition of a rich and mature culture but the work of a life beneath which there was practically no culture—the work of a builder destined to begin an age, not finish one. The part Picasso played with a clever irony, therefore, Tatlin took seriously, drawing conclusions that Picasso would probably have found, if not blasphemous, then barbaric and utterly unintelligible. Tatlin, however, was not mistaken; Russian artistic traditions—particularly icon painting—and the state of Russian artistic culture have not created the conditions necessary for transplanting a plant as slim and delicate as "French Cubism." . . .

Tatlin spontaneously skirted this very dangerous moment for the Russian artist, but the price was a reworking of French Cubism so complete that all that remained of it was a schema—merely the principle, like the immutable sign of our times. In his *Board No. 1,** essentially his only painting of a Cubist nature, only one structure is left—the only one without which Cubism is not Cubism at all: the work is built on a conjugation of planes or surfaces on the principle of construction; that is, movement within the work is not brought to a halt. Not only did everything else—variations on the cross-sections of the planes and playing on tones—not interest the artist, he rejected it, consistently and with considerable artistic tact.

The refusal to vary the cross-section of planes can also be defined as a struggle to strengthen the painterly surface. The essence of this struggle is as follows. Any phenomenon in painting is an event on a plane; the artist transfers the three-dimensional world, the world accessible to us in time, onto a plane where there is no real depth and no real time. The efforts of old European art to evoke depth by

**Board No. 1. Staro-Basmanaia* (panel, egg tempera, gesso, bronze, 1917, GTG).

means of perspective hindered the development of painting itself; the device was foreign and extraneous to painting. Equally unpainterly as a device was the Futurist shift whereby artists tried to bring time to life. French Cubism solved both these problems through the so-called system of coulisses and a painterly analysis of the object (where there was one). Its solution may have been in the spirit of painting, but the Cubist plane is overloaded with coulisses, and very often its sense of reality is destroyed by a juxtaposition of painterly elements that produces a new feeling of illusory, albeit painterly, depth. This does not discredit this understanding of the plane from the point of view of painting, but one cannot help noticing that it is traditional in Western European painting and runs counter to Russian art's icon traditions, which always carefully preserved the wooden panel as painting's material basis and avoided disturbing its two-dimensionality by even representing the sky. . . .

The same may be said of values—also not characteristic of Russian art, which advances and develops the technique of even and opaque coloration. Generalizing these two phenomena that typically distinguish French Cubism from its reworking in the traditions of Russian art, we can say that Russian art struggles against the dematerialization indigenous to Western European art and for the material basis of painting.

This struggle has not only helped transform French Cubism but also enabled Tatlin to escape it and embark upon a new path. This I define as not merely consciousness but the shaping of life, and, moreover, I detect two phenomena that accompany and are generated by this activity: the first is the new opportunity to broaden the circle of people for whom art is a need; and the second is the possibility of synthesizing the various art forms in the old European art: painting, architecture, the plastic arts, applied art, and so on.

Art seems to be recovering its "eternal" properties: unity and necessity.

54

Sillart

"Boccioni's Futurist Sculpture Exhibition" (1913)

After Tugendkhol'd's return to Moscow in 1913, *Apollon*'s most substantive Parisian correspondent was someone writing as "Sillart"; his real name remains unknown. Umberto Boccioni's one-man show opened on June 20, 1913, at the La Boêtie gallery in Paris. Its catalogue contained "A Technical Manifesto of Futurist Sculpture" (1912). Sillart's review appeared in *Apollon* (Apollo) 7 (1913).

. . . Boccioni's sculpture is ruthlessly theoretical. Dynamism, interpenetrating planes, the atmosphere, light . . . it's all there, the whole canon of Futurism down to the use of heterogeneous materials within a single work. Clay heads are bisected by wooden crosspieces; they support entire buildings and have eyes of glass and real hair (?); instead of cheeks you see bundles of light rays. Figures with titles like *Synthesis of Human Dynamism* and *Spiral Expansion of Muscles in Movement* resemble anatomical preparations with muscles minced into croquettes thrusting impulsively out from the body in a whirlwind of spirals.* There is a great deal of motion here, too much even, but the big question is whether it is plastic. Boccioni says that what to look for in his sculpture is not "a figure wrapped in its traditional line" but the figure as "the center of plastic movements in space," and he demands that the viewer "mentally construct its continuation (simultaneity) in space in order to perceive the form of these figures abstractly." Such abstraction may be suitable for constructing scientific diagrams, but a diagram is not a work of art. Boccioni's figures are precisely such diagrams. Sculptures such as *Force-Forms of a Bottle* or *Development of a Bottle in Space by Means of Form* (mediante il colore)† may interest a mathematician or a physicist, but I see nothing to do with sculpture in them. Boccioni wants to bring his viewers into the center of the sculpture and make them participants in his work. This is quite logical from the point of view of dynamism, but we have the right to ask whether the resources of the plastic arts suffice for such an operation. . . .

Last year the Futurists wrote in the foreword to the catalogue of an exhibition of their pictures‡ that their art was a reaction to Impressionism. This year, by contrast, Boccioni declares that the Futurists regard the Impressionists as their predecessors. There is indeed a significant link between them.

. . . the Futurists have transformed Claude Monet's external, static, and amorphous Impressionism into an Impressionism that is internal, dynamic, and synthetic. The impression's ephemerality is once again elevated to the basis of the work of art, but in a deeper, transcendental form. This is Impressionism at its highest, Impressionism taken to hallucination.

. . . Fragments of the concrete world are offered only as a concession to backward viewers in order to establish a bridge between them and the artist's refined perception. In principle, there is no place for material sensation in the work of art. The Futurist, the manifesto declares, is supposed to convey only the transcendental impression, its cerebral concentrate. But as the material world disappears, so—alas—does the basis for the plastic arts. The picture and the sculpture are transformed into a book of mysterious signs or table of hieroglyphs. This is the end result of the Futurists' aspiration to convey the unconveyable. In other words, *Futurism is destroying the plastic arts.*

**Synthesis of Human Dynamism* (1912); *Muscles in Movement* (1913). Neither sculpture has survived.

†*Force-Forms of a Bottle* (1913, destroyed); *Development of a Bottle in Space* (1913, Museum of Modern Art, New York).

‡"From the Exhibitors to the Public," foreword to the catalogue of the Futurist exhibition at the Bernheim-Jeune gallery, February 5–24, 1912.

55

Genrikh Tasteven

Futurism: Toward a New Symbolism (1914)

Genrikh Tasteven (1881–1915) came from a Moscow family of French extraction. He headed the editorial office of the *Golden Fleece*. In 1914 he organized Marinetti's trip to Russia. His book on Futurism was published in Moscow the same year.

THE AESTHETICS OF FUTURISM

In brief, the [Futurist] picture should be a synthesis of what you remember and what you see. Thus does Futurism supplement the theory of the Impressionists. Since psychic states cannot be portrayed on canvas, however, the Futurists are obliged to resort to conventional Symbolist techniques to present them.

This Symbolism is rather rational and naive. . . .

Another principle of Futurism is to put the viewer in the center of the picture. If Cubism rebelled against the vulgar focus on perspective by destroying the footlights between the picture and the spectator, Futurism wants to include the spectator in the picture itself, destroying the footlights between subject and object, so to speak. The Futurists seek this swallowing of the viewer by the picture not only in the sphere of visual sensations; they want viewers to be reincarnated into the picture, as it were, so that they feel they are within real space.

Such is the goal of Carrà's pictures *What the Tram Said to Me* and *Woman at a Window.** In this latter work the artist has attempted to depict not only real objects such as a street and window but also all the different associative images and visions flickering on the threshold of the unconscious. In the first place, however, even if such objectivized consciousness were possible, only a single moment of this constantly refreshed torrent of images, emotions, and moods could be grasped. The Futurists also forget that the viewer's personality is not a ready-made form that can be placed in these fixed experiences and that viewers will regard the picture as a foreign object. If Futurism did achieve its goal, Futurist pictures would become super-octopuses dragging viewers into them. After all, for viewers to fuse with a picture, all images fixed by association would have to coincide with those that arise in their consciousness. The task the Futurists have set themselves, therefore, is excessively rational and unrealizable. . . .

Despite the extremely rational and literary quality of their principles, the Futurists declare they are primitivists with a renewed sensitivity.

How little this forced primitivism resembles the genuine primitivism of Gauguin, which goes back to the eternal sources of creation, when art expressed the popular consciousness. Gauguin understood that in order to transform our art we have to

**What the Tram Said to Me* (1910–11, Städelsches Kunstinstitut, Frankfurt am Main); *Woman at a Window* (1912 private collection).

overcome culture within ourselves—overcome our little "I's"; the Futurists, on the other hand, want to reflect culture in its unenlightened aspect and quite simply hurl themselves into our Niagara of modernity. A certain artist once said that painting is expressive silence, but the Futurists probably define it as a deafening fanfare of colors. By and large, Futurism contains two tendencies: Symbolism in the literary (not painterly) sense; and an extremely superficial Impressionism. In time these two tendencies may produce something on the order of Futurist Neo-Wanderers. One need only look at pictures such as Boccioni's *The City Rises* and *Detour,* or Carrà's *Funeral of the Anarchist Galli,* or Russolo's *The Revolt,* where the subject clearly predominates over the painting, to realize that we are dealing here with the embryo of a *new Wanderers movement.** . . .

RELIGIOUS AND IDEALISTIC ELEMENTS IN FUTURISM

The contradictions of Futurist aesthetics, however, arise from contradictions in its overall cultural worldview. This worldview must be taken into account, since *Futurism is the first attempt at a new synthesis* since the failure of positivism. It would be highly unfair to see in it only nihilism and a summons to strip the soul. . . . One need only read the Futurist manifestoes to realize that hidden beneath these nihilistic formulae are elements of a new faith, a restoration of idealism. . . . Religious notes resound in this passionate apology for progress. Much as Futurism rejects the past in its entirety, it accepts the future *en bloc.* . . .

Thus [in Marinetti's novel *Mafarka le Futuriste*] the notion of personal and transcendental immortality that the Futurists so diligently buried with the declaration that the sense of the beyond must be destroyed has set sail anew in the form of a naively romantic daydream. In precisely the same way, after destroying everything transcendental, Nietzsche fashioned a new immanent immortality in his theory of the Eternal Return. That we are dealing with more than a poetic symbol is evident from Marinetti's manifestoes, which repeatedly refer to the possibility of externalizing the will. This is, of course, an antiscientific and philosophically naive idea, but psychology does not regard the will as a separate substance. This naive, fantastic dream shows that Futurism has not yet definitely accepted the world and that its revolt against the world and human nature and the "all too human" in us is still strong. This explains the revolt against the Eternal Feminine that neither Nietzsche nor the great individualists dared. Perhaps this unconscious religiosity concealed in a dark, unenlightened form beneath Futurism's nihilist husk is an extremely characteristic symptom. It indicates the new religious potentials that are without a doubt hidden within Futurism. In general, Futurism—like Hegel's pure spirit—contains all the opposites,

*Umberto Boccioni, *The City Rises* (1910, Museum of Modern Art, New York); Carlo Carrà, *Funeral of the Anarchist Galli* (1911, Museum of Modern Art, New York); Luigi Russolo, *The Revolt* (1911–12, Gemeentemuseen, The Hague).

both an implacable "no" and a dazzling "yes," both petty egoism and a great love of the future—an aspiration to sacrifice oneself for the sake of the future. But it is a vague love, not Verhaeren's enlightened emotion. The Futurists do not overcome contemporaneity internally, they accept it aesthetically. They do not transform its spiritual chaos into a new harmony, however, but merely react impressionistically to all phenomena in which they perceive elemental spontaneity. . . .

To summarize, then, Futurism is not an aesthetic school but above all a moral watchword or motto confronting all contemporary culture. Artistically, it is a bloc or coalition of schools and tendencies that have emerged from Symbolism, Romanticism, and the Parnassians under a common ideological platform: find the new beauty of our age, transform its emerging new idealism into artistic symbols, and express its deepest tendencies, its rebellious individualism and the emerging new consciousness of the masses. This is the enormous task our art faces.

56

Velimir Khlebnikov and Benedikt Livshits
"On Marinetti's Visit to Russia" (1914)

The Hylaea poets Velimir Khlebnikov and Benedikt Livshits distributed this leaflet during the St. Petersburg lecture by Marinetti on February 1, 1914. The translation reprinted here is from Vladimir Markov, *Russian Futurism: A History* (Berkeley: University of California Press, 1968), p. 151.

Today some natives and the Italian colony on the Neva's banks,* out of private considerations, prostrate themselves before Marinetti, thus betraying Russian art's first steps on the road to freedom and honor, and placing the noble neck of Asia under the yoke of Europe.

Persons who do not want any collar on their necks will be calm observers of such a black deed, as they were during the shameful days of Verhaeren and Max Linder.†

Persons of strong will are aloof. They know the laws of hospitality, but their bow is tightened and their foreheads show anger.

Foreigner, remember, you are in another country!
The lace of servility on the sheep of hospitality.‡

*This is evidently a reference to the bohemian frequenters of the Stray Dog cabaret on Italianskaia Street.

†The poet Emile Verhaeren and movie actor Max Linder visited Russia in November 1913.

‡This is an allusion to an episode in Gogol's novel *Dead Souls* (vol. 1, chap. 11) in which lace was smuggled across the border hidden in the fleece of sheep.

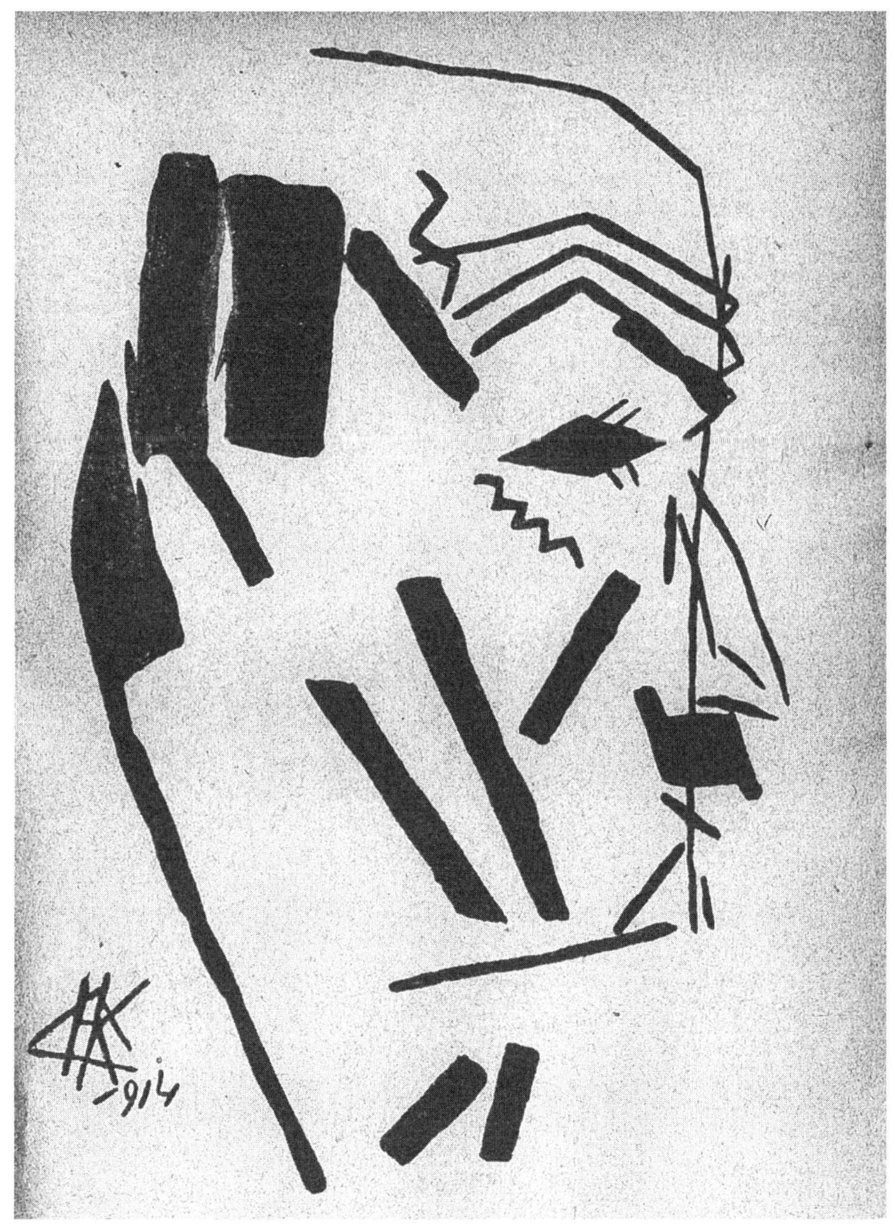

Nikolai Kulbin, *Portrait of Marinetti*, lithograph, 1914

57

Nikolai Berdiaev

The Crisis in Art (1917)

Around the turn of the century, the major Russian philosopher Nikolai Berdiaev (1874–1948) belonged to the "legal Marxists," for which he was persecuted. He later turned to Orthodoxy and developed his version of personalist philosophy. Berdiaev was deported from Russia in 1922 and settled in Paris in 1924. This text is an excerpt from a public lecture delivered and published in Moscow in 1917.

. . . We are witnessing a general crisis in art that is shaking it to its thousand-year foundations. The old idea of classical beauty has dimmed forever, and one senses that there is no returning to its images. Art is convulsively trying to escape from its boundaries. The borders separating one art from another and art in general from what is not art and is higher or lower than art are being violated. Never before has the problem of the relationship between art and life been so critical; never before has there been such a hunger to shift from the creation of works of art to the creation of life itself—a new life. There is an awareness of the impotence of the human creative act and the discrepancy between creative task and creative realization.

. . . In the old, seemingly eternal art, the human image and human body had firm contours and were distinguished from images of other objects—from minerals, plants and animals, rooms, houses, streets and cities, from machines and the infinite expanses of the world. Futurist art erases the boundary separating the human image from other objects and the enormous mechanized monster known as the modern city. . . . The human image disappears in this process of cosmic pulverization and exfoliation. The Futurists would enthusiastically kill off and incinerate the human image, which was always reinforced by the separate image of the material world. When the foundations of the material world were shaken, the human image was shaken as well. The dematerializing world penetrates humanity, and humanity which has lost its spiritual stability dissolves in the diluted material world. The Futurists demand that the center of gravity be shifted from humanity to matter. This does not mean, however, that they can be called materialists in the old sense of the word. Humanity disappears, as does the old matter with which it was correlated. . . . Marinetti's Futurist manifestoes are clearly hostile toward humanity and the human self. Herein lies concealed the basic contradiction of Futurism. The Futurists want accelerated motion but reject the source of creative motion—humanity. There is no other lever with which the Futurists could overturn the world. There is no real movement in Futurism; they are in the grip of a kind of global whirlwind, ignorant of the meaning of what is happening to them and essentially passive. . . . They are in the grip of the disintegrating material world. Futurism is enormously significant as a symptom, for it signals not only a crisis in art but a crisis in life itself. Unfortunately, the Futurists' agitational manifestoes predominate over artistic creation. In these manifestoes they express their changed sense of life, but they are powerless to express adequately this new sense of life in works of art. This creative impotence is especially noticeable in Futurist poetry and literature. They decrystallize the word, divorce it from the Logos. . . . The misfortune of Futurism is that it is turned backward; fettered to the past, it is too occupied with settling accounts and has not yet gone on to new creation in freedom. It is merely a transitional state, the end of the old art rather than the creation of a new art. . . .

The true meaning of the crisis in the plastic arts lies in their convulsive attempts to penetrate the material husk of the world, capture its more subtle flesh, and overcome the law of impenetrability. This is a radical break with antiquity. In the Christian world a Renaissance turned toward antiquity was still possible. The forms of the human body remained inviolable. The human body is a thing of classical antiquity. The crisis in art that we are witnessing is evidently the final and irrevocable break with all classicism.

58

R. Ia. [Roman Jakobson]

"Futurism" (1919)

Roman Jakobson (1896–1982), a prominent linguist, was a student at Moscow University who joined the avant-garde and published several poems signed "Aliagrov." This article was written for *Iskusstvo* (Art), no. 7 (1919), the newspaper of the IZO Department of Narkompros, where Jakobson worked briefly after the Revolution. In 1920 he settled in Prague and in 1941 moved to the United States. The translation here is reprinted from Roman Jakobson, *Language in Literature,* edited by Krystyna Pomorska and Stephen Rudy, translated by Stephen Rudy (Cambridge: Harvard University Press, 1987), pp. 28–33; published with the permission of the Roman Jakobson Trust.

It was in the twentieth century that painting first consistently broke off with the tendencies of naive realism. In the last century the picture was obliged to convey perception; the artist was a slave to routine, and he consciously ignored both everyday and scientific experience. As if what we know about an object were one thing, and the direct content of a presentation of objects were an entirely different thing—and the two completely unrelated. As if we knew an object only from one side, from one point of view, as if, upon seeing a forehead, we forget that the nape of the neck exists, as if the neck were the dark side of the moon, unknown and unseen. . . .

The Impressionists, applying the experience of science, had decomposed color into its component parts. Color ceased to be subjugated to the sensation of the nature depicted. There appeared blotches of color, even chromatic combinations, which copied nothing, which were not imposed upon the picture from without. The creative mastery of color naturally led to a realization of the following law: any increase in form is accompanied by a change in color, and any change in color generates new forms (a formulation of Gleizes and Metzinger).

In science this law was first advanced, it seems by Stumpf, one of the pioneers of the new psychology, who spoke about the correlation between color and colored spatial form: quality shares in changes of extension. When extension is changed, quality is also transformed. Quality and extension are by nature inseparable and cannot be imagined independently of one another. This obligatory connection may be opposed to the empirical connectedness of two parts lacking such an obligatory character, e.g., a head and torso. Such parts can be imagined separately.

The set *(ustanovka)** toward nature created for painting an obligatory connection precisely of such parts which are in essence disconnected, whereas the mutual dependence of form and color was not recognized. On the contrary, a set toward pictorial expression resulted in the creative realization of the necessity of the latter connection, where the object is freely interpenetrated by other forms (so-called Divisionism). Line and surface attract the artist's attention; they cannot exclusively copy the boundaries of nature; the Cubist consciously cuts nature up with surfaces, introduces arbitrary lines.

The emancipation of painting from elementary illusionism entails an intensive elaboration of various areas of pictorial expression. The correlations of volumes, constructive asymmetry, chromatic contrast, and texture enter the foreground of the artist's consciousness.

The results of this realization are the following: (1) the canonization of a series of devices, which thus also allows one to speak of Cubism as a school; (2) the laying bare of the device. Thus the realized texture no longer seeks any sort of justification for itself; it becomes autonomous, demands for itself new methods of formulation, new material. Pieces of paper begin to be pasted on the picture, sand is thrown on it. Finally, cardboard, wood, tin, and so on, are used.

Futurism brings with it practically no new pictorial devices; instead, it widely utilizes Cubist methods. It is not a new school of painting, but rather a new aesthetics. The very approach to the picture, to painting, to art, changes. Futurism offers picture-slogans, pictorial demonstrations. It has no fixed, crystallized canons. Futurism is the antipode of classicism. . . .

The overcoming of *statics,* the discarding of the absolute, is the main thrust of modern times, the order of the day. A negative philosophy and tanks, scientific experiment and deputies of Soviets, the principle of relativity and the Futurist "Down With!" are destroying the garden hedges of the old culture. The unity of the fronts of attack is astonishing.

"At the present time we are again experiencing a period in which the old scientific edifice is crumbling, but the crumbling is so complete that it is unprecedented in the history of science. But even that is not all. Among the truths being destroyed are ones which were never even uttered by anyone, which were never emphasized, so self-

*The Russian term *ustanovka* (orientation, set) is a calque for German *Einstellung,* a philosophical term designating apperception, the viewpoint or mental set crucial in the perceiver's constituting an object (editors' note).

apparent did they seem, so unconsciously were they used and posited as the basis for every sort of reasoning."* A particularly characteristic feature of the new doctrine is the unprecedented paradoxical nature of many of even its simplest propositions: they clearly contradict what is usually called "common sense." . . .

The basic tendencies of collectivist thought: the destruction of abstract fetishism, the destruction of the remnants of statics (Bogdanov, *The Sciences of Social Consciousness*).

And so the main lines of the moment are obvious in all domains of culture.

If Cubism, following Cézanne's behests, constructed a picture by starting from the simplest volumes—the cube, cone, sphere—offering its own sort of primitiveness in painting, then the Futurists in search of kinetic forms introduced into the picture the curved cone, the curved cylinder, collisions of cones with sharp, curved ellipsoids, and so on, in a word, destroying the mountings of volumes (see Carrà's manifesto).

Perceptions, in multiplying, become mechanized; objects, not being perceived, are taken on faith. Painting battles against the automatization of perception; it signals the object. But, having become antiquated, artistic forms are also perceived on faith. Cubism and Futurism widely use the device of impeded perception, which corresponds in poetry to the step-ladder construction discovered by contemporary theoreticians.

. . . Aristotle: "For men delight in seeing likenesses because in contemplating them it happens that they are learning and reasoning out what each thing is, e.g., that this man [in the painting] is that [sort of man]; for if by fortune one has not previously seen what is imitated, the likeness will not produce pleasure as an imitation, but because of its execution, or surface coloring, or some other cause of this sort." In other words, it was already clear to Aristotle that, alongside a type of painting that signals the perception of nature, there exists a type of painting that signals our direct chromatic and spatial perception (it does not matter whether the object is unknown or whether it has simply dropped out of the picture).

*It is indicated that this quotation and others, occurring in paragraphs omitted here, are from O. D. Xvolson, *The Principle of Relativity*, and N. A. Umov, *The Characteristic Features of Contemporary Natural-Scientific Thought*.

V

ART AND NATIONALITY

POLEMICS AND REACTIONS

The artists and critics around the art journal *Apollon* (Apollo) were trying to redesign the Russian national school on the model of the European—more precisely, the "Latin" (Franco-Italian)—tradition, which would pave the way for a contemporary high art [59]. Modern French painting was felt to embody a genuine national spirit of classical balance and order that could serve as a model for what was considered the rough, young Russian art.

On the contrary, "low" folk art and Russian medieval painting served as the medium of self-identification and source of renewal for the younger generation of the future avant-garde. These tendencies toward a national tradition were supported by the *Golden Fleece* and adopted by Larionov, who worked for the journal. The turn to archaic and "primitive" forms was programmatic for the early Russian Futurist artists, led by Larionov and Goncharova, and poets, led by Khlebnikov, and practically all the avant-gardists passed through some Neo-Primitivist phase. This tendency explored the national as well as the "tribal," the Russian along with the proto-Slavic, this last being deeply rooted in the undifferentiated—"organic," "anti-individualistic"—"East." It is no coincidence that the only manifesto of Russian artists at this time, published in Paris, expressed the "Asiatic" tendency particularly strongly [66].

One attempt to "sublate" the problem was the concept of everythingism *(vsiochestvo)* generated by Larionov's circle in the spring of 1913. Everythingism justified the extremely diverse experiments of Goncharova and Larionov by rejecting charges of eclecticism. The obvious allusions to Western (or Eastern) prototypes were acknowledged but radically reinterpreted: drawing on the French was not a sin, but a principle of national art [cf. 65]. Despite its intentionally sensational formulation, this idea reflected the views of the Symbolists and, in the final analysis, gave a paradoxical twist to Dostoevsky's idea of the Russian soul's "universality," which had become a commonplace in the modernist consciousness [60].

In the 1900s icons were discovered anew, both as an artistic phenomenon and as a manifestation of the national spirit. Medieval painting began to influence artists with Symbolist leanings as well as avant-gardists. Matisse's enthusiastic pronouncement about Russian icons, made in the course of his visit to Moscow in 1911, resonated broadly, and the icon began to be associated with modern art. The turning point in the reevaluation of icons was the March 1913 exhibition in Moscow dedicated to the tercentenary of the Romanov dynasty, which included over one hundred restored icons. At the same time, Larionov organized an exhibition of *lubok* works and icon designs or manuals that ran parallel to his major enterprise of the year, "Target," a provocative show of contemporary painting. Thus the icon was deliberately introduced into the new context of folklore "primitivism" and radical painting. Religious questions here were secondary. Not only did Benois establish common ground between medieval art and contemporary painting, but in asserting their kinship he also sought to correct the history of modern art's development [61]. This, in turn, provoked an extremely harsh rebuke from Burliuk and other avant-gardists [62].

With the transition from Primitivism to Cubism, the question of the avant-garde's national identity seemed to recede into the background, and explicitly anti-Western declarations became less frequent. At just this time, however, a messianic spirit became a distinguishing feature of avant-garde tendencies [75–77, 93].

59

Sergei Makovskii

"Art Survey" (1910)

Published in *Apollon* (Apollo) 10 (1910).

When I spoke about the anarchism of the Parisians being imitated by our young artists, I had in mind two tendencies of contemporary French painting: the chromo-luminarism of Seurat's successors, and the deformism of Matisse and to some extent Braque. . . . The first of these tendencies, however, is a kind of extreme (scientifically supported) conclusion drawn from the Impressionism proclaimed by Claude Monet, Sisley, and Renoir, so that despite the apparent "anarchy" of its drawing and colors, the art of a Signac or a Lucie Cousturier is a *continuation;* in the painting of the chromo-luminarists, this blindingly brilliant, unnatural mosaic of pink, blue, yellow, and violet brushstrokes is a purely technical development of what is by now the old principle of analyzing tones and the spectrum.

This painting follows a tradition of its own that is concerned exclusively with color—Pointillism—which should not be confused with the second, truly revolutionary tendency. I call it "deformism" to underscore one feature that is found in the works of quite a few innovators in the extreme camp of the "Salon des Indépendants," namely, the resolutely harsh, sometimes painfully contrived *rejection of the plasticity of traditional painting in favor of a new, recherché crudeness of form. . . .*

There cannot be two opinions of Matisse. He obviously "deforms" nature and consciously reworks God's creation in his own way. He does so not for the sake of stylistic schematization . . . but to achieve a *synthetic form* that is intended to have a vivid, rude, "lapidary" impact . . . that is transformed in the viewer's imagination into a plastic and colorful harmony. Matisse's method is profoundly theoretical; his art is to the highest degree calculated, cerebral, and distant from the notion of the "primitive." Having gone through a painful school of seeking and striving and passed in turn beyond Impressionism, chromo-luminarism, and Cézannism, he developed a "manner of seeing" of his own so personal and paradoxical that no innovator is likely to follow him without independently traveling the complex psychological road that brought Matisse to his latest works, which are at times completely inaccessible to even the very experienced viewer. Yet it is above all Matisse whom young artists imitate, and where?—in Russia! He is imitated by inexperienced pupils who often can barely wield a brush, youths who not only have not suffered through the complicated problems of contemporary painting but who are naively convinced that someone has revealed the truth to them. . . . I had occasion recently to discuss this sensitive subject with Matisse himself, who is well informed about our Russian artistic issues; he spoke with such grief of his many "followers": "Soon I will cease giving lessons entirely," he confessed. "The young want immediately what can be attained only through years of persistent work and ruthless self-criticism. I usually begin my instructions to my pupils with a piece of advice: only independent achievements and knowledge give you the right to be daring; be modest, *be banal*. . . . But it doesn't work." Here is a teacher pointing to a serious flaw in the very attitude of young innovators toward the problems of art. . . .

Reactionary critics, as we know, resolve this painful question simply: "painting à la Matisse is easier than à la Rembrandt or Rubens, so our 'semi-literate' artists are taking the public for a ride." To someone like Il'ia Repin, Matisse himself is "an illiterate inflated by Parisian boosters." What is there to say? This is a gross lie! This kind of thinking is outrageously ignorant naiveté! Il'ia Repin, after all, is a thousand times more "semi-literate" than Matisse! No, Matisse is too learned; his crudeness is refined and theoretical; it is a whole philosophy of drawing and painting. How inspired Matisse is, how beautiful and lasting his works, and how *appealing* they are to us are another matter. Personally, for example, *I definitely do not like him.* But that is no reason to shut your eyes to the authenticity of the young movement in art that has placed a halo around his name.

The indiscriminate imitation of Matisse is without question not an accidental phenomenon. If it is a mistake, it is a fateful mistake. The point is that Matisse's experiments—his "deformism," which does not shrink from any monstrosity or obvious disharmony and is sharply anarchistic in spirit and seemingly crudely contrary to the method of aristocratic "good taste"—this quest for *vitality at all costs,* ugly, cynical, barbarous even, but ardent, saturated with the blood of contemporary realism, satisfies a profound need today. As always, there is as much unconscious ideology here as purely artistic aspiration: a new civilization creates a new aesthetics; the morals of psychological freedom and the scientific worldview result in a gravitation toward "revolutionary" forms; democratic barbarism wants rapid and strong sensations for eyes sated with the kaleidoscope of the contemporary city; and the coming universal Americanization demands an art that is appropriate to the crude candor and impatient tempo of modern life. . . . We are looking, I repeat, at a spontaneous phenomenon long in the making that already has a history. Therefore to regard our young artists' excesses as a transitory illness or an imitation of something easier is an inexcusable mistake.

But how wrong it would be to conclude that deformism and anarchy are the only possible creative paths open to painting! Fortunately: (1) art never evolves in a *single* direction; (2) its conservative forces are just as effective as destructive innovation; and (3) alongside extreme modernism there usually develops the opposite tendency—a gravitation toward the past, a dreamy poeticization of obsolete forms. This tendency is especially noticeable today among the best Russian artists, who express their dream of the past and the "old world" through a refined graphic style and a fondness for bygone days and the quaint charm of the eighteenth century and the Empire period. And although they have nothing in common with the craze for Matisse, the latest triumphs of artists such as Bakst, Roerich, and Golovin are the best evidence that this refined stylism does not run counter to art's present tasks. . . . It is a profound delusion to think, as does our valiant youth greedily seizing upon the "latest word" from Paris, that contemporary stylism (stronger in Russia than in the rest of Europe) has had its day, or that the school of Russian stylism created by the World of Art has completed its role and will retreat and yield to innovative experiments à la Matisse. No, I am confident that the time has come for a *great decorative* style heir to everything accomplished in this area during the past decade. This style will not be barbarously devoid of traditions. On the contrary, in defiance of the modernists *à outrance* who prophesy that art will become coarser, it may once again resurrect the radiant harmonies of the Hellenic ideal. Twentieth-century humanity is sufficiently complex for both trends to develop in parallel. . . .

In art as in social life, the urge to move forward must be tempered by a sense of the historical and national soil. The soil of Russian painting is too poor for us to transplant in it all the capricious shoots of the West with impunity. Does the European future belong undividedly to the anarchic movement we have called deformism? Is it destined to sweep away the aesthetic traditions of "old Europe"? No one knows the answer to this. It is at any rate as distant as the United States of Europe and the triumph of socialism. . . . But until art's national features have been erased and as long as it develops in each country on the basis of tradition and the labor of previous generations, the painting of each nation will continue to exist independently. Even if Parisian "anarchism" did arise on French soil, I don't think we can call it a typical national phenomenon: developing parallel to it in France, after all, is a school continuing the traditions of the Grand Art of the eighteenth century and the Renaissance that has very little in common with Matisse or even Gauguin. However, this is not important. As the Capital of the World, Paris can permit itself even cosmopolitan luxuries, for it is rich in artists of all shades and justly proud of its great school of painting. Russia has yet to create its own painting. Russian artists do not have the right to divorce themselves from the soil. They have not yet earned it. However seductive the "last word" of the French, we are obliged to take into account the characteristics of our own Russian life, history, and national genius. . . .

60
Iakov Tugendkhol'd
"The 'Russian Seasons' in Paris" (1910)

Annual performances of Russian ballet abroad began in 1909. Parallel with the 1910 tour, an exhibition of Russian stage designers' works was held at the Bernheim-Jeune gallery. This review was published in *Apollon* (Apollo) 10 (1910).

. . . the very nature of nineteenth-century French painting and its technical revolution keeps it from being transferred to the stage. This is analytical painting—eternally searching, intimate, and *dynamic.* It is "anarchy in a golden frame," as Heinrich Heine once so aptly put it. Meanwhile theatrical painting, like all decorative painting in general, is art that is stabilized, completed, and static; the stage set is a premonition of the fresco; the theater is High Art in rough sketch. The stage designer cannot be the *initiator* in the area of painterly technique; he can only be the *completer.* This is why none of the best French painters had the temperamental vocation for stage design. . . .

This is also why it was logical for theatrical design to flourish in Russia. It is not because we have Mamontov and Teliakovskii,* who have invited artists onto the stage, but because Russian art is by nature *a synthetic rather than analytic art that transforms rather than creates, an art of concerted achievements rather than solitary acts of daring.* This is not to say that our painting is borrowed and eclectic, as is the Belgian, for example, but there is no denying that it has incorporated the achievements of the West. The critic of *Indépendance belge* is not so very far from the truth when he expresses the at first glance paradoxical thought that Korovin's set for *Ruslan* depicting an "*isba russe*"† could have been signed by Van Gogh, and Camille Mauclair is not so very mistaken when he declares that Alexandre Benois's nocturnal set for *Les Sylphides* is worthy of the renowned painter of "nocturnes" Whistler. But this does not mean that these artists are imitating Van Gogh and Whistler. It merely means that the principles of Van Gogh's and Whistler's art have been refracted through the prism of the Russian soul and realized as something supra-individual, inherited, and monumental. Bakst's set for *Scheherazade* contains a great deal of Oriental color and barbarian floweriness, and Charles Lalo is correct when he compares it with French stage sets: "We use delicate, refined nuances; the Russians employ vivid and pure colors based on sharp contrasts, and the intensity and depth they achieve startle us like the pictures of the great colorists." But was it not the pictures of the "great colorists" Delacroix, Manet, and Gauguin, those first martyrs of the bright palette, that deflected Russian painting from the Wanderers' lifeless path?

*Savva Mamontov (1841–1918), industrialist and patron of the arts, founder of the Moscow Private Opera (1885). Vladimir Teliakovskii (1861–1924), director of the Imperial Theaters (1901–17).

†A Russian wooden peasant hut. *Ruslan and Liudmila* (1842) is an opera by Mikhail Glinka, the first act of which was performed in Paris, with Korovin's stage design, during the 1909 tour.

Thus, when Russian painting absorbs the technical achievements of the West, it takes them with purely Slavic straightforwardness to their greatest intensity and elevates them onto a monumental pedestal. Raised amid the disharmony of life, it is not content with "colorful harmony in a golden frame" but dreams of transforming all reality through the magical power of colors. Since the days of Belinskii,* the theater, with its "rag clouds, wooden seas, and canvas trees," has been a haven for us from "reality," a temple to the decorative beauty and great art for which there is no longer any room in our little lives. Hence the love of "spectacle" that Maurice Denis considers typically Russian.† Hence the supremacy of painting on the stage that so amazes the French critics. In contrast to the French stage, where there are huge structures, complicated paraphernalia, and real properties but no painting, Russian artists have simplified, or rather, elevated decorative art to *decorative painting,* transforming stage costumes into living garlands of saturated color symbolizing the meaning of a musical drama. . . . On the Russian stage there is nothing "real" except real painting: not the illusion of truth but the persuasiveness of the illusion. Such is the revelation of Russian stage design. . . .

Let us not forget, however, that our artists (Vasnetsov, Polenov, and Vrubel') went over to the stage before anyone had heard of Gauguin, and although the logical consummation of Western explorations can be detected in the use of color in Russian stage sets, it is *essentially* an original phenomenon. Jusseaume, the critic cited above, advises the stage designer to travel a lot. Russian painting has always traveled—in distant ages and distant lands—not for the sake of archaeological collecting but to communicate with the soul of what is past and foreign. This "retrospective" aspect of our art (to use Sergei Makovskii's term) is the bridge that connects it to the stage. This is the "special gift Russians have over foreigners," "the gift for understanding other nationalities" noted already by Dostoevsky.‡ . . .

Most striking of all at the Russian exhibition of 1906 was the Western influence: at the sight of Somov's women and corners of Versailles the French critics were proudly convinced of the power of French culture, while in the works of Roerich and Vrubel' they saw only curiosities and anomalies. Today this could not happen. Now [at the exhibition at Bernheim's] Russian artists have come to Paris not as pupils taking an examination but as equals and also, with respect to stage design, as teachers.

Russian art is beginning to repay the West for what it has taken from it over the centuries. But let us not flatter ourselves: this new situation entails even heavier *obligations* than before. Let us not forget that the West has seen our art in holiday at-

*Vissarion Belinskii (1811–48), literary and theater critic.

†I take the liberty of citing this passage from a letter I received from Maurice Denis, although I do not agree with its first half: "You Russians have a passionate love of 'spectacle.' Sometimes you are not interested in the dramatic action, the pure music, and perhaps not even the talents of the performers. But what we understand so poorly in Paris—the beauty of the ensemble, delighting the eye—you always insistently demand" (Tugendkhol'd's note).

‡Inaccurate quotation from Fedor Dostoevsky's article "Apropos of the Exhibition," in *A Writer's Diary* (1873).

tire but not in everyday life. If only the holiday clothes of the "Russian season" are not discarded back in Russia!

61

Alexandre Benois

"Icons and the New Art" (1913)

Published in *Rech'* (Speech), April 5, 1913.

. . . For many years a handful of specialists studied and collected ancient icons—more out of reverence for their age and holiness than any interest in their aesthetic merits. In the diametrically opposite area of pure painting, there was an attempt to simplify and break free of Academy traditions, and artists searched for new laws of color. This phenomenon was global rather than only Russian and was centered mainly in Paris. Now we are witnessing a strange and highly significant meeting: the two tendencies have intersected and merged. Dead archeology has proved to be a living inspiration; the most zealous and daring innovators have found something relevant in what only recently seemed hopelessly obsolete. Russian "Futurists" of all possible stripes who had already gathered to set fire to the museums of ancient art have stumbled upon old treasures so congenial to them in spirit that wrath has given way to charity, and they do not conceal their desire to learn from these old men.

There is also a purely external explanation for this wonder. It was only a few years ago that icons became brilliant, colorful, and "contemporary." . . .

Only ten years ago the excavation of a "Pompeii of icons" would have made no impression on the art world. . . . Today, however, things are quite different, and you would have to be blind not to believe in the saving artistic grace of icons, their enormous power to influence contemporary art, and their unexpected relevance to our time. A fourteenth-century *Nikolai the Wonder-Worker* or *Birth of the Virgin* can, moreover, help us understand Matisse, Picasso, Le Fauconnier, or Goncharova. By the same token, through Matisse, Picasso, Le Fauconnier, and Goncharova we have a much better feeling for the tremendous beauty of these "Byzantine" pictures and the youthful, powerful, and life-giving force within them.

At any rate, two traits are inherent in both the ancient, rigorous, pious art sanctified by the church and history and the art of our day, which many continue to find clownish, frivolous, and charlatanical. One of these traits is the utter unwillingness to have anything to do with what we subsume under the word "realism." The other is a kind of voluptuous attitude toward color. Closely connected with the first of these traits is a tendency toward rigorous stylization; with the second, a quest for a musical quality on the order of sonorous contrasts rather than artful harmonics. . . . Studying the works of the Cubists, as in studying icons, the "counsels of reason" end and an insane dream, the logic of the unreal, begins, as mystical meaning is fully restored to art. . . .

Here someone has indeed brought together two mighty currents; however, if these currents are to form a single powerful and fruitful river, if only for a time, contemporary artists must not only accept the aesthetically "new" beauty of the ancient art we strangely find so relevant to us but also absorb it with their entire spirit and through this contact be spiritually regenerated . . . we must remember that what we now admire in icons is not just their brilliant colors, amazing linear qualities, and incomparable technique, but—and this is the main point—the depth of the spiritual life they reflect. It is not even so very important in what or whom these people believed; the most important quality of their painting is that they "lived by faith." They did not paint pictures merely to *amuse* themselves and others (whether aesthetically or quasi-scientifically) and regarded what they were doing as a spiritual feat. All of their devices can be copied superficially. . . . But if the art of our day is to become like the essence of their art, what is needed is a spiritual metamorphosis not only of individual persons, but of artistic creation as a whole.

62

David Burliuk

"The Noisy 'Benois' and the New Russian National Art (A Discussion on Art among Mssrs. Burliuk, Benois, and Repin)" (1913)

Structured as an imagined conversation between three artists, this pamphlet, published in St. Petersburg, was probably written in April 1913 in response to Benois's essays on icons and contemporary art [61].

With the arrogance of superficial Western culture, at first he [Benois] had no use for our National Russian Art. Did he write much in his *History of Russian Painting** on the *lubok* woodcut, the icon, the store sign? Did he note that, in the nineteenth century, led by Shishkin, we were slaves of the Germans? That Impressionism for us was merely a difficult word to translate? . . . Mr. Benois is full of the strength and courage to do battle with everything that is truly new . . . and now his praise of icons, and Goncharova, and Picasso must have some purpose, but what?

Here is the answer to this intriguing question. Modern Art has emerged in Russia.

The factors behind it: (1) Life itself; (2) the "rotten" West; (3) our national art (the shop sign, the *lubok,* and the icon).

The enemies of New Russian Painting, realizing that it made no sense to reject both Modern Art and the soil on which it arose (How can one reject France, for pity's sake? Although at first Benois and his blind followers did try to look down on this example of vivid courage and power. "Vandals and ignoramuses," they said. But then they were ashamed since they wanted to pass for "subtle" and cultured.), and a wondrous—and very political—thought occurred to them: praise what is safe to praise and praise it in a safe way. . . . Well, of course, if you're going to praise and shout

*See Alexandre Benois, *The Russian School of Painting* (New York, 1916); first published in Russian, 1902.

"Bravo!" praise something on the other side of the world: Paris. At the time, enemies of Modern Art such as Benois, Sergei Makovskii, and Shervashidze up and declared Russia an "artistic province of this Babylon, the Rome of our age!" There, there was where the real "Cubists" were—"we have only counterfeiters." There was where the real "talents" were—Russia had "wretched imitators." Let us love everything Western, which is genuine, trample our own, and spit on our "pitiful new shoots"! In a word, they turned Western art—the "best" "pictures"—into a huge boulder and set it rolling, crushing all that is New in Russian painting. We revealed to them this novelty in Western painting. We howled and cried in ecstasy over Cézanne, Gauguin, and Van Gogh, who had opened our eyes not to imitation but to the possibility of freedom; they opened our eyes to the falseness of the Lenbachs, Böcklins, Stucks, Zügels, Henri Martins, Besnards, Bonnats,* and the academics with and without the trappings of Impressionism. Our enemies accepted the new artists, pretending to like "Gauguin, who couldn't draw," and "hideous Picasso." . . .

Young Russian art got on its feet. The West and the great national art of our fatherland taught us one great truth, namely, that there is no definitive understanding . . . of form, line, or color instrumentation; that what you say about content, spirituality, and ideology (like a narrative tacked onto philosophy) is a crime before true art; that there is no definitive understanding of "beauty."

. . . And that there is only one path: "Is there a quest for something new?"

. . . That we must fear authorities. That we must believe both in our own art and the art of our homeland.

That Russia is not an artistic province of France!

That the time has come to declare our national artistic independence! . . .

That we must hate the forms that existed in art before us. . . .

But I appeal to everyone writing about the New Art! Stop the hypocrisy, be righteous, and do not follow Benois's example. Do not praise what you do not like. Express your indignation openly. Be as straightforward as Repin! . . . Demand your place in the museums! After all, the New Russian Art and Modern Western Art reflect the culture of our day. Academism, after all, is dead. Cézanne, Gauguin, and Van Gogh are classics, and the feeble so-called artists who fear the approaching bright light of the New Art will not triumphantly halt the procession.

63

Natal'ia Goncharova [Il'ia Zdanevich]

Foreword to the Goncharova exhibition catalogue (1913)

Natal'ia Goncharova (1881–1962) was trained at the Moscow School of Painting, Sculpture, and Architecture and participated in the *Golden Fleece* exhibitions and in other major avant-garde

*Heinrich von Zügel (1885–1941), German animalist; Henri Martin (1860–1943), Paul Albert Besnard (1849–1934), and Léon Joseph Florentin Bonnat (1833–1922), French painters.

shows of the 1910s. In 1915 Goncharova and her husband, Mikhail Larionov, left Russia, settling in Paris in 1918. This statement was published in the catalogue of her second one-person exhibition (in Moscow), in which she showed nearly 800 works dating from 1900 to 1913.

Elena Basner's archival research strongly suggests that the text's real author was poet and critic Il'ia Zdanevich (1894–1975), while a student at the Law School of St. Petersburg University, who became a mouthpiece for Larionov's group.* In 1913 he was developing the concept of everythingism *(vsiochestvo)* [cf. 65]. After 1921 Zdanevich lived in Paris, where he practiced his version of Dadaism under the pseudonym "Iliazd."

. . . At the beginning of my career I mostly studied the contemporary French. They opened my eyes, and I grasped the great significance and value of the art of my homeland and through it the great value of Eastern art. I have covered all the West has to give down to the present, as well as everything that my homeland, inspired by the West, has created. Now I am shaking the dust from my feet and moving away from the West, because I consider its leveling shallow and trivial. My road leads to the original wellspring of all the arts—the East. The art of my country is incomparably deeper and more significant than anything I know of in the West. . . . Where, if not the East, is the source of inspiration for all the Western masters we have studied and from whom we have not learned the main thing: not to imitate indiscriminately and not to seek individuality but above all to create works of art and realize that the East and we ourselves are the source the West draws upon? I hope my example and remarks will serve as a good lesson for those who understand their real meaning.

I am convinced that contemporary Russian art is developing so rapidly and has reached such heights that in the near future it will play a very prominent role in the life of the world. Contemporary Western ideas (principally from France; there is no need to mention others) are no longer of any benefit to us. And the time is not far off when the West will openly be studying us.

. . . I am shaking off the Western dust and find ridiculous and backward those who are still imitating Western models in the hope of becoming pure painters and who fear literariness worse than the plague. Equally ridiculous are those who preach individuality and assume there is value in their self even when that self is extremely limited. Not only are such ideas obsolete, but giftless individuality is as useless as bad imitation.

I am deeply grateful to Western artists for all they have taught me.

Now that I have conscientiously reworked everything of this sort that I could and have earned the honor of being ranked together with the contemporary masters of the West,† it is in fact in the West that I prefer to embark upon a new path. . . .

*Basner attributed this text to Zdanevich in an unpublished paper delivered at a conference on Larionov and Goncharova held at the Centre Georges Pompidou, Paris, in 1995.

†Goncharova had participated in such important exhibitions as the "Second Post-Impressionist Exhibition" (London, 1912) and the "First German Autumn Salon" (Berlin, 1913).

64

Aleksei Grishchenko

On the Ties of Russian Painting to Byzantium and the West, 13th–20th Centuries: Thoughts of an Artist (1913)

Aleksei Grishchenko (1883–1977) studied at the seminary and later graduated from the Department of Natural Science at Moscow University. He studied painting in a number of private studios and visited Paris in 1911 and Italy in 1913, the year he published this book in Moscow. His style was influenced by Cubism, Russian icons, and early Renaissance art. He emigrated in 1919 and moved to France in 1921.

The group of artists who represent our young art often read and hear that they are alienated from the traditional movement in Russian art and worship the Parisian innovators immoderately. . . . On the basis of irrefutable facts I shall attempt to show that their painting has deeply national tendencies and is indubitably linked to the best of earlier Russian painting. If we peer back into the ages we will see that painting came to us with religion from Byzantium, where at the time it was highly developed. . . . Rublev and Ushakov endowed the iconostases of the Moscow and Vladimir cathedrals with the majestic beauty of wholeness. Their consciousness and extremely rigorous skill were not inferior to that of their foreign counterparts Beato Angelico and the earlier primitivists Duccio and Cimabue. Elements of painting such as structure, plasticity of form and color, drapery, and strength and character of movement are developed in their works with utmost expression and precision. What a broad and bold use of disharmony in color, line, and plane! Their greatness lies precisely in their painting, which so excited the master painter Matisse, who discovered in Russian icons so much that was new and unexpected. It was he who acknowledged that our iconography is not inferior to the art of Giotto or the earlier primitivists Duccio and Cimabue. This is excellent evidence supporting the view that our old masters adhered to the principles of pure painting. Twentieth-century Paris strangely echoes barbarian Muscovy. . . .

During the reign of Peter the Great, life in Russia made a sharp turn toward Europe. . . . You would think it had come to a terrible precipice, that the old painting had come to an end, another mountain lay ahead, and then the new painting began. Nothing of the kind. Despite diametrically opposed starting points and an immoderate worship of completely dissimilar innovators, there is one trait that Russian painting retained both then and now, namely, a love for and highly developed skills in color, plasticity, and ornamental beauty. . . .

National painters never lost their originality in spite of foreign influences. The interrelationship of ideas in the art of different peoples can be traced through several millennia of human culture. This is how the arts evolved in Byzantium, Italy, and France, and that is how it will be in Russia.

Like the works of Monet and Degas from the 1870s through the 1890s, Matisse's decorative painting today is nourished by the juices of Japanese, Chinese, and even

А. ГРИЩЕНКО.

О СВЯЗЯХЪ

РУССКОЙ ЖИВОПИСИ

СЪ ВИЗАНТІЕЙ и ЗАПАДОМЪ

XIII—XX в.

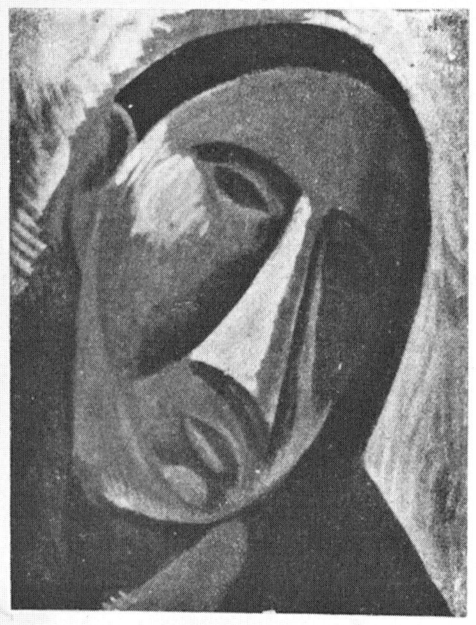

Съ 23 воспроизведеніями.

ИЗДАНІЕ А. ГРИЩЕНКО.

Cover for Aleksei Grischenko's *On the Ties of Russian Painting to Byzantium and the West, 13th–20th Centuries: Thoughts of an Artist* (Moscow, 1913)

Russian (icon) art, but this vivid decorative painter has lost nothing of his singularity. Despite the grumbling of obtuse nationalists, his artistic instinct forces him to draw fresh material for new constructions from all sources. This guarantees the healthy development of his artistic individuality.

. . . Unfortunately for Russian art, the brilliant movements of the Barbizons, Romantics, and Realists passed unnoticed. Corot, Millet, Delacroix, and Courbet—all these names were *terra incognita* to our homespun geniuses. Russian art paid dearly for the one time it tried to be "original," as a yawning chasm opened up and filled with rubbish.* . . .

Is it then surprising that a group of artists disgusted with this "traditional" movement in Russian art should follow the French genius by imitating their own glorious ancestors? In the midst of general decline and decay, Cézanne appeared as a mighty innovator. . . .

The relationship between the public and artists other than painters and Cézanne is being repeated before our eyes with amazing monotony and regularity in the case of another genuine contemporary painter. I am speaking of Pablo Picasso.

A true successor of Cézanne's great work, he is the most profound artist of our times. Unusually talented, Picasso has with dizzying rapidity already passed through several developmental stages. . . .

In 1910 he began to incorporate into his painting the Futurist principles of divisionism, dynamism, and complementarism. Henceforth the division of the object into parts became an obligatory element of his pictures. After taking the object apart, he re-creates it in a new and unusual form. Turning the rear or front, or the inner or outer sides of the components of the object toward the viewer, he distributes them on the canvas not arbitrarily but in accordance with the new principles mentioned above; the spirit of construction dominates here as well, only from this point on we see the objects in Picasso's pictures from several points of view, apprehending them in a fuller *(avec complément),* deeper, and entirely new way.

In his *Still Life*† Picasso cuts the violin into pieces and, as if he were looking inside it, places them on the canvas not haphazardly but according to a certain law, in order to bring out more deeply the interaction of the object's plastic masses; out of the violin's separate parts (sounding board, neck, strings, scroll) he constructs a whole that reveals more comprehensively and more plastically the violin's inner life, its rhythm and dynamics *(force dynamique).*

Up until now, movement has been conveyed as a static phenomenon, as one of an unbroken series of flash movements. Now Picasso has set himself the task of conveying the very sensation of movement *(sensation dynamique)* in the picture.

The Italian Futurists apply these same principles in their painting. Picasso, however, is a profound painter; in his hands the new method acquires a special cogency

*The reference is to the Wanderers.

†*Violin* (1912, Z.II.358, GMII).

and logic; works of this sort *(Compotier* and *Violin)* impress you as profound and natural. By contrast, despite their new method, the Italians are not far removed in spirit from their past compatriots, whom they so rightfully hate. There is something revolting in their jumble of French Pointillism and Impressionism and Klimt's German Symbolism. The movement the Italians have begun against the horrifying depravity and degeneration in contemporary art must be heartily welcomed, of course. Charting new paths in painting and implementing them, however, are not one and the same. For the latter, one must be born a profound painter and artist. Whether working in pencil, oils, or watercolors, Picasso has remained such an artist through all his periods beginning in 1901.

However, I do not think he will stay long within the confines of the new method; he himself regards his most recent works as a transitional stage. The future will tell. At any rate, Picasso's latest works clearly show the superficiality of the imitators (we also have quite a few), whom he not so long ago called dunces, much as Cézanne once spoke of his dull-witted, lifeless imitators. . . .

Roger Allard . . . says, "History itself has made it necessary to establish the new canon of painterly principles serving as the basis of the group of young artists that has rallied around the following ideals: to react as energetically as possible against instantaneous photographical representation, insidious narrative painting, and all the surrogates and epigones of Impressionism. To review the arsenal of painterly resources in order to rid it of the tinsel of retrospectivism, aestheticism, and decorative incrustation. To place between the perception of painter and viewer a single plate. Make no effort to please our bigoted eye with the chatter of colors and lines. All of the tendencies to which I all too briefly refer indicate, by and large, merely a desire to paint pictures; this is how arranged, constructed, made works must be understood—there is no longer any room for any Impressionistic notes, in which the deceit of false naturalness masks a profound paltriness. The sterility of efforts in the spirit of Impressionism needs no further demonstration."

The artists of the young Russian art are deeply convinced that painting is evolving authentically. They have begun building a bridge over the chasm of false realism and retrospective individualism to the best in their native art of the past. . . .

65

Mikhail Le Dantiu

"The Painting of the Everythingists"(c. 1914)

Mikhail Le Dantiu (1891–1917) studied painting at the Academy of Fine Arts in St. Petersburg and participated in all the exhibitions organized by Larionov. He died during World War I while serving in the field forces. This text was probably written in the spring of 1914 and intended for a public lecture. It was published much later, in *Neizvestnyi russkii avangard v muzeiakh i chastnykh sobraniiakh* (The Unknown Russian Avant-Garde in Museums and Private Collections), edited by Nina Gurianova and A. Sarabianov (Moscow: Sovetskii Khudozhnik, 1992), pp. 329–33.

. . . Nowadays all so-called innovators talk persistently about the "shift" as the principle that justifies the formlessness of their pictures. The original source of these "shifts" is always said to be Cézanne, the brilliant master from Aix who at any rate deserves a better fate than being the progenitor of the contemporary (especially Russian) Futurists. When all is said and done, what is this "shift"? When you look at Cézanne's pictures as a whole, you are struck by their amazingly good construction. He had to have a tremendous knowledge of art (perhaps intuitive—it makes no difference) to be able to create such classical forms in the age of Impressionism, when synthesis had been abolished and the primary impression had triumphed. Cézanne's canvases are so saturated with the equilibrium of painterly elements and objectness is understood so subtly as the object of composition that they will always be a model for painters. To give greater precision to his construction, in which he approximates the ancient masters of the golden age of painting, he skillfully introduces combinations of objects not only in color (a long familiar reflex) but also in form—a reflex lost by the art of the Academy, salons, and Impressionists. Only the academist, who approaches a picture from his knowledge of anatomy and perspective, can find any "shift" of form in Cézanne. From that point of view his faces are indeed done "incorrectly" and the perspective is "shifted" toward the canvas, but this is absolutely insignificant. The construction of his picture as an organic whole is impeccable—you could ask the artist for nothing more. Cézanne's followers have tripped on this "shift" of his. I am not speaking, of course, about followers such as Emile Bernard (the author of reminiscences of Cézanne, a little book that is less than useless) and the like but rather the Cubists. Among these we must single out Picasso, a master . . . who will of course become a classic (in our literature on art this word always has an ambiguous ring, but I understand it as something quite specific). Cubism in the works of its other representatives has manifested itself only as a treatment of real form and has not even approached synthesis. Metzinger is a typical academist. His proportions and drawing (despite the arrangement of the planes)—everything is anatomical and in perspective and fully corresponds to the work of a good, "competent" academist painter. The system according to which individual parts are distributed is a little different, but this does not affect the construction, and illusionism is not pursued so very zealously—but the difference is essentially very small. Gleizes is a naturalist inclined toward certain generalizations, but he does not go beyond external impressions with respect to either proportions or manner. His attempts at planar and even geometrical construction are so incidental, they seem unnecessary. Owing to his proximity to Picasso, Braque, a Romantic by nature, is the most synthetic of the group. It is difficult to say anything definite about Léger, Le Fauconnier, Picabia, Gris, Duchamp, Laurancin, and so on, since they are constantly making radical changes in their technique. Léger, the most striking of them, is still not free of the influence of Impressionism, some leavening of which is observable to various degrees in the works of all the painters mentioned here.

An analysis of the Cubists' works provides no grounds whatever for concluding that Cubism is a new painterly conception. As we can see, it has the most varied starting points. To superficial observers such as our Russian Burliuks, its treatment of planes seems like a great change in painting; even their declarations that "Cubism is the planar perception of the world," and so on, are meaningless, dilettantish phrases. The Cubists' sole achievements are their elimination of the aerial perspective of illusionism and their attempts to bring out the third dimension through a primitive division of the canvas—for which they are indebted to Cézanne and Picasso. By and large this is only a manner—a good, useful one, no arguing with that, but merely a manner. As they developed further, the Cubists were bound to run into Italian Futurism, whose theoretical premises . . . concern not painting as such but mainly its themes. . . . Yet if they really want to introduce a new concept into painting, then above all—to translate the language of painting into words—they will have to confront this "how." How can they combine their proposed themes with the inescapable laws of painting, and how are they to introduce them in a new way onto canvas? What new resources are available for this task? The people who want to burn down the museums and only acknowledge twentieth-century painting will never be able to answer these questions. Painting's resources are always the same, and no abstract theory is going to change them. They will change only if entirely new materials are invented. . . . The Futurists have not provided any new conception in painting and have merely proved that there is a single, immutable conception that has always been and always will be, that the organism of painting is viable only under certain conditions, and that all attempts to change it are useless. The Italian Futurists of whom I have been speaking all along are the direct descendants of the Neo-Impressionists (Seurat, Signac). Their aspiration to render motion through the division of form is entirely analogous to these latter artists' attempts to achieve a color interpretation of light through color divisionism. Neither group takes the whole into account, and composition is neglected. Boccioni, who treats divided real form, coincides in his painterly interpretation of it with Bosch . . . and in his picture *Le Rire** it is garnished with a sauce of Renoiresque Impressionism, an artificial combination that reveals his inability to join narrative and form. In his previous works *(La Danseuse, Le Confection)*† Severini's manner is close to Pointillism. Owing to his contact with the French, his later works (I am judging from reproductions) have produced much better synthetic constructions. The other contributors to the Futurists' first exhibition (Balla, Russolo, etc.) have even borrowed their forms from Hodler and the English graphic artists. They have devoted too much space to the theory underlying their art and are therefore obliged to join with the Cubists, whose form, at any rate, is incomparably more developed. The theses advanced by the Futurists' manifesto are nevertheless very significant. The main one has to do with motion. They have presented it as a division of real form and

**The Laugh* (1911, Museum of Modern Art, New York).

†Le Dantiu evidently has in mind Severini's *The Obsessive Dancer* (1911, private collection), and *La Modiste* (1910–11, private collection).

stopped there. In painting, however, this theme can be expressed much more richly and fully by means of an appropriate division of the surface of the picture. The Futurists' phrase "A galloping horse has not four legs but twenty"* adequately reveals their attitude toward craftsmanship. To a master, after all, it means absolutely nothing. If one understands the significance of lines, their interplay, and the space they delimit, one can combine them to express motion, heaviness, and so on. One can create a "motion style," which is what the real significance of Futurist painting activity essentially amounts to.

It is not my purpose here to analyze in detail all contemporary painting phenomena, so I will limit myself to the principal elements. Painting is presently developing at such an accelerated pace that new problems, tendencies, theories, and so on are constantly surfacing. We already know about Post-Cubism, Post-Futurism, Orphism (Simultaneism), and so on. These currents are still very undeveloped and have not produced any painterly forms of their own, and for the time being they draw on the achievements of Cubism and Futurism. Their academic nature, at any rate, deserves to be noted. To elaborate, by academic painting I mean painting in which theme and form diverge and do not directly interact and where there is consequently no organic construction. In this sense, with the brilliant exceptions of Cézanne and Picasso, the majority of Western painters have not renounced academism. The sensational Matisse is an academist who does not even conceal the fact with anything but bright and empty colors, but they are a dead giveaway. After Gauguin and Cézanne, the Western synthesists turned to the study of "primitive" art, finally realizing that only there could they find the lost knowledge of form, the absence of which is so keenly felt in any attempt at synthesis. As city dwellers raised on the masterpieces of the Louvre and the Vatican and lacking ready access to more needed materials in sufficient quantities, they were of course satisfied more quickly than they should have been. Although their skill and technique almost compensate for the shortcomings in their basic conception, their knowledge of form suffers many unavoidable compromises. I must point out one more great artist who stands completely apart. Although he is not connected with any theories or tendencies, the spontaneity with which he expresses his themes in a style peculiar to him alone makes him extremely interesting. I am referring to Henri Rousseau, a painter remarkable for his originality and perfection. Perhaps this is why he has remained on the sidelines and has not generated a school like the others.

With respect to the wealth of material at its disposal, Russian painting is in a special position. . . . It has absorbed the qualities of construction inherent in the Greeks, but it has not been merely imitative. Although its canons are based on Greek originals, the Novgorod school is extraordinarily distinctive. . . . If the West once participated in the life of Novgorod art, then why must influence necessarily come from

*"Manifesto of Futurist Artists" (1910). See *Manifesty ital'ianskogo futurizma*, translated by V. Shershenevich (Moscow, 1914), p. 11.

the West and not the other way around? Novgorod icons are incomparably better than the masterpieces of their Western contemporaries. . . .

When official Westernism was introduced into Russia during the reign of Peter the Great, it dealt a crushing blow to national art, which was violently forced to surrender its earlier positions. If it did not perish completely, that is only because art as such can never die. Simultaneously with the development of "state art," painting of the "high style," and the beginning of academicism, which assumed its final form later, we can note the development of the *lubok* woodcut—folk art that was spontaneous and therefore came from the tradition of the earlier "High Art." This was inevitable, and the forms of *lubok* painting very clearly bespeak this continuity. . . .

Contemporary Russian painting is in the same indefinite situation. Academicism, the Wanderers, and so on are not worth mentioning. Anyone who still fails to realize that these institutions were stillborn obviously has very little to do with art. To these two deceased may be added the pseudo-innovators of the World of Art, that hotbed of impotent decadence that has only lasted as long as it has thanks to the energies of intensely recruited new "forces" from among the young artists. . . . I prefer to proceed to "new" Russian art. The epithet "new" alone, on which the representatives of the Jack of Diamonds and the Union of Youth greatly insist, undermines any faith in their professionalism. Despite the abundance and size of the paintings annually exhibited by artists such as Mashkov and Konchalovskii, as an independent phenomenon the Jack of Diamonds does not exist at all. . . . The participants in these exhibitions lack both the boldness and the talent to go beyond epigonism. . . .

What connects a group of like-minded artists [Goncharova and Larionov] to these masters are the constant struggle with stagnation and imitation and the constant quest for new painterly forms that observes continuity in construction and style.

66

Georgii Iakulov, Benedikt Livshits, and Artur Lourie
"We and the West" (1914)

Georgii Iakulov (1884–1928) was a painter and stage designer whose ideas had much in common with Delaunay's Simultaneism. The poet Benedikt Livshits (1881–1939) was a member of the Hylaea group. Artur Lourie (1891–1966) was a composer. This manifesto was printed in St. Petersburg as a broadsheet in Russian, French, and Italian and sent to Apollinaire, who published it in *Mercure de France* on April 16, 1914.

In its creative quests (there have been no achievements!) Europe is undergoing a crisis manifested externally in a turn to the East. *It is beyond the West's power to understand the East* because it has lost all notion of the boundaries of art (philosophical and aesthetic issues are lumped together with artistic methods). *European art is archaic, and there is and can be no new art in Europe* because art is built upon *cosmic* elements. All art in the West is *territorial.* The only country that thus far has no territorial art is *Russia.* All work in the West is devoted to the formal achievements of the old art (the old aesthetics). All efforts in the West aimed at constructing a new *a priori* rather than *a posteriori* aesthetics are *doomed to disaster* because new aesthetics follow new art, not the other way around. Recognizing the different directions in which Western and Eastern art move (the art of the West embodies a geometrical worldview that proceeds from object to subject, whereas the art of the East embodies an algebraic worldview that goes from subject to object), we assert as *general* principles of painting, poetry, and music: (1) an arbitrary spectrum; (2) arbitrary depth; (3) the self-sufficiency of tempos as methods of implementation and of rhythms as constants. As special principles *for painting:* (1) a rejection of construction on the cone of trigonometric perspective; (2) dissonances (Georgii Iakulov). *For poetry:* (1) the continuity of the unitary verbal mass; (2) the differentiation of masses with various degrees of rarefaction—lithoid, fluid, and phosphenoid; (3) overcoming the accidentalist approach (Benedikt Livshits). *For music:* (1) overcoming linearity (architectonics) through inner perspective (synthesis [illegible]); (2) overcoming substantive elements (Artur Lourie).

67

Vladimir Mayakovsky

"Russia. Art. We" (1914)

Vladimir Mayakovsky (1893–1930), a member of the Hylaea group, began exhibiting in late 1912. Declaring war on two enemies—the past and the West—he equated "modern" with "Russian." This opposition was reinterpreted after the Revolution, when "Western/past" became "bourgeois" and "Russian" became "proletarian." His article was published in *Nov'* (Virgin Soil) on November 19, 1914.

Russia is struggling to avoid becoming the West's breadbasket. . . .

If people looked on the mighty state of Russia as a colony of Europe, they considered Russia's art a hopeless Kaluga.* The directors of taste are the capitals—Berlin, Paris, London.

The Russian is remarkable!

When he buys the most ordinary needle, nothing can make him choose the "Ivanov & Sons" brand. He will invariably demand a splendid "Excelsior."

Since what flashes in the hand of a Russian reaper swinging his scythe is a German "Solingen," . . . naturally no one would think of objecting, for example, to the fact that before the latest rebellion of the young the paw of dull-witted Munich lay on Russian painting.

The Shishkins and Aivazovskiis† are victims.

*Kaluga is a city southwest of Moscow.

†Ivan Shishkin (1832–1898), landscape painter, member of the Wanderers; Ivan Aivazovskii (1817–1900), painter of seascapes.

Russians have so little respect for themselves, they won't begin to acknowledge anyone as a great artist until he journeys abroad to Mecca to pay homage.

What do they get out of it?

Instead of the feeling of a Russian style and the cheerful spirit of our *lubok*—the frivolous glibness of Paris or the funereal gauntness of Munich.

It's time we realized that for us, "being Europe" isn't slavish imitation of the West or trotting along in leading strings tossed to us via Verzhbolovo,* but mustering *our own* forces to the same degree as they do *there!*

Far be it from me, of course, to think that everything that's not ours is rubbish.

But what a disgrace it is, for example, when the German repertory of all those Wagners and Hauptmanns was tossed out of Russian theaters and we were left with almost no theater!

And this at a time when a constellation of young Russian artists—Goncharova, Burliuk, Larionov, Mashkov, Lentulov, and others—have already started to resurrect genuine Russian painting, the simple beauty of [painted] shaft-bows and signs, the anonymous ancient Russian icon painting that is the equal of both Leonardo and Raphael.

Society has to abandon yesterday's jeers and change its attitude toward these artists and their construction of the temple of the new Russian beauty.

*A railway station on the Russian-German border; presently Virbalis, Liithuania.

RUSSIAN AND SOVIET CRITICISM AFTER THE REVOLUTION

VI

THE INTERNATIONAL OF ART AND THE GREAT UTOPIA

The Bolshevik leaders regarded art mainly as a means of propaganda and education. Like Lenin [68], most of them shared a negative view of contemporary trends in art in favor of a nineteenth-century realism. The fact that the Bolsheviks entered into a brief alliance with the leftist artists who from 1918 through 1921 led the Visual Arts Department (IZO) within the People's Commissariat of Enlightenment (Narkompros) did not change this situation. These artists' ambition was to establish a new universal revolutionary art using an innovative approach to organizing a new type of nationalized public museum that would help to legitimize contemporary art.

In early 1919 the "leftists" organized the Museum of the Culture of Painting in Moscow and the Museum of Artistic Culture in Petrograd. These collections framed the contemporary art movement as part of an interdependent international process. However, the avant-gardists' attempts to obtain Shchukin's and Morozov's paintings were unsuccessful. Muratov's project [72] represented the concept of the more conservative group of modernists, for whom the defense of Russia's European orientation after the October Revolution took on special significance.

Creating a new "proletarian" culture was among the proclaimed goals of the Revolution. Although the content of this notion varied, it remained extremely exclusive. Typical of the 1918–20 period were attempts by Party journalists and Marxist scholars [70] to discover the sources of proletarian art in works devoted to the workers by artists from the industrial countries (Kollwitz, Brangwyn, Constantine Meunier, etc.). Attempts to make realism the model for the new art aroused opposition from the most politicized cultural force—the Proletkult [69].

Between 1918 and 1920, Russia's increasing isolation proved conducive to various projects to found a worldwide association of artists. In late 1918, IZO Narkompros established an International Bureau that included Anatolii Lunacharskii, Nikolai Punin, Vladimir Tatlin, and Vasily Kandinsky. The bureau developed the "International of Art" project (a magazine with this title was compiled but never published). The world's transformation in the International had to become an act of artistic creation [75–77]. Spreading Russian slogans in the West became more important than having European art return to Russia.

As the political and economic embargo was being lifted in the years 1920–23, the question that came to the fore was to what extent Russian art should be connected with the West. Many participants in the debate were convinced that Western culture was undergoing a crisis, but its causes and consequences were interpreted differently—in Marxist, Christian, and Spenglerian terms. Recognizing the crisis did not mean rejecting the Western heritage; a return to the European values represented in art could be regarded as an antidote to political and cultural radicalism [83]. On the contrary, politically engaged critics related to Constructivism and Lef (Left Front of Arts, organized in 1922) believed in the international character of contemporary art but assumed that only what they called productionist, or propagandistic, art could give any meaning to the formal experiments of the European avant-garde [82, 92]. Obviously, the very notion of a relationship with "Paris" and of Western culture generally would also have to be reevaluated.

The wide variety of views on the future interrelationship of Russian and Western art was made possible by the relative intellectual pluralism of the early 1920s. By the middle of the decade that situation had changed, as indicated by Punin's debate with Tugendkhol'd [86–88]. The latter's arguments showed that international cultural ties were now inevitably being regarded in the context of antagonistic social systems.

In the early 1920s conservative isolationism came back into play. The AKhRR (Association of Artists of Revolutionary Russia) concept of "heroic realism" implied a return to pre-Impressionist conditions. Rather than creating any new idea, its critics merely combined prerevolutionary journalistic truisms about the aping of Western art with a Marxist scheme that established a direct dependence between art and society's class nature [85]. Banal though this construction was, however, it became a powerful weapon in the debate.

68

Clara Zetkin

Reminiscences of Lenin (1924)

Clara Zetkin (1857–1933) was a leader of the Communist Party of Germany and a friend of Lenin. Published soon after Lenin's death in 1924, her memoirs reflect a conversation she had with Lenin sometime between September 22 and 28, 1920. Since Lenin left no writings on art, the Soviet system constructed "Lenin's theory" of art retrospectively, regarding Zetkin's memoirs as a canonical source. The excerpt here is reprinted from Clara Zetkin, *Reminiscences of Lenin* (New York: International Publishers, 1934), pp. 12–13.

[Lenin said:] "But of course we are Communists. We must not put our hands in our pockets and let chaos ferment as it pleases. We must consciously try to guide this development, to form and determine its results. In that we are still lacking, greatly lacking. . . . We are much too much 'Iconoclasts.' We must retain the beautiful, take it as an example, hold on to it, even though it is 'old.' Why turn away from real beauty, and discard it for good and all as a starting point for further development, just because it is 'old'? Why worship the new as the god to be obeyed, just because it is 'the new'? That is nonsense, sheer nonsense. There is a great deal of conventional art hypocrisy in it, too, and respect for the art fashions of the West. Of course, unconscious! We are good revolutionaries, but we feel obliged to point out that we stand at the 'height of contemporary culture.' I have the courage to show myself a 'barbarian.' I cannot value the works of Expressionism, Futurism, Cubism, and other isms as the highest expressions of artistic genius. I don't understand them. They give me no pleasure."

I could not but admit that I, too, lacked the faculty of understanding that, to an enthusiastic soul, the artistic form of a nose should be a triangle, and that the revolutionary pressure of facts should change the human body into a formless sack placed on two stilts and with two five-pronged forks. Lenin laughed heartily. "Yes, dear Clara, we two are old. We must be satisfied with remaining young for a little longer in the revolution. We don't understand the new art anymore, we just limp behind it."

"But," Lenin continued, "our opinion on art is not important. Nor is it important what art gives to a few hundreds or even thousands of a population as great as ours. Art belongs to the people. It must have its deepest roots in the broad mass of workers. It must be understood and loved by them. It must be rooted in and grow with their feelings, thoughts, and desires. It must arouse and develop the artist in them. Are we to give cake and sugar to a minority when the mass of workers and peasants still lack black bread?"

69

Aleksandr Bogdanov

"Our Critique. Essay One: On Artistic Heritage" (1918)

Bogdanov (pseudonym of Aleksandr Malinovskii, 1873–1928) was a prominent Bolshevik leader and Lenin's political and philosophical rival. After the October Revolution he worked in the Proletkults, which were meant to become "incubators" of proletarian culture. In 1920 Lenin placed the Proletkults under Party control and removed Bogdanov from the leadership.

Bogdanov believed that a work of art automatically transmits the class worldview contained within it and that therefore practically everything created by artists of the past was dangerous for proletarians. This essay was originally published in *Proletarskaia kul'tura* (Proletarian Culture) 2 (1918).

. . . In his sculptures the Belgian artist Constantin Meunier depicts the life and culture of the workers. His statue *The Philosopher* is an image of a worker-thinker absorbed in some important philosophical problem. The naked figure gives a integral and powerful impression of intense thought focused on one thing and struggling to overcome enormous invisible resistance.

What is the artistic idea of the statue? The organizational problem is how to combine heavy physical labor with mental labor and intellectual creation. . . . If you peer into the figure of the "philosopher"—which is always filled with contained exertion, each visible muscle gripped by restrained tension that does not translate into external action but seems to retreat inward—the remarkably clear and complete, ingenuously persuasive solution that presents itself is that "*thought itself is physical exertion;* it is identical with labor; there is no contradiction between them, so separating them is artificial and transient." The conclusions reached by the exact science of physiological psychology fully corroborate this idea, but it is much clearer and more comprehensible when it is embodied in art. And its tremendous significance for the proletariat needs no demonstration.

Our critique, however, must inquire as to which class or social group viewpoint this artist adopts in his works. The answer will be that although he represents workers, he does not do so as an ideologist of the working *class;* the viewpoint is that of labor, but not of *collective labor.* The worker-thinker is presented as an individual; absent or only very vaguely, almost elusively outlined are the ties that fuse the efforts of his thought to the physical and intellectual efforts of the millions who make it a link in the global chain of labor. With respect to social position, artists are intellectuals; accustomed to working individually themselves, they fail to notice the degree to which the method and the tasks addressed by their labor derive from the collective labor of all humanity. The viewpoint of the worker intelligentsia differs little from that of the bourgeoisie—it is just as individualistic. Here as well our critics must supplement what Meunier could not provide.

Thus do the tasks of proletarian criticism of the art of the past define themselves. When it accomplishes them, the working class will be able to master firmly and use independently the organizational experience of millennia that is crystallized in art.

70

Vladimir Friche

"The Art of the Labor Commune" (1918)

Vladimir Friche (Fritzsche, 1870–1929) was active in the Social-Democratic movement beginning in the 1890s, and joined the Bolshevik Party in 1917. Even before the Revolution, he analyzed literature and art from a Marxist perspective as an instructor at Moscow University. Considered the leading Marxist cultural theorist in the 1920s, he influenced Ivan Matsa, Aleksei Fedorov-Davydov, and other critics. This essay was published in *Vestnik zhizni* (Messenger of Life) 6–7 (1918).

Like religion and philosophy, like literature and science, art is an ideological superstructure on the social base. Its flowering and decline, content and style, and evolution are all ultimately predetermined by the aggregate of socio-economic conditions obtaining in a given period. As soon as a social formation recedes into the past, the art it has generated dies out with it. . . .

Owing to the October Revolution, today we are on the boundary dividing two worlds: dying bourgeois civilization, and embryonic communism. What, then, are the prospects of art in the labor commune? . . . In the labor commune once again, as in ancient Hellas and the Middle Ages, art will become a social and public phenomenon. The art of palaces and salons will yield to the art of the square and the streets. The possession of the few will become the property of all. . . .

Grown up on the ruins of the absolutist and aristocratic world and completely absorbed in its mercenary dealings and squeezing surplus value out of the workers, modern bourgeois society would seem at first glance to offer very little material for transforming society into a festive fairy tale. Yet artists manage to change even this prosaic trade fair into a picture of distinctive beauty. This time they have woven it out of gigantic towering skyscrapers, mineshafts plunging deep into the earth, locomotives rushing along rails, blazing, roaring factories, and the wheels and cables of wonder-working machines. Under the brush of artists such as Brangwin, Meunier (not his sculpture but his painting), Bianco, and a great many others, the life of the industrial bourgeois age has once again become a holiday celebrating the beauty of steel and iron, smoke and motion. . . .

The more attentively these artists looked into the industrial bourgeois society around them the more clearly they discerned, chained and nailed to the rock, the tragic figure of Prometheus, who from dawn to late night created this world of marvels and riches. Then suddenly gazing out at the viewer were Botticelli's and Raphael's madonnas, the kings of Velásquez and Van Dyck, Watteau's knights and ladies, the petty bourgeois of Manet and Renoir; unexpectedly looking at us were the degenerate proletarians of Käthe Kollwitz and the gaunt, embittered faces of Roll's and Adler's striking workers.

The artists of the bourgeois industrial age watched a new image almost alien to the art of the past slowly emerge, more and more distinctly, out of the smoke of the blast furnaces and factories and to the cries of the suffering and rebellious proletariat—the image of labor that nourishes and creates the world. Timidly, hesitatingly, they set about surrounding it with a halo of poetry and beauty. Thus were born the pictures celebrating labor by the English Pre-Raphaelite Madox Brown and the French naturalist Roll. The poet Verhaeren's Belgian friend Meunier also tackled the problem, but his . . . ambitious monument to labor was never finished.

Thus did the artists of the bourgeois industrial age pave the way for the artists of the labor commune.

Under the brush and chisel of the latter, life will once again become a holiday of beauty, the creative and revolutionary beauty of labor. . . .

71

Decree of the Soviet of People's Commissars on the Nationalization of the Sergei Shchukin Art Gallery (1918)

Shchukin emigrated to France in August 1918, and his collection was nationalized soon thereafter by this decree, which was signed by Lenin. Pavel Muratov may have helped draft this document, issued on October 29, 1918, for several of his writings contain similar wordings. Until early 1919, Muratov held a position in Narkompros and worked on nationalizing private collections.

Whereas the Shchukin Art Gallery represents an exceptional collection of great European painters, primarily French artists of the late nineteenth and early twentieth centuries, and by virtue of its artistic quality is of national significance for popular education, the Council of People's Commissars decrees:

1. The art collection of Sergei Ivanovich Shchukin is declared to be the property of the Russian Socialist Federative Soviet Republic and is hereby transferred to the authority of the People's Commissariat of Enlightenment on the same bases as other state museums.
2. The building in which the gallery is located, . . . all furnishings, and the adjoining plot of land constituting the former property of S. I. Shchukin are hereby transferred to the authority of the People's Commissariat of Enlightenment.
3. The board supervising the museums and conservation of works of art and antiquities in the People's Commissariat of Enlightenment will immediately develop and implement new administrative principles for the former Shchukin gallery and its activities in accordance with present requirements and tasks in the democratization of the artistic and educational institutions of the Russian Socialist Federative Soviet Republic.

72

Pavel Muratov

"The Museum of Western Art in Moscow" (1920)

Published in *Khudozhestvannaia zhizn'* (Art Life) 3 (1920).

What Moscow . . . wants is not a "surrogate Hermitage" but a strong and viable organism of its own that in its way is no less powerful than the Hermitage. The city is capable of organizing and developing its own Museum of Western Art. Thanks to the collections of S. I. Shchukin and I. A. Morozov, . . . Moscow possesses a selection of the most recent Western European masters unmatched by any European capital except Paris. Here it is important to add that we do not perceive or want to establish any boundary between "old" and "new" Western European art. In our eyes, Manet and Cézanne are the immediate successors of the great Venetians and Spaniards. Their place is in the Louvre and the Uffizi alongside Velásquez, El Greco, Zurbarán, Veronese, and Tintoretto.

We are firmly convinced that a museum containing the Barbizons, Delacroix, Courbet, Manet, the Impressionists, Cézanne, and the so-called Post-Impressionists can fulfill the same *aesthetic and educational* function as a museum containing the works of the Venetians, Spaniards, and Dutch. Both will *in equal measure open the viewer's eyes and provide an introduction to the great art of Europe.*

From here the appropriate practical conclusion is easily drawn. Prioritizing a broad aesthetic education, the [Museum] Section [of Narkompros] can and should organize the Moscow Museum of Western Art around the works of contemporary Western European masters. . . . As soon as feasible, Moscow will systematically collect for the state museum the newest Western painters who are not represented in sufficient quantity or quality in formerly private collections. Gaps must be filled in the holdings of Manet and Courbet. It will be a relatively simple matter to bring the collections of the Impressionists, Cézanne, Van Gogh, and Gauguin to the desired level of completion. Moscow will also face the extremely interesting and absorbing task of presenting the "post-Cézanne period" in painting as it deserves to be shown and has not yet been shown *anywhere.*

Perhaps only then will it be understood and recognized that, in the fifty years between 1870 and 1920, French painting approximated in creative intensity the best periods of the Renaissance, and its achievements were equal to those of the Dutch school as a whole. Thus, the extremely vital goal of the Moscow Museum of Western Art is firmly rooted in the cultural organism of our entire age. If this objective can be met, the museum will directly and creatively influence all active manifestations of contemporary artistic culture. No museum, it seems to me, could set itself a more desirable goal.

73

Vasily Kandinsky

"The Museum of the Culture of Painting" (1920)

In 1914 Kandinsky returned to Russia. From 1918 to 1921, when he emigrated to Germany, he was a member of the Art Department of Narkompros (IZO) and led the Monumental Art Section of the Institute of Artistic Culture (INKhUK). From June 1919 to October 1920 he also served as director of the Museum of the Culture of Painting. He was replaced there by Rodchenko, who served until July 1922 and who rejected the incorporation of foreign artists. The museum merged with the Tretiakov Gallery in 1924.

Originally published in *Khudozhestvennaia zhizn'* (Art Life) 2 (1920), Kandinsky's essay is reprinted here from *Kandinsky: Complete Writings on Art,* edited by Kenneth C. Lindsay and Peter Vergo, translated by Peter Vergo, vol. 1 (Boston: G. K. Hall, 1982), pp. 439–40; text © 2009 Artists Rights Society (ARS), New York/ADAGP, Paris.

The Museum Commission has defined the character of the Museum of the Culture of Painting as follows:

"The Museum of the Culture of Painting shall have as its goal to represent the different stages of purely pictorial attainment, pictorial methods and resources in all their fullness, as expressed in the painting of all periods and peoples."

Methods that have enriched the resources of pictorial expression, solutions to the problem of the correlation of color-tones, the correlation between the color-tone and the application of color, compositional methods—i.e., the building up of the whole composition and of its individual parts, their treatment, the overall *facture,* and the structure of parts, etc.—these are examples of the criteria that shall determine the acquisition of the works by the museum.

It follows from this that the Museum of the Culture of Painting will not try to show in its entirety the works of any one artist, nor to trace the development of the above problems solely in any one period or country, but will show, independently of any trends, only those works which introduce new methods. In this manner, the Museum of the Culture of Painting is distinguished by its definite approach to the question of evaluating the products of different epochs: it will classify the historical development of painting from the point of view of the conquest of the material, both real and ideal, as a purely pictorial phenomenon. In this way the Museum, having set itself purely technical-professional objectiveness, will in the same time be seen as indispensable for the masses, who until this time have never in any country had a collection capable of opening the way to this branch of painting, without which the complete understanding of art is unthinkable.

Being of the view that museums and repositories of art in the Russian Republic should contribute from their own resources to the general state reserves, the Department has taken steps to obtain from the Moscow collections of Western European art those works which are regarded as essential for the Museum of the Culture of Painting, and which, at the same time, can be removed from these collections without detracting from their scope and effectiveness.

. . . The Museum Department [of the People's Commissariat of Enlightenment], in accordance with the principle and necessity of the Museum of the Culture of Painting, has agreed that a series of works by French artists should be selected from collections of Western European art (principally from the galleries of Shchukin and Morozov). For this purpose, pictures by Braque and Van Gogh, Gauguin, Derain, Le Fauconnier, Matisse, Manet, Monet, Picasso, Pissarro, Rousseau, Renoir, Cézanne, Signac, Vlaminck, and Friez were chosen. . . .

74

Varvara Stepanova

Diary Entry (1919)

This diary entry from March 27, 1919, is translated from Alexandr Rodchenko and Varvara Stepanova, *Budushchee—edinstvennaia nasha tsel'* (Future Is Our Only Goal), edited by Peter Noever (Vienna: Austrian Museum of Applied Arts; Munich: Prestel, 1991).

Anti's [Rodchenko's] thoughts can be summarized more or less as follows.

French painting should not be mixed with Russian painting, for Russian painting goes its own way, even if we stubbornly refuse to see the fact, don't value it, and bow down to Westerners. Putting the pictures of Russian artists in Shchukin's and Morozov's museums amounts to admitting our own bankruptcy and burying our own past, which is as rich as that of French or any other art. Above all it has to be made perfectly clear that Russian painting has not inherited the Western tradition, and what it does reflect of the West detracts from the essence of Russian painting.

We go our own way; our painting is so distinct from that of the West that it is stupid and sinful to heap them together. The essence and significance of Western painting is easel painting—a picture of set dimensions adapted to fit a room, a study, or a museum. This is its meaning and purpose; this is the external feature and internal painterly component of Western painting. Western painting explores the light and volume of forms. Western painting can never be compared with Russian painting, for the latter is diametrically opposed to it. Externally Russian painting observes no set dimensions—canvases can be enormous or tiny. Internally it explores color and plane and aspires to conquer space of any dimensions whatever. Thus it is clear that Western painting is essentially easel painting and synthetic, whereas Russian painting is decorative and analytical. The problems addressed in the painting of the West and the East, therefore, are completely different, and the one cannot be compared with the other. Russian painting takes its source from the icon, which is a decorative ornament—that is, a value unto itself—in contrast to applied ornament, which does not live an independent life and is merely an appendage to an object. This great decorative element of color and light is the prime mover of a Russian painterly culture that we do not value, that we do not know. Our worshippers of Western easel painting are profoundly mistaken when they close their eyes and suppress within themselves that which is peculiar only to us.

This, incidentally, is in general typical of Russians—failing to see their own beauty, they idolize the West, which has already disintegrated and become obsolete. I hope that my remarks will not be taken for a national appeal, for that is not at all my intention, but I simply want to explain the difference and incongruence between our paths of development and Western painting.

Our painting must be taken out onto the streets, onto the fences and roofs. . . . That is why we cultivated icons, shop signs, and *lubok* woodcuts. And it is clear to me that we must create and show our Russian culture of painting, which we unfortunately consider worthless, invariably attempting instead to follow in the leading strings and at the bidding of the West. . . .

75

Nikolai Punin

"The Third International" (1919)

First published in *Iskusstvo kommuny* (Art of the Commune), March 16, 1919.

. . . The proletariat is united—science and art should also be united. The International, the Third International—what further schools and currents are needed? Can science and art really expect anything more effective than the International? I don't think so. Let's not think so.

The tasks the Third International faces are enormous. At present they are practical in nature, but the time will come for theory, a theory of culture, and then the Communist International will confront nationalism and individualism in science and art, face them in order to leap over them. I believe leaping is precisely what it will do, for that is what will solve them.

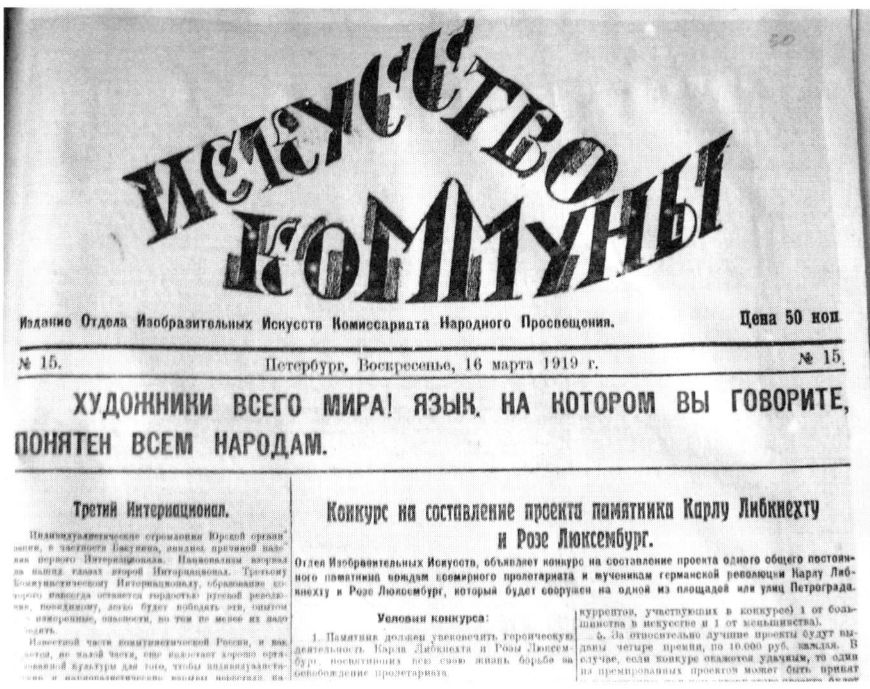

Искусство коммуны

Издание Отдела Изобразительных Искусств Комиссариата Народного Просвещения. Цена 50 коп.

№ 15. Петербург, Воскресенье, 16 марта 1919 г. № 15.

ХУДОЖНИКИ ВСЕГО МИРА! ЯЗЫК, НА КОТОРОМ ВЫ ГОВОРИТЕ, ПОНЯТЕН ВСЕМ НАРОДАМ.

Третий Интернационал.

Конкурс на составление проекта памятника Карлу Либкнехту и Розе Люксембург.

Отдел Изобразительных Искусств, объявляет конкурс на составление проекта одного общего постоянного памятника вождям всемирного пролетариата и мученикам германской революции Карлу Либкнехту и Розе Люксембург, который будет сооружен на одной из площадей или улиц Петрограда.

Условия конкурса:

Nikolai Punin's article "The Third International" in *Iskusstvo kommuny* (Art of the Commune), March 16, 1919. The headline reads: "Artists of the World! The language you speak is clear to all nations."

Quite a lot has been said about the contemporary arts and sciences being above nations, above personality, and even above classes. This is a language that everyone today understands. As for the supra-class character of science and art, that premise has been refuted rather convincingly; suffice it to mention Franz Mehring's immortal work on Lessing.* Nor is it difficult to prove the nationalism and individualism of contemporary scientific and artistic practice. . . . Science and art should be international and collective, but thus far they have not been.

Will they be? Yes, they will. This is as inevitable as the European socialist revolution, as inevitable as tomorrow and the year 1920. Our task, if we want to creatively master the life we have been granted, is to bring closer this hour of the triumph of communist culture, the hour of the Revolution's triumph in science and art. What we want is not to wait for it to arrive but to create its arrival, for only those who sense victory while their enemies are still asleep can be victors.

In this respect as well our greatest hope is the Third International. . . .

*Franz Mehring, *Die Lessing-Legende* (1893).

76

Konstantin Krainii [Umanskii]

"The International of Art (The Tasks Confronting the International Union of Fine Arts Workers)" (1919)

Konstantin Umanskii (1902–45) was sent to Europe in 1919 as an "ambassador of the arts." His 1920 survey of contemporary Russian art (*Neue Kunst in Russland, 1914–1919*) influenced radical German artists. For many years he worked as a journalist and diplomat, serving as ambassador to the United States from 1936 to 1941. This article was published in *Iskusstvo* (Art), September 5, 1919.

. . . What tasks will confront artists organized in an international federation? These will be essentially the same professional, economic, social, cultural, ideological, and aesthetic factors that have already motivated Russian artists to take the initiative to organize. Thus the International Federation of Fine Arts Workers would be, above all, a powerful economic organ called upon to carry out a complex task, namely, to determine once and for all the social and material conditions the state should provide. For only through an international exchange of national experiences and through the internal practice of each national artistic group, etc., can the complex problems squarely confronting artistic life today be articulated; closest to such a practical task for an ideal International Federation would be the formation of an international jury competent to judge the art of the whole world. They, rather than the newspaper scribblers, would evaluate the achievements and determine the fate of world art. In its theoretical work the international association of artists would, of course, promote collective art rather than the individualism that in the waning years of capitalism has been manifested so prominently in rivalry, publicity seeking, and aestheticism. Expanding national art on an international scale will stimulate a huge demand for the international exchange of works of art by creating a solid link between the arts of all peoples, through exhibitions, museums, the circulation of products of the art industry, books, "ambassadors of art," international congresses, competitions, and so on. The balanced distribution of artistic forces, the establishment of a new ethics for the artist-worker, and the bold proclamation of the slogan "art for the workers" are some of the other tasks facing the International Federation, and it is on their successful fulfillment that the renaissance and flowering of international proletarian artistic culture will depend.

77

Vasily Kandinsky

"The Great Utopia" (1920)

This essay first appeared in *Khudozhestvennaia zhizn'* (Art Life) 3 (1920). It is reprinted here from *Kandinsky: Complete Writings on Art*, edited by Kenneth C. Lindsay and Peter Vergo, translated by Peter Vergo, vol. 1 (Boston: G. K. Hall, 1982), pp. 444–47;

. . . the Russian artists, in their call to their colleagues, also wrote of their desire for an international art congress.* One must hope that active steps and real measures will soon be taken in this connection, so as to bring about the first world congress of art on an unprecedented scale.

It seems to me that this congress should adopt a theme of a real, albeit utopian character. Without a doubt, one of the most forcible questions in art, as regards both its internal and external significance, concerns the forms, methods, scope, possibilities, and present and future attainments of *monumental art.*

Naturally, questions of this kind cannot be decided by a congress only of painters, or only of representatives of the three main branches of art, which would, in the end, only succeed in finding general subjects and problems—that is to say, a congress of painters, sculptors, and architects.

To consider the question outlined, it would be necessary to attract representatives of all the arts. . . . The real collaboration of *all* branches of art on *one* real task is the only way of finding out (1) to what extent the idea of a monumental art has matured, both in its potential and in its concrete form, (2) to what extent the ideas about such an art developed by different peoples are related to each other, (3) to what extent the different realms of art (painting, sculpture, architecture, poetry, music, dance) are prepared for this kind of genuinely collective creation, (4) to what extent the representatives of different countries and different arts are prepared to speak the same language regarding this most important subject, and (5) how far the actual realization of this idea, which is still in its infancy, can be carried.

. . . One must conclude that a congress would constitute a curative means of heroic proportions, which would bring this illness to a crisis of unprecedented force. After such a crisis, the still-ailing elements would fall prey to the disease of separation, while the remaining healthy ones would be united with unprecedented strength by a bond of mutual attraction.

. . . A theme for the first *Congress of Representatives of All the Arts of All Countries* would be the building of an international house of art and the working out of plans for its structure. Such a structure would have to be designed by representatives of all the arts, since it would have to accommodate all branches of art, not only those which already exist in reality, but also those which have existed and which exist only in dreams—without any hope of these dreams ever being realized. This edifice should become *for all nations the house of utopia.* I believe I would not, in fact, be the only one to rejoice if it were given the name "The Great Utopia."

*The call from Russian artists was forwarded to Germany by the artist and former prisoner of war Ludwig Baehr (1871–?) and was published there in several periodicals (cf. *Das Kunstblatt* 4 [1919]).

78

IZO Editorial (1921)

The newspaper *IZO* (Visual Arts), the IZO Department's last publication before it was dissolved, came out once, on March 10, 1921. This editorial reflects the mood of young artists who had absorbed the ideas of production art and were awaiting the triumph of the Artists' International.

. . . we can see two fundamental features that will determine further development. First, the art of all peoples is aligning itself to find a common solution to what are basically the same problems; art is moving away from nationalism and toward the International. Second, contemporary creative artists of all countries have begun to sense that art cannot go on like this, that they cannot move art forward until life around them has changed. . . .

Now that we have begun to get access to the foreign press, we see that the ideas tossed into the world by our International Bureau have borne fruit. We see that an international exchange of exhibitions has already begun. . . .

All of this, however, is being run on a private footing by groups or international societies that merely enjoy the patronage of their governments. In addition to international exhibitions, contact is being reestablished through a number of art periodicals that devote a lot of discussion to international connections. Some information on Russia gets through as well, and an entire book on Russian art was even published there recently.* To us everything in it is old news and quite distorted, but judging by the foreign press's reception of the book, there is enormous interest in us and what is going on here. They expect us to save them. We believe that they will save themselves, but our struggle and our accomplishments and our mistakes will undoubtedly show them the way.

Thus we approach our activity in Europe not with words, not with a mass meeting, but with works, with something concrete.

This matter can and will be resolved through an exhibition. Not a circle or a society, but the state as a whole will show the West that we have known how to destroy, but that with all the vital forces at our disposal we are building something new. This will be reinforced not only by the "pure" art of aesthetic value created by artists but also by the accomplishments of the new school (the State Free Art Studio). We will then come face to face with everything in the West that is vital and congenial to us, and this is how the Comintern of the Arts will be founded. . . .

*Konstantin Umanskii's *Neue Kunst in Russland, 1914–1919* (Potsdam: Kiepenheuer; Munich: Goltz, 1920).

79

Abram Efros

"We and the West" (1920)

Abram Efros (1888–1954) studied law at Moscow University and in 1911 began his career as an art journalist. After 1917 he became one of the most influential critics continuing the Modernist tradition. He worked for Narkompros, the Tretiakov Gallery, and many other institutions. In the 1930s and 1940s he was repeatedly criticized for "formalism" and in 1949 was exiled to Tashkent.

The article is a response to the Soviet-Estonian treaty signed on February 2, 1920, marking the first break in Russia's political isolation. It was published in *Khudozhestvennaia zhizn'* (Art Life) 1 (1920).

. . . There are not enough art supplies, no technical literature or general fiction, no ties to the world of Western art, no contact with the study of art; we know nothing about new discoveries in artistic culture, new names that have become famous, new currents that are shaking up the drowsy world of the old schools. But at the moment we have other things on our mind. We must frankly admit that what especially stirs our imaginations now are all the simplest and most vital things for which we have been so unbearably starved. We dream of tubes of paint, instrument strings, picture hooks and twine, lacquer, reproductions, paper, sheet music, etc., etc.—everything needed to prevent the immediate collapse of the artistic structure that we try, stubbornly, gritting our teeth, to hold together with homemade string and reinforce with homemade pegs.

But art's turn will come as well. How will we greet it? Quite obviously, with great interest, greedily. But that is not the point. The point is whether Russia will continue in her old attitude toward the West as a *pupil to a teacher,* or whether, after *what* we have gone through and *how* we have gone through it, after the great war and the great revolution, we will greet Europe differently, more independently and more discriminatingly—perhaps in some respects completely independently? Will Russia cease simply *borrowing* as before, or will she begin selecting critically, aware that in some areas of artistic production she is if not more experienced then more *significant* than Europe?

Renewed relations with the West confront us with three areas of European artistic life: artistic technique and knowledge, free artistic creation, and the state-sponsored construction of artistic culture. In the area of technique and knowledge, of course, we must and will be *students* who will study and adopt everything that the West has so consummately created. And we will probably be doing so for a long time—perhaps years. Here the new Russia, unlike the old, must be a *perceptive and persistent* pupil and not just skim the surface haphazardly as before.

Nor should we abandon our apprenticeship in the area of artistic creation. New forms of art, new artistic theories, a new palette, new music, and new theater are emerging as before in the West, whose benign hegemony is indisputable. Our artists will be drawn to Paris as before in search of a laboratory of leftist art among the nests of bohemia, and people in the music and theater world will turn to Germany and the innovations of its superb professionalism. However, there is something in which we are *ahead* of Europe, and although embryonic and imperfect, our undertakings are nonetheless new, important, and instructive, and our experience will be the *first* experience the West will study: the area of mass, proletarian, collective art, the workers and peasants' theater, the Proletkults, the folk art communes, mass musical and theatrical productions, and so on. . . .

In the third area we have all the advantages. The state-directed construction of artistic culture has developed in Russia on an unprecedented scale and according to a well-administered plan. The West has nothing like that. . . . Bearers of the living artistic culture of Russia accustomed to *opposing* the powers that be are now participating in the government, and they are participating as *an authority,* because the state has almost if not completely handed over its levers of power to them. . . .

. . . Russia is now a huge artistic laboratory—a laboratory as large as the entire state, and here we will not be rushing through the doors that have opened wide into Europe but will be waiting for visitors to come to us.

80

Nikolai Punin

Tatlin (Against Cubism) (1921)

From 1916 to 1924 Punin was Tatlin's close friend. His concept of the "independence" of Russian art was much influenced by Tatlin's approach to materials and the creative process. This excerpt is from his book on Tatlin published in Petrograd in 1921.

. . . the position of the Russian school is such that its continued existence depends to a considerable degree on the intensity of the struggle with Paris; as for Tatlin, there seems to be no better way to demonstrate his importance than to make him the starting point of what in the final analysis is an unavoidable campaign against France. . . .

Many masters of the Russian school whose significance I by and large do not intend to refute represent an abysmal muddle of traditions and methods. Tatlin is among those who have a clean line of evolution. In certain cases strength of talent is nothing but willpower. In their unselfish wanderings around the world, Russian artists of recent decades most often return to Paris, where the only genesis they find is Manet–Picasso. . . . The fact that Gleizes and Metzinger anticipated the forms of objective beauty does not mean that they foresaw *culture.* In Picasso's works the study of materials was reduced to a play with textures, the basis of the game being *"nous voulons les nuances encore"* (Verlaine). Picasso cannot be taken as the dawn of a new era. When analyzed, contiguous periods will always have something in common, but "can it [logic] ever really make wine be the same in the retort of the chemist and the glass of the gourmet?" Picasso is at any rate on the other side of the crisis; it is not even a question of invention, artistic culture, or traditions. The future belongs to those who are amazingly incapable of understanding beauty *(Beaux-Arts),* for that is what destroyed "beautiful France." The beautiful became French once and for all beginning with the Impressionists, but this did not make Frenchness European, let alone human. Thanks to the intensive work of the French school, art became identified with the romantic, the individual, and the aesthetic, but it thereby ceased to be classical, realistic, and professional. The thousands of kilometers separating Paris and Moscow allow us to see the approaching wave of professional classical realism. . . .

The eye of the French artist is limited by his free personality and "aesthetic" sentiments; it is enfeebled and enslaved. Restoring it means restoring a realism that is equally necessary and obligatory. We regard the violation of real relations to be the greatest mistake of the dying (French) school. Art that has been raised on false relationships, hypertrophied feelings, and illusion is diseased art. An eye deprived of objective criteria pays too much attention to details; little by little art itself becomes a detail; it elevates the incidental to the obligatory, prefers the individual to the classical. The Impressionists transformed painting into an art of life, and the Cubists are determined to renew painting; together with painting it is necessary to renew reality—that is, life itself—in its entirety. The generations of artists who will find in art the strength to cleanse traditional realism will reinforce the achievements of recent decades. Then the period from Monet to Picasso will be regarded as the crisis of European art, after which, owing to this crisis, classical European Realism—deeper, richer, and reborn—will shine even brighter. The professors of the Academy who accuse Manet–Monet of degeneration had their reasons, but their misfortune was that they themselves were corpses. . . .

81

Jansen

"On the Exchange of Art Exhibitions with Western Europe" (1921)

The Dutch artist Jansen (pseudonym of Jan Proost, 1890–1943) came to Moscow as a member of the Executive Committee of the Comintern in 1920. In 1926 he left the Party. Jansen was executed by the Nazis during World War II. This essay was published in *IZO* (Visual Arts), March 10, 1921.

Western Europeans find it striking and strange that Russian artists and art studio apprentices should express such enormously respectful interest in everything "new" going on in the "artistic" sphere in Europe. . . .

Only in the social soil of Soviet Russia can a new art be created.

Only when this new soil has been created in Western Europe, only then, in contact with this new art, can it draw vital new juices for itself.

In conclusion, the question arises as to what Russian art expects to gain from exhibiting abroad works done during the Revolution. Are we trying to bring revolution to Europe? There is nothing to say against that. You know, though, that art is one means of distracting attention from revolution, and capitalism regards it as an anesthetic, just like religion.

But why else would young artists want to exhibit abroad? Surely not for this.

They expect that recognition in the West will help them in their struggle with the moribund trends of the old men—the former artistic lackeys of tsarism and the bourgeoisie. . . .

If the young hold the petty bourgeois spirit of the old men in such contempt, though, how can they expect help from the reactionary and counterrevolutionary art critics and other pseudo-intellectual lackeys of the Western bourgeoisie?

And vice versa. How significant will exhibitions of Western artists be in Russia as long as only Russia possesses the social foundation on which a new art can be built? . . .

Here we must be aware of our own strength and calmly go on building.

If we cannot build because something or even a great deal is lacking, then fine—it does no harm to realize that it is not art that is the basis of the new society but the other way around: a new art can be built only on the basis of a new economy.

So first help build a new economic life; this is the most important thing and it will take all forces. As for the West, let them first make a revolution.

82

Boris Arvatov

"Toward Proletarian Art" (1922)

Boris Arvatov (1896–1940) was a theoretician of production art and a member of Lef. In 1919 he joined the Communist Party and in 1920 was a commissar during the Soviet-Polish war. Arvatov strongly believed that art is entirely determined by economic factors and possesses no specific qualities. This essay was published in *Pechat' i revoliutsiia* (Press and Revolution) 1 (1922). He ceased publishing after the 1920s because of a mental disorder resulting from a contusion he suffered at the front.

. . . More and more subjective impressions, more and more expressive effects, more and more self-sufficient play of emotions—this is the path the picture has traveled from Delacroix to Courbet, Courbet to Monet, and Monet to Van Gogh. Sooner or later the object must lose all meaning in the eyes of the bankrupt personality, and it is no surprise that Van Gogh's epigones now number among their leaders the Russo-German artist Kandinsky, who has turned the picture into an abstract play of pure colors governed by a single law—the metaphysical fantasy of a painter who spits on real life.

Only Cézanne, a mason in painting and a hermit in real life, opened up new horizons by tackling the constructive and technical use of the material of painting. Here as well, however, the bourgeoisie found itself at an impasse: Cézanne's school, which with Picasso's help developed the teacher's principles, limited its constructions to the same few feet of canvas enclosed again and again in that accursed frame. Contemporary artists are incapable of shaping real life or embellishing a "real" thing; with the arrogance of upstarts they have left that to the house painters.

It would be strange if bourgeois painters did not suffer from their divorce from life; man, even when he neglects humanity, remains a social animal nonetheless. In fact, running throughout the history of the latest painting is an urge toward the fresco and an escape from the bounds of the rectangular frame that holds painting captive. But how to find this fresco? Zero, after all, will always be zero; without life you cannot create life. The artists, however, were more cunning. In broad daylight, in front of everyone, they began stealing . . . they began stylizing. Puvis de Chavannes, Maurice Denis, Henri Matisse, and many others who raised the banner of artistic reaction decided to use the lines of Giotto and the colors of the savages to delight our age of electricity and proletarian revolutions.

Others, languishing in hopeless isolation but failing to understand that life cannot be transformed by art and that, on the contrary, only the transformation of life will liberate art, either fled society or put a bullet in their brains. But Gauguin's Tahitian pilgrimage, which realized Grandfather Jean-Jacques's sentimental utopian ideal, and Van Gogh's suicide did not save art but merely demonstrated their own bankruptcy. Van Gogh may have understood better than anyone else the reasons for the decay of art; it was not for nothing that he awaited help from the socialists. The whole point, however, is that one must act rather than await, and not alone but along with the great vanguard of humanity that through victories and defeats, neither intoxicated by the former nor nonplussed by the latter, marches ahead of everyone toward the harmonious society rising up before them. This vanguard is the proletariat, which alone through the class struggle will cast off the old world that is strangling art; only the proletariat's artists will lead the battle for the creative transformation of life under the banner of international communism. . . .

. . . when they have seized power, the proletarians will not depict beautiful bodies but will cultivate real, live, harmonious individuals; they will not draw a forest but will plant parks and gardens; they will not decorate walls with mechanically suspended pictures but will adorn the walls themselves; they will not take color photographs of elegant clothes but will manufacture clothes in their workshops. All this bourgeois classification of genre artists, portrait painters, and *nature morte* painters will plunge into oblivion, and their place will be taken by artists who are metalworkers, woodworkers, textile workers, and electricians, the friends and coworkers of their great class. *Art will organically coincide with productive labor. . . .*

Thus only the dictatorship of the proletariat will make the machine a docile and supple tool in the hands of the collective—a tool as sensitive and mobile as the brush in the hand of the individual artist. The brush will be needed to study and construct the materials of painting in the technical laboratory: their density, texture, and color, their application to living reality. Here the proletariat will utilize with unprecedented might the achievements of the bourgeois "constructivists" (the Cézanne–Picasso–Tatlin school), transforming individualistic play with the "end in itself" into the creation of real forms and transferring painterly constructions from the picture to the real object. . . .

83

Pavel Muratov

"Predictions" (1922)

Published in *Shipovnik* (Dog Rose) 1 (1922).

Although we have been separated from the West for eight years, we can state with full certainty that nothing important or decisive has happened in European art during these years. We are convinced of this by the books and magazines, newspaper articles, and letters from foreigners and compatriots that reach us from time to time. The artistic Paris of 1922 is clearly a spectacle that differs little from what it was in 1914. Although there have been some changes in intensity and direction in the artistic energies of Germany, this is a temporary and local phenomenon whose significance should not be exaggerated. . . .

Neither the war nor the Revolution has had any influence on art. Everyone should acknowledge this quite sincerely, with neither delight nor distress. . . . It is in any case wrong to view art as a result. Art is, of course, profoundly linked to the march of history and the fate of culture, but this link is of an entirely different order. Yes, it is still man's keenest and most sensitive psychic apparatus, which is exactly why it neither reflects nor repeats events: it foretells and forewarns. Foresight is art's historical function. . . .

Post-Impressionist art distinguished itself in the European culture of 1900–1914 by a level of alarm and intensity that was unusual for the period. There was something "suspicious" about its willingness to accept any extreme or harshness and its readiness to take the shortest path to its end. Amid the overall apparently smooth and slow course of events, art was struck by an inner fever that made it quake. . . .

From this point of view, the pause observed in art after the war is easy to explain. Contemporary art has already survived its passion; now it is merely living out the upheavals that nourish it. . . .

The unprecedented predominance of abstractions is amazing. Today's artists think in abstract categories of color, composition, space, form, and texture. It is incorrect to think that they were taught to do so by the art critics and historians. Artists have always taught the critics, not the other way around. If there had been no Cézanne or Picasso, the formal method in the history of art would never have developed to the same extent. Our artists perceive unusually keenly the differentiated principles of objectness and thingness in the world without responding to the concrete diversity of objects or the fluidity of things.

Their attitude toward man is also crucial. Man is the beginning and end of everything in classical and Western European art. Anthropomorphism was the basic worldview that made this art possible. . . .

European humanism is dying, and because it was the soul of the old Europe, Spengler is right to announce its imminent demise. Culture or civilization—we will ignore the fact that these terms are debatable. One thing is in any event clear: the culture or civilization of the future will be neither humanistic nor connected by a thousand threads to antiquity. Modernity is breaking these threads; the Hellenic cycle of history that lasted to the twentieth century is coming to an end. . . .

. . . Not-Europe proved stronger than Europe. At the same time, the collective proved to be a fortunate rival for the nation, because America, Australia, South Africa, and Canada are not nations but collectives. Thus was a blow dealt to the two basic notions of modern history—Europe's predominance and the purely European notion of the nation.

. . . For all its material and technological might, America remains essentially the same wild land as in the days when it was populated by polecats and Indians. Canada and Australia, for all their tilled fields and elegantly and well-ordered cities, exemplary schools, and numerous universities, remain a perfectly blank spot in terms of intellectual culture. . . .

It turns out one can live splendidly without one's own art, poetry, God, or historical and national spirit. The Hellenic European world has yet to know or see such human constructs. . . .

. . . Next in line is not only the awakening but the emancipation of the East, whether through revolution or some other means. Despite the peaceful colonizing and civilizing facade it has adopted, Europe has for a long time taken the position of the East's traditional enemy. . . . One day the culture of modern India, modern China, modern Japan, and modern Persia will emerge as a rival—a civilization of the East we do not know and have not foreseen because it is as distant from the ancient cultures of the East from which it derived as the culture of Renaissance and Baroque Europe are from the great civilization of Greece. . . .

The history of art clearly distinguishes only two noncontiguous and nonintersecting lines of development—the art of Hellenism (the West) and that of China (the East). An abyss separates these two artistic principles, and an abyss certainly separates the complex worlds of outlooks, thought, emotions, and sensations they conceal. The artistic language of the East (China) and India, which has not been touched by Hellenism, is utterly unintelligible to us. We cannot penetrate beyond the surface of this art. We catch expressions without fathoming the essence of what is being expressed. . . .

There is a third participant, however, that views the contrast between the principles of East and West from the side, so to speak. All the collections in America's exemplary Boston Museum of Fine Arts are divided into two equally prominent sections of Oriental and Western art. It contains fewer Titians, Velàsquezes, and Rembrandts than London, Paris, or Berlin, of course, but many more works by the masters of ancient Japan and China. America in general abounds in collections of Oriental art. Its equal interest in the art of *them* and *us* underscores its present role as a third party. . . .

It would be fruitless now to try to guess the shape of these potential Alaskan-Siberian, Japanese-Mexican, Chinese-Californian, and Indo-Peruvian arts in the distant future. Their hypothetical existence does not fill us Europeans with optimism, for there is no question here of our cultural and artistic achievement. To those who feel they are in the bosom of a single European civilization, the notion that humanistic and Hellenic Europe is ending, the collective will dominate over the nation, and the East will triumph over the fragments of European culture must seem like the end of the world. This notion should sharpen our sense of Europe's historical unity, so that art once again becomes man's keenest psychic apparatus, because it alone in the years of our great discord and strife can express that notion.

. . . Contemporary art, a single European art with its center in Paris, is the most durable of the links uniting the European nations. Besides this "horizontal" link, however, it supports an even more precious "vertical" one. More powerfully than the ephemeral traditions of manners and mores, it unites us with our past. It contains the sources of eternal resurrection and rebirth. . . .

84

Vasilii Chekrygin

"On the Emerging New Phase of All-European Art" (1922)

Vasilii Chekrygin (1897–1922) participated in the radical "No. 4" exhibition in 1913, but by the end of the decade his attitude toward Cubism and Futurism had changed completely. He was among the founders of the Makovets society in 1922. This article was published in its journal, *Makovets* 2 (1922).

. . . The inexplicable commonality in the character of the new art that has manifested itself here and in the West simultaneously obviously emanates from the depth of the new artist, who is now on the path to recovery. This comes to us as a gratifying necessity, the only "objective," genuine path for pictorial art that does not contradict its nature (creating images) and therefore leads to new possibilities, to revelations carrying all the force of conviction. As we examine the typical features of new Russian and Western works, we cannot fail to note that the path they have marked out (not always clearly and distinctly, sometimes noticeably dependent on the old schools) is nothing but the now salutary "realism of the naive," which speaks in living images of beauty, which it assumes is an indubitable "realizable but not yet realized reality."

This objective relationship of the artist to the world is creating a language that everyone is greeting with relief as a liberation from the subjective arbitrariness that had led to a Tower of Babel.

Facing the world, the new artist seems to be in contact with the concealed being of nature and to perceive true reality—beauty as the idea of wholeness and total unity—not only contemplatively or speculatively but also in creative action.

This clearly observable "realism of the naive" that seeks out the true image and essence of things, of course, is not at all that naive. The path by which contemporary (artistic but of course not scientific) analysis of the perception and creation of form arrived at is complex. The sophisticated and wide-ranging experience this new European phase has inherited makes it all the more valuable and significant.

The contemporary artist is a philosopher and metaphysician. Speculation as an abstract spiritual activity accompanies but does not contradict his sense of the world. Like the poet, he clothes abstract schemes in visual images of immediate reality, perceiving the idea of unity that "shines through matter" as the beauty that reveals reality.

These are the features we see in the emerging outline of all-European art, which since Impressionism has been in the grip of lonely subjective explorations that have generated countless mutually intolerant currents claiming to possess the whole truth. . . .

85

Viktor Perelman

"From the Wanderers to Heroic Realism" (1923)

A year before he wrote this report, the painter Viktor Perelman (1892–1967) praised the Post-Impressionists highly and offered a positive evaluation of the French influence on Russian art.* After the founding of AKhRR (Association of Artists of Revolutionary Russia) his position changed radically. This paper was delivered at an expanded session of the AKhRR presidium and Party faction in October 1923. It is reprinted here from *Assotsiatsiia khudozhnikov revoliutsionnoi Rossii. Sbornik vospominanii, statei, dokumentov* (Association of Artists of Revolutionary Russia. Collection of Memoirs, Essays, Documents), compiled by I. V. Gronskii and V. N. Perelman (Moscow: Izobrazitel'noe Iskusstvo, 1973).

. . . The dialectical method so brilliantly applied by Marx enables us to analyze a number of contemporary artistic currents and schools from the perspective of their profound connection with economics; thus the dialectical method is destined to be the reagent that tries and tests the authenticity of the latest art theories based on an analysis of the political and economic conditions of their specific historical period. Production relations are the principle, the political and economic frame, on which historical conditions embroider the elegant pattern of the plastic arts. . . .

Only now is it becoming clear that the dizzying path from Signac, Cézanne, and Picasso to our abstractionism and the wild "Dadaists"—all of this in the course of some thirty to forty years—represents the progressive decay of the visual arts. This process is the natural result of the decay of capitalism, one consequence of which is the appearance of so-called leftist tendencies in art. Precisely because the first element to decay in the visual arts was the least stable one—color—we may be able to see what a long and agonizing line back we must follow. Need we knock on an open door and argue the specific bourgeois and decadent character of prerevolutionary Futurism? . . . To what but developing capitalism do we owe the definitive tragic divorce of form and

*V. Perelman, "The Konchalovskii Exhibition," *Vestnik iskusstv* (Messenger of the Arts) 5 (1922): 28.

content in the Western visual arts of the 1870s, and to what but capitalism as it entered the phase of global rot, the period preceding the world war, do we owe the appearance of the Fauves? . . . You had to have something with which you could deafen yourself and get all worked up—this is where Picasso's smashed violin comes from. . . . At that time one could either toady to the capitalist cultural machine, which is essentially what Marinetti's Italian Futurism did, or, in the presence of a sated bourgeoisie aware of the approaching social disaster, enjoy digging in the rotting waste of the decayed visual arts. For the future art historian, the canvases of Picasso, our Kandinsky, Malevich, and their ilk will be the most obvious and irrefutable proof of the insane horror of the impasse that gripped the world bourgeoisie. . . .

If all of the deposits that have accumulated on Cézanne are stripped away—if, so to speak, he is "dug out"—you will see him as he really was: a man "thinking about life, brush in hand," a self-taught artist from whom you can learn to love art and self-sacrifice for the sake of art, a man whose feats you can admire, but a man and artist whose specific sight defects constitute the principal content of the art of his innumerable imitators. . . .

Cézanne knew nothing about art that speaks to the masses. Because of his social roots, he essentially could not even imagine the possibility of such art. He once remarked aptly that "art speaks only to an extremely limited circle." Further on we shall see that Malevich's and Kandinsky's "philosophy of art" was constructed along the same lines, thereby demonstrating its specific decadent bourgeois essence.

Cézanne is an extremely significant example, for he is the father of the so-called leftist currents in art. Valloton was once asked what he thought of Cézanne. "Cézanne," he answered. "Oh, I respectfully walk on by!"

In the same way, without either ignoring Cézanne's formal achievements or regarding him with excessive enthusiasm—sometimes respectfully and sometimes disrespectfully—the young realist artists who in 1922 advanced the watchword of "heroic realism" in Russian art walked on by. This small group was untouched by the universal, almost psychotic enthusiasm for Cézanne among most artists. Perhaps this is why this group is now destined to save the Russian school from Cézannist and post-Cézannist infatuations.

We must first of all very critically review a pseudo-law that the majority consider axiomatic. I am speaking of the conviction that Russian art cannot survive without French art and that Russian art has no choice but to acknowledge the hegemony of Paris and repeat what French art has already done. . . . We must only emphasize that the basic elements of French art of the latter half of the nineteenth century and the beginning of the twentieth emerged quite understandably and naturally but on our soil they are an alien plant we have no need to cultivate. With no intent whatever to lapse into superfluous Slavophilism, we can state that since the October Revolution we have been following our own course of development, whose significance is enormous for world development. . . .

86

Nikolai Punin

"A Response to French Artists" (1924)

Once diplomatic relations were resumed on October 28, 1924, links with France could be restored. The immediate impetus for the polemics involved was probably the publication, in *Zhizn' iskusstva* (Life of Art) 1 (1924), of a letter from Sergei Romov, the leader of the pro-Soviet art group Strike, or Blow (Udar), in Paris [cf. 115, 116]. This response to that letter was published in *Zhizn' iskusstva* 26 (1924).

. . . Over the past few decades, Russian art has been greatly indebted to French artistic culture—this none of us will hide from you—but the years of separation from the West, which have had an especially profound effect on art, have taught us to get along without Paris; whether that is to our credit or discredit is not for us to judge, but the influence of Guys, Monet, Signac, Gauguin, Van Gogh, Matisse, Cézanne, Derain, Braque, and Picasso is weakening, and Russian art is now addressing and to some extent accomplishing, tasks that may seem to you barbaric and devoid of traditions.

I do not know whether or not you believe in that which is called the East, but I think that under any circumstances you should not be indifferent to the fact that your culture, of whose strength and authenticity you cannot but be aware, has lost its influence over a large and young country such as ours.

On the other hand, we, whose attention to Paris has been shown not only in words but in deeds, cannot but desire to be close to you again, for you are still the sole bearer of the best artistic traditions of Europe.

Among you artists of France, however, there are evidently some who cannot stand the Soviet government and do not want any sort of rapprochement with Soviet Russia. I would like to address them as follows.

Why do you spend so much time thinking about our government? Why should you artists think anything about any government? . . .

In this preliminary letter I am calling upon you to be indifferent to that which essentially has nothing to do with art. Thus we want to arrange exhibitions, and we feel that political relations should play no role whatever in this matter.

87

Iakov Tugendkhol'd

"Once Again on French Artists and Us" (1924)

Published in *Zhizn' iskusstva* (Life of Art) 29 (1924).

. . . Contemporary French art as well, of course, which just recently experienced a period of great flowering (the Matisse-Picasso-Derain-Maillol-Bourdelle pleiade) is entering a decline that is typical of the twilight of bourgeois culture in general. Here

Comrade Punin is *absolutely wrong* when, attempting in his article to persuade French artists to overcome their antipathy toward Soviet Russia and enter into contact with Russian artists, he can find nothing better than to summon them . . . to *political apathy.* . . .

No, Comrade Punin, artists are not merchants and bankers who can recognize Soviet Russia for the sake of economic gain and try to close their eyes to her government. Some French artists cannot help thinking about the government because *they are very intimately connected* with their government. These are the artists who are commissioned by mayors to immortalize various heroes, adorn new churches, and, like the loyal Catholic Maurice Denis, paint the Virgin Mary surrounded by the generals of the imperialist war. There are other French artists, however, who *should* not ignore the government, but for *different* reasons.

These are the best and youngest French artists who—as I mentioned earlier—have reached the dangerous boundary of degeneration. Degeneration, because the contemporary French social order provides no outlet for the inner forces and artistic tendencies in early twentieth-century French art. I mean first of all the decorative-monumental trend of Puvis de Chavannes, Gauguin (although he has not been given a chance to do murals), and Matisse (and who in France afforded him the same opportunities as Shchukin, Morozov, and certain Americans?). There is no place under the present "government" for this monumental mural painting. Second, I have in mind the constructive tendency that was present in Cubism, the aspiration of Cézanne and the early Cubists to a monumental transformation of the world, which, however, remained on canvas. The volumetric and spatial experiments of French artists found no outlet into life because this life does not go beyond erecting new churches of steel and concrete—the last word in French culture. In all other respects it is nourished as before by the antiquarian styles with which Le Courbusier vainly struggles in *L'Esprit nouveau.*

France was the first to thrust upon our consciousness the search for volume—the hunger to compress forms and endow them with strength, organic integrity, and architectonics. This was a tendency that, as during the Renaissance, might have resulted in the flowering of a great monumental architectural style. Alas, in France itself it led nowhere! Even volume itself disappeared from the painting of Picasso, Braque, and Léger. Their painting became flat, ornamental, and florid, displaying qualities characteristic of the art of the decadent period: mannered, effeminate, and *jolie.* The French artist reached a dead end; art that possessed explosive force and could lead to the creation of new vital forms collided with the inert wall of conservative life. . . .

French artists have something to learn from Soviet Russia. We as well, of course, have not yet progressed beyond the stage of paper projects with our ideas for gigantic palaces of labor, but the door through which art can pour out into life has opened wide for us and our artistic thought. We have *something worth working for* in the laboratories, so that laboratory experiments can then become reality. . . .

88

Nikolai Punin

"The USSR and French Artists" (1924)

Published in *Zhizn' iskusstva* (Life of Art) 37 (1924).

. . . when I say to leave the government alone I mean don't mix art with politics, issues of the moment, and all of the incidentals and ugliness of the day.

Period. That is, if even Comrade Tugendkhol'd needs a patriarchal blessing, I will repeat Trotsky verbatim: "We must not treat art like politics." I repeat this with special emphasis because today the problems of art and the problems of politics are so entangled, art has lost so much of its significance and become so hackneyed, people have become so accustomed to the disgraceful exploitation of art and art workers, and artistic culture itself—owing to constant pressure on the part of politics—has experienced such a degree of putrescent decay that what we need is not to talk but to scream about it all.

After all these explanations Tugendkhol'd is knowledgeable enough to understand that when I speak of the government and politics I do not at all mean any sort of "social order," much less the October Revolution, but only the "actions and instructions" engendered by circumstances today.

. . . Tugendkhol'd says that French art, which aspires to monumentality and spatial expansiveness, has suffocated because supposedly the bourgeois government will not give it a chance, and he even writes: "French artists have something to learn from Soviet Russia."

After that it is natural to expect him to show what French artists have to learn from us and give some examples of how our government has opened up broad possibilities to the new monumental art. Alas, this he does not do. Referring to monumentality he modestly pleads: "We as well, of course, have not yet progressed beyond the stage of paper projects with our ideas for gigantic palaces of labor . . . " and so on. Tugendkhol'd has told the truth here—a much more frightening truth than he thinks.

We have no advantages. The new art, monumental or visual, is just as unrecognized in Moscow and Leningrad as it is in Paris. It is still waiting to be recognized, and this recognition will come not from the government, that is, from those who are occupied with politics, but from the masses—the socially and economically organized society that will finally create a culture that can breathe life and strength into the new art. . . .

Our Republic is poor and culturally weak and helpless, and it is silly to try to hide this from the West. It is silly to invite Western artists to learn from us and assure them that the wall they face by the kindness of their government does not exist here; this is deception. We have made a great revolution, but the time is very far off when this revolution will bring with it a new culture that can be contrasted to the "bourgeois" West. Until that time has come it is more dignified to work and struggle openly with our lack of culture than it is to boast of our nonexistent culture to people who are truly cultured.

VII

NEW VISIONS OF WESTERN ART

In the early 1920s, Russia broke out of its political and cultural isolation of the early postrevolutionary years, as artists, critics, and writers traveled to Europe and shaped Russian views of postwar Western art [87–92, 94]. Evaluation of new phenomena was dictated to a large extent by critical essays or even reports people heard. Most characteristic in this respect was the evolution of attitudes toward Picasso. For the Russians, Picasso's art in 1920 was believed to be practically the same as it had been in 1914. But in early 1921, Russia began to hear about Picasso's return to the "Ingres tradition." By the mid-1920s the focus in Russia was no longer so much on the contrast between Cubism and Neo-Classicism as on their interconnections. The Cubism of the 1920s, which in Russia had been called "aesthetic" (in contrast to the "analytic" and "synthetic" periods of its development), was regarded as resulting not only from the further development of the movement's initial principles but also from the impact of social factors.

The Soviet press, of course, was uneven in its treatment of artistic phenomena. The political situation demanded that both avant-garde and figurative art deliver a clear message. Despite lively Russian interest in German art in the early 1920s and a good knowledge of Expressionism, artists such as Beckmann and Klee were underrepresented. The rejection of Dadaism and Surrealism [89, 115] derived not only from the Bolsheviks' materialism but also from the Puritan attitudes characteristic of much of the intelligentsia, which was hostile to the demonstrative combination of the irrational and the sexual. In contrast, the critics of the mid-1920s tried persistently to elucidate the realist tendency in French painting by devoting attention to Friesz and Segonzac as well as to figurative tendencies in Italian art. In postwar European art, Russian observers also focused on the spread of contractual relations between dealers and artists, which were taken as evidence of the avant-garde's integration into the art market.

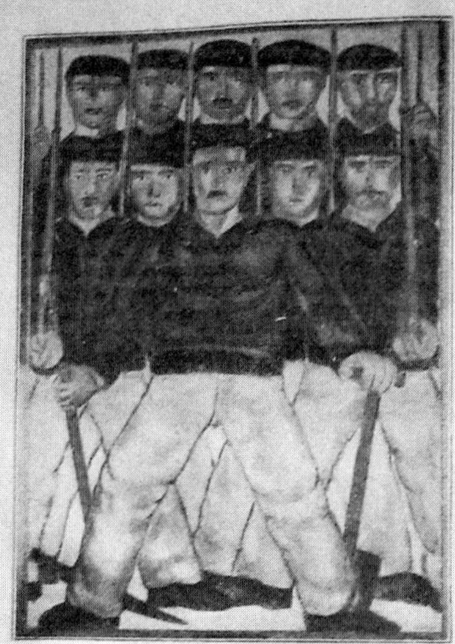

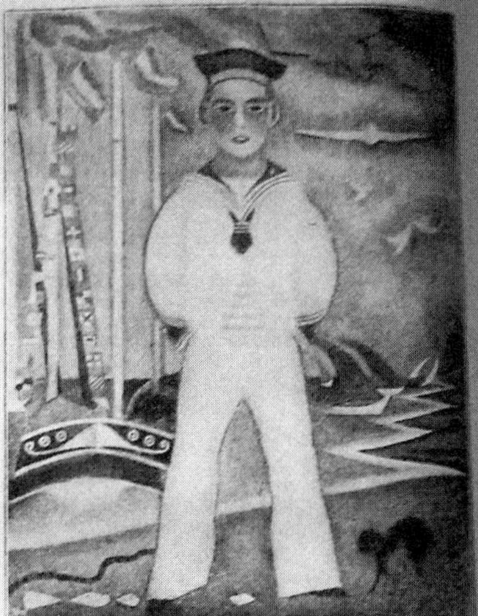

П. Альма — *Красные.* *П. Альма.* — *Матрос.*

ЗАМЕТКИ О СОВРЕМЕННОМ ИСКУССТВЕ ГОЛЛАНДИИ [1])

Что происходит в Голландии в области искусства? Я полагаю, что русские о том не могут быть хорошо осведомлены. Между [illegible] движение в искусстве у нас достаточно важно для того, чтобы вам дать небольшой отчет и несколько репродукций.

В живописи, скульптуре и архитектуре и у нас, как в России, есть свои консерваторы, умеренные и левые.

Наши консерваторы придерживаются традиций Гаагской школы (конец XIX века). Это школа импрессионистов-тоналистов. Эти художники очень хвалимы буржуазией, они воспроизводят чувства, которые они любят, чувства индивидуальные, интимные.

Более важности имеет группа художников-мистиков, пре-рафаэлитов. В их главе назовем *Торопа*, *ван-Конненбурга*, *Роланда Хольста*. Их картины и их рисунки вдохновлены великими стилями. Это отражения средневековые, далекие сны.

Художники более центрального положения подверглись влиянию француза Сезанна. Это влияние не всегда было благоприятным. Правила валеров и конструкции, которые были созданы Сезанном по логической потребности, ими воспринимаются слишком подражательно, а не переживаются. Другие художники центра вдохновлены ван-Донгеном, не имея, однако, острой выразительности и колорита этого франко-голландского художника.

Часто узнаешь и влияние ван-Гога. Ван-Гог был великой индивидуальностью, но он никогда не искал общих правил для искусства. Его влияние на других художников всегда было более или менее подражанием его личности.

Теперь мы подходим к искусству новому со всеми его оттенками. Новое искусство, которое не хочет больше вдохновляться древними стилями, которое хочет дать новые формы и идеи, вдохновленные нашим временем. Между новыми мы имеем тоже наших «декадентов», наших «пуристов» и др. Но в их формах возможно порою найти и первые камни для постройки будущего. Здание, которое мы сможем начать постройкой только после революции. Картины *Мондриана* исходят из импрессионизма. Из субъективного впечатления на него природы, он строит свою композицию на полотне. Он находит в этих картинах некие всеобщие правила, но содержание в них отсутствует.— Художник *ван-дер Лек* менее философичен. Его цель более материальна. Его картины являются лишь предлогом для живописи в сотрудничестве с архитектурой. Архитектор должен давать чистую архитектуру, живописец—чистую

[1]) [illegible]. Автором данной небольшой статьи, весьма удачно [illegible] примером с запада на наши художественные [illegible], является недавний гость Москвы, член III Конгресса Коминтерна т. *П. Альма*, художник-коммунист (автор картины «Красные», здесь помещенной). Приехав в Россию с специальной целью ознакомиться с русским новейшим искусством, т. Альма наибольше интереса выказал к [illegible] пролетарскому творчеству.—Намечаемая же им в конце статьи возможность международного объединения художников, стоящих на почве коммунизма, делает его весьма желанным сотрудником «Творчества».—С другой стороны [illegible] связь с западом позволяет надеяться, что на страницах нашего журнала будут появляться аналогичные чисто-информационные статьи о положении искусства в Европе, от которой слишком долго было оторвано наше художественное творчество.

60

An example of growing Russian interest in contemporary Western art was Peter Alma's article "Notes on Contemporary Art of Holland," illustrated with Piet Mondrian's painting, which appeared in *Tvorchestvo* (Creation) 4–6 (1921).

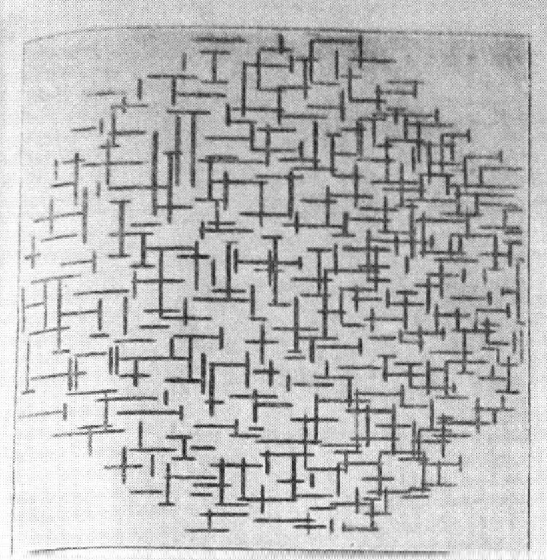

Мендриаан. *Композиция.*

живопись (это для него—цвет без содержания). Архитектор и живописец так создадут сообща здание. Ван-дер Лех является основателем этих принципов, и рядом с ним имеются последователи более или менее талантливые.

Эти два последние художника являются утопистами, первый со стороны идеологии, второй с материальной точки зрения. Их принципы родились слишком рано и основаны на возможности эпохи гармонии и культуры. Мы живем в переходное время. Далекие от того, чтобы утверждать, что утописты («футуристы») не имеют права на существование, мы в то же время нуждаемся в искусстве, которое бы исполняло свою работу непосредственно в сотрудничестве с народом, революционными массами. Некоторые художники это понимают, и я вам дальше расскажу о группе художников-коммунистов, которая сформировалась с этой целью в Голландии.

Между скульпторами нет такого различия в идеях. Часто можно угадать влияния египетского и буддийского искусства в их работах. Скульптуры, которые создаются в Голландии, являются скорее статистическими, а не динамическими, как я их много вижу в России.

В противовес России мы имеем большое движение в архитектуре. Несмотря на то, что в общем эта архитектура является барочной, стилизованной и иррациональной, можно было бы сказать, что есть архитектора, которые ищут более логического зодчества. Отцом современной архитектуры является *Берлаге*. Он построил биржу в Амстердаме. Ирония судьбы захотела, чтобы архитектор с коммунистическими наклонностями построил храм капитализма. Это здание просто, в больших массах. Это — рациональная архитектура.

Молодая архитектура есть реакция на основанный им рационализм. Молодые ищут применения различных материалов в своих зданиях, и можно сказать, что с большой ловкостью делают это.

Из заметок этих вы видите, что развитие искусства у нас идет тем же путем, возможно с некоторыми различиями, как и в других странах. Потребность найти новые основы в искусстве столь же интернациональна, как и в экономике. Все наши опыты ведут более или менее прямо к коммунизму. Теперь, когда наша борьба сделалась международной, интернациональные сношения между художниками стали необходимыми. И в искусстве должны мы разрушить границы и организовать борьбу против международной буржуазной идеологии. Чтобы начать эту работу также и в Голландии, мы организовали в этой стране группу художников-коммунистов [1]).

Эта группа ищет связи с аналогичными коллективами других стран. Мы хотим поддержать рабочих в их революционной борьбе средствами искусства. Мы хотим начать международную борьбу против буржуазной идеологии, в настоящее время сгнившей, против буржуазной идеологии, которая повсюду задерживает развитие человечества, зарю коммунизма.

Петрус Альма.

(Перевод А. А. Сидорова).

[1]) Секретариат—P Alma, Hobbemastr Amsterdam, Holland.

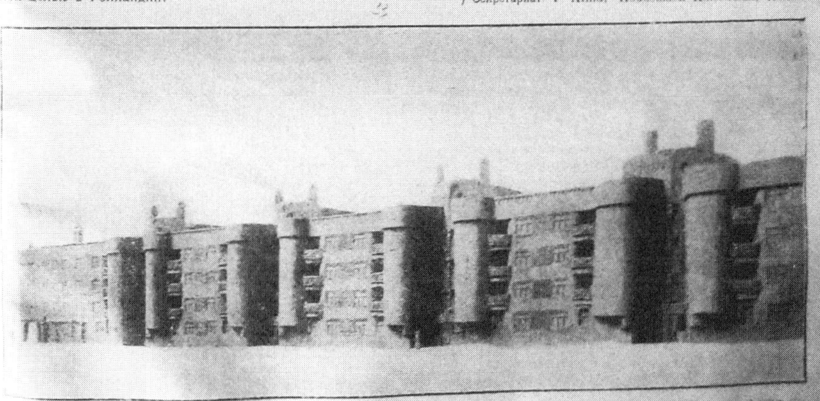

[illegible] *Проект здания.*

89

R. Ia. [Roman Jakobson]

"Letters from the West: Dada" (1921)

On his way to Prague in July 1920, Jakobson visited the "First International Dada Fair" in Berlin. In his description of the Dada movement he applies formalist categories such as the "laying bare of the device" and draws parallels with the practice of the Russian Futurists. The review was originally published in *Vestnik teatra* (Herald of the Theater) 82 (February 1921) and is reprinted here from Roman Jakobson, *Language in Literature,* edited by Krystyna Pomorska and Stephen Rudy, translated by Stephen Rudy (Cambridge: Harvard University Press, 1987), pp. 38–40; published with the permission of the Roman Jakobson Trust.

. . . Dada honorably perceives the "limitedness of its existence in time"; it relativizes itself historically, in its own words.* Meanwhile, the first result of establishing a scientific view of artistic expression, that is, the laying bare of the device, is the cry: "The old art is dead" or "Art is dead,"† depending on the temperament of the person doing the yelling. The first call was issued by the Futurists, hence "Vive le futur!" The second, not without some stipulations, was issued by Dada—what business of theirs, of artists, is the future? "À bas le futur!" . . . The laying bare of the device is sharp; it is precisely a laying bare; the already laid-bare device—no longer in sharp confrontation with the code *(à la langue)*—is vapid, it lacks flavor. The initially laid-bare device is usually justified and regulated by so-called constructive laws, but, for example, the path from rhyme to assonance to a set toward any relationship between sounds leads to the announcement that a laundry list is a poetic work. Then letters in arbitrary order, randomly struck on a typewriter, are considered verses; dabbles on a canvas made by a donkey's tail dipped in paint are considered a painting. With Dada's appeal, "Dilettantes, rise up against art," we have gone from yesterday's cult of "made things" (say, refined assonance) to the poetics of the first word let slip (a laundry list). What is Dada by profession? To use an expression from Moscow artistic jargon, the Dadaists are "painters of the word." They have more declarations than poems and pictures. And actually in their poems and pictures there is nothing new, even if only in comparison to Italian and Russian Futurism. Tatlin's "Maschinenkunst," universal poems made up of vowels, round verses (simultaneism), the music of noise (bruitism), primitivism—a sort of poetic Berlitz. . . .‡

But the crux of the matter lies elsewhere, and the Dadaists understand this. "Dada is not an artistic movement," they say. "In Switzerland Dada is for abstract (nonob-

*It was the *zaum* (trans-sense) poet Aleksei Kruchenykh who drew this comparison. See A. Kruchenykh, I. Kliun, and K. Malevich, *Tainye poroki akademikov* (Secret Sins of Academic Artists) (Moscow, 1916).

†The slogan at the Dada fair was "Art is dead. Long live the new machine art [Maschinenkunst] of Tatlin." The Dadaists borrowed the notion of machine art from K. Umanskii's article on Tatlin in *Der Ararat* (January 1920); cf. Umanskii's *Neue Kunst in Russland, 1914–1919* (Potsdam: Kiepenheuer; Munich: Goltz, 1920).

‡Maximilian Berlitz (1857–1921), Austrian pedagogue, creator of a method of intensive foreign-language study.

jective) art, in Berlin—against."* What is important is that, having finished once and for all with the principle of the legendary coalition of form and content, through a realization of the violence of artistic form, the toning down of pictorial and poetic semantics, through the color and texture *as such* of the nonobjective picture, through the fanatic word of transrational verses *as such,* we come in Russia to the blue grass of the first celebrations of October† and in the West to the unambiguous Dadaist formula: "Nous voulons nous voulons nous voulons pisser en couleurs diverses." Coloring *as such!* Only the canvas is removed, like an act in a sideshow one has grown tired of. . . .

One should take into account the background against which Dada is frolicking in order to understand certain of its manifestations. For example, the infantile anti-French attacks of the French Dadaists and the anti-German attacks of the Germans ten years ago might sound naive and purposeless. But today, in the countries of the Entente there rages an almost zoological nationalism, while in response to it in Germany there grows the hypertrophied national pride of an oppressed people. . . . Against this background, the Dadaist Fronde is quite understandable. At the present moment, when even scientific ties have been severed, Dada is one of the few truly international societies of the bourgeois intelligentsia.

By the way, it is a unique Internationale; the Dadaist Bauman lays his cards on the table when he says that "Dada is the product of international hotels." The environment in which Dada was reared was that of the adventuristic bourgeoisie of the war—the profiteers, the nouveaux riches. . . . Here, amid the "cosmopolitan mixture of god and the bordello," in Tzara's testimonial, Dada is born.

90

El [Lazar] Lissitzky

"Exhibitions in Berlin" (1922)

Veshch' (Thing, or Object), an international review of contemporary art, was published in Berlin in 1922. This article appeared in the third and last issue of *Veshch'*. Its editors, the journalist and writer Ilya Ehrenburg (1891–1967) and the artist El (Lazar) Lissitzky (1890–1941), considered Constructivism the mainstream of postwar art. El Lissitzky lived in Germany from 1921 to 1925.

In Berlin there are a lot of shops, galleries, art dealers, studios. Art is exhibited everywhere. An exhibition opens. Its own crew drops by. After that, one and a half oddballs a day.

You think you're going to find contemporary things at Sturm. But that steamer is

*See Richard Huelsenbeck, "Introduction," in *The Dada Almanach*, edited by Richard Huelsenbeck (Berlin, 1920). English edition presented by Malcolm Green (London: Atlas Press, 1993), pp. 13–14.

†On the occasion of the first anniversary of the October Revolution, artists from the military camouflage school painted the grass of Alexander Garden outside the Kremlin walls.

now a fragile little rowboat. Recently some Hungarians were shown there. Related now to Russia through revolution, in their art as well they have been fertilized by us. Moholy-Nagy has overcome German Expressionism and is moving toward structure. Against the background of octopus-like German abstract art, Moholy's and Peri's precise geometrism is reassuring. They are making the transition from composition on canvas to construction in production, in real materials. . . .

The French have no metaphysics. Léger. A large canvas from the classical period of Cubism and a new one from 1920 (*City* . . .). In the former, the rich and fertile, earthy brown texture of painting. In Cubism, just recently a bastard, even the myopic are beginning to recognize the features of its father—the Louvre. The culture of the new painting no longer comes from the museum but from the picture gallery of today's street—the sounds and dense colors of the lithographic poster, the black glass sign with superimposed letters. The color of aniline-lacquered electric lights.

Just now Sturm is featuring Kurt Schwitters and L. Kozintseva-Ehrenburg.* Schwitters has the brain of a writer but also an eye for color and a talent for materials. Together they produce confusion. His drawings assembled of various materials are visually satisfying. But he has not progressed beyond his earlier works.

There are two cultures of painting at Sturm—the French and the German. For the artists of the former the brush is a bow with which to draw sounds from paint and canvas, yet they overburden the picture with elegant detail. For the latter it is a pen to register ideas, yet they cover the picture with smears. A Russian culture of painting is beginning to emerge now that fills the material of the canvas or board with the material of the paint, *robustly coloring the entire surface.*

Arkhipenko, who entered Germany through Sturm, has by now also been through Gurlitt (the butcher's shop of the Corinths, the Slevogts, and the like). If this is typical of the sculptor's popularity, then it also rattles the brains of the aesthetes, dealers, and critics, who are beginning to fear letting modernity through. (Yet they all arrived after the third bell, so to speak.) Arkhipenko is coming to an end. Through materials and relief contemporaneity is disappearing from painting. Arkhipenko colors his reliefs and is driving plastic art back into painting. The result is prettiness. One accomplishment is certain—form determined by relief and counterrelief. But why do it in Tanagra figurines? It is a pity that Arkhipenko spent these years outside Russia. The great tasks we at one time assigned sculptors, to say nothing of the whole tempo of our artistic life, might have led this remarkable artist to valuable achievements. Now the gilt of salons lies on all his works.

Kandinsky is exhibiting some new works with Wallerstein. The titles are new. Not "compositions" as earlier, but now the more precise: "circles on black," "blue segment," "red oval," "with square shapes." Everything else is as before. True, sprinkled into the vegetation running beyond the square of the canvas is a clear geometrical shape, but

*Ehrenburg's wife, Liudmila Kozintseva, held the exhibition in May.

it as well is so dispersed by color that it cannot contain the chaos. From Russia Kandinsky brought a more conscientious approach to solidly filling the canvas. But, as before, there is no wholeness, no clarity, no work of art.

91

Leon Trotsky
"Futurism" (1923)

Among the Soviet leaders, Leon Trotsky (1879–1940) was the most tolerant toward contemporary art. According to Trotsky, most of the essays in *Literature and Revolution* (1923) were written on Lenin's suggestion. The article here, which originally appeared in *Pravda* on June 26, 1923, was accompanied by an earlier letter on Italian Futurism addressed to the Italian Communist leader Antonio Gramsci (September 8, 1922). The translation is reprinted from Leon Trotsky, *Literature and Revolution* (New York: Russell and Russell, 1957), pp. 126–61.

Futurism is a European phenomenon, and it is interesting because, in spite of the teachings of the Russian Formalist school, it did not shut itself in within the confines of art, but from the first, especially in Italy, it connected itself with political and social events.

Futurism reflected in art the historic development which began in the middle of the nineties, and which became merged in the World War. Capitalist society passed through two decades of unparalleled economic prosperity which destroyed the old concepts of wealth and power, and elaborated new standards, new criteria of the possible and of the impossible, and urged people towards new exploits.

At the same time, the social movement lived on officially in the automatism of yesterday. The armed peace, with its patches of diplomacy, the hollow parliamentary systems, the external and internal politics based on the system of safety valves and brakes, all this weighed heavily on poetry at a time when the air, charged with accumulated electricity, gave sign of impending great explosions. Futurism was the "foreboding" of all this in art. . . .

Futurism originated in an eddy of bourgeois art, and could not have originated otherwise. Its violent oppositional character does not contradict this in the least. . . . In Italy, the interventionists (that is, those in favor of intervention in the War) were the "revolutionists," that is, the Republicans, Free Masons, social Chauvinists and Futurists. Last of all, did not Italian Fascism come into power by "revolutionary" methods, by bringing into action the masses? . . . It is not an accident, it is not a misunderstanding, that Italian Futurism has merged into the torrent of Fascism; it is entirely in accord with the law of cause and effect.

Russian Futurism was born in a society which passed through the preparatory class of fighting the priest Rasputin, and was preparing for the democratic Revolution of February, 1917. This gave our Futurism certain advantages. It caught rhythms of movement, of action, of attack, and of destruction which were as yet vague. It carried its struggle for a place in the sun more sharply, more resolutely and more noisily than all preceding schools, which was in accordance with its activist moods and points of view. To be sure, a young Futurist did not go to the factories and to the mills, but he made a lot of noise in cafés, he banged his fist upon music stands, he put on a yellow blouse, he painted his cheeks and threatened vaguely with his fist.

The workers' Revolution in Russia broke loose before Futurism had time to free itself from its childish habits . . . and before it could be officially recognized, that is, made into a politically harmless artistic school whose style is acceptable. The seizure of power by the proletariat caught Futurism still in the stage of being a persecuted group. And this fact alone pushed Futurism towards the new masters of life, especially since the contact and rapprochement with the Revolution was made easier for Futurism by its philosophy, that is, by its lack of respect for old values and by its dynamics. But Futurism carried the features of its social origin, bourgeois Bohemia, into the new stage of its development.

. . . Through the outer layer of this poetic revolt was felt the pressure of deep social forces, which Futurism itself did not quite understand. The struggle against the old vocabulary and syntax of poetry, regardless of all its Bohemian extravagances, was a progressive revolt against a vocabulary that was cramped and selected artificially with the view of being undisturbed by anything extraneous; a revolt against impressionism, which was sipping life through a straw; a revolt against symbolism, which had become false in its heavenly vacuity. . . . If we survey attentively the period left behind, we cannot help but realize how vital and progressive was the work of the Futurists in the field of philology.

. . . It is just as difficult to strip Futurism of the robe of the intelligentsia as it is to separate form from content. And when this happens, Futurism will undergo such a profound qualitative change that it will cease to be Futurism. This is going to happen, but not tomorrow. But even today one can say with certainty that much in Futurism will be useful and will serve to elevate and to revive art, if Futurism will learn to stand on its own legs, without any attempt to have itself decreed official by the government, as happened in the beginning of the Revolution. The new forms must find for themselves, and independently, an access into the consciousness of the advanced elements of the working-class as the latter develop culturally. . . .

92

Vladimir Mayakovsky

"A Seven-Day Inspection of French Painting" (1923)

Mayakovsky spent the last three months of 1922 in Berlin. Through Diaghilev he obtained a French visa and spent the week of November 19–25 in Paris. He described impressions of his trip in a number of newspaper articles and in a book that remained unpublished during his lifetime. This essay was first published in Vladimir Maiakovskii, *Polnoe sobranie sochinenii* (Complete Collected Works), vol. 4 (Moscow, 1957), pp. 218–53.

THE ART OF PARIS

. . . Before the war, Paris was the same Entente* as it is now. Just as today the ministries of Germany, Poland, Romania, and dozens of other countries are under the direction of Poincaré;† then, even more than now, artistic schools and trends were born, lived, and died according to the dictates of artistic Paris.

Paris commanded:

"Expand Expressionism! Introduce Pointillism!" And everyone in Russia immediately began painting only in little dots.

Paris proposed:

"Consider Picasso the patriarch of Cubism!" And the Russian Shchukins threw themselves and their money into acquiring the biggest, most extravagant Picasso.

Paris terminated:

"Futurism is dead!" And the Russian critics immediately began requiems so that the next day they could bring forth the very latest Parisian "Dada"—that is what they called it—the Paris fashion.

The newspaper and magazine critics (as always, artists who have despaired of a career in painting) were simply bowled over by Paris.

The revolution and innovations of Russia's artists were sentenced to death in their absence: it had all been done long ago and better in Paris. . . .

For eight years Paris got along without us. We got along without Paris.

I entered Paris with trepidation. I looked around with studious conscientiousness. With the attentiveness of a rival. What if once again we turned out to be a provincial backwater?

PAINTING

Appearance (what vulgar critics call form) has always dominated in French painting.

In the real world this forced Parisians' inventiveness into haute couture, resulting in so-called Parisian chic.

In art it resulted in the predominance of painting over all the other arts—painting as the most prominent, best-dressed art.

Today as well, painting is the most widespread and influential art in France.

The picture occupies a prominent place in the apartment furnishing projects exhibited at the Salon.

Cafés like the Rotonde are packed full of pictures.

A seafood restaurant is for some reason decorated with Picabia landscapes.

Every few steps there is a shop with an exhibition.

Enormous buildings are honeycombed with studios.

*The Entente was a military alliance between France, Great Britain, and Russia, joined by other states during World War I.

†Raymond Poincaré (1860–1934), French prime minister.

France has produced hundreds of famous names in art.

For each artist with a big name there are a thousand who have only a last name. For each one with a last name there are thousands whose first name and last name are of interest to no one but their concierge.

You must plug your ears to the humming of dozens of mutually lethal theories; you must be very familiar with earlier painting to get a complete impression and avoid falling into the grip of the bacterial spawn of pictures by some utterly insignificant artistic school.

Let's take the scheme of things from before the war: Cubism is the leader; Cubism is attacked by a bunch of color painters known as the Simultaneists; off to the side a bunch of nonpartisan "wild" artists remain neutral; from all sides, an ocean of enormous canvases by innumerable academists and salon hacks, and darting in from one side, getting in everyone's way, some "last word" or other.

Armed with this scheme, I go from trend to trend, exhibition to exhibition, canvas to canvas. I think to myself, "This outline is only a guide. I must unveil the face of contemporary French painting." I make desperate sallies away from the scheme. I search for a discovery in painting. I wait for some new problem to be posed. I glance at the corners of paintings, looking for at least a new name. All in vain.

Everyone is in his proper place.

There is only the perfection of manner, more rarely of skill. Even that is for many artists a retreat, a decline.

As before, Cubism is the center. As before, Picasso is the commander in chief of the Cubist army.

As before, the coarseness of the Spaniard Picasso "refines" the ever-so-pleasant greenish Braque.

As before, Metzinger and Gleizes go on theorizing.

As before, Léger is trying to return Cubism to its main problem—volume.

As before, Delaunay is warring irreconcilably with the Cubists.

As before, the Fauves Derain and Matisse go on painting picture after picture.

As before, there is a last word in all of this. At present these obligations are borne by the all-negating and all-affirming "da-da."*

And as before . . . all of the bourgeoisie's orders are filled by innumerable Blanches.† Eight years of the most bustling lethargy. . . .

For the first time a new achievement in art has flown in not from France but from Russia—Constructivism. I'm amazed to find that the word even exists in the French vocabulary.

Not the Constructivism of artists who make useless gadgets out of useful wire and tin. The Constructivism that understands the artist's formal work only as engineering needed to shape all of our practical life.

*A play on the Russian "da" (yes).

†The reference may be to Jacques-Emile Blanche (1861–1942), who painted scenes from Brittany.

Here the French artists will have to learn from us.

Here you won't get anywhere with something you think up in your head. To build the new culture you need a clean place. You need the broom of October.

And what is the soil for French art? The parquet floors of the Paris salons!

THE "AUTUMN SALON"

2,395 items (not counting arts and crafts).

And the "Autumn Salon," after all, is merely one of several exhibitions in Paris.

Counting about four exhibitions a year, this means 10,000 pictures. Bear in mind that no more than ten percent of the total production is exhibited. That comes to the respectable figure of 100,000 pictures a year. . . .

I look for the Cubists.

Here's Braque. Eighteen solid works. I stop in front of two decorative panels. What a step backward! Definitely substantive. Swarming with caryatids. So nice and smooth. Gray-green-brown. Not the old Braque—iron-hard, resolute, with extraordinary taste—but licked and softened by the Salon.

Léger. You can pick him out immediately by his vividness and anti-aesthetic use of color. But even his anti-aestheticism, which in his studio seemed to be a revolutionary force, has been salonified here as well and simply become a trivial quirk.

You look at the neighboring, quite decent academist pictures, and you think, if you put all this in the same frame and shaded the edges slightly, wouldn't it all run together into a single decorous picture-porridge? Cubism has become quite domesticated, quite tame.

Warmed up on the schools, I turn to individual artists.

Matisse. Decrepit. Insignificant. A little head and a little figure. . . . I feel a slight unpleasantness, like standing next to pictures by our own Bodarevskii.*

Van Dongen. *Neptune.* Even more unbelievable: an old opera singer with a trident. Yellow-green—an onion omelet. In the rear, a steamer. Wretched painting, tawdry little allegory.

The rest is even drearier.

Picabia is to some extent an exception. His picture *The Principle of French Painting*—a black man against a white background and a white woman against a black background—is interesting. But even the problem itself is formalistic. It is in any case not the solution to a painterly problem.

. . . I am worse at jingoism than anyone else in Russian art. I have welcomed artistic ideas in Paris in the same way I express my enthusiasm for new ideas in Moscow. But there aren't any anymore!

This does not mean I don't love French art.

I have *already* loved it. I am not rejecting my old love, but it has passed into

*Nikolai Bodarevskii (1850–1912), a painter who began exhibiting with the Wanderers in 1880.

friendship, and soon, if you don't go forward, it may be no more than simple acquaintanceship. . . .

But of course Russian picture production is no match for Paris. Paris stands many heads taller. Paris is number one.

Of course, I would give our entire Jack of Diamonds style for a single variation from this cycle of Picasso's or Braque's.

That's not the point.

The point is that the age has called the existence of pictures into question. And of their painters in general. It has called into question the existence of a society that contents itself with the paltry artistic culture of decorating with Salon pictures. This culture has outlived itself. To the French I gladly concede first place in the painting of pictures.

I say that our *peintres* should stop painting pictures because the French paint better. But the French should stop painting, too, because they can't paint any better. . . .

THE MERCHANTS

Paris is swarming with art shops. I inspect two of the most important—Simon Rosenberg's and Leon Rosenberg's. These words, of course—"merchant," "shop"—would grate on the French ear. These merchants are considered bearers of taste, bearers of the artistic ideas of France. Artists surrender their best pictures to these merchants, who exhibit the best Picassos, the best Braques, etc. . . .

These merchants make the artists' reputations. It is they who spot the genius, buy his pictures for a song, pile them up in their basements, and when he is dead trumpet the fame of the deceased through the reviewers in their service and sell his masterpieces for many tens and hundreds of thousands of francs.

These merchants maintain Picasso's reputation. Day in and day out these merchants force the entire world to be interested in him. . . . Wicked tongues say that the heightened interest in Ingres, a mediocre pseudo-Classical graphic artist, is due to the fact that one of these Leons accumulated a large number of his drawings. There was an immediate turn to Classicism in French art. This is of course a schematic, black-and-white account of things, but in this scheme the franc nevertheless plays the leading role. All French artists are either working for these merchants or trying to leap over them and break through their blockade. . . .

PICASSO

The first studio to visit in Paris, of course, is Picasso's. He is the painter with the greatest sweep and world significance. In the middle of an apartment decorated with pictures long familiar to all of us from photographs is a stocky, gloomy, energetic Spaniard. Typical both of him and of other artists I visited is a passionate love of Rousseau. All the walls are hung with his pictures. The eye of the refined Frenchman evidently seeks repose in these utterly artless, utterly simple works. One question interests me immensely—namely, Picasso's return to Classicism. . . . I can dispel any misgivings. Picasso has not returned to any Classicism whatsoever. His studio is full of the most diverse works, from a quite realistic little scene in blue and pink done in the style of ancient art to a construction of tin and wire. . . . There is a coarsely realistic portrait of a woman and an old dismantled violin. And all of these works are dated the same year. His large, so-called realistic canvases—those women with enormous round arms—are of course not a return to Classicism, or, if you insist on using the word "Classicism," then this is the assertion of a new Classicism. Not a copy of nature, but the realization of all previous Cubist study of nature. What you see in these leaps from technique to technique is not a retreat but the casting about of an artist who has reached the limits of formal achievement in a certain manner and is trying to apply his knowledge but cannot find any such application in musty French reality.

I look at the catalogue of a Russian art exhibition in Berlin lying there on a table.* I ask, "Are you really happy to be taking a violin apart again for the thousandth time so that you can make a tin violin that can't be played, no one wants to buy, and is only destined to hang on a wall for the artist's personal enjoyment?"

Here in the catalogue is Tatlin. For some time now he has been appealing to artists to make the transition, not in order to mangle beautiful pieces of tin and iron but so that this iron, which at present produces only tasteless structures, can be shaped by artists.

"Why," I ask, "don't you transfer your painting to the walls of your parliament building, for example? Seriously, Comrade Picasso, that way more people would see it."

Picasso silently shakes his head.

"You have it good. You don't have to worry about Monsieur Poincaré's police."

"To hell with the police," I advise him. "Take a bucket of paint some night and go over there and paint. Our Strastnoi Boulevard has already been painted!"

Although she hardly believes that my suggestion can be implemented, there is a slight flicker of horror in Madame Picasso's eyes. But the serene pose of Picasso, who is obviously accustomed to the fact that he will never paint anything but pictures, restores the domestic calm.

DELAUNAY

Delaunay is Picasso's complete opposite. He is a Simultancist. He is searching for ways to paint pictures whose form is created not through weights and volumes but solely through color. (He is the spiritual father of our own Iakulovs.) He is thoroughly embittered. The Cubism covering all the canvases of French painters gives him no rest. The merchants are not after him. There is nowhere and no reason for him to acquire Classicism. All of him, even his back, even his hands, not to mention his pic-

*Catalogue of the 1922 Berlin exhibition "Erste Russiche Kunstausstellung."

tures, is on a feverish quest. He sees that the walls erected by the taste of the French salons cannot be breached by talking, and by circuitous routes he is also approaching revolution. In the pictures he unrolls for me, even old ones from 1913 and 1914, in the Eiffel Tower familiar to us from photographs, which he shows surrounded by storm clouds and collapsing on Paris, for example, he tries to detect some premonition of revolution.

He listens enviously to accounts of our holidays, when an artist is given a building and a school is given a city block, and the artists can decorate it any way their imagination desires. This idea is congenial to him. Even in his studio his pictures are so huge that they look more like walls than canvases. . . .

Through art, too, he has come to recognize the grandeur of the Russian Revolution. He writes down several dozen addresses, asking that they be passed on, that the art world of Russia correspond with him and enter into an exchange with him. He is entertaining the idea of coming to the RSFSR, opening a school, and bringing French painting there to be rejuvenated.

For the time being, though, he wears the ball and chain of the Parisian everyday around his ankle, and he discharges his outbursts of enthusiasm by painting the doors of his own studio. Also a slice of life.

I don't think he did this "from the heart." At any rate, he definitely envied my return to the land of revolution. He sent his greetings to the Russian revolutionaries of art on behalf of their French counterparts, he asked me to say that they are the ones who are on our side, and he asked the Moscow airport to accept as a gift the two enormous canvases of his that I liked the most: an expanse of colored air cleft by propellers.

BRAQUE

Braque is for sale (not figuratively but in actual fact) more than any other artist of Paris. Throughout—in his surroundings and his person, he tries to preserve the classical dignity of the *peintre.* You have to give him credit—he always balances very tastefully between art and the Salon. Revolutionary French Cubism's temperament is squeezed into respectable forms acceptable to all. There are angles, but they are not too sharp or Cubist. There are luminous spots of color, but not too forceful or Simultaneist. To all my questions as to what is available from his latest works to show to Russia, he has a haughty excuse: "There aren't any photographs; it's at so-and-so's shop. . . . Sorry, there aren't any pictures, they've all been sold." This man has no interest in revolution.

LÉGER

Léger—of whom the illustrious connoisseurs of French art speak with a certain condescension—made a very deep and pleasant impression on me. A stocky man who looks like a true worker-artist who regards his labor not as divinely ordained but as an interesting, useful craft equal to other practical crafts. I examine his important painting. His aesthetics of industrial forms is gratifying, as is his fearless use of the coarsest realism. Striking as well is his workmanlike attitude toward color, so different from that of other French artists, which he regards not as a means of conveying atmospheres but as a material with which to paint things. His attitude toward the Russian Revolution is a worker's attitude that is also free of aestheticism. It gladdens me to note that he does not showcase his big and little accomplishments or make any artistic effort to throw revolutionary dust in your eyes, but puts art aside and asks about the Russian Revolution, about life in Russia. His enthusiasm for the Revolution is obviously not an artistic pose but simply a "businesslike" attitude. He is interested less in where and how to exhibit if he comes to Russia than in the technical matter of getting there and how to apply his knowledge to help in construction.

The moment I mentioned that my comrades might be interested in his painting he responded to me not like a merchant artist trembling over his treasures but simply said:

"Take it all. If something won't fit through the door, I'll lower it to you from the window."

"Goodbye," he had learned to say in Russian as we parted. "I'll be coming soon."

The four artists listed here exhaust the various types of Paris artists.

GONCHAROVA AND LARIONOV

Russian artists do not play any special role in the painting of France—or at least no one talks about it. True, their influence is indisputable. When you look at Picasso's latest works you are amazed at the color, the carousel of tones in his pictures and his studies of decorations. This is undoubtedly the influence of our colorists Goncharova and Larionov. At work here as well is the arrogant attitude of victorious France toward Russians who refuse to recognize their indebtedness. Facts mean nothing to us. Paris is better at everything. . . .

It is good to note the attitude of these artists toward the RFSFR, for they do not whine or insinuate the attitudes of the émigrés. Theirs is a businesslike attitude. Their own, long expected, and in no way surprising business. No questions about the "landmarks."* Traveling to Russia is a technical detail.

It is pleasant to state on the basis of this example that revolutionaries in art remain revolutionaries to the end. . . .

*The reference is to the title of the collection of essays by Russian émigré intellectuals, published in 1921, *Smena vekh* (Change of Landmarks), in which they called upon their fellow émigrés to return to Russia and help the Bolsheviks rebuild the country.

The early twentieth century in art was occupied with solving purely formal problems.

Not the mastery of things, but only a study of the techniques and methods of this mastery. . . .

The French were the leaders in this area.

If you take some abstract task—presenting the form of a human figure using the simplest planar generalizations—then Picasso is of course best.

If you take some third dimension of a still life shown not as it seems but in its essence, by unfolding the depth of the object, its hidden aspects, then of course Braque is best.

If you take color in its essence, unmarred by the incidentals of the various reflections and penumbras, if you take line as an independent ornamental force, then Matisse is best.

By 1915 this formal work had been taken to its limit. . . .

Naked formalism had given all it could. . . .

We are left with an "either/or."

The first is the "either" of Europe: use the results to satisfy European taste. This taste is not complicated. It is the taste of the bourgeoisie. The worst part of the bourgeoisie—the nouveaux riches grown wealthy from the war. This taste can only be satisfied by manufacturing pictures for the apartment of the private speculator who can buy the artist's "fire" to illuminate only his living room (the state does not count, for it is always trailing behind artistic taste and is unable to support this entire army of painters materially). . . .

No, it is not to make pictures that the best people of the world have studied the techniques of coloring and illuminating life. It is not in the salons that their discoveries should be applied, but in life, in production, in the mass work that embellishes the life of millions.

But this is the "or"—the "or" of the RSFSR. The "or" of any country washed clean by the workers' revolution. Only in such a country can the application and content (painterly, naturally, not thematic) for all this formal work be found. . . .

This is designing, this is the highest artistic engineering. The industrial artists of the RFSFR must be guided not by the aesthetics of the old artistic manuals but by the aesthetics of economy, convenience, expediency, Constructivism.

But this "or" is for the time being not for France.

First it must go through the great purge of a French October.

In the meanwhile, despite all our backwardness in technology and skills, we, the art workers of Soviet Russia, are the leaders of world art, the bearers of avant-garde ideas.

All of this, however, has yet to pass from theory into realization in practice, and to do that we must still learn, above all from the French.

93

Aleksandr Rodchenko

"Rodchenko in Paris: Letters Home" (1927)

From March to June 1925, Aleksandr Rodchenko (1891–1956) worked on the Soviet exposition at the "International Exhibition of Modern Industrial and Decorative Art" in Paris. Two years later, in 1927, excerpts from his letters to his wife, Varvara Stepanova, were published in the second issue of *Novyi Lef,* along with Mayakovsky's poem "To Our Youth." The poem and letters continued a campaign begun by Osip Brik in the preceding issue of the journal, which attempted to present Lef as a major rival of contemporary bourgeois art.

MARCH 25, 1925

Yesterday, as I was watching people dance the foxtrot, I very much wanted to be in the East rather than the West. But I have to learn how to work in the West, organize things, and then work in the East.

How simple and healthy it is, the East, and only from here do you see that clearly. Here, although they steal the dances, dress, colors, gaits, types, and everyday culture of the East, everything—they turn it into something so loathsome and vile that there's no East at all in it.

Yes, but others sit and work, and it is they who are creating a high-quality industry, and again it's disappointing that on the best ocean liners, airplanes, and so forth, again you will keep on finding these foxtrots, and powders, and endless bidets.

The cult of woman as an object. The cult of woman as moldy cheese and oysters—it's gone so far that "ugly women" are in vogue now—women like rancid cheese, with long, skinny hips, flat-chested and toothless, and with hideously long arms covered in red blotches; women à la Picasso; women made to look like "Negroes"; women made to look like "hospital patients"; women made to look like the "dregs of the city."

And again the man, creating and constructing, shivering all over with this *"great contagion"* this *global syphilis of art.*

Here you see where it leads. Here are its luxuriant blooms.

Art without life, art that robs the simplest people here, there, and everywhere and turns all this into a hospital.

We will eat excrement in a silver wrapper, hang our dirty pants in a golden frame, and copulate with a dead bitch.

APRIL 2, 1925

. . . Why did I see it, the West? I liked it more before I saw it. Take away its technology and it's a nasty pile of dung, helpless and puny. . . .

I dislike and disbelieve everything here and I can't even hate it. It so resembles an old artist with well-made gold teeth and a fake leg. That's Paris, which I wasn't interested in before but did respect.

APRIL 23, 1925

I visited the "Salon des Indépendants"—such nonsense and lack of talent. The French really are played out. Thousands of canvases and all of them rubbish, truly provincial; even worse than I expected. Really, after Picasso, Braque, and Léger it's empty, there's nothing. Nonobjectivity, our Russians pant as they bring their works from Moscow. They're better than the rest, but gradually they lapse into dubious taste and that's the end of them.

R[abinovich]* introduced me to D[oesburg, the leftist Dutch architect]. No sense in it, since he doesn't speak Russian nor I French, so we looked at each other and parted. For some reason everyone is taking a terribly good look at us, that is, the people at the pavilion; they're probably wondering what Bolsheviks look like.

MAY 4, 1925

. . . And so . . . just as before there was nothing worse than to be a Russian, now there is nothing better than to be a Soviet citizen, but there's a "but." . . . It means you have to work and work and work. . . . The light from the East is not only the emancipation of the workers; the light from the East is a new attitude toward humanity, women, and things. Our things in our hands should also be equal—comrades, not black and gloomy slaves as they are here.

94

Iakov Tugendkhol'd

The Artistic Culture of the West (1928)

Tugendkhol'd's book, published in Moscow in 1928, consists of previously published essays. The texts here are excerpts from his review of the 1924 "German Exhibition" and an article on French painting based on his impressions of his 1925 visit to Paris, where he organized the Soviet section of the "International Exhibition of Modern Industrial and Decorative Art."

GERMANIC ART

. . . The Moscow exhibition immersed us in the overall atmosphere of modern Germanic art and allowed us to draw certain conclusions—mainly, that it is highly eclectic. In a certain sense, though, this very eclecticism is the new feature of Germanic art which attests that it has shed its recent calm, self-assured, and self-sufficient nature. Germanic art has always fed on its own juices, so to speak. Strengthened by its victory over France, the German empire had too high an opinion of itself to borrow anything from elsewhere. . . . At a time when French art was characterized by a sense of measure, clear plastic harmony, the cult of form, and a balance of line and color,

*Isaak Rabinovich (1894–1961), stage designer.

Я. ТУГЕНДХОЛЬД

ХУДОЖЕСТВЕННАЯ КУЛЬТУРА ЗАПАДА

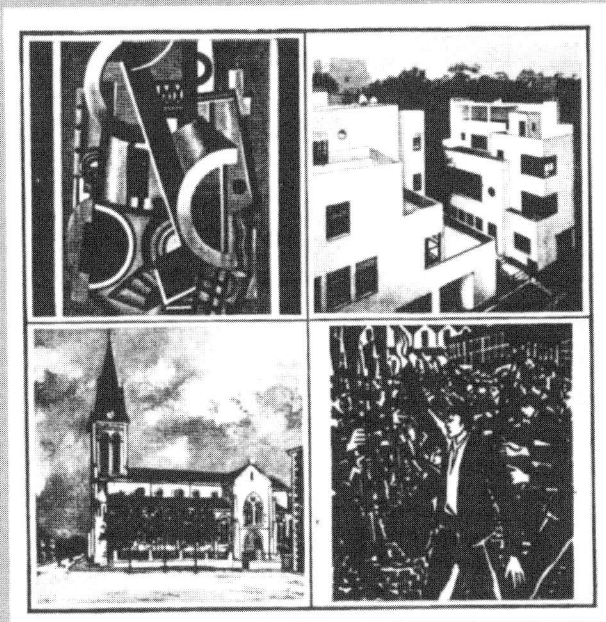

ГОСУДАРСТВЕННОЕ ИЗДАТЕЛЬСТВО

1928

Cover for Iakov Tugendkhol'd's *The Artistic Culture of the West* (Moscow, 1928)

Germanic art always kept abstract or naturalistic content in the foreground. This *cerebralism,* although a great intellectual virtue, explains its backwardness in painting. In French art, emotion dominates over consciousness; in Germanic art the intellect and reflection have dominated over direct feeling. French art is synthetic; German art, analytic. Hence the hypertrophy in it of line over color; hence the graphic and "colored" rather than painterly quality of German painting (Dürer, Cranach, Leibl); and hence, finally, the passionate, painful, and almost tragic attempts . . . to break the fateful vicious circle of Germanic art in order to join the world culture of painting and conquer this elusive "painterliness." . . .

Germanic Impressionism, which lagged behind Paris by some twenty years, has only very weakly impregnated Germanic art with color. . . .

The second and equally tardy wave of French influence was Expressionism, a reaction against Impressionism that took as its slogan the greatest possible expressiveness of the artist's inner image. . . . For the time being, of course, the German epigones lag behind their teachers' level of painterly culture, and their colors are still raw and mealy. However eclectic contemporary German art is, though, it does have one thing to its credit: it has escaped its dead end, opened its narrow national circle, and absorbed what it lacked, namely, French color. This is only the first step, but it is a big one that is obvious to anyone who has seen the prewar painting of Germany and can compare it with Germany's art today.

Of course, it would be unfair to deny the specifically German *originality* of Expressionist painting, the heightened passion and tense and torturous pungency of these canvases. . . . The individual's emancipation from the bonds of militarism, the liberation of spontaneous forces and inner energy, the assertion of the individual and subjective emotions—this was the first slogan of the intelligentsia that survived the war. This is the origin of Germanic Expressionism, a trend that in the written word, graphic art, painting, and stone strives for maximum nakedness and "expression" of the artist's inner emotions. What methods and paths are followed to achieve this is unimportant, whence the incredible eclecticism of "Expressionistic" art. . . .

Because these individualist artists fled a horrible reality and sought "emancipation" only privately, in their inner world, rather than in the collective and in active struggle, however, they withdrew into mysticism, metaphysics, and abstraction. . . . Nor can it be denied that besides the aspiration to "unmask," the unusual attention that contemporary Germanic youth pays to sexual motifs and to portraying prostitutes is clearly decadent. . . . Eroticism is the blood sister of "mysticism," and the two together are the daughters of social reaction. . . .

CONTEMPORARY FRENCH PAINTING

. . . it must be noted at the outset that the heroic Sturm und Drang epoch of French art is *over.* . . . The art of postwar France is no longer the pictures of those amicable collective efforts devoted to a single goal that we saw earlier in Impressionism, Cézannism, and even Cubism. Formal skills have advanced even more, but the combative ardor of French art has cooled somewhat; its pulse throbs less rapidly, and its slogans have become trivial. Everyone is working out of inertia and in isolation. This is why they are so fond of theorizing and writing articles. An era of individualism and eclecticism has come. . . .

For all its excesses, the first period of Cubism (1908–13) had some positive features. There was a unanimity that made it difficult to distinguish the works of one Cubist from another, Picasso from Braque. This was a logical movement, a natural reaction to amorphous, superficial, purely painterly Impressionism. . . . [But] analysis defeated synthesis in Cubism. The abstract, un-French element triumphed over the visual and essentially realistic French tradition. Picasso's metaphysics triumphed over Cézanne's realism.

This second period of Cubism began after the war, when the previous cult of three-dimensionality was replaced by the *cult of the plane*. . . . From the formal point of view, this new tendency of Cubism is clearly a step forward. The ascetically gloomy and chalky-stony palette has been replaced by abundant color. But this new, unusually refined, and subtly elegant play of color arabesques and all this amazingly sophisticated texture, like the almost graphic style of these works, are somehow too aesthetic, Alexandrine, and Parnassian and combine with something extremely eclectic suggestive of the tastes "of all peoples and ages." . . .

It is interesting to compare with this Epicurean stage of Cubism another trend whose name would seem to indicate the polar opposite: "Purism." For all their rationalism and apparent hostility to Picasso's metaphysics, though, their ultimate aspirations and entire "goal-oriented attitude" do not go beyond hedonism. . . .

Léger's art is a brilliant example of modern material "being" conquering subjective "consciousness." Léger's art is the product of the latest mechanical war and its tanks, battleships, armored cars, and human "troglodytes" encased in armor. Léger's art is the fruit of modern industrialized France, which has emerged from the war as a major metallurgical power. Léger's art is more industrial than France; he is already more Catholic than the pope. Léger's art is the fetishism of the machine. . . .

Picasso is a realist; Picasso is a Neo-Classic; Picasso is the author of entirely verisimilar portraits of a downright beautiful woman . . . this, of course, was quite an event, regarded by some as "treason" and by others as his latest "trick." In reality, however, it was not so terribly unexpected. It was a return to his old pre-Cubist experimentation, which he now has simply given a more ingenious . . . and commercially appealing form. . . .

Once again, as in the Cubist period, we have to ask which will win out in contemporary Neo-Classicism—its healthy aspiration toward reality and clarity, or its postwar weariness from creative activism and color experimentation? . . .

Very likely, contemporary French art combines the classical striving for "organization" and "order" with the rebellious temperament of Romanticism. If the Romantic elements now germinating are to attain full growth, however, French art must go through what the revolutionary generation of Delacroix and Daumier did: social passion. Otherwise, all its Romanticism is shooting blanks. Whereas in the art of contemporary Germany we have seen profound humanity and genuine human agitation (which sometimes becomes hypertrophied psychologism), French art by contrast still lacks new inner "content" to melt the breaking ice of its formalism. In this sense, the fate of French art may be seen as inextricably bound up with the development of French society.

95

Ia. T-d [Iakov Tugendkhol'd]

"The Art of Contemporary America" (1928)

This review is a rare example of Soviet critical attention to the art of the United States. The printmaker Louis Lozowick (1892–1973), one of the founders of the John Reed Club, visited the USSR in 1923, 1928, and 1932. There was an exhibition of his works in January 1928 at the Museum of Modern Western Art. Tugendkhol'd's review appeared in *Krasnaia niva* (Red Field) 2 (1928).

America . . . is the land of gigantic engineering feats and architectural colossi. The land of dizzying industrial progress. The land of the New York skyscrapers, Minnesota grain elevators, Pittsburgh steel mills, Oklahoma oil derricks, Butte copper mines, and Oregon sawmills.

Does it, however, have its own art? This is a question many have asked, and it must be answered in the affirmative. Although American art has developed to a significant degree under French influence, it has its own distinctive character. The latest American painting and graphic art display the engineering spirit that is so specific to life in America.

There was a time when world art, alarmed by the growth of technology that "disfigured" nature, was in a kind of opposition to urban culture, rejecting it and seeking salvation from the cities in the lap of nature. This attitude gave birth to landscape painting, and it was the philosophy in particular of the English aesthete Ruskin.

In this respect, the latest American art takes a healthier position. It is in step with the age and does not attempt to distance itself from technological progress. Among the talented representatives of this young American art is Louis Lozowick, who recently visited Moscow as a guest for our October celebrations.

Lozowick is in every respect a man of his age and a genuine American artist. He does not flee the city—on the contrary, he is in love with the technological might of the time and the architecture of today's cities. His lithographs are paeans composed of lines and patches, paeans to New York and Chicago. His landscapes are cityscapes in which massive buildings take the place of trees and hills. Yet there is a crucial and extremely positive difference between Lozowick's "urban aesthetics" and that of his Italian Futurist predecessors.

The Futurists so worshipped technology that they deified urban culture and along

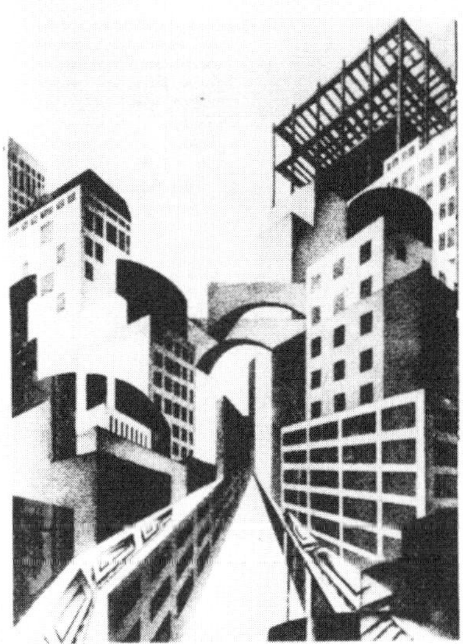

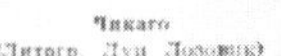

Чикаго
(Литогр. Луи Лозовик)

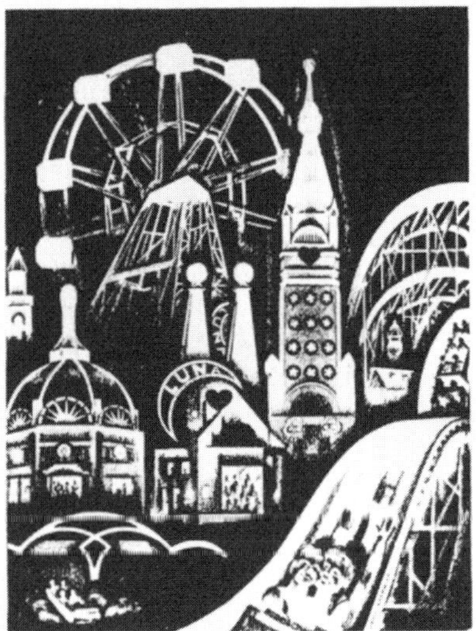

Луна-парк в Нью-Йорке
(Литогр. Луи Лозовик)

Искусство современной Америки

Америка... Страна гигантских инженерных достижений, колоссов архитектурного строительства. Страна головокружительного индустриального прогресса. Страна небоскребов Нью-Йорка, элеваторов Минеаполиса, стальных мельниц Пицбурга, нефтяных вышек Оклагомы, медных шахт Бюта, лесопильных заводов Орегоны...

Есть ли, однако, у нее свое искусство, своя живопись? Вот вопрос, который интересует многих и на который надо дать ответ положительный. Правда, новейшее искусство Америки возникло в значительной степени под влиянием французского искусства, но все же ему присуща и своя, особенная, характерная нота. Новейшая американская живопись и графика являются проявлением того же инженерного духа, который так специфичен для американской жизни.

Было время, когда мировое искусство, напуганное ростом техники, «уродующей» облик природы, пребывало в своеобразной оппозиции к городской культуре, не «принимало» ее и искало спасения от городов на лоне природы; так именно возник в живописи пейзаж и такова в особенности была проповедь английского эстета Рескина.

Новейшее американское искусство занимает в этом отношении более здоровую позицию. Оно идет с веком наравне и не отмежевывается от великого прогресса техники. Таков именно и один из талантливых представителей молодого американского искусства Луи Лозовик, недавно побывавший в Москве в качестве гостя на наших октябрьских торжествах.

Лозовик — человек чисто современной формации, подлинный художник-американец. Он не убегает из города, наоборот — он влюблен в техническую мощь современности и в архитектуру современных городов. Его литографии — песни, сложенные из линий и нитей в честь Нью-Йорка и Чикаго; его пейзажи — пейзажи чисто городские, в которых вместо деревьев и гор — громады домов. Но есть существенное и чрезвычайно положительное различие между всей «эстетикой города» Лозовика и его предшественников, итальянских футуристов.

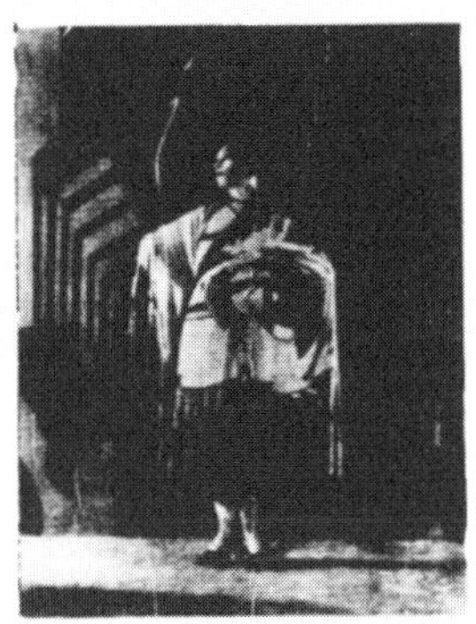

«Индустриализованное» платье.
(По рис. Луи Лозовик)

Последние в своем преклонении перед техницизмом доходили до подлинного обожествления городской культуры, а вместе с нею и самого капитализма со всем его «динамическим» хаосом. Лозовик, как и некоторые другие молодые художники Америки (группирующиеся вокруг журнала «Новые Массы», напр. Гроппер, Робинзон Бейкон, Майнер), близок к социализму. Он умеет отличить отрицательные черты сегодняшней городской культуры, сегодняшнего «города желтого дьявола», от имеющихся в них плодотворных начал — тенденций истинно рационального прогресса. И Лозовик не рабски отображает современный американизм, а претворяет его художественно по-своему.

Из вертикалей труб, из параллелей рельс, из квадратов улиц, из кубов зданий, из цилиндров нефти, из арок мостов, из феерии городской электрификации он создает свое [illegible]-геометрическое, строго организованное и гармонически-уравновешенное целое. Хаос современного города он превращает в стройно упорядоченный «ансамбль»; в его пейзажах — точная и четкая красота инженерии, величавость монументальных масс, пафос бетона, стекла и стали.

Быть может, это не столько город настоящего, сколько полуфантастический сон, город будущего — город, как чудо техники, как триумф творческой воли и научной мысли человека. И однако, в некоторых своих городских грезах талантливый художник доходит до чрезмерных фантасмагорий, и тогда кажется, что он забывает о самом человеке, о трудящемся человечестве, которому нужна ведь не только городская культура, но и зеленая земля. Истинно социалистическая культура, это — синтез техники и природы...

Я. Т—д.

Iakov Tugendkhold's "The Art of Contemporary America," in *Krasnaia niva* (Red Field) 2 (1928), with lithographs by Louis Lozowick with it capitalism and its "dynamic" chaos. Lozowick, like other young American artists grouped around *The New Masses* such as Gropper, Robinson, and Minor, is sympathetic to socialism. He is able to distinguish the negative features of contemporary urban culture—the present-day "city of the yellow devil"*—from its fertile elements and its tendencies toward genuinely rational progress. Rather than slavishly reflect contemporary Americanism, Lozowick transforms it artistically in his own way.

Out of the vertical lines of smokestacks, square blocks of streets, parallel rails, cubes of buildings, cylinders of oil tanks, arches of bridges, and fireworks of urban electrification he creates geometrical patterns and strictly organized and harmoniously balanced wholes. He transforms the chaos of the modern city into rigorously ordered "ensembles"; his landscapes display the precise and clear-cut beauty of engineering, the majesty of monumental masses, and the passion of concrete, glass, and steel.

Perhaps this is not so much the city of the present as the still semi-fantastic city of the future—the city as a marvel of technology, the triumph of human creative will and science. Yet in some of his urban visions this talented artist produces excessive phantasmagorias, and there it seems he has forgotten humanity—laboring humanity, which needs not only urban culture but also green countryside. Genuinely socialist culture merges technology and nature.

*The title of Maxim Gorky's 1906 essay on New York.

VIII

EXPRESSIONISM AND GEORGE GROSZ

The term "Expressionism" was used sporadically before the war but did not become common until 1919. The next year it was adopted by an obscure group of young Russian poets influenced by the Moscow Imaginists.*

Russians embraced Expressionism—unlike Cubism—not as an integral poetics but as a specific *Lebensgefühl,* a philosophy of art opposed to Naturalism and Impressionism, even as an ideological construct charged with liberating German art from its dependency on the French [96]. Expressionist painting was little known in Russia and never received genuine recognition. Expressionist graphic art, by contrast, was highly esteemed as a truly original phenomenon.

For the majority of Soviet critics, the crucial issue was art's social and educational function, which required of the artist a clear demarcation of positive and negative elements and did not permit differing political and ethical positions, thus presuming an objectivized and clear artistic language. Expressionist art did not meet these requirements.

Critics greeted the 1924–25 "First All-German Exhibition" in Moscow, Leningrad, and Saratov (see p. 247)—the first major show of Western art after the Revolution—with extraordinary interest and unusual unanimity. The exhibition showed that Expressionism was already being supplanted by the socially charged art of activism, variants of figurative painting (*Neue Sachlichkeit* and "Verism"), and geometrically oriented architecture and industrial design that bore similarities to Russian Constructivism. The realistic works in the exhibition, however, reflected a shocking nihilism and cynicism that Soviet critics felt had penetrated even the art of "revolutionary" artists and appeared even in the portrayal of "positive heroes" [99, 104]. Initially, Soviet critics had regarded the Expressionists as the revolutionary proletariat's allies from the intelligentsia and petty bourgeoisie. By the late 1920s, radical Marxists were condemning Expressionism as the style of "decaying capitalism."

The Russian audience considered George Grosz one of the most vivid figures in the art of postwar Europe. Immediately regarded as a phenomenon that encompassed several relevant problems, he assumed the role of a kind of "anti-Picasso"—an artist who ignored Cubism and who was not afraid of being "literary" and political. For a time Grosz had even been a member of the Communist Party of Germany. The Russian artistic consciousness had been searching for a language adequate to the demands of the revolutionary present and found it in Grosz.

Grosz spent several months in Russia in 1922 (and much later developed an ex-

*See Vladimir Markov, "Russian Expressionism," in *Expressionism as an International Phenomenon,* edited by Ulrich Weisstein (Paris: Didier, 1973).

tremely critical view of Soviet reality).* His portfolio, *Das Gesicht der herrschenden Klasse* (1921), was added to Lenin's Kremlin library. Mayakovsky brought several of Grosz's albums back from Germany in late 1922, and Russian articles about him began appearing in 1923 [100, 101]. Between 1923 and 1933 his works were featured in at least five exhibitions.

Grosz had as substantial an influence as an "artist of contemporary life" as the impact of his style was limited. His evolution from Dadaism to Communism, from épatage to political journalism, made him extremely attractive to the supporters of Lef [102]. In the Russian context, Grosz assumed functions accorded no other foreign artist. His graphic cycles powerfully influenced the Soviet viewer's image of the entire Western world.

Beginning in the mid-1920s, however, a number of German Communist critics charged that Grosz was incapable of rendering the heroism of the revolutionary proletariat. The artist responded with his autobiography, published in the Soviet weekly *Prozhektor* (Searchlight) 14 (1928; see pp. 251–53).† In the early 1930s the Soviet attitude toward him began to waver, and he was virtually forgotten for decades.

96

Vladimir Weidlé

"Notes on Western Painting: 1. The End of Expressionism" (1923)

Art historian Vladimir Weidlé (1895–1979) visited Germany in the fall of 1922. In 1924 he settled in Paris and wrote literary and art criticism. The excerpt printed here, which originally appeared in *Sovremennyi zapad* (Contemporary West) 3 (1923), is a response to a lecture by Wilhelm Worringer (October 1920), which Weidlé knew from Worringer's book *Künstlerische Zeitfragen* (Munich, 1921).

Expressionism is an invention. It was not something that existed and was discovered; it did not exist and so was invented as something useful to have. It is indebted to a handful of theoreticians not only for its fame but for its very existence. . . . All of its properties were worked out in advance, all of its manifestations were foreseen, and once its brief life had passed before the eyes of its inventors and the public with the regularity of a well-organized experiment, all that remained was—no surprise here either—to pronounce it dead.

[Expressionism] represents only a brief period of theoretical experimentation characteristic of Germany alone. "Impressionism" was not a good name, but the names of great artists will be connected with this paltry word forever. The word "Expressionism" has a more exact meaning, and in the future it will be associated with many

*See George Grosz, *An Autobiography,* translated by Nora Hodges, foreword by Barbara McCloskey (Berkeley: University of California Press, 1998), pp. 161–82.

†Charles Harrison and Paul Wood, eds., *Art in Theory, 1900–1990: An Anthology of Changing Ideas* (Oxford: Oxford University Press, 1992), p. 393.

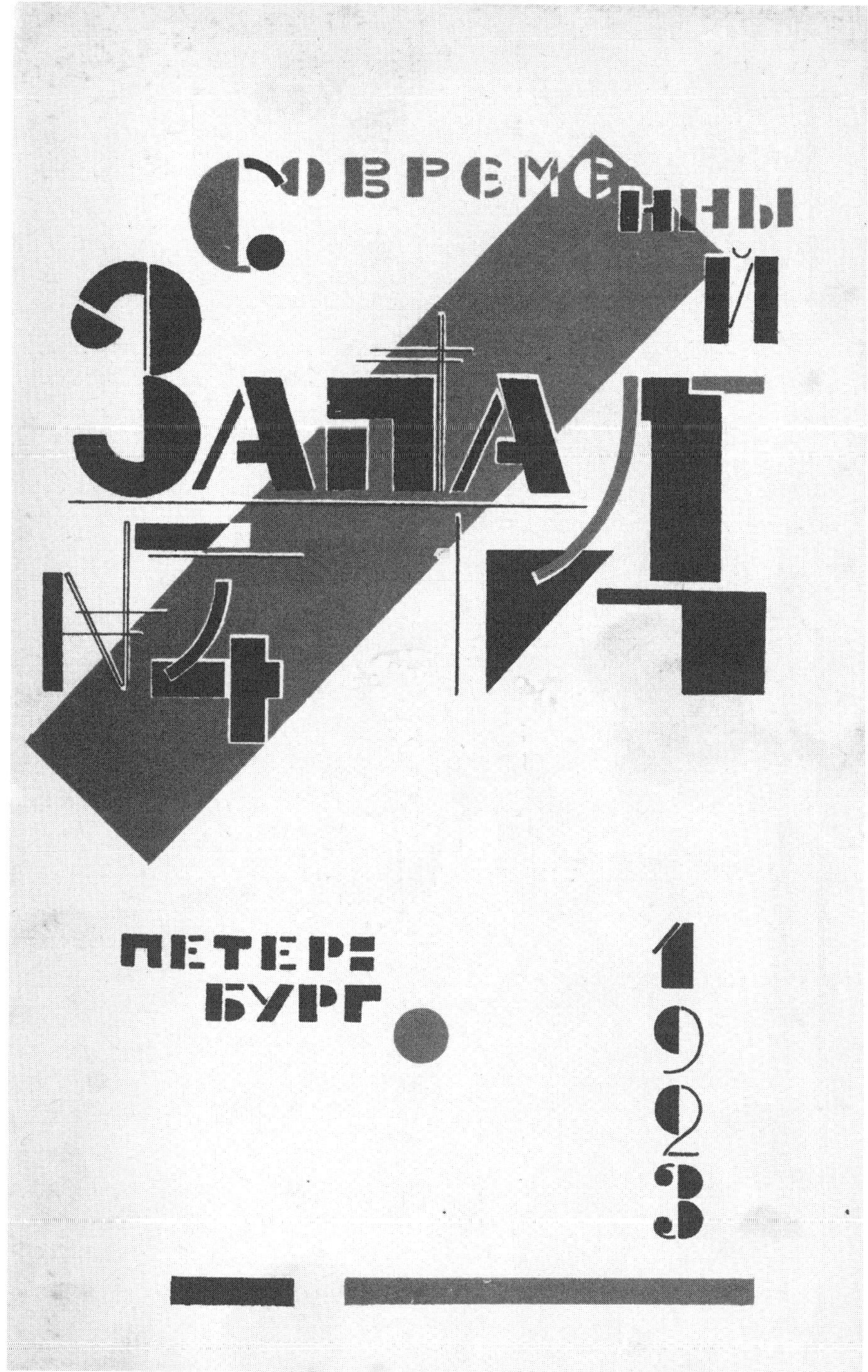

Cover by Iurii Annenkov for *Sovremennyi zapad* (Contemporary West) 3 (1923), in which Vladimir Weidlé's "Notes on Western Painting" appeared opinions and intentions and a little atrocious painting. . . . I could easily write a book about contemporary Expressionism after all the books written on the subject; the only insurmountable difficulty would be illustrating it, for any illustration would reveal the text's innate groundlessness. Here, finally, I come to the main point: regardless of how good Expressionism was in theory, in practice it inflicted incalculable damage on German painting. The theorists can move on as solemn as ever to something else, but the artists will have to heal, and the cure will be difficult. For too long they have been told about spontaneous "expression" and brilliant whimsicality; grasping even more superficially something that was not very deep to begin with, they believed that the idea was more important than the realization, that the intention—what was on the outside, the obvious, what could be described in advance—was worth more than the picture and in fact was the picture. This happened in a country that has had no artistic tradition, no discipline of taste or craftsmanship, since the chaos of the nineteenth century, when so many great talents perished, crippled by loneliness, never having reaching their potential precisely because there were not enough obstacles to their development. Expressionism here is merely the freedom of incoherence—not the great incoherence that comes of abundance but the puny variety born of poverty. Furthermore, Expressionism is a system of exaggeration, sterile self-aggrandizement, and self-deception that takes weak nerves for a paroxysm of emotion and the inability to concentrate expression for the hypertrophy of expressiveness. The artist tries to give the picture a spiritual content that he himself lacks.

. . . But the Expressionists are interpreted here [in Ludwig Justi's guide to the National Gallery in Berlin] with such competence and such contagious and self-evident clarity! Explaining them is a true pleasure. Their pictures were generated by and created for commentaries. And here they are explained historically, aesthetically, and philosophically. . . . The entire success of Expressionism in Germany is based on its extraordinary suitability for interpretation. . . . But nothing is more inert than these new rooms in the German museums. You can wander for hours among plans and ideas, among unrealized conceptions and enfeebled fantasies, and when you finally feel the insurmountable need to escape this tiresome non-being and descend one floor in the crown prince's palace and return to the Cézanne still lifes you have seen so many times before, what strikes you especially and wins you forever is not the perfection of the craft or the solidity of the construction *aere perennius,** not the wholeness or the profundity, but the divine concreteness of this pot, these flowers and fruits.

**Aere perennius*, "more lasting than brass." From Horace's ode "Exegi monumentum."

97

Boris Arvatov

"Expressionism as a Social Phenomenon: Apropos of Eckart v[on] Sydow, *Die deutsche expressionistische Kultur und Maleri* (Berlin, 1920)" (1922)

In a lecture delivered in Moscow on December 8, 1921, the leftist Hungarian art critic Alfred Kemeni contrasted Constructivism to Expressionism. Arvatov offered a similar juxtaposition in this review of von Sydow's book *German Expressionist Culture and Painting,* published in *Kniga i revoliutsiia* (Book and Revolution) 6 (1922).

. . . Expressionism is extremely revolutionary. Its deadly hostility toward the conservatism of traditions, its struggle against everything old, and its spurts, its impetuous spurts into the new—all this marks every step the Expressionist takes. In the political sphere, moreover, the Expressionists stand out as determined radicals; their banners are bright with socialism, anarchism, and communism; their hatred of the bourgeoisie and capitalism knows no bounds nor end; and the proletariat is their love and their hope!

. . . which social group masses Expressionism's combat brigades around itself?

Von Sydow's answer is precise and definite: the sector of the German intelligentsia that is analogous to the illustrious Russian intelligentsia in its social and cultural structure and outlook. They are members of the free professions, that is, people whose labor has not been collectivized by the successes of capitalist technology, people who create individually, helpless and solitary individuals who have felt the heavy burden of the bourgeois social machine's stoppages and breakdowns, who were crippled by the war, and who hate capitalism but are rootless and therefore have no life or historical path of their own. It is hardly surprising that at a time when the society that gave birth to them is crumbling they should try to flee it like rats from a sinking ship. But society cannot be escaped; it must be overcome. These cherished wards of the bourgeoisie, who turned away from it at a critical moment for the sake of self-preservation, are attempting to save themselves by pinning their hopes on the only class they see as vibrant—the proletariat. . . . Von Sydow is quite right in noting that the Expressionists talk about the workers not because they love them, but because they have ceased to love the bourgeoisie and nothing remains but to love the proletariat. . . .

Beginning with the Post-Impressionists, the history of recent Western European painting divided into two main and sharply delimited currents: the first has its source in Cézanne, the second in Van Gogh. The first found its way into production art by way of Picasso and Tatlin (Russian Constructivism must be considered its forerunner), and so laid out a path to the vital art of the proletariat. The second came, by way of Matisse, Paul Klee, Kokoschka, and Kandinsky, to the dead end of an idiosyncratic, subjectively emotional, and formally anarchic game played with pure colors and lines. The social bearer of Constructivism is the progressive, revolutionary, primarily technical intelligentsia; the social bearer of the latter movement, that is, Expressionism, is . . . the backward, idealist, homeless intelligentsia. It is of course no coincidence that Constructivism put down roots in Soviet Russia, whereas Expressionism lives in the Germany of Scheidemann and Stinnes.* . . .

Constructivism and Expressionism share only one feature: both reflected the disintegration of easel painting as they progressed from schematic representation to complete abstraction. If the former solved objective, material problems (the texture and properties of materials, etc.), however, the latter merely used material to achieve subjective, emotional, and mystical expressiveness. Constructivism was interested in reality, focused on technology, and step by step accumulated experience for the future; Expressionism didn't give a damn about reality, aimed for sensual effect, and accomplished only one thing: it dug its own grave.

. . . Thus, Expressionism is an organized tool of the declining bourgeoisie—an original tool in the sense that its blade is supposedly aimed at the bourgeoisie itself. We now see in Germany a new, genuinely revolutionary movement in art that has declared all-out war on the pseudo-socialist aesthetes. This movement has been fertilized by the ideas of Russian Constructivism; from its very first steps, this movement took its place beneath the banners of the Communist Party. Thus begins the end of Expressionism. The class war in art is a function of the class war in economics and politics. . . .

98

Nikolai Radlov

"Introduction" to Georg Marzynski's *The Expressionist Method in Painting* (1923)

Nikolai Radlov (1888–1942) studied art history at St. Petersburg University and painting at the Academy of Fine Arts and contributed as a critic to *Apollon.* He and Evgenii Braudo edited a collection of translations of German articles on Expressionism: *Ekspressionizm* (Petersburg, 1923). He also wrote this introduction to the Russian translation (Petrograd and Moscow, 1923) of Marzynski's *Die Methode des Expressionismus: Studien zu seiner Psychologie* (Leipzig, 1920).

. . . Whereas Cubism and Futurism are cultivated by small groups of connoisseurs and theorists scattered around the globe, Expressionism is entirely free of this caste character. It is concentrated in one country but is developing with a breadth and depth which suggest that it is attuned to profound features of the national spirit. The theory and practice of Cubism, Dadaism, and so on mainly interest the "initiated"; they remain alien to the artistic culture of the broad masses and exist almost exclusively in the laboratory. By contrast, Expressionism is organically rooted in the very heart

*Philipp Scheidemann (1865–1939), leader of the German Social Democrats, prime minister; Hugo Stinnes (1870–1924), influential German industrialist.

of German art and has influenced even the oldest art associations. . . . Its theory has long interested everyone from philosophers and art historians down to scholars of the museum variety, and its "style" also permeates official art, even including government-issued postage stamps. . . .

Expressionism is a protest against the ingrained principles of Impressionism, but in a broader sense it is a protest against the entire formal, technical art of France. Even more broadly it is a protest against the very nature of contemporary European intellectual culture.

Hence the national coloring of Expressionism. . . . These features, however, . . . are incidental. Today, after France's cruel victory, the German spirit is rising purified and brightened, perhaps aware that the chauvinist attitudes of wartime are only the final stains of the hostile culture against which German Expressionism has taken up arms. . . .

Contemporary mankind's task is to make artists once again feel and experience rather than just perceive the world, create rather than reproduce the world, and fill despiritualized, ready-made nature once again with the living, vibrant, and mysterious spirit that the scalpel of materialism amputated.

. . . Craft, calculation, and skills, you see, inhibit this outpouring of creative energy. They muddle the pure wellspring of experience, wrap the artist's bared emotion in contrived and impersonal forms, and act as a barrier between the artist's soul and the perceiver's.

Whatever the philologists might say, *Kunst* has nothing in common with *Können*. The more immediately, naively, and unskillfully the artist's agitation makes itself felt, the more clearly his original divine spirit is revealed.

Thus, the absence of formal theory is not an incidental shortcoming of Expressionism but its formal theory.

This theory holds both the weakness and the strength of Expressionist art. Its strength lies in its psychological premises, which are broad enough to be applied equally to the artistic creation of all types of tools without circumscribing the artist's individual freedom through any technical doctrine. . . .

Those who have cultivated their taste on the formal traditions of Italian or French art, which is always balanced, even in ecstatic moments, and always "classical," even in revolutionary moments, will find this art monstrous and repellent.

If we are to understand it and see the unity of psychological and metaphysical premises in the artist's "abstract" effusions of agitation as well as in the childlike babble of his ideas of the world and in his hysterical communion with the mysterious spirit of nature and humanity, and if we are to come to accept or even to love this rebellious, inarticulate, "ugly" art, in which the ugliness of corporeal form is almost a canon, we need a new and different focus and approach to art. . . .

Is "ugly," ecstatic, formless art—art in which the artist's intense thought and mystical insights have left their mark down through the ages—really so alien to European man? Does it really need any new justification? . . .

99

Nikolai Tarabukin

"Apropos of the German Art Exhibition" (1924)

Nikolai Tarabukin (1889–1956) graduated from law school but became known as a theoretician of production art. In the early 1920s he taught at various institutions, including Proletkult, and was the academic secretary at INKhUK (Institute of Artistic Culture). In 1924 he became a corresponding member of GAKhN (State Academy of Artistic Sciences). Tarabukin was never prosecuted, but in the early 1930s he ceased publishing and concentrated on teaching. This essay on the "First All-German Exhibition" appeared in *Pechat' i revoliutsiia* (Press and Revolution) 6 (1924), along with articles by Tugendkhol'd [cf. 94] and Fedorov-Davydov.

German artists want to be active. . . . Unlike "our" Jacks of Diamonds, they are not passive contemplators of landscapes, fruit, and earthenware dippers. They are not illustrators of events or chroniclers, not even those with "red carnations" in their lapels, like the Russian AKhRR. . . . Unlike many Russian graphic artists and caricaturists in today's magazines, they do not just "comment" on the "latest news." To the extent that the exhibition justifies the generalization, German artists are active participants in public life.

. . . *Russian artists are antisocial by conviction.* As represented by the qualitatively and quantitatively most substantial branch of the Jack of Diamonds, they have not only consciously eliminated socio-political and socio-philosophical thought as a means of orienting themselves but have also as a matter of principle limited the content of their art to aesthetic and formal problems. . . .

I am well aware that the anarchist ideology and purely individualistic protest in many of the German artists' works are alien to us and inappropriate for contemporary Russian society. The purpose of the present article and lack of space prohibit analysis of the hidden social essence of the German artist's anarchist protest, which has gone so far that it has lost all foundation and become naked nihilism: protest for the sake of protest, destruction for the sake of destruction, utterly unscrupulous sneering without reason or any desire for reason. . . .

In addition to the two main points presented above about German artists—their extremely keen social awareness and their active role—I will contrast another two facts that are present in German painting and absent from Russian art, namely, the former's *dynamics of form and intensity of expression.* A majority of works—not only xylography, etching, and drawing, but painting as well—are informed by a *dynamically developed theme.* Beginning with the principles of composition and ending with line and the psychological portrayal of characters that are sometimes executed with amazing expressiveness and poignancy, certain exhibits* are very deeply shocking. . . .

As for the outburst of "indignation" that has often greeted the slight pornography and sex in the Germans' pictures, it would not hurt anyone who is especially upset

*For example, Dix's works on war themes (Tarabukin's note).

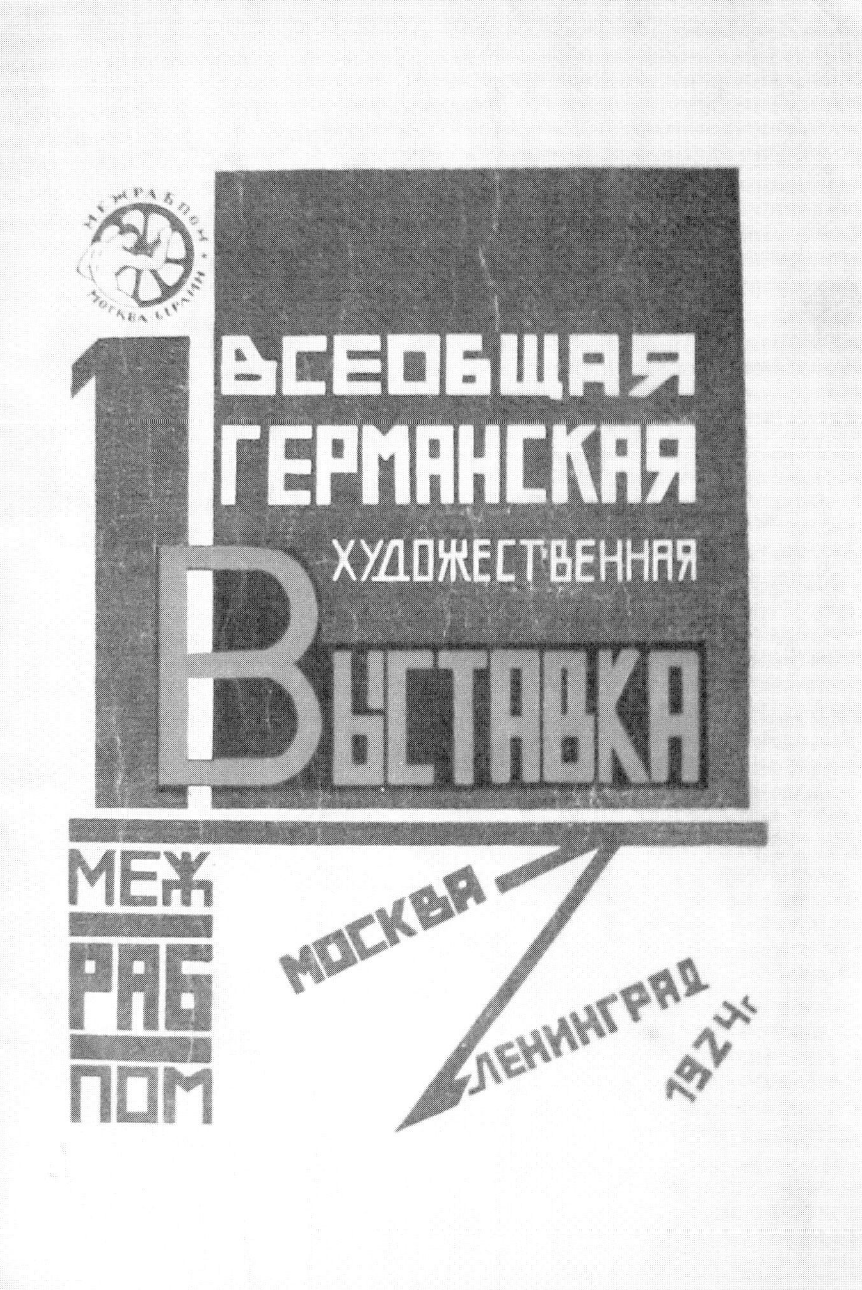

Cover of the catalogue for the "First All-German Exhibition" (Moscow, 1924)

to survey quickly the grand epic of the art "of all times and peoples" and recall the brief and expressive description of it in L. Tolstoy's caustic but in many respects accurate essay ["What Is Art?"]: to an overwhelming degree, art was and remains a "smear of sexual abominations." Dix does this with the acuity of a contemporary citizen of the capital of an imperialist state, and he could not, of course, use the good-natured devices of a Bocaccio.

Since I have not set myself any formal goals, I may remain silent about the purely technical features of German art. The reproach leveled at the exhibition of this art, that there is not the slightest trace of "painting" in the sense of Veronese's or Rembrandt's color and "values," is a valid criticism. German artists are not painters but graphic artists even in painting. But that was true even in the distant past. . . . In counterbalance to Titian the Germans had L. Cranach. The predominance at the German exhibition of graphic art in the narrow sense of the word, however, is a highly significant symptom of the social goals and active position described as fundamental above. Because mass distribution is more portable and flexible, graphic art, whether done as engraving or executed photomechanically and connected with magazines and books, is by its very form better suited than the unique object of easel painting to fulfill an active social role. Thus, the role that German art wants to play naturally makes it gravitate toward graphic art. . . .

Having noted the German artists' basic position, we see visitors leaving the exhibition speaking of the "feelings" and thoughts that arose under the influence of the pictures they have seen. If nothing else, they are disturbed by the negative impact of the "ideas" the German artists have expressed in visual form. No matter that this impact is essentially negative. It is positive in principle, for *impact* is what we expect of contemporary art. . . .

100

Osip Brik

"Ecce Homo" (1923)

The philologist Osip Brik (1888–1945) was one of the founders of the Society for the Study of Poetic Language (Opoyaz) and a member of Lef. From October to December 1922 he accompanied Mayakovsky to Berlin. This essay was published in *Ogonek* (Little Flame) 19 (1923).

. . . Once you have seen enough of Grosz's drawings [in *Ecce Homo*], you cannot look without disgust at the people who served as his theme. In the street, in restaurants, in streetcars on the boulevard—you see them everywhere, and you see them as Grosz makes you see them. . . .

Viewing Grosz's works you immediately think of drawings on fences, on walls, and in prisons, lavatories, and schools. This is no coincidence. Grosz understands very well that you cannot struggle with the bourgeoisie while continuing the traditions of the art it has produced. You have to find another approach, and what could be more natural than to look for it where none of these traditions exist, where "ignoramuses" attempt by the simplest devices to achieve their goal, which is to express an idea as keenly and clearly as possible and to make the maximum impression with minimal resources.

Unlike many pseudo-leftist artists, however, Grosz does not "stylize" or work in the primitivist "manner." He borrows the energy, intensity, and "below-the-belt" punches of fence paintings* but uses all the power of contemporary painterly technique to develop these qualities, and this distinguishes his works from the drawings of the fence artists and the "artistic naiveté" of aesthete stylizers.

Grosz's works are inconceivable apart from the political objective they serve. They cannot be regarded from an "artistic" point of view. Their technical strengths do not protrude but enter completely into an overall visual effect of enormous agitational tension. It is only afterward, when the first burning impression has cooled, that you begin to distinguish the devices Grosz used to achieve this impression. Herein lies his enormous skill.

Grosz is a very prominent contemporary artist. It is, of course, no coincidence that he is a Communist and that he has studied in the school of radical leftist trends in art. It is only in such a combination that the creators of today's artistic culture can appear and succeed.

And the bourgeois authorities confiscate their works. That is no coincidence either.

101

Abram Efros

"George Grosz" (1923)

Published in *Sovremennyi zapad* (Contemporary West) 3 (1923).

George Grosz is the only name in art that postwar republican Germany has tossed over its borders. We can evidently assume that the law so clearly at work in Russia today operates to a greater or lesser degree in all countries: a rapid, rather abundant, and brilliant accrual of new names in literature accompanied by a temporizing, stagnant, and unpromising marking of time in art. German Expressionism, of course, is first and foremost a *literary* school. In art it is mainly a "theory" transferred here by analogy to literature and reinforced with an appropriate number of historical artistic masterpieces and formal aesthetic theorems. The young Expressionist writers of Germany have formed a *school* as easily and organically as the German artists dubbed Expressionists have failed to form anything integral. . . . The only authentic distinguished figures of recent years to have matured in wartime and postwar Germany are George Grosz and Paul Klee. Klee, however, remains and cannot but remain a "purely

*The reference is to the Futurists' "Decree No. 1 on the Democratization of the Arts," authored by Mayakovsky, Kamenskii, and Burliuk (*Gazeta futuristov* [Futurists' Newspaper], March 1918).

local," typically German phenomenon that seems to satisfy a quirk of taste and a fondness for "aging child prodigies." He has still not overcome this organic flaw, nor does he seem to think he should. Grosz alone has achieved the stature of an extra-German, broadly interesting, almost European phenomenon.

The social and political atmosphere of Europe and the idiosyncrasies of Grosz's talent have contributed in equal measure to this standing. Here is an artist who does not know the meaning of the words "shade," "nuance," and "undertint" and who is maximally passionate and keen in everything, in his artistic techniques as much as his sense of self. Just to be able to launch a heavy projectile he would sooner miss hitting a sparrow with a cannon than fire a smaller bullet. This explains why he is so controversial. He arouses the same degree of passion in his critics and viewers. Each time he presents something he somehow forces you to define your attitude toward him very precisely, although this attitude is not aesthetic, or rather, more personal and political than aesthetic. People attack him with their fists and defend him with their fists, but fists are the main argument for and against Grosz in both cases. In the final analysis, to be able to evaluate him as a purely artistic or, I should say, socio-artistic phenomenon, one evidently has to be a foreigner rather far removed from the atmosphere that nourishes him. It then becomes obvious that one is not at all obliged to declare him either a positively first-class figure—as do his friendly and partisan critics—or a nonentity feeding on the passions of society, as the hostile side would have it. That he is not a genius is, of course, clear. Even in the context of German art, which is generally provincial ("Germany is a good European province"), Grosz is nothing extraordinary, or at least not so very extraordinary that his artistic merits need be ascribed any definitive significance. Naturally, his art is even less simply "Bordell und Irrenhaus," as *Münchner Zeitung* two years ago laconically summarized the opinion of the sedate and respected family press. His combination of a rather striking talent with extremely striking politics suffices to assure his pungency and success. In this relationship everything is in its proper place. The political element of Grosz's art is, of course, more powerful than its purely aesthetic significance, but genuine and original skill is needed for the magnificent, loud, and piercing scream of politics to penetrate with such clarity and precision.

This means above all that Grosz's art is filled to the brim with content. And that, of course, distinguishes Expressionism as a whole. . . .

So many artists have unsuccessfully taken up Grosz's themes during the past five years of revolution in Russia! They all lack what Grosz's drawings abundantly, brimming over, possess almost unbearably: genuine political passion.

Grosz has an almost physiological effect on the viewer: you are short of breath, you clench your teeth, and everything goes dark before your eyes; to discharge the energy welling up inside you you want to fight, crush, beat someone, scream, howl. Grosz accompanies the advancing revolution in its most seething depths and its

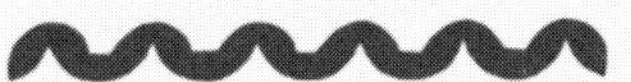

Жорж Гросс.

МОЯ ЖИЗНЬ.

Автобиография, написанная специально для „Прожектора".

Родился я в Берлине 26-го июля 1893 года. Еще будучи маленьким мальчиком, я мечтал стать художником. Позднее я посещал академию в Дрездене, а потом, из материальных соображений (ради стипендии)— художественно-ремесленную школу в Берлине. В 1912 году впервые я поехал в Париж — и безо всякого к тому побуждения вернулся обратно—хотя старательно рисовал этюды в эскизной студии Калароссі (известная мастерская в квартале Мон-Парнасс) и посещал Лувр.

Жорж Гросс. Рисунок к «Солдату Швейку» на сцене театра Пискатора. «Будьте добры, повернитесь направо!».

Пестрая жизнь улиц и кафе привлекала меня, в сущности, больше всего; там у меня уже было в то время смутное ощущение, что я должен попробовать выразить и передать в живописи нечто подобное тому, что выражал Золя в своих произведениях.

Три месяца в Париже пролетели быстро и незаметно. В Берлине я рисовал для заработка каррикатуры в юмористические журналы — конечно, я охотно обслуживал бы и более солидные издания, но не было ни одного работодателя, который бы захотел испробовать меня, как художника; ведь я был слишком неизвестен. Одно время я думал было стать заправским художником-иллюстратором, и передо мной заманчиво маячила „Премия

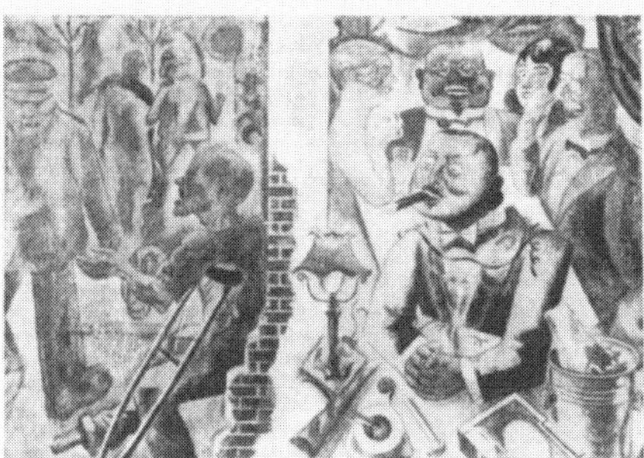

Жорж Гросс. Внутри и снаружи. (Масло. 1926).

Менцеля", об'явленная „Берлинер Иллюстрирте Цейтунг" [1]) для художников-иллюстраторов (гонорар в 3.000 марок). Я мечтал уже о путешествиях вокруг света, видел себя смелым предприимчивым репортером большой газеты на солидном окладе. Недосягаемыми и достойными зависти казались мне знакомые американские художники.

Мать моя долгое время готовила и вела хозяйство в офицерском собрании, так что я до некоторой степени имел представление о солдатах и офицерах.

Это была одна сторона юношеской поры: — достаточно оптимистической и неверной кажется она мне теперь; что касается другой стороны, более темной, относящейся ко мне лично, то она тоже была налицо: подстерегающая, полная сомнений, часто бессмысленно мотающая из стороны в сторону, она проявлялась в виде человеконенавистничества и недовольства собою и людьми.

У меня всегда была склонность к раздумью и наблюдению, и, когда разразилась война, я был уже совсем серьезным и вдумчивым человеком.

[1]) „Берлинер Иллюстрирте Цейтунг"—самый распространенный в Германии иллюстр. еженедельник. *Прим. пер.*

Патриотическая шумиха, которая увлекла за собой самых культурных из моих товарищей, меня не привлекала вовсе. А когда пал Льеж,

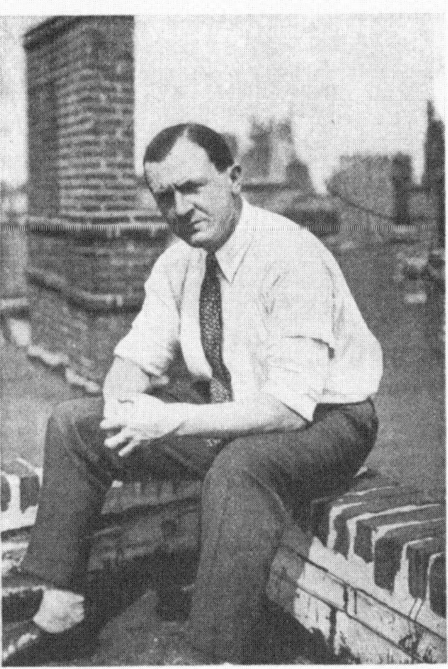

Жорж Гросс.

и все кругом торжествовало, я считал это „газетной уткой" и чувствовал себя так, как после хорошей порции розог.—Я упоминаю об этом незначительном факте лишь потому, что он характеризует мое необыкновенно сильное предубеждение и скептическое отношение к печатным листкам вообще, а особенно к экстренным выпускам, которые сыпались дождем с неба, как тогда.

Однако, я слишком отвлекаюсь... Впредь обещаю не выходить из рамок рассказа и постараюсь быть кратким.

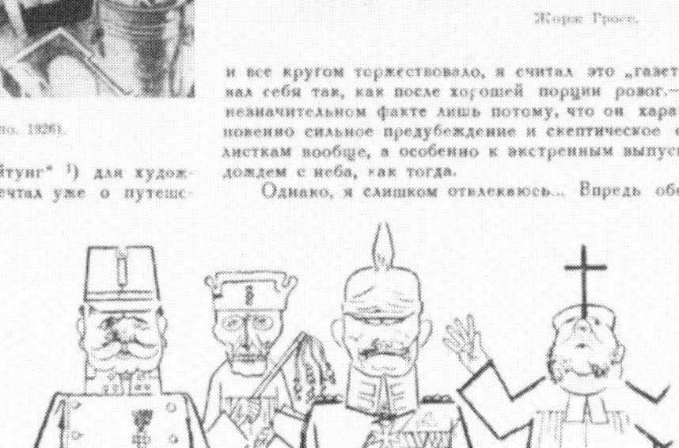

Жорж Гросс. Рисунок к «Солдату Швейку» в театре Пискатора. «Солдатское начальство».

Когда я думаю о своей жизни в деревне и маленьких провинциальных городках, о периоде детства, о школьном периоде или о „Вильгельмовском"— отмеченном появлением у меня усов, или о „ура-политическом" военном—сколько воспоминаний о смешном, тяжелом и забавно-трагическом...

Итак, 1914 год—и мировая война. Я сразу стал солдатом — был военнообязанным. В 1915 году был снова отпущен, получив на фронте острое воспа-

George Grosz, "My Life," *Prozhektor* (Searchlight) 14 (1928) ление мозга вследствие контузии и, так как в то время не было еще такой нужды в пушечном мясе, как потом (все думали, что через какие-нибудь полгода будет заключен мир) — я был отпущен на родину для несения гарнизонной службы. Великолепное началось для

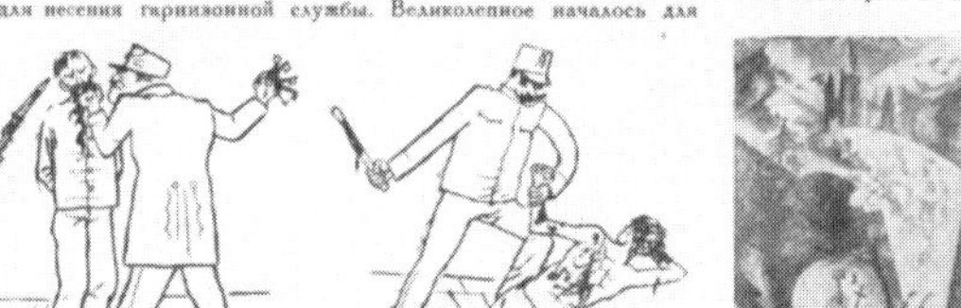

Жорж Гросс. Рисунок к «Солдату Швейку». «А ну-ка, поговори у меня!».

меня время, чудное, восхитительное время, когда все было пропитано символикой войны, полно „неподдельного патриотизма"; когда каждый пакет искусственного меда украшался „железным крестом второй степени"; когда на каждом письме сзади наклеивалась надпись: „Боже, покарай Англию!" Восхитительное время консервных колбас из раковин!.. Удивительное время, когда старые кожаные чемоданы перерабатывали в солдатские ботинки и доказывали, что политура — питательная вещь; чудесное время, когда жиры добывались из овощных и фруктовых семян, а знаменитый военный „мус" был так едок, что проедал дыры на скатерти. Только человеческий желудок способен был выдержать все это!

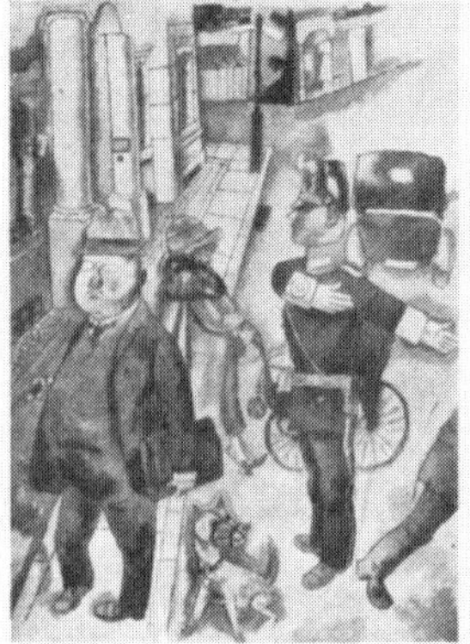

Жорж Гросс. Снова в Германии. (Акварель, 1926)

Шел 1916 год. Крупные наступления поглощали целые поезда людей. Потом настал 1917 — „великая демобилизация" — как замечательно удачно выразился генерал Людендорф. Я тоже был демобилизован в то время.

Прибыл я тихий и скромный в Грос-Брессен — барачный поселок близ Губена. Держал я себя, однако, как ярый противник войны. Проделал я фантастическую, типично-прусскую комическую Одиссею. В заключение, благодаря возобновившимся болезненным припадкам, был отослан для наблюдения в нервную лечебницу в Герден.

До этого еще в Берлине я сочувствовал молодой литературе и искусству.

В 1915 году, после моего первого увольнения с военной службы, я познакомился с поэтом Теодором Дойблером и по его рекомендации посылал рисунки в „Вейсе Блеттер", — журнал, который издавал в Цюрихе Рене Шикеле. — Это были скромные листки с демократично-пацифистским направлением. Теодор Дойблер писал к моим рисункам статьи. Он первый — так сказать — открыл меня для „высшей" литературы и искусства, толкнул меня на этот путь. Ему я обязан многим и об этом именно хочу здесь упомянуть.

В 1916 году основался маленький кружок „Новая Молодежь", в который вступил и я. Одним из активнейших среди нас, — настоящим отцом нашего журнала — был В. Герцфельде, впоследствии владелец „Малик-Ферлаг". В то время это был приветливый, похожий на картинку гимназистик, в коротких штанах, с манерами хорошо воспитанного школьника. Он писал стихи и пламенно интересовался литературой и искусством.

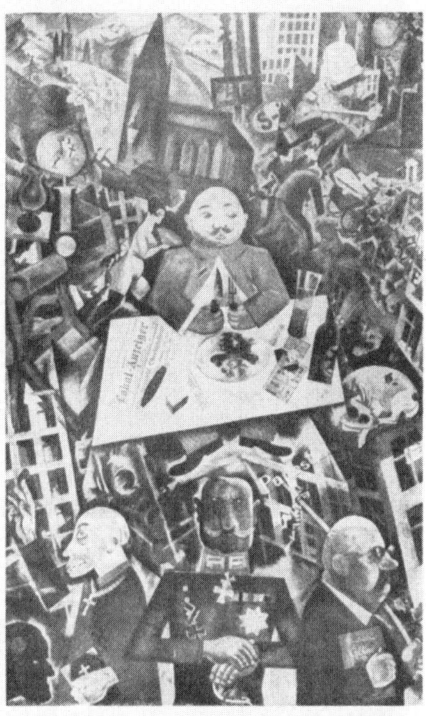

Жорж Гросс. Германия — зимняя сказка. (Масло, 1917—18).

Само собой разумеется, что все мы были настроены антимилитаристически и ненавидели всю эту барабанную шумиху. „Новая Молодежь" сначала, конечно, была аполитична, но мы были пацифистами, и характер журнала выразился в некоторых статьях и стихотворениях, а также в культурническом интернациональном уклоне.

Но я опять потерял нить рассказа...

Итак, после пяти месяцев испытания и строгого наблюдения, я был выпущен из Герденской лечебницы и признан годным для несения лишь нестроевой, гарнизонной службы. Это было в конце 1917 года: надвигался уже 18-й год. Тут я встретился с Юнгом, Гертфильдом и Хюльзенбертом. Последний приехал из Цюриха с идеей „дадаизма"[1]). Это значит, что „Дада" стало в Германии тем, чем оно есть теперь, лишь благодаря нам. До того времени „Дада" было случайным названием, на которое опирались опыты чисто формальной эстетики. Теперь, под его флагом мы об'явили и повели войну против всей распущенности, отсталости и расхлябанности

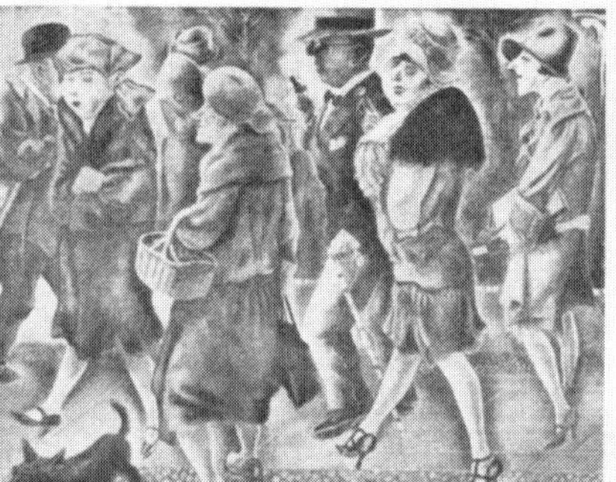

Жорж Гросс. На модной улице. (Курфюрстендамм). (Масло, 1926).

[1]) „Дадаизм" — крайне левое течение в зап.-европейском искусстве. Прим. пер.

в немецкой литературе, искусстве и философии. С едкой бранью обрушились мы на так называемые „священные ценности человечества". В. Гергфельде тем временем был мобилизован. Журнал „Новая Моло-

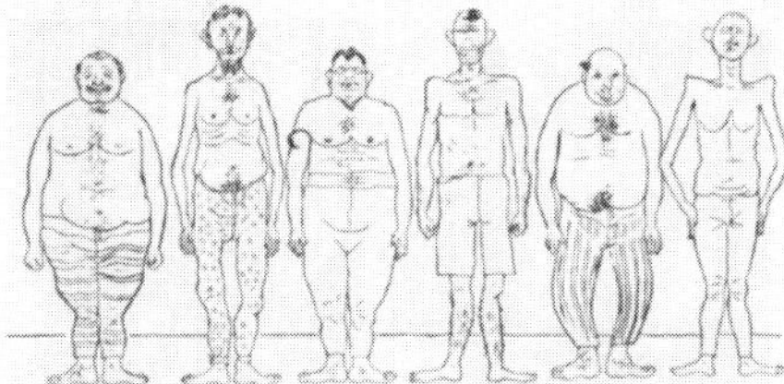

Жорж Гросс. Рисунок к постановке «Солдата Швейка» в театре Пискатора.

дежь" под руководством Гертфильда вырос и стал лучше печататься. Косвенно, благодаря Югу, журнал стал политическим — и потому был тотчас запрещен.

Для историков культуры следует упомянуть еще о том, что в 1917 году открыт был „фотомонтаж" — столь высоко ценимый теперь родной брат клеевой работы, а также были испробованы новые способы печатания, и над ними проделывались разные эксперименты. Мой друг Гертфильд, маленькие грязные ручки которого всегда полны были свертков, клише, художественных снимков, предназначенных для напечатания и подклейки, получил тогда прозвище „монтера", — позднее это слово переделали в „монтаж" (Гертфильд один из первых гениально подбирал и подклеивал снимки, чтобы придать им силу и тенденциозность).

Это было необычайно оживленное время. Франц Юнг, демонический знаток человечества, тянул нас всех за собой, не интересуясь тем, хотим мы этого или нет. Много было выпито — за спорами об искусстве и тут Юнг был главарем. Еще многое можно было бы вспомнить, но время не терпит и места мало. Хочется еще только сказать о том, что тогда уже появился Эрвин Пискатор и председательствовал на одном из утренников „Дада" немного позднее, в 1919 году. Война приходила к концу без песен и без колокольного звона. Пангерманский сон рассеялся. — Матросы забаррикадировали улицы и воцарилось радостное анти-офицерское и анти-правительственное настроение. Те, которые занимали высокие посты, торопились снять свои мундиры и скрывались в мышиные норки, потому что в то время шутки были плохи с одичавшим на фронте „солдатьем". И у многих сорвали погоны и отобрали оружие. Мне да и всем нам казалось, что внезапно распахнулись ворота, проник свет, — так казалось — но, к сожалению, очень скоро эти ворота были опять заколочены и заперты на двойной замок. Это побудило многих из нас к определению своей политической позиции — нас, лучших, а за нами ринулись спартаковцы в неумолимую борьбу с буржуазией и ее ставленниками Эбертом и Носке.

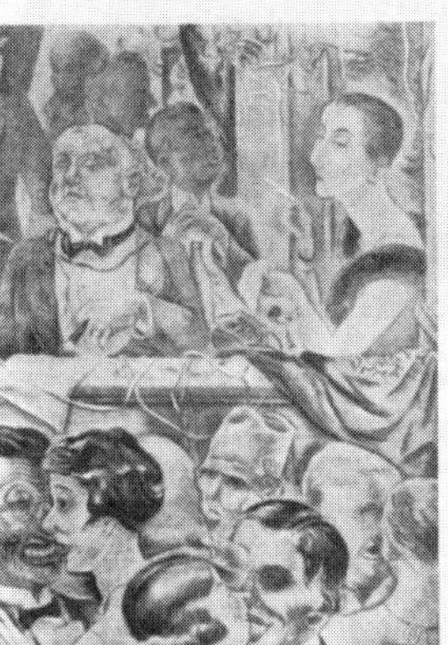

Жорж Гросс. В ложе. (Масло, 1927).

В 1919 году я вступил в ГКП. Основана была коммунистическая сатирическая газета „Плетка", которая резко выступила против социал-предательских спекулянтов и повнившихся вновь „белогвардейцев Носке". Я напечатал в „Плетке" много моих карриктур и рисунков. Все же наше издание неоднократно запрещалось, и даже потом, при „свободе печати", оно не смогло продолжать своего существования за отсутствием средств. Теперь оно, уже давно не существует, и только в голове некоторых верных учеников сохранилось воспоминание о нем, как о лучшем опыте создания настоящей коммунистической сатирической газеты. Но уцелели тысячи политических рисунков. События оплодотворили мою продуктивность, и чувство справедливости влекло меня к революционному делу.

В 1922 году я предпринял путешествие в Россию.

В 1917 году начал я писать революционные картины. Во время войны я написал картину „Германия — зимняя сказка". Здесь я изобразил картинку из современной жизни: „вечного" буржуа в виде центральной фигуры, с окружающей его декорацией — качающейся мировой кулисой, — буржуа, вечно пришитого к тарелке с картофельными клецками (и в ней тонет революционер-матрос). Внизу троица: священник, генерал и учитель с черно-бело-красным ореолом — символика немецкого воспитания и крепости — но с Гете под мышкой. Год тому назад я написал еще несколько картин сходного содержания: „Солнечное затмение" и „Падение общества", „Внутри и снаружи" и „Агитатор". Две из них в настоящее время находятся в фойе театра Пискатора — буржуазные художественные магазины не охотно показывают такие „реалистические" картины и отрицают их за тенденциозность. Я хочу приступить к целому циклу такого рода картин, которые, по восхитительному выражению художественного жаргона, „хочется попробовать языком". Я хочу доказать, что и сегодня, как во времена великих художников, популяризировавших идеи католической церкви, можно художественно изобразить и представить волнующие народ идеи. Я знаю наверно, что сейчас в каждой стране есть сотни тысяч недовольных, которые имеют лишь смутное понятие о новом искусстве и культурных потребностях. Без лишних фраз я хочу сказать, что в изобразительном искусстве пошлые темы „Уют среди апельсинов", „Жертвоприношение" — или даже „Симфония в красном" вызывают лишь умеренное стремление филистеров к чему-то „новому".

В заключение мне хочется сказать следующее о моей работе в целом:

Часто товарищи, считающие себя особенно „умными", возражают против моего изображения рабочих: „Пролетарии — в моем изображении

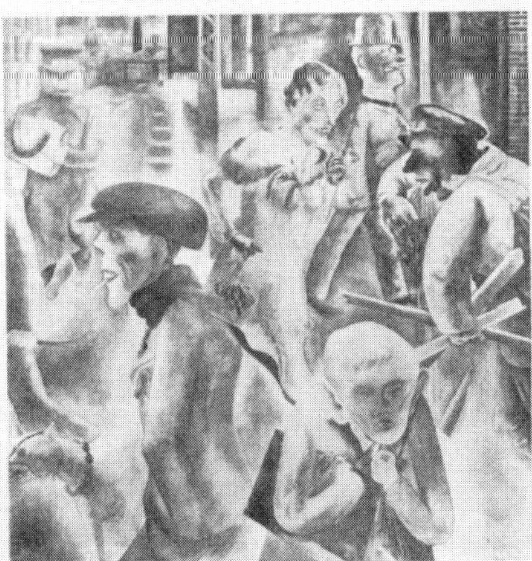

Жорж Гросс. Мрачная улица. (Масло, 1926).

с их точки зрения — не настоящие пролетарии, а ходульные, какими их видит „мелко-буржуазно-анархично" и пристрастно художник Гросс". Они хотят этим сказать, имея в виду идею роста рабочего класса, что именно такого растущего пролетария следовало бы изображать, как „положительную" идею. Но я не считаю нужным удовлетворить требования „ура-большевизма", который представляет себе пролетариат гладенько причесанным и в древнем героическом костюме.

Я, по крайней мере, не могу себе представить пролетариат другим, чем таким, каким я его изображаю.

Я вижу его еще угнетенным — еще внизу общественной лестницы — плохо одетого, плохо оплачиваемого, в мрачных, вонючих берлогах и очень часто одержимого мещанским стремлением „ввысь".

Кроме того, я совершенно не верю в то, что лишь путем односторонней, восхваляющей и фальшивой идеализации можно служить пропаганде.

Нельзя же изображать всего рабочего в стиле агитплакатов, с засученными рукавами и толстыми бицепсами.

И нельзя, исходя из такого сусального представления о рабочем, говорить, что я неверно изображаю его с пропагандистской точки зрения. Всякий художник стоит на базе своего времени. Надо помнить, что германский пролетариат в своей массе еще не дошел до такого сознания своей силы, как рабочий Советского Союза.

Помочь рабочему понять его угнетение и страдание — заставить его констатировать открыто свою нищету и свое рабство, пробудить в нем самосознание, пробудить его для классовой борьбы — вот задача искусства.

И я служу этой задаче.

Перевод с рукописи А. Л.

strongest, simple watchwords. This is why one needs no special explanations, approaches, or justifications to understand him. He has sided with German communism as resolutely and unreservedly as he once declared himself a Dadaist when he thought that "Dada" was the artistic hypostasis of radical leftist revolutionary socialism. He is overflowing with the "ecstasy of destruction"—each drawing of his targets something the revolution should attack. . . .

. . . Grosz's mastery is in direct proportion to the scale of his theme. The simpler his theme, the more remarkable his power. He has managed to rid himself of something from which even the best masters of political caricature, even the artists of *Simplicimus,* could not break free. . . . They could not and did not want to be "vulgar," as every great man of the masses is obliged to be. Grosz has this vulgarity, and he has made it a source of power and style. The more vulgar he is, the more significant. The real medium for his skill, therefore, is the linear drawing. When he attempts complex art, he immediately sinks and becomes "one among many," lowering himself to epigonism, picking up crumbs from Chagall, laboring over the recipes of the Futurists, sometimes not so badly, more often badly—always far from the uniqueness that distinguishes his graphic works. It is in any event only these that make Grosz a figure of European stature with his own artistic periphery. "Grosz's influence" has now begun to make itself rather widely felt, and even among young French artists, who would seem to be insulated from foreign influence by the tried and tested independence of French art, Grosz is a palpable presence, for example, in Cocteau's drawings.

102

Viktor Pertsov

"Foreword" to the Russian translation of George Grosz and Wieland Herzfelde's *Art Is in Danger: Three Essays* (1926)

Viktor Pertsov (1898–1980) was a critic, a member of Lef, and subsequently the author of the official Soviet three-volume work on Mayakovsky (3rd edition, 1976). Just a year after Grosz and Herzfelde's work appeared, it was translated into Russian as *Iskusstvo v opasnosti* (Moscow and Leningrad, 1926).

. . . Grosz provides an interesting description of the latest aspirations of German painting. He notes an important pattern according to which it is the radical "leftist" artists—who would seem to be concerned only with narrow problems of form and style—who have broken with pure art and become champions of art that activates the masses.

Here there is a perfect parallel with our nonobjectivists and Cubists, from among whom our present production artists have arisen.

Grosz is keenly aware of the power of modern technology, and in his evaluation of the German Constructivists' significance he quite correctly notes art's potential to dissolve in industry and industry's definitive role in the evolution of the newest art (rather than the other way around, as certain Russian Constructivists maintain).

The artist should become an integral part of the industrial army, and in this case Grosz goes so far as ultimately to admit the disappearance of the artist as such (to be replaced by the engineer, architect, etc.), or to subordinate the artist's task completely to the goals of the proletarian class struggle. In the latter case, the artist should immediately become an agitator.

To Soviet ears, Grosz's calls to bourgeois artists to join the ranks of the struggling proletariat sound rather naive. He clearly overlooks both the possibilities for creating new art forms and the new artists that the growing working class is producing quite independently and organically from its own ranks. After all, even Grosz himself—a vanguard artist and human being—finds it difficult to imagine himself working under Soviet conditions. It is entirely uncertain whether this master of visual images that unmask bourgeois society would be able to cope with the standards of the triumphant working class that our age demands of the artist. . . .

103

Anatolii Lunacharskii

"Art Is in Danger" (1926)

Anatolii Lunacharskii (1875–1933) joined the Social Democratic movement in 1895. In 1907, while living abroad, he started contributing articles on contemporary European art to a number of Russian newspapers. In 1913 he began publishing in Lenin's newspaper, *Pravda,* and upon his return to Russia in 1917 he joined the Bolshevik Party. In Lenin's administration he headed the People's Commissariat of Enlightenment (Narkompros) and continued to be active as an art critic. This response to Grosz and Herzfelde appeared in *Novyi mir* (New World) 3 (1926).

Georg Grosz is one of today's most talented graphic artists. Brilliant and original, a caustic and penetrating caricaturist of bourgeois society and a staunch Communist, he has written three essays on the present situation of art. I had the pleasure in Berlin to review almost everything that has come from his hand.*

The powerful talent and powerful bitterness of his works are truly amazing. The only fault I can find is that at times his drawings are too cynical. . . . But this does not prevent Grosz from being a militant and noble artist with basically positive ideas.

. . . Pertsov's foreword does not explain or supplement but instead conceals and distorts this very gifted German artist's healthy and splendidly expressed ideas.

Indeed, Grosz admits only two paths for art, one being ideological production art, which he describes with an even stronger word: "tendentious." Everything else he

*Lunacharskii met Grosz in Germany in 1925–26.

considers profoundly bourgeois and decadent, and for everything else he predicts death, specifically at the hands of photography and the cinema. His statement of the matter is harsh, but it coincides with the position of Narkompros. . . .

Grosz declares that the production artists are killing art and are fusing entirely with technology and engineering. . . . "In Russia," he says, "Constructivism represents the hypnosis of the artist by industry, so to speak. There is a great deal of beauty in industry and the machine. Rural Russia with its reviving industry is in love with the idea of industry, so to speak, and the artists, often quite thoughtlessly, reflect industry's outward appearance, so to speak. . . . " In the West, on the other hand, . . . Constructivism has no future, for industry in the West is too serious and powerful and cannot bear to stand next to what I personally view as an attempt to ape industry. . . .

Grosz emphasizes, however, that consciously or unconsciously, the artist is always an agitator and that art rises to a colossal new level when it devotes itself to serving the ideology of the new class. This is the position that we at Narkompros as well have always considered necessary to support. Instead of stressing the coincidence of these positions, Pertsov's presentation of Grosz's ideas overshadows the significance of his message. . . .

For all proletarian connoisseurs, of course, Grosz is a master not of visual stereotypes but of social analysis and synthesis in extremely economical visual images. The point is not the stereotype but the individual viability of each of Grosz's caricatures and the fact that hidden beneath the external naiveté of the drawing the inner power of eye and hand enable you to penetrate as attentively as possible into the depths of the phenomenon being portrayed. . . . Grosz is not a "master of stereotypes" but a master of types; this makes him a realist, although like all realist caricaturists . . . he of course appropriately deforms the objects he is depicting. . . .

IX

CREATING A MODEL FOR REVOLUTIONARY ART

The Soviet state supported relations with Western artists sympathetic to the Revolution, its primary goal being to strengthen Soviet political influence in the West. But the role of the foreign artist "allies" was not limited to political objectives. One of the principal tasks of the revolutionary regime was to create the new society's "proletarian" or "socialist" culture, whose various conceptions allowed a relatively limited range of past phenomena to serve as reference points or sources [cf. 70].

In the 1920s, a critical discourse formed around the work of the "revolutionary" artists. But despite events such as the extensive exhibition of revolutionary art in Moscow in 1926 [105], no integral tradition of this art really existed. Among the many connected issues were art's social utility and its educational and structuring impact on human behavior. Another inevitable question was the relationship between ideological content and form: among the Western artists considered revolutionary there were practically no major figures developing modern poetics. Such artists did not appear until the 1920s, but their language was often too radical and their political positions insufficiently orthodox (Grosz, Rivera).

Despite the publicity given to Masereel, Steinlein, and Kollwitz, their influence was insignificant. Politically active, aesthetically innovative artists were drawn deeper into the Soviet context. Thus Diego Rivera's arrival in the Soviet Union in 1928 came at the same time as a renewed interest in monumental art. John Heartfield's visit in 1931 coincided with debate on the "creative method" of Soviet art [111]. The reception of the *monteur* followed the traditional pattern in Russia—various groups attempted to make the Western artist a "model" contemporary master and to impose their interpretation of his work on the public. At first Heartfield was directly drawn into Soviet artistic life, but he was the last Western artist to play such a role. The turn to Socialist Realism made Soviet artists look to the Russian Realist artists of the second half of the nineteenth century, such as Il'ia Repin and his fellow Wanderers.

When Stalin turned to intensified class struggle and sharper distinctions in the international workers' movement, critics of the late 1920s and early 1930s became particularly selective in their attitudes toward "revolutionary" artists. Both Kollwitz and Grosz ceased to meet the new criteria. In contrast, pro-Communist associations of Western artists whose works were useful for propaganda purposes, such as the ARBKD/BRBKD (German Association of Revolutionary Artists/German Alliance of Revolutionary Artists) in Germany and the John Reed Club in the United States, began playing an active role. The International Bureau of Revolutionary Artists, which in reality was designed to promote Comintern policies among the Western intelligentsia, was founded in 1930.

The mid-1920s saw two basic approaches to the development of Soviet art—one traditionalist, the other avant-gardist—which on the whole corresponded to two different conceptions of art: art as the reflection of reality, and art as a means of organizing life. In both cases, the relationship to Western art was key. For instance, Lunacharskii believed that the evolution of socialist art was connected with a return to a "Grand Style" patterned on the Renaissance. Contemporary and recent Western art lost out in this respect [107, 108].

The second conception was born of the effort to appropriate international avant-garde trends, as was most clearly formulated in the works of the assimilated Hungarian émigré Ivan Matsa (János Mácza) [106] and the program of the October group (1928). Among the partisans of this concept were members of the Lef circle, art critics such as Fedorov-Davydov, and a number of foreign Communists [104]. As a rule, they rejected any fruitful influence of "individualist" and bourgeois easel painting on socialist culture, favoring instead art that contributed to shaping an integral social environment (architecture, industrial design, photomontage, etc.). This doctrine originated in the notion of the structural link between socialism and imperialism: by borrowing highly organized production, the former resolved the basic contradiction of capitalism between collective production and private exploitation. Thus a great many rationalistic trends became the predecessors of socialist art.

The latter concept was rejected by Stalinist critics around 1930, and its supporters had to perform public penance [118]. The former, traditionalist doctrine became the natural background for the Socialist Realism of the 1930 to 1950s, which almost totally ignored (officially, at least) the experience of modern Western art.

104

Aleksei Fedorov-Davydov

"On the New Realism in Connection with Western European Trends in Art" (1925)

Aleksei Fedorov-Davydov (1900–1969) studied at Kazan University and the Institute of Archaeology and History of Art of the RANION (Russian Association of Scientific Research Institutes in the Social Sciences) in Moscow. In the 1920s he held a number of positions, both in academia and in journalism. From 1931 to 1934 he headed the Department of New Painting at the Tretiakov Gallery, and in later years he taught at Moscow University. In this article, published in *Iskusstvo trudiashchimsia* (Art for the Laborers) 17 (1925), Fedorov-Davydov argues with critics such as Lunacharskii who considered Expressionism and Italian figurative painting of the 1920s useful to Soviet art.

Now, it seems, hardly anyone would disagree that our contemporary painting is more and more clearly aspiring toward a kind of new realism. Its most unreserved advocates are the AKhRR artists. Although they have written realism on their banner, however, our contemporary artists do not agree on the meaning of the term. Realism, after all, can be understood in two ways: in the sense of naturalism, that is, the attempt to render the surrounding world as it is, as objectively as possible; and in the sense of the realistic worldview of materialism in painting, which is as revolutionary as materialism in philosophy. At least with respect to their goal of creating monumental art it is the AKhRR artists who are most responsive to the demands of today, which is why the question of a new realism becomes especially urgent. To understand and evaluate AKhRR, we must understand what sort of realists they are. We are not likely to err if we say that they understand realism in its essentially naturalistic, thematic, generic sense.

Here—setting aside the question of talent—is perhaps the principal reason why they cannot genuinely reflect our revolution. Naturalism's passive methods cannot convey enthusiasm and heroism.

It is extremely interesting to examine what is going on just now in the West. Our critics are trying to present two trends there as being in harmony with our contemporary reality: Neo-Classicism, which is found partly in France (Derain) and mainly in Italy (Oppi, Casorati, and others); and Expressionism, which we saw at the German exhibition in Moscow. Let us take a closer look at these tendencies and see what they have to offer. First, Neo-Classicism. Quite correctly perceiving in it the desire to recover a long-lost monumental style and a break with all the otherworldly visions and logical abstractions of Cubism and the like, some of our critics, even some Marxists, think that these aspirations are very much in keeping with our own. Seeing in Neo-Classicism the bourgeoisie's desire to gird itself morally in the ongoing struggle with the working class, they believe that revolutionary art should assimilate this trend's aspiration toward organization, order, and discipline because it corresponds to the spirit of the proletariat, which will turn it against the bourgeoisie. This view is mistaken. Neo-Classicism as a whole is reactionary and as such we find it completely unacceptable. One need only look at the works of Oppi or Casorati to sense that this is decadence elevated to monumentalism and recast in classical forms. Neo-Classicism is not a step forward but the desire to eternalize all the old accomplishments of Cézannist Post-Impressionism. The land of Neo-Classicism is the homeland of fascism for good reason. This Classicism in fact represents the end of a culture that is about to crumble. Never in the history of art has Classicism been the starting point of the new art of a new age.

Expressionism has far greater claims to being revolutionary. It makes sense that there are so many Communists and sympathizers among the Expressionists. In the dialectics of changing styles, elements in the birth of a new style are always closely interwoven with the disintegration of the preceding style.

The German exhibition showed us that Expressionism no longer exists as a specific artistic style, that abstract Expressionist transrationalism is a thing of the past, and that the characteristic Expressionist effusion of the inner trembling of its "soul" (Marzynski)* has been replaced by the timid representation of social reality outside the soul. German art is decadent not because it is Expressionist but because it is hys-

*Cf. Georg Marzynski, *Metod ekspressionizma v zhivopisi* (The Method of Expressionism in Painting) (Petrograd, 1923).

terical, because it is confused, half-insane howling about the "death of culture." However, Expressionism's passion, poignancy, emphasis on the typical, and aversion to details, as well as the agitational content that saturates it, are positive features that we can and should master. I call this forceful but realistic passion and dynamism Expressionist Realism. Realism that aspires to be revolutionary must be a realism which does not register with the objective indifference of a camera but judges and evaluates and rejects, which proclaims its own unique, vital, and real reality, the only reality of which it wants any part. Such were Courbet and the early Wanderers.

If we are bound to take anything from Neo-Classicism, it is the "conscientiousness" of its masters. Although we accept the passion of Expressionism, we must not accept its ideological and technical disarray. The high demands of craftsmanship, the consideration and synthesis of all the achievements of the latest painting—all of this is needed to produce "strong" works. Today it is as masters of their craft that artists must approach their work. The work of art is above all a well-made thing.

105

Abram Efros

"Revolutionary Art of the West (The State Academy of Artistic Sciences Exhibition)" (1926)

The "Revolutionary Art of the West" exhibition—the first attempt to bring together politically activist works—was organized by GAKhN (State Academy of Artistic Sciences) and the All-Union Society for Foreign Cultural Contacts (VOKS). Besides paintings and works of graphic art, the exhibition featured books by "revolutionary" writers, posters, and satiric journals—over three thousand items in all. More than forty artists participated in the visual arts section. The exhibition opened on May 16, 1926, at the Rumiantsev Museum in Moscow. As a member of GAKhN, Efros helped organize the exhibition. This essay was published in *Prozhektor* (Searchlight) 11 (1926).

. . . Almost nothing has been accomplished in art. In this sense we have not been reunited with the West. It is as though the blockade was never lifted. Our painting, sculpture, and graphics are in isolation. They have been left to fend for themselves. This is all the more difficult in that Russian art was always nourished by the West. There was more here than a simple connection. Our young trends were born, grew, and were shaped under the direct influence of leftist European groups. Paris was the real capital of Russian art. Separation from the West has meant the loss of defining models. Traditional provincialism is beginning to feel itself the master of the situation. If you're standing behind a fence you don't need to button your pants. Our art is already displaying phenomena indicating that its inner forces have been perverted and are moving unsteadily. The absence of leftist trends and the present growth of the graybeard tendencies of the Wanderers loudly signal danger.

We need showings of Western art. Even the exhibition of German artists brought to Moscow a year and a half ago was useful. True, it was also provincial, but there was a breath of the West in it. Not many were seduced by it, but it did make many stop and think. If these young Germans didn't do it the right way, at least they did what had to be done. . . .

Now the window to the West is again open. The State Academy of Artistic Sciences exhibition has brought together a remarkable set of materials and is unusual and doubly interesting because it combines the West and the Revolution. At present nothing is more crucial to Russian art than these two problems. The artists from Europe and America who have come together in the exhibition propose a number of solutions. Whatever they are, they are equally important and instructive. They can be opposed, but not ignored. They are all the more impressive in that all the leading names and characteristic tendencies are represented. Moreover, they have been brought together here for the first time. This is the Western art that the West does not know. The West is familiar with individual artists but has never attempted to join and compare them. This task fell to us instead. . . .

The general features of the exhibition are simple and sharp. It spans the first quarter of the century, 1900 to 1925, representing two generations of artists separated by the world war who do not resemble each other, differing formally and artistically as much as they do socially and politically. The completeness and wholeness of the change are remarkable. A new worldview is arrayed in a new artistic form. . . .

This does not mean that all leftist art is revolutionary, but it does mean that all revolutionary art is leftist. This is one of the most important lessons to be learned from the Academy exhibition. The watershed of exhibition rooms dividing the older from the younger artists is immediately apparent, for on each side you are confronted by a different social feeling and a different formal system. On the social level there is a transition from socialist to communist groups; on the artistic one there is a shift from genre to synthetic realism.

The older generation is represented by three basic names: Brangwyn, Steinlen, and Kollwitz. . . . Käthe Kollwitz is the most tragic, tenacious, and profound. Perhaps that is why of all the older artists she seems closest to us. Sometimes she even feels like our contemporary. Her best works are striking. The old-fashioned quality of certain inner and formal features is hardly noticeable. If she could only refresh and hone her technique she could be accepted almost as a teacher. . . .

The art of the younger generation . . . is *active* throughout. It strikes a blow, incites an uprising. Such is the second half of the exhibition. Artistic form here is a weapon. It whips life rather than merely registers it. . . . Here there is but a single voice. We are therefore less aware of the difference in talents than we are of their monolithic thrust. . . . But this does not prevent a lively rivalry among the various leftist schools within the generation. There is competition for the keenest artistic devices and forms, which open like a broad fan. Here there are shades of Expressionism (the Germans Grosz, Beckmann, and Felixmüller; the Czech Reichental), Neo-Realism (the German Dix), Monumentalism (the Austrian Nistler, the Dutchman

Alma), Primitivism (the Dutchman Bieling, the German Seiwert), Neo-Classicism (the Hungarian Bortnyik), Orientalism (the Hungarian Uitz), Synthesism (the Belgian Masereel), etc., etc.—an International of "-isms"!

. . . Here there are as many promises, as many realities, as much future as there is present. Let me be even more precise: everything is boiling so rapidly that there are bound to be bubbles. But it is *boiling!*

This is what we need. In art, mistakes are less harmful than silence. Young art is right even when it hits a false note. These may seem like aphorisms, but in fact they are a simple summation.

106

Ivan Matsa (János Mácza)

The Art of Contemporary Europe (1926)

Ivan Matsa (János Mácza, 1893–1974) was a political activist in the Hungarian Soviet Republic (1919) who moved to Moscow in 1923, after living in Vienna. He was head of the art section of the Institute of Literature and Art, a division of the Communist Academy. He was also one of the founders of the October art group. In his later years Matsa taught at Moscow University. In this book, written in 1922–24 but published in 1926 (Moscow and Leningrad), Matsa presents what seems to be the first detailed account of the Central and Eastern European avant-garde.

PURIST AESTHETICS, MACHINE AESTHETICS, AND CONSTRUCTIVISM

No artistic phenomenon of recent years has produced such a wealth of formal and methodological achievements as Cubism. Cubism, which pursued its basic point of view to its logical conclusion in the experiments of *Bildarchitektur* and Suprematism, reduced the analysis of forms and colors to maximum simplicity, provided an elementary doctrine of painting as a whole—that is, a methodology for analyzing the forms and composition of all types of pictures beginning with the drawings of primitive man—and also formulated a scientific system of form and colors for the further development of painting.

This development is expressed in the art (and even more in the theory) of the former French Cubists Ozenfant and Jeanneret [Le Corbusier], the founders of "Purist aesthetics." . . . "Purist aesthetics" rejects the primacy of the psyche in human emotions and acknowledges a material, physiological primacy. . . . Furthermore, the Purists are leading Cubism out of its impasse and moving from the Cubists' "geometrical order" to the "geometrical and mathematical order of our life and reality."

In this way renascent Cubism has arrived at "machine aesthetics" (Fernand Léger, *Machine Aesthetics,* Paris, 1923). which at first glance seems to resemble the Futurist principle, which also took the aesthetic appreciation of machines as its point of departure. The crux of the matter, however, lies elsewhere. The Futurist viewpoint is that of a petty bourgeois who has grown up in the city but lags behind the rapid de-

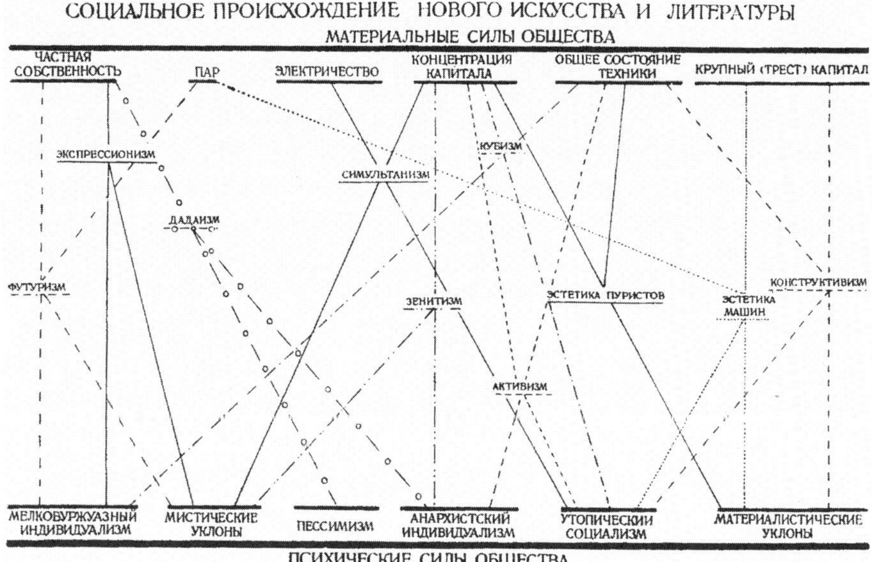

Diagram showing "social genesis of new art and literature" from Ivan Matsa's *The Art of Contemporary Europe* (Moscow and Leningrad, 1926)

velopment of urban life. He is essentially passive and merely wants to enjoy the dynamics of urban life and modern life in general but is not interested in building it. The new Cubist, on the other hand, is a son of the industrial, capitalist social system. He feels that he has not only the right to enjoy himself but also obligations toward the society in which he lives. . . .

Now we have a very clear picture of the course of development that resulted in Constructivism. The sociological aspect of this development is as follows:

1. Acknowledgment of coercion by big commercial and industrial capital in the evolution of art (Scheerbart).
2. Acknowledgment of the social role and utility of art and the observation that art has evolved in accordance with industrial production (Léger, *Machine Aesthetics*).
3. Acknowledgment of certain *materialist* principles in the synthesis of modern art (Ozenfant and Jeanneret, *Purist Aesthetics*).

The formal aspect of this development is as follows:

1. Study of the real relations among geometrical forms as an achievement of Cubism *(Purist Aesthetics).*
2. Study of the real relationship between abstract geometrical forms and the "geometrical order" of industrial life *(Machine Aesthetics).*
3. Glass as a new material and architecture as the central art form (Scheerbart).
4. The overall result is the acknowledgment of things in art.

If we now combine all these features, we will have a general description of Constructivism.

For what is the "constructive principle" in art? Nothing but the reconstruction of art on the basis of real fundamental forms—not through composition, but through the *mathematical and mechanical interrelationships of things.*

. . . The new artist of the new capitalist age builds and produces practical, useful *things* or *designs for such things.* He is an artist, a technician, a mechanic, and an architect.

For him, movement is not aesthetic beauty, as it is for the Futurist, but a mechanical or physical process possessing not only a principle but also a definite function. For him, color and form are not empty aesthetic elements but living realities with their own real value. For him, painting, sculpture, and architecture as such do not exist—there is only one "universal art," which encompasses elements of painting, sculpture, and architecture. In the final analysis, for him there are no "arts" in the old, primarily aesthetic sense of the word, but, from both the practical and the aesthetic points of view, there is production as the collective unity of industry and art—the union of human aesthetic desire and creative will.

It is in this aspiration for unity that the Constructivists' "revolutionary" quality or the source of their revolutionary tendency is to be found.

. . . Objectively, although the capitalists do not acknowledge Constructivism, its art is nonetheless the ideological expression of the capitalist age. The centralization of the various art forms and Constructivism's general tendency, which is expressed in the mechanization of all phenomena and which views technology as the summit of life and almost totally rejects the ideal of earlier art—individuality—all these features clearly show that Constructivism's tendency coincides with the tendency of capitalist production, which, according to Marx, also expresses "the expansion of objective productive forces at the expense of subjective productive forces." . . .

Yet there is one point in Constructivism through which it can attach itself to the Revolution, namely, its realization that as long as class society exists, neither the capitalist class nor any other class will acknowledge "the necessity of immediately implementing the union of industry and art" and that therefore no one will provide the means for implementing this union.

But if the Constructivists have understood this, what are they to do? Either abandon Constructivism as unfeasible for the time being and adapt themselves to agitational art or do what the Constructivists in the West are doing: create designs and make amusing toys or, finally, work for the Revolution and at the same time pursue laboratory experiments as such. . . .

THE PROLETARIAT AND THE DIALECTICAL SIGNIFICANCE OF MODERN ART'S FORMAL AND METHODOLOGICAL ACHIEVEMENTS

. . . We have at our disposal the materialistic Marxist method, which enables an objective critique of all issues. We must utilize this method and apply it to new artistic and literary phenomena, which exist and *have their own objective significance* apart from our subjective rejection of them.

In short, the proletariat, as the revolutionary class and builder of communist society, must look on modern art in the same way as it does all phenomena of the past; that is, it must embrace and master all achievements *that are viable elements in social development.* This viewpoint has found acceptance not only with respect to material phenomena and systems of production but also, for example, relative to the forms of feudal art. It has not been accepted only with respect to the latest petty bourgeois and capitalist art and literature. And this is entirely wrong.

After all, if we are seizing and mastering all viable forms of the past, then it goes without saying that we should also seize and master those forms that are closest to us and are *advanced by the industrial forms* closest to us. This is not "logic" but a necessity determined by the dialectical course of social evolution. . . .

The prewar schools of art—Expressionism, Neo-Primitivism, Futurism, and Cubism—and the movements brought forth by the period of petty bourgeois despair—Dadaism, Tactilism, and Haptism—display primarily destructive tendencies. . . . Either their forms and methods are a conscious (Cubism) or unconscious (Expressionism, Neo-Primitivism, Futurism) *analysis;* or they are simply a conscious (Dada) or unconscious (Tactilism, Haptism) mimicking of earlier artistic and literary forms and methods.

The viability of these forms was exhausted as soon as the result of their analysis was used for construction. Here the school "died," and all that remained were the form and method simply as a means of development: the *broad rhythm* of the Futurist poem, the nervous *enthusiasm* of the Expressionist expression, the *geometrical form* and *constructive approach* to the method of constructing these forms and the sarcasm of the Dadaists as a method of approach to social problems. . . .

On the other side are tendencies that developed after the imperialist war as capitalism consolidated and awareness of the social significance of industrial production and technology grew.

Of course, these tendencies—such as Scheerbart's "glass architecture," Purist aesthetics, machine aesthetics, and Constructivism—used the formal and methodological achievements of Cubism, but they gave geometrical form a new meaning: instead of a purely artistic, representational function, they are concerned with the expanded, "objectively realistic," and utilitarian significance of the work.

Although the views of the artists of this latter category are still too aesthetic, and although in their works one also finds real phenomena abstracted or at least dissociated, they are nevertheless taking an important step toward a materialistic understanding of art.

They are generating above all a new understanding of "things" and "creation," in the sense that the "artistic thing" is the same sort of material product as, say, a machine and is produced in the same deliberate and material manner as a machine.

That both the object and the machine are isolated in their works and become extra-social phenomena is another matter.

Second, beginning with *Bildarchitechitektur*, the new artists turned their attention to the *biological* and *physiological* aspect of aesthetic relations and looked for "physical laws" in the interrelationship of forms, colors, lines, planes, and space. (Incidentally, it is interesting to note that Einstein's theory of relativity has thus far had no influence at all on the solution of these problems, due to modern art's absolutist aspirations.)

Third, attention has been drawn to the problem of *texture* and expanding the range of artistic *materials*. The modern artist is no longer satisfied with paints, canvas, plaster, and so on, but uses glass, iron, cement, and all sorts of industrial materials. This development, of course, has been influenced by capitalist production and technology. But can we *completely deny* the significance of these formal and methodological achievements simply because they developed in the period of capitalism? *Of course not.*

On the contrary, we must master all of these viable formal and methodological achievements in order to test them in our practice.

For only practical implementation can show us the relationship of the achievements of modern art and literature to our reality. And our reality and the reality of the Western proletariat consist in the class struggle, in preparing the broad proletarian masses for the coming revolution, and in the road leading to the dictatorship of the proletariat.

Perhaps this seething reality of ours will not produce "art" in the broad "monumental" sense of the word but "only" propaganda in the forms of art and literature. Perhaps we will be able to use only a small percentage of the formal and methodological accomplishments of modern art and literature. But there is no doubt that in this small percentage the best of them will come over to us, and they will remain dialectically significant for the next phase of social evolution as well.

107

Anatolii Lunacharskii
"Discussion on AKhRR" (1926)

In 1926 AKhRR (Association of Artists of Revolutionary Russia) organized "The Life of the Peoples of the USSR," a huge exhibition shown in Moscow and Leningrad. That summer and fall, the Leningrad weekly *Zhizn' iskusstva* (Life of Art) launched a discussion of the event; most of the participants in the debate strongly criticized AKhRR for demagoguery and provincialism. The essay by Lunacharskii from which this fragment is taken was published in *Zhizn' iskusstva*, no. 34.

. . . We know that contemporary society—prerevolutionary society here and the society that is still dominant in Western Europe and America—is little interested in the content of art. Fashion there is set by snobs—people who in art look above all for interesting aesthetic, technical, or simply sensational gimmicks. Entire generations have been raised on such things, as have a great many of our critics. Repudiating oneself is difficult. It is difficult to declare that something on which you have worked a great deal and which has become your pride and joy, so to speak, is of little value. It is all the more difficult because these artists are in general not very sensitive to their new audience and tend to think that people dressed "in caftans and work blouses" simply don't understand anything. Europe and America, moreover, are still and will for a long time yet be engaged in various "formal" experiments, and this helps formalists think that the reason they are not understood here is that our revolution has disastrously lowered the public's cultural level. Formalist artists can always say of themselves that they are on the level of Europe and not of these Asiatics who are just learning to babble like children. . . . Comrades who share the views of "moderate" formalism should remember that their belief in the progressiveness of the art of the 1890s is entirely unfounded. Fromantin argued long ago that not a single artist of his time was able even to copy a picture such as de Hooch's *A Sick Child,* let alone paint it.* . . .

Art can regress under certain conditions. In the introduction to his *Toward a Critique of Political Economy,* Marx very definitely establishes that the rises and falls in the development of art do not coincide with regression or progress in science and technology. Ever since artists began painting for the market and art entered into the overall market system, the quality of artistic production has hopelessly declined. . . . The artists of Lef merely claimed to have a highly developed technique. In actual fact, among them it was impossible to tell whether someone had a real painterly technique, because by pleading deliberate infantilism, simplification, deformation, and so on, they could conceal utter incompetence and the most naked lack of talent behind a facade of self-confidence. . . . The study of technique and skills is essential. There are individual artists in the West today (some of whom were represented at the exhibition of revolutionary Western art in Moscow) who are worth studying. Most of all, of course, the masters of realistic periods must be studied, for to express the content that is vital to us we need a stronger, unusually striking, aesthetically and ideologically expressive, stylized—that is, transformative—and stirring realism.

108

Emelian Iaroslavskii

"Against Leftist Phrase Mongering and Unfair Criticism (Apropos of Comrade A. Kurella's Article)" (1928)

On September 30, 1927, the German Communist activist and critic Alfred Kurella (1895–1975) read a paper at a Komsomol meeting at VKhUTEIN (Higher State Artistic-Technological Institute) in Moscow. Early the following year, the conclusion of his lecture was published in a journal edited by Nikolai Bukharin.† Emelian Iaroslavskii (pseudonym of Minei Gubel'man,

*Eugène Fromentin, *Les Maîtres d'autrefois* (1876). See *The Old Masters of Belgium and Holland* (Boston, 1882), pp. 173–77.

†A. Kurella, "Khudozhestvennaia reaktsiia pod maskoi 'geroicheskogo realizma'" (Artistic Reaction behind the Mask of Heroic Realism), *Revoliutsiia i kul'tura* (Revolution and Culture) 2 (1928).

1878–1943), a prominent Party functionary, wrote a rebuttal for *Revoliutsiia i kul'tura* (Revolution and Culture) 3 (1928). Himself an amateur artist who exhibited with AKhR (Association of Revolutionary Artists), Iaroslavskii—along with Defense Minister Kliment Voroshilov—was AKhR's highest-ranking patron.

. . . Comrade Kurella sheds tears because "the development of contemporary painting that began with the great French Impressionists seems to have stagnated; it is as though it never existed." *So why has it stagnated? Because in Western Europe as well it did not arise out of the needs of the struggle of the proletarian masses.* The sated bourgeoisie pounced on the new art as a titillating novelty. And Comrade Kurella cannot name any Western European artists who have created models of leftist proletarian art *that could not be united under the AKhR banner.* Conversely, he will have to admit that Impressionism, Cubism, and other forms of leftist and arch-leftist art in Western Europe have served and are serving the interests of the bourgeois classes splendidly. Comrade Kurella would like to get out of all this extremely cheaply. How does he explain the fact that French Impressionism is alien to the workers, that Cubism, Constructivism, and the other forms of leftist art are alien to the workers? He ascribes it to the *backwardness* of the workers. . . . Excuse us, Comrade Kurella, but we are inclined to place far greater trust in the feeling and intuition of these tens of thousands of workers, who . . . *graduated from the school of the civil war and who are themselves participants in the Revolution, its makers. They want the artist to show them what they have been through and what they have created. They have a right to demand that artists give this to them. And the artists, if they want to be artists of the Revolution, are obliged to do so.*

As Comrade Kurella says, of course, "tens and hundreds of thousands of workers are weighed down by the legacy of capitalist enslavement and systematic cultural stupefaction." But really, Comrade Kurella, are you so naive that you don't understand that exhibitions are visited by the *most advanced* workers and peasants, who are at any rate less influenced by "the legacy of capitalist enslavement and systematic cultural stupefaction" than the bourgeois intelligentsia, which is in raptures over the Impressionists, Cubists, and Futurists? We are inclined to maintain just the opposite—*that worship of the "modern art" of the West is a kind of worship of the bourgeois art of the epoch of the decline of capitalism.*

109

Alfred Kurella

"From 'Russia's Revolutionary Art' to Proletarian Art: Responses and Questions for the Critics" (1928)

Published in response to Iaroslavskii [108] in *Revoliutsiia i kul'tura* (Revolution and Culture) 6 (1928).

. . . Here we have a classic example of a Marxist analysis of art history! How are we to understand the fact that the proletariat cannot be interested in anything in the capitalist world that does not "arise out of the needs of the struggle of the proletarian masses"? . . . As we try to penetrate the complex process by which art has evolved in the early twentieth century, however, we have arrived at somewhat different conclusions. Intertwined in this evolution are elements of decadence and elements of the progressive struggle between representatives of the big industrial bourgeoisie and the petty bourgeois traditions in art. The story of art from the early Impressionists to Suprematism and Constructivism is the story of how the stagnant, naively self-assured naturalism of the pre-imperialist bourgeoisie was routed under the bombardment of new, complex forms of life; it is the story of the liberation of art from its traditional rut and of attempts to adapt the language of all the arts to encompass a new, ever more complex reality; this, of course, is the story of the "discovery" of the mastery and technique, and so on, of the old masters from whom the naturalists had distanced themselves, thereby immeasurably lowering the quality of their painting.

And the proletariat is supposed to ignore this entire tremendous process and return to the anarchic art of the petty bourgeois "masters" of the latter half of the nineteenth century? . . .

Proletarian art regards the art of the past as a stage in the preparation . . . of a new style corresponding to proletarian ideology. Not only the art of past revolutionary periods (Giotto, Bruegel, Goya, and others) but also the revolutions in styles in the bourgeois art of recent decades provide a rich body of materials to develop it. Futurism, Cubism, Suprematism, and Constructivism can partly be explained as attempts by artists expressing the ideology of monopoly capitalism to find, as a counterweight to the humdrum naturalism that is a feature of the early capitalist period, a new form suitable to the complexity of contemporary life and serving as a better guide to it. . . .

110

Aleksei Mikhailov

"Diego Rivera" (1929)

The Mexican painter Diego Rivera was invited to Moscow for the celebration of the tenth anniversary of the October Revolution and remained in the USSR from the fall of 1927 to mid-May 1928. He became a founding member of October and harshly criticized AKhR. In April 1928 he participated in the fourth OST (Society of Easel Painters) exhibition. In his public pronouncements, Rivera called upon Soviet artists to make use of medieval and folk traditions, in particular the icon, in the creation of a new art.

Mikhailov (1904–?), a critic once close to the October group, later wrote widely on Russian architecture and Soviet publishers. This essay was published in *Vestnik inostrannoi literatury* (Messenger of Foreign Literature) 5 (1929).

. . . Mexican social conditions must be considered the fundamental and decisive factor in the evolution of Diego Rivera's art. An active participant in the revolutionary Mexican peasant and worker movement, he is naturally and inevitably confronted by the problem of how to link art to the revolutionary struggle. . . .

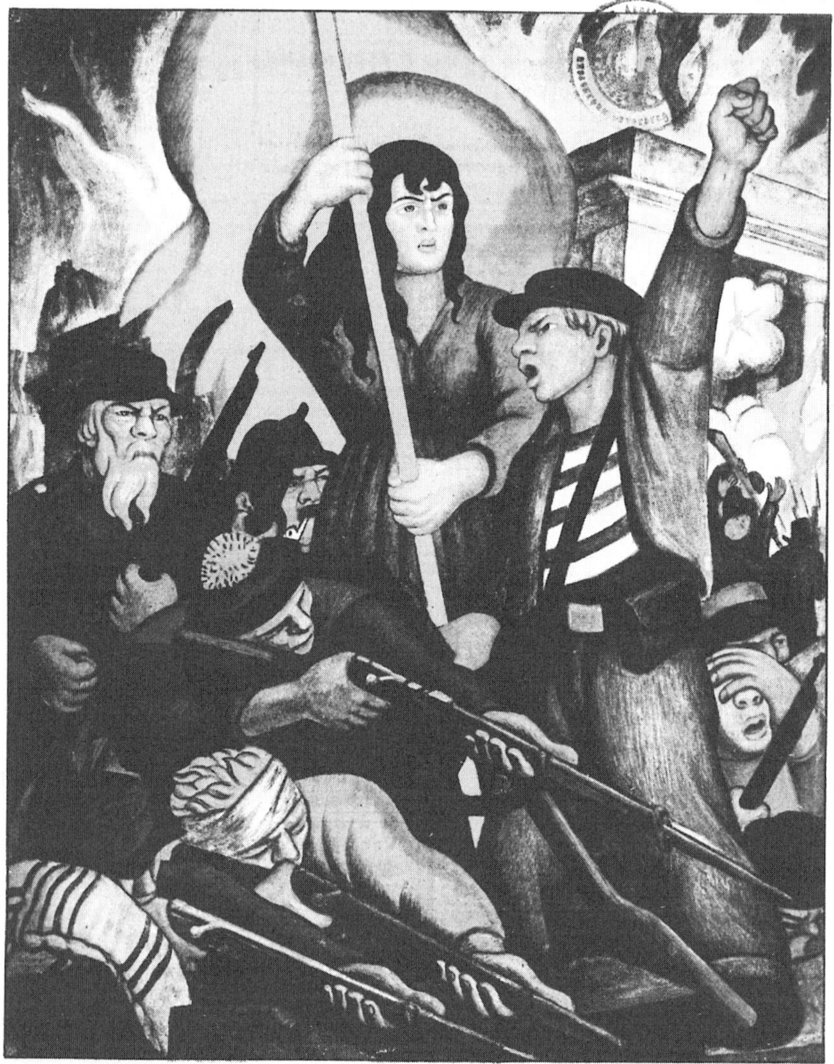

Diego Rivera, *The Paris Commune*, cover for *Krasnaia niva* (Red Field) 12 (1928)

He has concluded that it is necessary to create monumental fresco art using, on the one hand, the latest achievements of bourgeois artistic practice (especially Cubism) and, on the other, the devices that once were an inseparable part of ancient Mexican art, which had features of a collective mentality. These techniques solved the problem of the national coloring of the new Mexican art. At the same time Diego Rivera wants to use the art of the thirteenth and fourteenth centuries, when fresco painting reached its peak. He is so fascinated with fresco painting that he calls it *"die kollective Kunst par excellence."* From our point of view, of course, this is something of an exaggeration, since the fresco is only one means by which art can be socialized and is needed only where industrial artistic production, which solves the problem of creating genuine mass art most satisfactorily, is weakly developed. In Mexico, however, where the industrial arts are not developed at all and where the monumental and fresco forms are the high point of the national artistic heritage that must serve as the point of departure, for the time being the fresco really is the most progressive form of painting intended for the broad masses. . . .

Rivera's works are above all art, and the fact that he was awarded first prize at the American art exhibition in 1925* shows that even bourgeois circles were forced to acknowledge their great artistic value. Diego Rivera appeared before bourgeois public opinion fully armed with the artistic achievements of all preceding ages, which he has used skillfully and critically in his own art. This is why in his works we do not find new themes forced into old forms or the inability to embody a revolutionary theme in genuinely artistic and profoundly meaningful images. And this is why his art has such irresistible power.

. . . In the vast majority of his works a profoundly revolutionary content is combined with indisputable formal perfection. In scenes depicting labor, Rivera shows himself to be a great master of composition. His workers live in organized rhythm, and they really are alive and not simply attached or posing next to machines. Here he combines the principles of organized, constructive composition with monumental forms full of movement, once again showing how inadequate it is to think that monumentality implies something huge and static.

Rivera's frescoes contain numerous unrealistic devices. It might seem that this would disturb the concrete diversity of the representation, but if we look closely at the faces of the people in his works, we will see how well he has managed to emphasize the uniqueness of each figure and movement and how skillfully he combines fantasy with a realistic approach. His unrealistic devices are merely a means of expressing reality most effectively and forcefully; they focus our attention on the most important elements of the action, the typical expressiveness of the faces, and so on.

Despite all the variety of the whole, such devices enable Rivera to show the dialectical and interlinked unity in this diversity.

*Rivera won a prize in the "Pan-American Exhibition" of the Los Angeles County Museum of Art for his *Flower Day* (1925, LACMA).

111

Aleksei Fedorov-Davydov

"Militant Art: John Heartfield, Proletarian Artist" (1932)

In 1931 the International Bureau of Revolutionary Artists invited John Heartfield to Moscow to work on a number of projects. In November and December 1931 he had a one-man show in Moscow, where some three hundred of his works were displayed. This review appeared in *Brigada khudozhnikov* (Artists' Brigade) 1 (1932).

. . . The principle of photomontage—the free compositional combination of different photographs—makes it possible to compare and combine in a single work different points of view, multiple planes, and rich play on the different scales of the individual images. Its representational possibilities are expanded even further by devices such as angled shots, multiple exposures on the same plate, stretching the film, imprinting, and so on, and finally, the superimposition of drawing or writing. If for the Western European formalists this new presentation of an object through comparison with another object, this new construction of space, and so on, are significant in and of themselves, then for us all these possibilities of photomontage acquire significance only as a means of constructing a new image and revealing new content.

It is not difficult to see that the correct use of the devices and techniques of photomontage offers enormous possibilities for the dialectical presentation of phenomena. The dialectical creative method in the visual arts may be described briefly and, of course, far from thoroughly, as one which reveals the universal even as it presents the unique in all its true concreteness and political and social relevance—a method that in the singularity of the visual image offers a dialectical notion of process and the movement and unity of opposites; ultimately, it provides an evaluation of phenomena that reveals their true nature in both their intrinsic and their indirect connections.

Let us return to Heartfield. I do not at all mean that his creative method is wholly and completely a dialectical, that is, proletarian method. . . . Here I merely want to note the elements by which phenomena are presented dialectically in his works and, proceeding from these, to capture in some measure the tendency or direction in which this dialectical method in photomontage should develop. The photomontage artist can arbitrarily juxtapose things and phenomena, tearing them out of their "real" environment, so to speak, and placing them in an "unreal" one. The content of this method will vary depending on the new position in which people and objects are placed and what new statements are made about them in this way. Objects and people can be put into a fantastic, mystical, and so on, environment, and into false, contrived, purely external and formal connections. But these new connections can be more real, that is, more true, than random "real" ones.

Thus the phenomenon can be situated in a position that cannot be perceived in reality but that, in Hegel's terms, reveals the real in the existing. Heartfield puts a little picture of a battleship into the hands of the Social Fascist* Müller. From the point of view of visual verisimilitude this is unreal, but from the point of view of the dialectical revelation of the role of German Social Democracy in the growth of imperialist armaments, it is realistic—it is "real." . . .

Heartfield does have his shortcomings, however, and they are in fact quite significant. . . . He has not rid his works of elements of formalism and mechanism. A formalist attraction to color and texture and to shifts and sharp contrasts is a vestige of his Dadaist past, and it is still alive in works such as the colorful cover of the book *Deutschland, Deutschland über alles* and the photomontage of a ballerina's foot thrust into an inkwell. His *Man,* in which the contemporary philistine is shown as an empty coat hanging on a nail, is to a significant extent a play on differences in photographic texture, and precisely this formalist work is at the same time an example of a mechanical approach to theme. This approach is a remnant of an idealism in his art that he has not yet entirely eradicated. . . .

Significantly, Heartfield is much stronger in satire and protest and at showing the negative than he is at showing the positive. It would be useless to search for the class ideals of the proletariat in his works for they do not present the "destructive spirit" as a "creative spirit." But of course it is this that is the unity of opposites constituting the dialectical presentation of the revolutionary proletariat.

To summarize, to what extent can Heartfield be called a proletarian artist, and is his art proletarian art? As was stated above, there are elements of the dialectical revelation of phenomena in his works that are mostly critical of capitalism and show the revolutionary movement of the proletariat. At the same time, however, there are persistent remnants of formalism and mechanism. But to realize the extent to which the petty bourgeois intellectual Heartfield has already mastered the proletarian creative method, one need only compare him with such fellow travelers of the Western European proletariat as Grosz, Dix, and Masereel. . . . For them the revolutionary theme was merely a single brief stage. After unmasking the horrors of war, the hypocrisy of the capitalist order, and its evils and contradictions, they returned to an inoffensive genre (Masereel), bourgeois portraiture (Dix and Grosz), or, at best, abstract, "Tolstoyan" moralizing (Masereel). This is not at all what we see in Heartfield's works. His connection with the proletariat is not fleeting but continuous; his art has developed and is developing in the midst of harsh reaction and the persecution of the Communist Party and the revolutionary trade union opposition. He works day in and day out in the German Party and participates in its "everyday" struggle. . . .

We can with certainty say of Heartfield that developing for him means developing, expanding, and enriching his creative method by deepening and genuinely mastering materialist dialectics and overcoming his mechanical and formalist errors. He has consciously put his art at the service of the proletarian revolution, and it is a weapon of the Party. This is why Heartfield is a proletarian artist.

*Stalinist pejorative term for Social Democrats.

X

CHANGING VIEWS OF WESTERN ART

The first postrevolutionary French exhibition in Moscow ran from October to November 1928 and attracted nineteen thousand visitors. Its organizers encountered resistance from art dealers, and as a result major artists—including Picasso, Matisse, and Braque—were not in the show. Most observers agreed that the exhibition nevertheless provided an adequate picture of Parisian art and introduced a number of new trends and artists (including Maurice Utrillo, Amedeo Modigliani, Giorgio de Chirico, Max Ernst, and Constantin Brancusi). More than half the works were by "Russian Parisians." The exhibition undermined the prevalent view of French art as the realm of harmony; critics applied the term "Expressionism" to French painting, and the generally negative attitude toward German Expressionism was projected onto it as well.

The exhibition, which summed up thirty years of artistic ties with Europe, took place at a time when major Soviet critics, with few exceptions, had reformulated the relationship between the USSR and the West. Soviet art was envisaged mostly as realist and pursuing a new social mission. The majority of artists and critics expressed no doubts about the necessity for relationships with the Western cultural tradition [112, 114, 116], though October and AKhR (Association of Revolutionary Artists) disagreed on this point. In April 1930, an article by Frida Roginskaia [117] set the direction of the propaganda campaign conducted by AKhR and its successor, RAPKh (Russian Association of Proletarian Artists). Sergei Romov's essay [116] served as a pretext, but the real goal was to change the criteria for contemporary Russian art and subsequently to establish control over artistic life. As a result, all aspects of Soviet art that had a "French" pedigree were automatically devalued. The vocabulary of political demagoguery was combined with a deliberately rude tone that terrorized opponents. The theoretical background of this campaign was found in Plekhanov's writings [20, 46], but AKhR-RAPKh critics went much further in vulgarizing Marxist ideas and reducing art to ideology.

This propaganda campaign contributed to the capitulation of AKhR-RAPKh's main rivals: October [118] and other art organizations. For the first time, the threat of being shut down hung over the Museum of Modern Western Art [120], and in 1933 four major paintings from its collection were sold to the United States, Van Gogh's *Night Café* among them.

The anti-Western attack met almost no resistance. Osip Mandelstam was apparently the only person to express publicly his highly individual view of French painting, using his poetic autonomy to negate the extremist rhetoric [121]. In the late 1920s several subjects that already belonged to the history of modern art became topics of discussion for Soviet criticism, among them Cézanne and Impressionism. The cult of Cézanne, which was noticeable in the very first writings on him after his death [22] and was re-

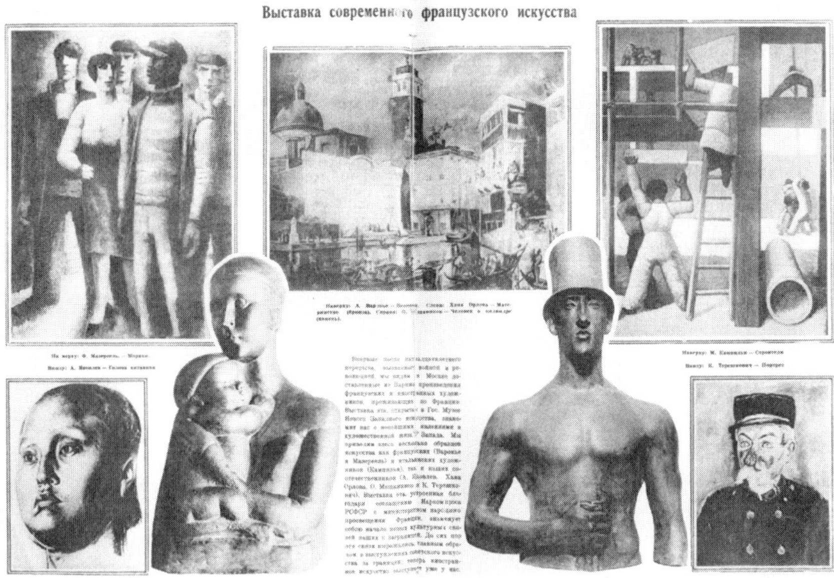

Выставка современного французского искусства

Article on French exhibition in *Krasnaia niva* (Red Field) 41 (1928)

inforced by the Russian translations of Emile Bernard's book (1913), reached its apogee following the Revolution [122]. For a time Cézanne became the "model" of the contemporary artist who supported a balance between the spontaneous and the intellectual, the concrete and the abstract. The growing interest in Cézanne was related to the problems associated with the very existence of representational art.

Cézanne exerted a significant stylistic influence on Russian painting in the 1920s, particularly the Jack of Diamonds painters, who comprised a broad, influential, and extensive figurative school [123]. Abram Efros aptly captured the ambivalence of the Cézannist tradition: "this is a genuinely painterly system . . . this is a system that is genuinely realistic . . . [but] nowhere are there so many mediocrities. Russian Cézannism has become a haven for the *juste milieu.*"* Not surprisingly, therefore, in the following decade no other Western artist was subjected to such a precipitous and radical reevaluation [124].

In the late 1920s Impressionism emerged in Russia as a painting style connected with a new turn toward visual experience. But at the same time, renewed Impressionist poetics could express an individual worldview that stood in opposition to contemporary collectivist and rationalist doctrines. Furthermore, the Impressionists occupied a key position in the "history" of contemporary art then taking shape. Discrediting this phenomenon thus meant rejecting the entire subsequent development of modern painting in general. On the other hand, a carefully constructed retrospective view made it

*Abram Efros, "Vchera, segodnia, zavtra" (Yesterday, Today, Tomorrow), *Iskusstvo* (Art) 6 (1933): 35.

possible to "justify" the avant-garde that had grown out of Impressionism and to demonstrate its realist and national sources [125]. Significantly, Malevich also turned to Impressionism at this time, in 1928–29 painting a number of "Impressionistic" pictures, which he dated to 1903–4.*

By the late 1920s, Impressionism's reputation among Russian critics had been undermined. Impressionism was interpreted as an art of passive reflection incapable of developing socially significant, integral painting [127]. Marxist radicals adopted Plekhanov's critique of Impressionism [20], and the movement was interpreted as a manifestation of unconscious "subjective idealism," which amounted to a condemnation of both French painters and those contemporary Soviet artists whose works bore the imprint of their influence [129]. Lunacharskii played a certain part in Impressionism's defense. In 1933 he joined the discussion with an essay on Renoir that was a kind of "aesthetic testament" [128]. In defending optimistic Impressionism as a model for Soviet artists, Lunacharskii in effect was also asserting the stylistic diversity of Soviet art. In the 1930s Impressionism remained at the center of the discourse about modern art and was subjected to ideological criticism, but it continued to influence Soviet art.†

112

Boris Ternovets

"The Contemporary French Art Exhibition in Moscow" (1928)

Published in *Pechat' i revoliutsiia* (Press and Revolution) 7 (1928).

. . . We can see . . . that the relationship between Russian and French art had to develop on an entirely different basis than before the Revolution. If before the war shoots of French art grew splendidly when transplanted to Moscow soil, now they were hardly going to enjoy such successful growth. The art of France, which developed in surroundings foreign to us and reflected the distant attitudes, needs, and tastes of French society, evokes a different reaction and is regarded differently than was the case before the Revolution. . . .

We have no right now to expect the sort of "infection" that was possible twenty years ago from the clash with the art of Paris. The impact of French art now will no doubt be narrower and limited to industrial-technological and formal artistic problems. . . . The basic tasks confronting Soviet art and the art of Paris are very different, but acquaintance with the method of posing and solving these problems cannot but be profoundly instructive for us. . . .

*See Elena Basner, "Malevich's Painting in the Collection of the Russian Museum (The Matter of the Artist's Creative Evolution)," in *Kazimir Malevich in the Russian Museum* (St. Petersburg: Palace Edition, 2000).

†See Matthew Cullerne Bown, *Socialist Realist Painting* (New Haven: Yale University Press, 1998), pp. 192–95; Alison Hilton, "Holiday on the Kolkhoz: Socialist Realism's Dialogue with Impressionism," in *Russian Art and the West: A Century of Dialogue in Painting, Architecture, and the Decorative Arts,* edited by Rosalind P. Blakesley and Susane Reid (De Kalb: Northern Illinois University Press, 2006), pp. 195–216.

Cover of the catalogue *Contemporary French Art* (Moscow, 1928)

There is much to suggest that Moscow was profoundly impressed by two works by Utrillo. *House on Rue Mont-Cenis* and *Street in Montmarte** are not among his very best works, yet they are rather typical of him. . . . Utrillo's art satisfied the new de-

*This picture (1914–19) was acquired by the State Museum of Modern Western Art and is now in the Pushkin Museum in Moscow.

mands and moods of postwar French society. It was the life-giving rain for which the soil parched by the long rule of formalism thirsted. His painting marks the return to French art of a deeply intimate, inspired feeling for the world that is far from the fleeting, superficial glance of the Impressionists. Utrillo loves what he paints and paints only what he loves. . . . Profound and incompletely formed neo-Romantic tendencies account for the interest in Utrillo, just as they have created the posthumous fame of Modigliani. . . .

The influx of young forces into the Cubist camp has ceased, and now young artists are more inclined to follow new watchwords (Surrealism). More important than these external failures, however, are the inner transformations that have matured during these years within the Cubist system itself. . . . The analytical and investigative nature of Cubism's early experiments is now giving way to a dominant decorative principle. In this rejection of earlier explorations it is impossible not to see the influence of the declining atmosphere of postwar France. The political reaction cannot but be reflected in all areas of social life, and it is accompanied by mistrust of all innovation. The sensualism typical of contemporary French culture is expressed in art by a heightened interest in the sensual perception of artistic values. In this atmosphere, the flowering and success of Braque's works are understandable. No less characteristic of the development of Cubism is Picasso's evolution. It is in his art that these new tendencies toward decorativism have first fully manifested themselves. In the absence of works by Picasso himself, "aesthetic Cubism" is fairly well represented at the exhibition by the talented Marcoussis,* the cultured, somewhat eclectic Survage, and the young, showy Lurçat. In such surroundings, artists such as Léger and Ozenfant seem more and more lonely. . . .

Although he is older than the other sculptors participating in the exhibition, Brancusi seems like the youngest and boldest. The golden brilliance of his *Bird,* which cuts through space like a flashing sword, is striking and moving. A fanatic of pure sculpture, in his aspiration to generalization Brancusi approaches a maximum schematization of the image, which he takes to ovoid and spherical bodies. These laconic generalized forms do not seem empty, however, but are persuasive and acute. Sometimes, as in *Bird in Space,* he approaches the creation of an image that is absolute in its precise wholeness and maximally tensed. His impressive skill and technical mastery are worth noting, particularly in his metal sculptures.

. . . The experience of this initial French exhibition should be continued. We should try to make it the first link in a continuous chain of annual foreign exhibitions. Soviet art needs this contact and competition with the art of the West. Only such encounters will make it "competitive" and battle-hardened, revealing gaps and shortcomings and forcing it to tackle the problems posed by life with new zeal. The West's experience cannot leave us indifferent. We must use its artistic and technical achievements just as we are using European accomplishments in science and technology. . . .

*Louis Marcoussis (originally Marcus, 1882–1941), Polish-born French painter.

113

Ts. Plotkin

"The French in Moscow" (1928)

Published in *Ekran* (Screen) 42 (1928).

There was a forty-minute line stretching from the Museum of Western Art to the Military Academy. The workers' side-buttoned and checkered shirts were lost amid the woolen suits and foreign jerseys.

In the general hubbub, at quite a distance from the doors, young people ran through the names of Masereel and Orlova, Campigli and Chagall.

Morozov's palace is suitable for a gentleman's private collection, but the museum there is cramped and has no room for a large exhibition. Languorous pink "panneaux" hang over the stairs.* The impatient eyes of the street crowd do not dwell on them. They dash past these artificially dreamy "compositions" and their haze of refined nobility. Their eyes search for something brighter and livelier. And they find it in the first room of the exhibition.

Masereel's *Group of Sailors* stands out crudely against the background of the wall, its tense inner animation capturing the visitors' attention.

The sailor lads stride along, heads gaily tilted back. Striding along with them is a chance female companion from the harbor. This is not a demonstration, nor is it of course a parade. Perhaps they are marching on the nearest tavern to bathe their rebellious youth and restless recklessness in liters of cheap beer. But at the moment, these men who are laborers of the sea but not its masters walk proudly, resolutely, almost belligerently.

Here in the very first room of the exhibition devoted to French art, the line that was compact on the street breaks up, and everyone goes their own way.

Side-buttoned and checkered shirts stand riveted to three of Masereel's canvases. The woolens and jerseys rush on into the interior, to the "Russian" rooms and the Dutchman Dongen. . . .

Chirico's "archeologists" sit bulkily in their academic chairs. Hung with the excavated burden of millennia, their faceless skulls bowed, they really do resemble citizens wearing gas masks who have sat down to rest. Their skulls are gas masks to protect them from life. This is practically the only attempt at social satire in the exhibition's "foreign" section. But the Italian artist is only being derisive; there are no sparks of unfeigned indignation in him, and his canvas is therefore unconvincing and unexciting. . . .

The woolens finally get something close to their hearts—van Dongen's *Silver Chemise.* On a pillow lies a young woman, a refined, prettyish creature with deep brown eyes. Her silver shift is about to fall off. Thrilling lewdly, the viewers linger around her. This is a well-filled "social order" of the bourgeoisie, which is titillated by semi-nudeness.

*The stairway in Morozov's home was decorated with a three-part panel by Bonnard: *On the Mediterranean* (1911, Hermitage) and the paired *Early Spring in the Countryside* and *Autumn: Picking Fruit* (1912, GMII).

Французы в Москве

Очерк *Ц. ПЛОТКИНА*

От Музея западной живописи к Военной академии растянулась очередь в 40 минут. Косоворотки и ковбойки терялись в хвосте коверкотовых пар и заграничного трикотажа.

В общем гомоне, на изрядном расстоянии от закрытых дверей молодежь перебирала имена Мазерэля и Орловой, Кампильи и Шагала.

«Морозовский» особняк пригоден для барского коллекционирования. Музею в нем тесно, широкой выставке — негде развернуться. Над лестницами розовеют томные «панно». Нетерпеливые глаза уличной толпы не останавливаются в них. Они бегут мимо надуманно-мечтательных «композиций», мимо дымки изысканного благородства. Глаза ищут более яркого и жизненного. И находят в первом же зале выставки.

Мазерэлевская «Группа матросов» грубо выделяется на общем фоне стены, приковывает внимание зрителя напряженным внутренним под'емом.

Весело вскинув головы, шагает матросская «братва». Случайная портовая подруга шествует рядом с ними. Это не демонстрация и, конечно, не парад. Может быть, в поход в ближайшую харчевню, чтобы буйную молодость, неприкаянную бесшабашность залить литрами дешевого вина. Но сейчас — эти труженики моря, но не его хозяева — ступают гордо, уверенно, почти воинственно.

Уже здесь, в первой комнате выставки «Французского искусства» — единый на улице «хвост» раскалывается, самоопределяется.

Косоворотки с ковбойками приковываются к трем полотнам Мазерэля. Трикотаж и коверкоты стремительно уносятся вглубь — к «русским» комнатам и голландцу Донгену.

— Что это за Осоавиахимы?

«Археологи» Кирико грузно расселись на академических креслах. Увешанные ископаемыми грузом тысячелетий, со склоненными черепами без лиц, они действительно напоминают граждан в противогазах, присевших отдохнуть. Их черепа — противогазы от жизни. В «иностранной» части выставки — это почти единственная попытка дать социальную сатиру. Но итальянец только умен и насмешлив, искры неподдельного чувства, негодования в нем нет и поэтому его полотно маловразумительно, не волнует.

Женские портреты Модильяни и «Балаганы» Лафоржа острее, неожиданнее. «Молодая шведка» и «Маленькая Жанна» подкупают непосредственностью своих некрасивых лиц.

У скульптурных портретов Орловой останавливаются обе зрительские струи. Бронзовый бюст «Рубина» поворачивает на подставке вхутеиновка. Она ищет тайны мастерства, которым изваян этот мужественный бюст — одинаково выразительный, четкий, убедительный с любой точки поворота.

Рядом с «Рубином» — наивная жизнерадостность «Моего мальчика» и почти бунтующая сила «Молодого американца».

„Мой мальчик" — Орловой.

Коверкотовая публика обретает, наконец, свое родное. Это «Серебряная рубашка» Вандонгена. На подушке — молодая женщина с глубокими коричневыми глазами и утонченною красивостью. На «честном слове» держится ее короткая серебряная сорочка. Около нее подолгу застаиваются, похотливо млеют. Это хорошо выполненный «социальный заказ» буржуазии, смакующей «полуголенькое».

Дальше — «Русские из Парижа». Эмигранты перемешались здесь с «уехавшими», молодежь со стариками. Из семи комнат выставки русские заняли три. Количество здесь явно господствует над качеством.

Между мотивами Мазерэля и Кампильи и «русскими» комнатами пропасть не менее глубокая, чем между «Группой матросов» и «Серебряной рубашкой». В 1923 г. Юрий Анненков завоевал почетное место портретами к 5-й годовщине Красной армии. В 1924 г. он «уехал» в Париж. Его картины безусловно одни из лучших на выставке, но от них веет внутренним холодом и они отголосков в зрителе не будят.

Шагал «уехал» в Париж еще раньше Анненкова. В выставленной им серии «Мертвых душ» чувствуется, однако, большая близость к нашим темам сегодняшнего дня. Они показывают новое отношение к литературным типам, вскрывают их так, как сделал это Мейерхольд в «Ревизоре».

„Строители" — Кампильи.

Во всех трех «русских» комнатах это единственная работа, насыщенная острым социальным содержанием.

В целом, выставка для рядового зрителя не представляет большого интереса, поскольку содержание ее отвечает требованиям, которые пред'являют к художникам заказчики — буржуазия.

Но нашим художникам выставка даст неизмеримо больше. Нашему молодняку надо учиться на хороших образцах, а мастерски сделанными полотнами выставка «Французского искусства» далеко не бедна.

Ему нужно критически усвоить, переварить блестящие достижения французской школы и применить их к темам, которыми живет наша, советская страна.

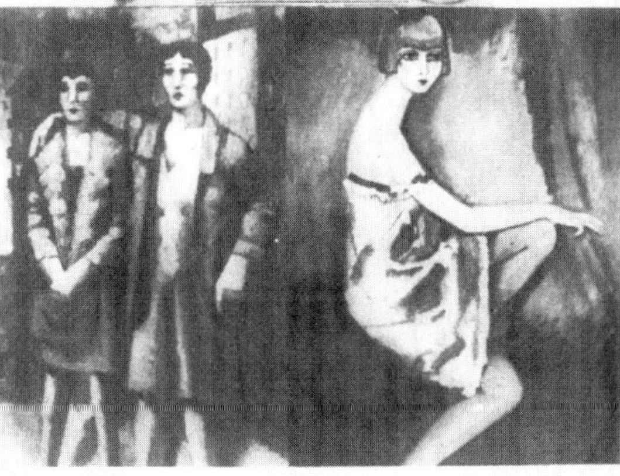

Направо — „На улице" Мазерэля.

Налево — „Серебряная рубашка" Вандонгена.

11

Ts. Plotkin, "The French in Moscow," *Ekran* 42 (1928)

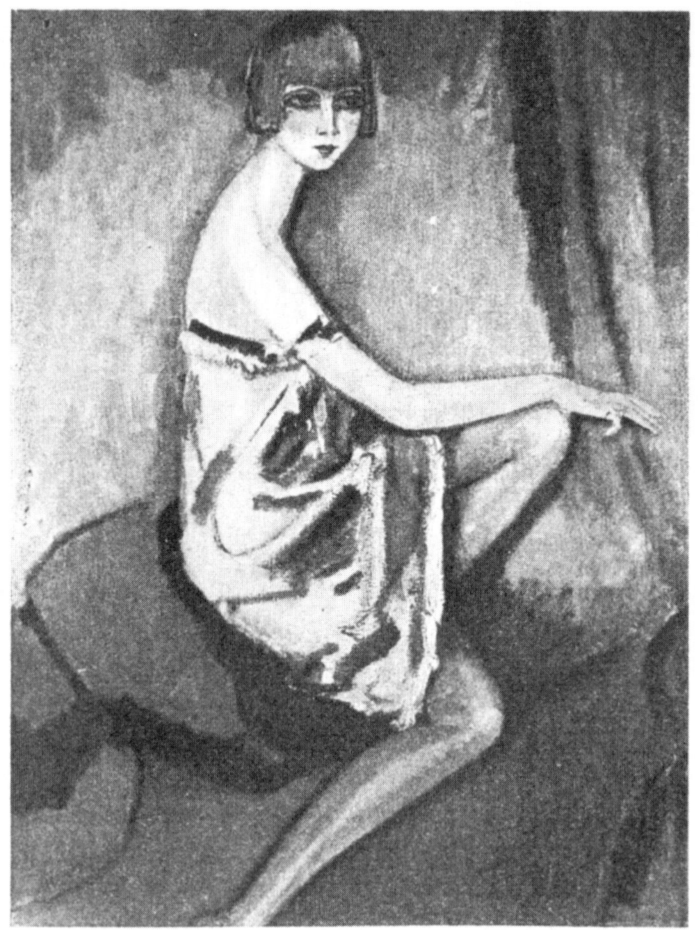

Ван-Донген, Кес.
№ 24. Серебряная сорочка.

Van-Dongen, Kees.
La chemise d'argent.

Kees Van Dongen, *The Silver Chemise*, 1919 (published in the 1928 catalogue *Contemporary French Art*)

Farther on are the "Russians in Paris." Young and old, émigrés and others who simply "left," mingle. The Russians take up three of the seven rooms of the exhibition. Quantity obviously predominates over quality.

The chasm between the motifs of Masereel and Campigli* is no less deep than that between *Group of Sailors* and *The Silver Chemise.* In 1923 Iurii Annenkov's† portraits done for the fifth anniversary of the Red Army gained him an honored place in the museum. In 1924 he "left" for Paris. His pictures are certainly among the best at the exhibition, but they breathe an inner chill and get no response from the viewer.

Chagall "left" for Paris even earlier than Annenkov. The pictures of his *Dead Souls* series exhibited here, however, feel close to contemporary themes.‡ They show a new attitude to literary types, unmasking them as Meyerhold did in *The Inspector General.***

In all three of the "Russian" rooms, this is the only work with any social content.

On the whole, the exhibition is of little interest to the ordinary visitor because it gives the bourgeois customers what they want.

The exhibition, however, has immeasurably more to offer our artists. Our young offspring must learn from good examples, and the French art exhibition is far from devoid of masterly executed canvases.

Our artists must critically process and master the brilliant achievements of the French school and apply them to themes that are relevant to our Soviet land.

114

Nikolai Punin

Vladimir Vasil'evich Lebedev (1928)

Vladimir Lebedev (1891–1967) was an artist close to the avant-garde. From 1924 to 1933 he headed the department of children's books at the Gosizdat publishing house in Leningrad. Punin wrote this book on the occasion of Lebedev's one-man show at the Russian Museum in 1928.

. . . Impressionism, Cézannism, and Cubism are almost inseparable from theory, but who is prepared to speak the language of theory about Matisse or Utrillo or Modigliani? In addition to terms and notions, one needs finely calibrated feeling to speak about these artists because their art is different.

I remember very well a certain fundamental thesis professed by the overwhelming majority of artists about twenty years ago. It ran something like this: the only possible fruitful work we can do in art is on the means of expression, for what we want to express is given to us and is not for us to change or improve. It was this thesis that

*Massimo Campigli (1895–1971) was represented by *The Seamstresses* (1925) and *The Builders* (1928); the former was acquired by the State Museum of Modern Western Art and is presently in the Hermitage.

†Iurii Annenkov (1889–1974), graphic artist and painter who employed Cubist and Futurist devices.

‡Between 1923 and 1925 Marc Chagall did a series of illustrations of Nikolai Gogol's *Dead Souls* for Vollard's publishing house.

**Vsevolod Meyerhold staged Gogol's 1836 comedy in 1926.

contributed to the broad development of so-called formal experiments in recent art and set its seal on the period preceding the present one.

Today hardly anyone would be willing to define his attitude toward art in this manner. The means of expression no longer appear to exist separately from that which is expressed, and with respect to the latter we are no longer so very powerless as it once seemed. Anyone with a good ability to feel will express his feelings well, and if a particular work of art is bad, it is bad not just because the artist lacks the means to say something but because he has nothing to say. Form and content are inseparable: as we work on feeling we are thereby also working on expressing it.

Recently I had the opportunity to glance through some reproductions of a series of Picasso's drawings and another series by Matisse. It was instructive. Even when he paints from life, Picasso remains essentially formal: he sees the world through art (an aggregate of devices) and superimposes the stony weight of his "style" on his vital perception. This, of course, is not to say that his works lack content—where there is form there is content—but life takes its revenge by draining the warmth from artists who build walls around themselves, even if these walls are built of art itself. However much Picasso has amazed and devastated us with his great inventions, the world of his feelings is as cold as a lunar landscape; you cannot believe that a man could feel like that, that he could see like that and still feel. By contrast, even when Matisse wants to be formal, he remains spontaneous and alive, and albeit sometimes frustrated or suppressed, a sensation of life palpitates in the most crucial elements of his art. I have drawn this parallel not to demonstrate the difference between Picasso and Matisse but to describe the change that has taken place in art over the past few years. Of note is the fact that Matisse seems more contemporary than Picasso; his development is a genuine movement in time, whereas Picasso seems to be frozen in the midst of his ideas. Matisse's proximity to contemporary art, which has already been noted by a very broad circle of artists, suggests that formal problems are no longer a source of inspiration. . . .

. . . The traditions of the Russian school of painting are, of course, weak and unstable. Our age, like all previous ages of Russian art, is hampered by this instability, so that there may seem to be no basis for attempting to express the feelings of our time through the limited means at the Russian artist's disposal. In comparison with the mighty artistic culture of Paris, the resources of Russian art are paltry; Paris today is for us what sixth- and seventh-century China probably was for the art of the Far East, Byzantium for the art of the medieval East, and Italy for the Western European Renaissance. Yet we must not draw false conclusions from this and make a dogma of what is inevitable only at present. After all, our historical role is now becoming extremely special; not only are we not living by what Europe lives, but we could not live like that. However keenly we sense our apprenticeship to Paris, we are nonetheless doomed to independence. It would, of course, be foolish to interpret this independence as independence from French artistic culture; nor do we have any inclination to do so. But we live and feel differently than they do there, and we therefore want our own language of painting and plastic arts. It is in this sense that I speak of the feelings and real face of our age.

. . . Unlike many Russian artists who come under some influence or other and begin seeing and feeling with the other's eyes and heart, Lebedev has always remained true to himself; he has not been infected by anyone else's emotionality without assimilating their worldview; the enormous experience of the French masters was for him not the experience of life but only the experience of a school, which he wisely used not to develop his individuality but to become a better artist. Paraphrasing Renoir, we could say of Lebedev that you study art in museums, but museums are not made to live in. French artistic culture is for us a museum, and no other museum is its equal; we are living on the eastern periphery of Europe, where there is no Louvre, no Montmartre, no Latin Quarter, and none of the traditions of our life resemble those of Paris. French art cannot and should not be anything for us but a school. To understand this means to take the correct attitude toward Parisian influences; given our weak and unstable artistic culture they are inevitable, but at the same time they should always remain formal. . . .

115

Sergei Romov

"From Dada to Surrealism: On Painting, Literature, and the French Intelligentsia" (1929)

Sergei Romov (1883–1939) moved to France in 1906. In 1922–23 he edited the Russian-language journal *Udar* (Strike, or Blow) and was the leader of the artistic group of the same name, which was loyal to the Soviets. During the 1920s he headed the art section of the French Communist newspaper *L'Humanité.* In 1928 he returned to Russia. He was executed during Stalin's purges.

Romov's article, published in *Vestnik inostrannoi literatury* (Herald of Foreign Literature) 3 (1929), was the first significant Soviet review of Surrealism in the visual arts. On the official level, Surrealism never met with a friendly response.

. . . If some of Surrealism's experiments have proved possible in literature, where the word keeps pace with the image and images are in the final analysis realized and expressed in words, in the plastic arts the Surrealists' problem appears to be completely insoluble because the plastic image should and can be presented only in space, and the process of concretizing it is more protracted and complex. All that remained for them was to find an absolute nonobjectivity about which neither Larionov with his Rayonnism nor Malevich in his search for Suprematism could even dream.

. . . Max Ernst and Yves Tanguy are above all painters; moreover, they are a definite kind of painter. Despite a considerable measure of literariness that is characteristic of them as well, they produce an enchanting impression through the self-sufficient image in the narrow or broad sense of the word. In their pictures the elements of painting—paint, color, and palette—are dominant. Their magical devices never entirely overshadow the painterly means they employ. . . . This is why I think that these two artists should be singled out from among all the Surrealists, for their experiments and intentions may develop broadly and become a very interesting phenomenon in painting.

For the first time in recent years, both Ernst and Tanguy have begun rehabilitating the image, which has been eclipsed by the narrow formalism of previous schools, and they are working to achieve lyrical expressiveness not only by means of technical painterly devices of color but through form and theme, albeit abstract ones thus far.

. . . As for Man Ray, he is a photographer, not an artist. True, he sometimes allows himself the luxury of a vaguely scandalous painting, but only very rarely, and fortunately it never moves or upsets anyone. For him it's like a bout of fever or a toothache that hurts for a while and then goes away. He is doing approximately the same thing in photography as Rodchenko is in art, although by different means. The only difference is in his repertoire and more sophisticated equipment. It is the same montage principle, except that Man Ray puts it through the very intricate laboratory manipulations to which he subjects photographic positives and negatives, producing extremely amusing results, or more exactly, tricks and stunts. . . .

Masson's painting reflects a very complicated intellectual and artistic chemistry in which the reagents and reactions produce very fantastic effects, although it would be more correct here to speak of alchemy rather than chemistry. . . . You stand there looking at his pictures and have no idea what he intended or wanted.

Arp has solved all plastic problems with an enviable naiveté and simplicity, reducing all plastic images to highly simplified and arbitrary forms. Considerable imagination is needed to understand them as well.

Joan Miró's works have the entertainment value of a fireworks display. Sometimes they act like a rocket exploding in mid-air in unexpected bursts of colored stars. But once the mirage has passed and the first blinding effect is over, you are left staring at a void, the blue expanse of an ordinary evening sky. His canvases possess a decorative graphic quality and attractive colors, but underneath there is nothing but emptiness or hooklike cabalistic symbols. It is simply impossible to understand or feel anything in them, for they are no longer plastic images but crazy graphics devoid of any emotional content or significance. . . .

Despite their loud references to Marxism and dialectical thought, and for all their extreme leftist phraseology, their paintings are utterly eclectic. . . . The Surrealists are rootless intellectuals who in politics are romantic dreamers and petty bourgeois mystics.

116

Sergei Romov

"Contemporary French Panting" (1929)

Sergei Romov's article, published in *Iskusstvo v massy* (Art to the Masses) 7–8 (1929), was an important commentary on Soviet publications dealing with the 1928 French exhibition. Although Romov did not support AKhR (Association of Revolutionary Artists), he published the essay in its journal, which at the time was the only specialized periodical devoted to art.

. . . Because of its mistakes and weaknesses, the Moscow exhibition failed to provide any clear idea of the contemporary state of French painting. Many progressive French artists have undergone considerable development and greatly refined their formal achievements and aesthetic problems since the war, and a study of their present works in comparison with their prewar art would have been extremely beneficial. Then perhaps it would have been clearer how organic the revolutionary trends were throughout the nineteenth century and how all schools from Romanticism to Cubism found their synthetic resolution in contemporary French painting. If, with very few exceptions, there are almost no Cézannists in France today, Cézanne's lessons nonetheless were not in vain. The Impressionists may now be represented only by the mediocre epigone d'Espagnat, but Bonnard and Matisse transformed Impressionism into majestic, major-key painting that is the best proof of its historical significance. . . .

It is time to abandon the superficial criticism and subjective judgments that are sometimes hastily borrowed from bourgeois chroniclers for whom the study of art is usually merely colorful anecdotes and aesthetic phrase mongering and begin a more scholarly examination of Western, especially French, art.

We must also have done with the smug arrogance of those artists who subsume all of Europe's artistic achievements under the extremely vulgar and empty formulas "rotten, foxtrot art" or "jazz-band formalism."*

They may find it surprising to learn that these judgments coincide precisely with the opinions of reactionary art critics in the conservative bourgeois press.

Subjectivism and vulgar oversimplification are equally harmful. *We must under no circumstances allow the accumulated formal and technical treasures of bourgeois Europe to be lost to us. . . .*

Without prejudging the fate of easel painting, we can say that if it gradually moves from the dominant position it has enjoyed in bourgeois society to a secondary or more auxiliary status, it will in any case never disappear altogether.

And since it will continue to exist, we will inadvertently encounter all of the problems French painting has brought to the fore.

Derain is especially instructive in this regard. It is as though he has absorbed all the wisdom of French painting. Everything in his works is structured on experience and observation. No metaphors or eloquence! He has reduced his entire effort to the problem of color and the monumentalism of form. His palette has been simplified to the point of miserliness. He uses five or six colors, achieving chromatic expressiveness through the color's power and intensity. He concentrates everything, taking from his observations only what is central and best corresponds to his compositional intent. . . .

We must also evaluate Henri Matisse differently. Although not so much Matisse

*Quotations from former AKhR leader Evgenii Katsman's article "K voprosu ob AKhRovskoi samokritike. Stranitsy iz dnevnika" (On AKhR Self-Criticism. Pages from a Diary"), *Iskusstvo v massy* (Art to the Masses) 3–4 (1929).

himself, perhaps, as Raoul Dufy, who is completely unknown in the USSR and who as one of the most consistent of Matisse's companions-in-arms has managed to realize Fauvism's basic intentions most fully. Moving away from the analytical Impressionist fragmentation of light in nature and toward its synthetic artistic transformation, he has discovered a compositional rhythm and a tension and resonance of color never achieved by Matisse himself. . . .

To gloat over Cubism's demise, assured that it was just another whim of fashion, is incomprehensibly obscurantist. Cubism confronts us with many problems that we cannot simply ignore, such as *the relativity of light and the contradictions between volumetric and two-dimensional painting* that André Lhote has attempted to solve synthetically, and the problem of *overcoming Italian perspective,* which has been variously resolved by such major and genuinely cultured artists as Georges Braque, Albert Gleizes, and Leopold Survage. Despite their contradictions, each of them individually is significant in the development of the monumental fresco, which our socialist construction is bound to develop enormously.

Finally, thanks to Cubism, we have encountered the problem of a new style to reflect the age of machine technicism. On the one hand are the Purists; on the other, Fernand Léger has raised the question of the mass-produced thing and its influence on contemporary art. . . .

Today it is ridiculous to fear the ideology of bourgeois Europe. We are separated by different approaches to and utterly different perceptions of the surrounding world. Socialism is the highest stage of human development, and we have broken with the bourgeois ideology of capitalist Europe once and for all. Despite the temporary respites that history may grant it, the social crisis that Europe is experiencing must inevitably and fatefully bring it to social revolution. Europe will be forced to catch up with us. In the meantime we should borrow the technical advancements it has made during its period of cultural growth.

117
Frida Roginskaia
"Against the Cult of the French" (1930)

Frida Roginskaia (1898–1963) published extensively as an art critic in major Soviet newspapers and magazines. She became a member of the bureau of the AKhR (Association of Revolutionary Artists) Art History Section that was established in early 1930. This essay appeared in *Iskusstvo v massy* (Art to the Masses) 4 (1930).

. . . If "we must also have done with the smug arrogance of those artists who subsume all of Europe's artistic achievements under the extremely vulgar and empty formulas 'rotten, foxtrot art' or 'jazz-band formalism,'"* then it would not hurt to put

*Cf. same quotation on p. 287.

an end as well to all this bowing and scraping to Cézanne's "wisdom," to which Romov refers without quotation marks, uttering profound maxims on this art's universally recognized "formal and technical riches."

"Vulgar arrogance" toward modern Western art has infected not only the artists attacked by the author of the article but also Marxist theoreticians such as Plekhanov and Mehring. Moreover, all statements on recent art by Marxist leaders (for example, Rosa Luxemburg) have been extremely negative and by no means laudatory. Very unfortunately, Lenin never confronted this issue head-on, but when he happened to touch on modern art even in passing his opinion of these trends was always negative (his talk at VKhUTEIN [Higher State Artistic-Technological Institute],* his conversation with Clara Zetkin, and so on [68]). It is widely known that Plekhanov considered bourgeois art irrepressibly degenerate. . . .

Even if we accept the view that the formal culture of contemporary Western painting is extremely well developed—which in my opinion is entirely incorrect—even then it cannot be concluded that it is useful to us. *It is not relevant to a single fundamental formal problem* confronting proletarian art. It has no socially significant themes and consequently is ignorant of many formal problems that are inseparably connected to those themes. I shall indicate a few such problems: (1) the composition of a mass scene, (2) the socio-psychological features of characters, (3) the presentation of collisions through the expressiveness of human figures, gestures, and facial expressions. Are these not formal problems? *And is it not true that in this respect French painting is on an extremely low level?* Finally, does our painting not face the task of finding a language that is fiery and contagious but intelligible to the broad masses, that is, a language diametrically opposite to that spoken by Western painting?

Usually the partisans of Western art attempt to support their enthusiasm on a Marxist foundation by arguing that the basis of proletarian art has been dialectically laid in the painting of the latest period of capitalism. If this process is complex with respect to arts such as literature and the cinema, in which the pressure of the mass consumer is certainly bound to exert some influence, with respect to painting such a formulation of the question does not withstand scrutiny. . . .

Finally, we must expose the error in the combined notion of "formal and technical" properties. The notion of form is as relevant to ideology as it is to content, and, like content, it should be distinguished from technique. If we pose the question to mean that "the technical riches of bourgeois Europe are extremely important to us and should be exploited to the fullest," we will be quite correct. But what does this mean? In the case of architecture, for example, it will mean the use of reinforced concrete and other modern construction materials as well as the many improvements that enhance the amenities of a building. In the case of the production arts it means using technological and industrial experience in the form of, say, improved chemical

*On February 25, 1921, Lenin visited the student commune (dormitory) at VKhUTEMAS (Higher Art and Technical Studios). In conversations with the students, he expressed his negative view of Futurism.

dyes, improved fiber processing, better methods for the mass reproduction of various sorts of products, and so on, but it does not at all involve the actual architectural structure of a building or the *designs* that are provided by the artist and disseminated to the mass consumer.

When Comrade Romov talks about using the "formal and technical" riches of French painting, what he has in mind is, of course, not improved oil paints or better methods for priming a canvas. He is talking, of course, about Western painting's *aggregate of formal devices*, that is, *ideology rather than technique.* It is high time that AKhR specifically put an end to the idealistic notion that a veil of Soviet content can be stretched onto the framework of the alien form generated by a social environment diametrically opposite to our own. Lax Impressionist form as well as abstract Cubist form and morbidly pessimistic Expressionist form are all equally unsuitable and dangerous to proletarian art (which, of course, does not mean that AKhR should return to Naturalism). However much we might want to do so, we cannot agree with Comrade Romov's view that, since we have put an end to bourgeois ideology once and for all, "it is ridiculous to fear the ideology of bourgeois Europe," for it is now, during this period of intensified class struggle, that frivolous victory celebrations are so inappropriate. . . .

118

Ivan Matsa (János Mácza)

"To the Highest Level!" (1931)

Matsa's text, published in *Za proletarskoe iskusstvo* (For a Proletarian Art) 3–4 (1931), is an example of ritual ideological penance. He is responding here to a lecture at the Communist Academy by Iu. Ianel' attacking his views.*

. . . Unable . . . to analyze in the present article all the many mistakes committed at various stages of Marxist art criticism as a whole, I shall dwell on those I myself have committed. . . . I do so not to "confess" but to remove the positions that I consider erroneous and that therefore may in practice become an obstacle in the struggle for the correct line of development in proletarian art.

Such was above all my attitude toward the use of the artistic heritage, which resulted in a distortion of the Leninist concept. The essence of this mistake was that in my works I incorrectly focused only on bourgeois art of the imperialist phase. I believed that from this art we must take all elements connected with the growth of industrialism, the objectivization of the artistic process, the struggle between the well-

*See Iu. Ianel', "Mekhanisticheskii 'organizatsionnyi' printsip v kontseptsii t. Matsy" (The Mechanistic "Organizational" Principle in the Concept of Com. Matsa), *Literatura i iskusstvo* (Literature and Art) 4 (1931). See also L. Roshchin, "Iskusstvovedcheskie oshibki t. Matsy" (Com. Matsa's Errors on the Fine Arts), *Za proletarskoe iskusstvo* (For Proletarian Art) 3–4 (1931).

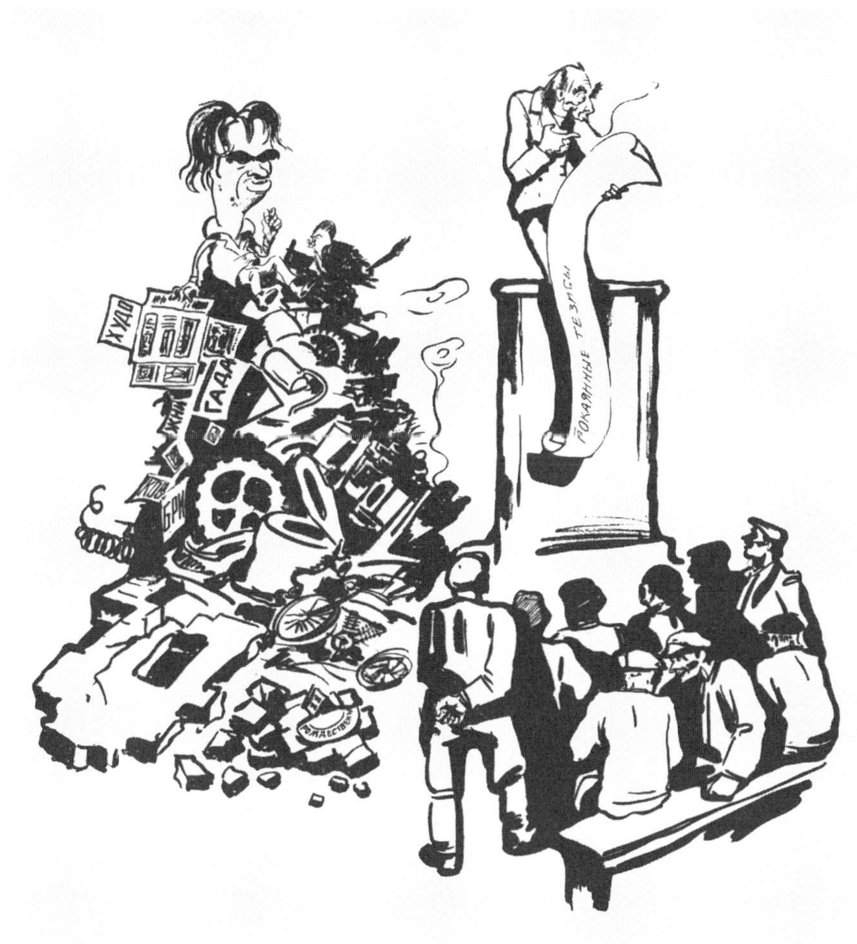

Cartoon of Ivan Matsa's ideological penance in *Za proletarskoe iskusstvo* (For a Proletarian Art) 3–4 (1931). On the left is the VKhUTEMAS (Higher Art and Technical Studios) rector Pavel Novitskii, another scapegoat of the AKhR-RAPKh critics.

organized big bourgeoisie and the anarchy and intuitivism in the art of some of the petty bourgeoisie. This mistake of mine was intimately connected with my past as an art historian, when, among "leftist" activists in the capitalist West, I waged a struggle against philistine vulgarity and empty "art for art's sake" and wholeheartedly joined the "left" front of bourgeois art and myself became a representative of its rationalistic, "Constructivist" tendencies. The problem, however, was not only that I could not distance myself quickly enough from the "nightmare" hanging over me or that even as I criticized the art of the big bourgeoisie I was objectively encouraging it nonetheless, but also that my "objective-critical" attitude toward this art was objectively transformed into an incorrect attitude and became an incorrect, un-Leninist appraisal of the capitalist relations of the imperialist West and an underestimation of the decay of capitalism. In political language (and we are obliged to translate all our appraisals into political language) this is called the right-wing opportunist deviation. Thus do *"left-wing" excesses become the right-wing deviation*—and that is what happened in my case. Not until I understood this "metamorphosis" did I realize the essence of my mistake, which I not only repudiated but in practice began to correct by providing in my paper before last (on the creative method) a different approach to tradition in the development of proletarian art based on the Leninist view of the cultural heritage. . . .

119

Aleksei Mikhailov

"Comrade Bogorodskii's Trip Abroad" (1931)

Fedor Bogorodskii (1895–1959) was a commissar who worked with the Cheka and the Revolutionary Tribunal from 1918 to 1921. After he graduated from VKhUTEMAS (Higher Art and Technical Studios) in 1924 and joined AKhRR (Association of Artists of Revolutionary Russia), Bogorodskii was allowed to study abroad. He became known for mediocre paintings of revolutionary sailors and homeless orphans. In the years 1928–30 he lived in Germany and Italy. Upon his return to Moscow Bogorodskii arranged an exhibition featuring mainly his landscapes, still lifes, and nudes. Mikhailov reviewed the show for *Brigada khudozhnikov* (Artists' Brigade) 3–4 (1931).

. . . Bogorodskii's assignment was to *critically select and assimilate the aspects of bourgeois art that are most valuable from the viewpoint of the tasks confronting proletarian art.*

As you look through his works, however, you become convinced *first, that this assimilation has been insufficiently critical and, second, that he has chosen some dubious points of departure. . . .*

The exhibition shows that while abroad Bogorodskii did not study the classics of the rising bourgeoisie at all but concentrated instead on epigones of bourgeois art such as Dufy, Utrillo, and Derain, while ignoring the monumental and realistic art of the past and the "Neo-Realist" and Constructivist trends of the present.

The exhibition shows that while abroad Bogorodskii lightly abandoned socially topical themes and accepted the apolitical themes of bourgeois art.

Heroic Realism yielded to the eclecticism so typical of contemporary French painting.

These facts are a good lesson. They splendidly demonstrate that cultivation of the slogans and practice of the old AKhR leads to an uncritical acceptance of the bourgeois art of the *most recent period* (for which the association's members have no critical use) and not even the *most recent period as a whole* but its most unprogressive, decadent trends. . . .

It was not Ghirlandaio, or Masaccio, or Michelangelo who became Bogorodskii's "teachers." He did not even follow the path once traveled in Italy by Diego Rivera.

Having returned to the USSR, Bogorodskii demonstrated through his exhibition the danger of moving away from proletarian art. . . .

120

Dmitrii Lebedev

"The Museum of Modern Western Painting Must Live!" (1930)

The probable closure of the museum in 1930 was opposed by the influential newspaper *Komsomol'skaia pravda* (Young Communist League Pravda), which traditionally maintained strong ties with leftist artist circles and severely criticized the anti-Western attitude of AKhR (Association of Revolutionary Artists). This essay was published in *Komsomol'skaia pravda* on March 12, 1930.

The jingoism of tsarist Russia, of course, could not popularize the ideas of the new painting, which rejected obsolete, hackneyed forms and searched for new ways of perceiving and treating phenomena in the visual arts. The founding of the Museum of Modern Western Painting was made possible only by the October Revolution, which expropriated the most valuable masterpieces from their private consumers—generous merchant "philanthropists" who sometimes did not even understand the works of art that they "patronized.". . .

Whereas most "classical" picture galleries are essentially merely archival collections of museum rarities, during the Revolution the Museum of Modern Western Painting became the only gallery in the world that featured almost all contemporary Western European painting. The school of artistic mastery that it represents is the keenest, most hostile enemy of the old "classical" ways. . . .

The entire constellation of artists who discovered new artistic techniques and new ways of perceiving things (Monet, Degas, Derain, Valloton, and others) are all here; it is in Soviet Moscow that genuine, impartial appreciation of them is to be found. These artists' enormous social and cultural significance consists in the fact that, unlike the epigones of the classical painters, they understood and reflected in their art the flimsiness, transitoriness, and doom of the capitalist order.

The decision to close and move this museum is muddle-headed economically as well, for owing to its monopoly position the museum attracts a great many foreign sightseers who bring us much-needed foreign currency. Given proper work on the part of our tourist organizations, we can increase this stream of visitors even more.

The Museum of Modern Western Painting must live. Closing it would mean not only the elimination of an extremely valuable art collection, but also the politically impermissible refusal to patronize the most progressive and revolutionary trends in Western European art.

121

Osip Mandelstam

"A Journey to Armenia: The French" (1933)

In spring 1930 the poet Osip Mandelstam (1891–1938) visited Armenia. His book *A Journey to Armenia*, where this fragment on the Museum of Modern Western Art was published, provoked negative reviews (including one in *Pravda*, August 30, 1933). In May 1934 Mandelstam was arrested for the first time.

This excerpt, originally published in *Zvezda* (Star) 5 (1933), is reprinted here from *The Noise of Time: The Prose of Osip Mandelstam*, translated with critical essays by Clarence Brown (San Francisco: North Point Press, 1986), pp. 211–13.

Now I stretched out my vision and sank my eye into the wide goblet of the sea, so that every mote and tear should come to the surface.

I stretched my vision like a kid glove, stretched it onto a shoe tree, onto the blue neighborhood of the sea. . . .

Quickly, rapaciously, with feudal fury, I inspected the domains of my view.

One puts the eye like that into a wide goblet full to the brim so that a mote will come out.

And I began to understand what the obligatory nature of color is—the excitement of sky blue and orange football shirts—and that color is nothing other than a sense of the start of a race, a sense tinged by distance and locked into its size.

Time circulated in the museum in accordance with an hourglass. The brick siftings would come running as the goblet emptied itself and there would be the same jet of golden simoom from the little case at the top to the bottle on the bottom.

Hello, Cézanne! Good old grandfather! A demon for work. The best acorn in the forests of France.

His painting was certified on the oak table of a village notary. He is as incontestable as a will executed by a man sound of mind and possessed of his memory.

But what captivated me was the old man's still life.* Roses that must have been cut in the morning, solid and rolled tight, unusually young tea roses. Exactly like little scoops of yellow ice cream.

On the other hand, I took a dislike to Matisse, a rich man's artist. The red paint of his canvases fizzes like soda. He knows nothing of the joy of ripening fruits. His mighty brush doesn't heal the vision but gives it the strength of an ox, so that the eyes become bloodshot.

Enough already of this carpet chess and odalisques!†

Persian whimsies of a Parisian *maître!*

The cheap vegetable pigments of Van Gogh were bought by accident for twenty sous.

Van Gogh spits blood like a suicide in furnished rooms. The floorboards in the

*Cézanne, *Flowers* (1902–3, R.894, GMII).

†Matisse, *The Painter's Family* (1911, Hermitage).

night café are tilted and stream like a gutter in their electric fit. And the narrow trough of the billiard table looks like the manger of a coffin.

I never saw such barking colors!

And his streetcar conductor's vegetable-garden landscapes! The soot of suburban trains has just been wiped from them with a wet rag.*

His canvases, smeared with the omelette of an accident, are as clear as visual aids—as the charts in a Berlitz School.

The visitors move about with little steps as though in church.

Each room his its own climate. In Claude Monet's room there is a river air. Looking at Renoir's water you feel blisters on your palm as though you'd been rowing.†

Signac invented the maize sun.

The woman who lectures about the pictures leads the cultural workers behind her.

To look at them you'd say a magnet was attracting a duck.

Ozenfant worked out something surprising by using red chalk and gray slate squirrels on a black slate ground and modulating the forms of glass-blowing and fragile laboratory equipment.‡

But you also got a nod from Picasso's dark blue Jew and Pissarro's raspberry gray boulevards, flowing like the wheels of an immense lottery with their little boxes of hansom cabs, their fishing-pole whips pitched on their shoulders, and the shreds of splashed brain on the kiosks and chestnut trees.**

But isn't that enough?

Generalization is already waiting, bored, at the door.

To anyone recuperating from the benign plague of naïve realism I would recommend the following method of looking at pictures.

Under no circumstances go in as if you were entering a chapel. Don't be thrilled or chilled, and don't get glued to the canvas. . . .

With the stride of a stroll on a boulevard: straight on!

Cut through the huge heat waves of the space of oil painting.

Calmly, with no excitement—the way little Tartars bathe their horses in Alushta††—lower your eye into what will be for it a new material ambiance—and remember that the eye is a noble, but stubborn, animal.

Standing before a picture to which the body temperature of your vision has not yet adjusted itself, for which the crystalline lens has not yet found the one suitable accommodation, is like singing a serenade in a fur coat behind storm windows.

When this equilibrium has been achieved, and only then, begin the second stage

*Van Gogh, *A Road in Auvers after the Rain* (1890, GMII).

†Renoir, *La Grenouillère* (1869, GMII).

‡Amedée Ozenfant, *Drawing on Black Background* (1928, GMII).

**Picasso, *The Old Jew* (1903, Z.I.175, GMII); Pissarro, *Boulevard Montmartre* (1897; Hermitage) and *Avenue de l'Opéra* (1898, GMII).

††Alushta, a town in the Crimea, populated mostly by Tatars before the 1944 deportation.

of the restoration of the picture, the washing of it, the removal of its old peel, its external and late barbaric layer, which is the linking of it to sunny, solid reality.

With its extremely subtle acidic reactions, the eye, an organ possessed of hearing, which intensifies the value of the image, which multiplies its accomplishments by its sensual insults (which it fusses over like a child with a new toy), raises the picture to its own level; for painting is much more a matter of internal secretion than of apperception, that is, of external perceiving.

The material of painting is organized in such a way that it stands to lose nothing, and that is its distinction from nature. But the probability of the lottery is inversely proportional to its feasibility.

And only now does the third and last stage of entering the picture begin: when one confronts the intention behind it.

Now the traveling eye presents its ambassadorial credentials to the consciousness. Then a cold treaty is established between the viewer and the picture, something on the order of a diplomatic secret.

I left the embassy of painting and went out into the street.

So soon after having left the Frenchmen I found the sunlight to be a phase of some waning eclipse, and the sun to be wrapped up in foil.

Near the entrance of the cooperative stood a mother with her son. The boy was tabetic, respectful. Both were in mourning. The woman was sticking a bunch of radishes into her reticule.

The end of the street, seemingly crushed by binoculars, swerved off into a squinting lump; and all of this, distant and linden-lined, was stuffed into a string bag.

122

D. Mel'nikov

"Cézanne and Cézannism" (1921)

Tvorchestvo (Creation) was published by the Moscow Soviet and edited by Vladimir Friche [70]. The journal advocated a "transformed realism" and criticized avant-gardists. This essay was published in *Tvorchestvo* 4–6 (1921).

. . . With the appearance of Impressionism we witnessed the beginning of a new era in painting. "Let there be light!" said the Impressionists. And light became painting's basic problem.

Essentially, though, it was a chaos of light—something fragile, intangible, an "apparition," as Cézanne said of Claude Monet. "We must move on," says Cézanne, and he creates dry land. He is the first to give the Impressionists' painting a solid body, a mass with a definite density, weight, and volume, and to endow it with an unusual sense of materiality. "Essentially, light does not exist in painting," he says to counterbalance the Impressionists.

Cézanne was the first materialist in painting. He criticized Pissarro for "anarchic theories," saying that he had only approximated nature. Cézanne was a theoretician and scholar. He created a new theory as he "thought about painting, brush in hand." . . .

"Imagine Poussin reworked in harmony with nature," he said.

Our young questing artists should remember this, particularly after the recent rather piquant published confessions of such a Cézannist as Pablo Picasso. Picasso's drawings "à la Ingres" indicate he has gone down this classical, genuinely Cézannist path. Derain, another talented follower of Cézanne who continues his work, has definitely joined the Primitivists. The road to Cézanne's "classicism through nature" lies through the Primitivists and early Gothic.

. . . Cézanne, Gauguin, and Van Gogh represent three completely different temperaments that bear comparison with three others: Leonardo da Vinci, Raphael, and Michelangelo. . . . The difference, however—and it is enormous—is that the first three are Primitivists and stand *at the beginning of a new road,* as Cézanne himself admitted, whereas the latter three represent the culmination of the entire preceding epoch. They are genuine classics, and the range of their genius is therefore enormous and broad. Our age is merely awaiting the appearance of such universal geniuses.

If with respect to theory Impressionism is close to socialism, it is a utopian socialism that has no firm ground or base beneath it. To continue the analogy, the "materialist" Cézanne's temperament and mentality could be compared with Karl Marx, except that Marx has become the purest classic of scientific socialism, whereas Cézanne, a Primitivist himself, merely foresaw the age of classicism. He is but one of the first landmarks on the road to classicism. His art does not know the *picture,* for Cézanne had *no creative imagination.* He was merely a "painter," an honest "art worker," an innovator and inventor, but not a creator who perfects a system, not a Leonardo da Vinci; he was a "brilliant bourgeois" close to him in spirit but not a universal genius. For this reason we can appreciate him only as an innovator and inventor, the first artist to find the right path, but for this reason as yet imperfect and inarticulate. . . .

123

David Arkin

"R[obert] Fal'k and Moscow Painting" (1923)

In 1910 Robert Fal'k (1886–1958) began exhibiting with the Jack of Diamonds group and developed a highly personal interpretation of Cézanne's work. In the 1920s David Arkin (1899–1957) wrote extensively on art and design; he later switched to the history of architecture and sculpture. This article was published in *Russkoe iskusstvo* (Russian Art) 2–3 (1923).

. . . *Cézanne* is almost a magical word for Russian painting. The name has for a long time signified something much more than a great artist: it stands for an entire system of painting, a system that would, of course, be called by some other term were there a more suitable Russian, Latin, or other word.

Cézanne's role in new Russian painting is enormous, and the whole Moscow group have been called Cézannists for good reason. The prevalent opinions about the character of this "influence" and about the nature of "Cézannism" itself, however, are very superficial and quite simply mistaken. . . .

In the history of French painting, Cézanne was a way-station on the high road of Impressionism. Far from slowing forward movement, this station was a turning point on the brink of the "light" abyss to which oil painting had brought Impressionism.

In Russian art, Cézanne was once again destined to restore *painting* and assert the painterly principles of the picture. There, he did not allow painting to atomize into sunbeams and diverted it from the shores of naturalistic illusion. Here, he steered the differentiation process into the channel of painting.

Not so long ago, a very witty man called Russian painting "art in greasepaint." Much of the work done by the Moscow group was devoted to putting on the greasepaint of "Cézannism." Guided by their exceptionally healthy instinct to begin with Cézanne and an elaboration of his system, for a long time the only way Moscow painters could approach their task was by interpreting its isolated individual elements. What came to the fore as a result was a purely superficial thematic kinship with Cézanne that led to talk of "influences," "imitations," and so on.

In reality, Moscow painting was only preparing to master Cézanne. To use a medical term, we might call this long period of preparation the "latent" period of the Cézanne "affliction." Its length varied for different masters, ending earlier for the most mature of them, Konchalovskii, than for others. But it was only Fal'k who emerged from this period to find himself for the first time, and his Cézannism can no longer be described as greasepaint, but is his true artistic face. . . .

The master's mature period began with what on the surface was a certain delay. Arriving to supplant the Cézannism of isolated individual techniques was a Cézannism of integrally organized pictorial vision—a system for processing the material of painting. Fal'k and his contemporaries had followed the line of least resistance, introducing into their painting discrete "new" properties of texture, composition, color, and so on. In Cézanne's painting as well, after all, what was noticed most was his notorious "volume"; we were also enticed to do so by the famous passage in "the Gospel according to Bernard" on the geometrical and three-dimensional principles of painterly expression. Fal'k needed to follow the differentiation of material to its logical conclusion, and when at the end of this journey painting appeared to him naked and stripped of all literary and narrative stratifications, he approached the knowledge and use of this material from a completely different angle. Cézanne's system consists not in the elimination of the theme, or subject, or representation, but in an assertion of the primacy of *color,* and it is this point that contemporary painting is approaching after all its analytical purgatories. . . .

Now that painting has differentiated, having eliminated the theme and attempted to eliminate the subject, it will not go back along the same line. In the pictures of Fal'k and his comrades the significance of the theme is restored, but the subject figures in another, purely painterly sense, corresponding to the demands and properties of the material and the techniques for handling it. Painting evolves not in a straight line but in a spiral: horizontally it passes through earlier points, but on entirely different vertical planes. After the assertion of the theme we can clearly note today the *return of narrative*—not, however, in the sense of the "narrative content" of a picture as was the case before the process of differentiation. The subject is returning as a definite constitutive element of painting. Fal'k's most recent works clearly show that theme has entered his art, and no longer as a narrative envelope alien to the material of painting but from within, out of the construction of the very art of painting and its interrelationship with reality, a relationship that is completely different from that of literature, and who knows, is perhaps much closer and more intimate. The very *formation of narrative* therefore obeys different laws that can be determined only if the theme is regarded as a definite element in the processing of painterly material. We are *on the eve of a new narrative painting* (just as all of Cézanne is narrative), and this is the essence of the change taking shape in the latest works of the Moscow artists. . . .

124

Nikolai Tarabukin

"The Still Life as a Problem of Style" (1928)

This article, published in *Sovetskoe iskusstvo* (Soviet Art) 1 (1928), is related to Tarabukin's unpublished book, *The Problem of Style in Painting* (1927). Although he was known for his devotion to the great French artist, it appears to be the most extreme criticism of Cézanne in the Soviet press of the period.

. . . The spirit of the still life has conquered almost all of contemporary painting. Instead of "soul" there is "construction"; instead of the living organism of art, the inert mechanism of a craft. Cézanne was the first to look at his surroundings without "emotion," so it made sense when his friend Bernard called his painting "meditation with brush in hand." Cézanne was the first to see the world as an aggregate of inert things and to approach the non-object as though it were an object as well. It was he, the terrible vivisectionist, who deprived artists of their living human perception of the world, leaving them only their "eyes," which gape and skim the peripheries of objects and "feel" only the world's outer and superficial chromatic husk. It was he who deprived artists of a feeling "heart" and a brow capable of reflecting philosophically on the world, leaving them only to "consider" and "calculate" like artisans how to use color to "construct" a real object on a plane. He replaced the philosophy of art with several practical recipes for the painter's craft. It was he who transformed the painting of life into the painting of death, depriving art of its social significance and restricting its influence to the professional milieu. It was under his pressure that art descended from the heights of a social fact to the "arcade" of the *vernissage.* It was his painting more than anyone else's that begot a flock of cawing "carrion-crows of aesthetics" who limited the problem of art to the mechanical question of "how, how, how" to make something and forgot that there is also a formidable "what." Beginning with Cézanne, whose art served as a green light on the road to all the formal contrivances of Cubism, Futurism, and Suprematism, painting came to treat the human face as it would a bottle or a teapot, and living nature as an inert mock-up.

The still life as we understand it is devoid of narrative. The narrative is action unfolded in visual forms. No matter how simple, it can be conveyed verbally in a coherent story. Cézanne's *natures mortes* are not amenable to such paraphrase, for they have no action or theme. Looking at them, you can only enumerate the objects represented on the canvas and indicate which object is next to which. The Dutch still lifes of the seventeenth century have a theme. They are like genre paintings, portrait representations of beautiful things for which the artist feels a tender love and attachment; in a sense, they are lyrical novellas. . . .

In the golden age of the Dutch *Stilleven,* the burghers were still just beginning to conquer their half of the world. The situation changed radically in Cézanne's time, the age of developing capitalism, when the thing acquired a fateful power over its owners, subjugating human consciousness. What reigns in Cézanne's canvases is not "life" but the "power of things" over human consciousness. Humanity is subordinated to the thing, rather than the other way around. Humanity itself is transformed into a thing. All of nature becomes a thing—soulless, inert, an *objet inanimé,* and the work of art becomes a still life. . . .

The still-life worldview is capturing all forms of contemporary art and is by no means limited to painting. In sculpture, for example, Lipchitz, Wauer, and others have abandoned the living image to "cobble together" abstract masses they call "constructions." In architecture, Le Corbusier advocates eliminating the contemporary dwelling with its "familiar" everyday "odor" and proposes using an American technology that makes it possible to build houses in standardized "series" that can be transported and "unfolded" anywhere, buildings that are no longer immovables and have been transformed into "tools" just like the automobile, airplane, and so on. In literature, adventurers following in the footsteps of Marinetti, who "set words free," cultivate "transrational poetry," a peculiar "sound" writing that not only emancipates speech from rules of grammar but also robs language of any human meaning. Phenomena of the same order in music include the compositions of Schoenberg, Roslavets, and to some extent Stravinsky, the early Prokofiev, and others. . . .

The still life, a product of the power of things over human consciousness, reflects the highly exacerbated contradictions in contemporary Western European civilization. The still-life worldview is one of those pages in the history of artistic culture that speak of man's submission to everything material that man has created to liberate himself from the power of nature but, owing to the abnormality of life's social aspects, has turned against man and imprisoned him. Relations among human beings have acquired the illusion of relations among things. In the words of Karl Marx, man has become a "fetishist of things." . . .

The still-life worldview asserts the power of the inert over the living and acknowledges the dominance of submission over creation. The still life denies life and creation and consequently also denies the profound, genuine essence of art. . . .

125

Nikolai Punin

"Mikhail Larionov's Impressionist Period" (1928)

In the 1920s Punin tried unsuccessfully to organize a one-man show for Larionov at the Russian Museum. He dates Larionov's Impressionist period to 1902–6, although works employing Impressionist techniques continued appearing until 1908. The essay was included in *Materialy po russkomu iskusstvu* (Materials on Russian Art), vol. 1 (Leningrad, 1928).

. . . Larionov was and always will be a realist; his direct and vibrant perception is the basis of his talent and has never failed him.*

This extraordinary immediacy enabled him to rework Western European formal influences into a national Russian tradition. Larionov's Impressionism is original in the sensation it bears, and this is his third characteristic trait. He managed to link French Impressionism and Russian painting traditions. While many of his contemporary Russian Impressionists, sometimes even Korovin, give occasion for comparisons to German or Scandinavian Impressionists, Larionov permits no such comparison; moreover, for all his closeness to the French, his Impressionist works differ from theirs in their special, "somewhat coarse" painting and lyricism, which is alien to the French masters. . . . In the period following Impressionism he stressed the independence of Russian artistic traditions and opened a broad front in the struggle against urban, Western-influenced art in order, as he put it, to rework the "provincial" forms and traditions of the people. This struggle issued organically from his entire past and was shaped by the essence of his talent. This is why his Impressionism is especially dear to us—it links Russian art's painting past with the latest trends. The inherited realistic painting tradition runs from Vasil'ev and Surikov through Larionov. A certain number of artists who characterize the "line of realism" in Russian art can be grouped around this tradition. This line is weak, of course, and not always easy to trace in the various nonrealistic branches of Russian artistic culture. All the more deserving of attention is the artist who was able to carry the pure culture of painting through the motley polyglotism of Russian art and show a path that is rich and alive to all who care to see.

*I think that the theory of "Rayonnism," advanced by Larionov in 1912–13 as a barrier against certain rationalistic tendencies in Cubism, is also—in practice, at least—the fruit of very subtle realistic comparisons (Punin's note).

126

Amshei Niurenberg

"The Pissarro Exhibition: Letter from Paris" (1929)

The painter Amshei Niurenberg (1887–1979) wrote art criticism in the 1920s and published a book on Cézanne in 1926. He reviewed the March 1928 Pissarro exhibition at Durand-Ruel's gallery in *Iskusstvo v massy* (Art to the Masses) 1–2 (1929).

The exhibition demonstrates the viability of Impressionist ideas, *the very ideas* that radically changed our artistic attitude to our surroundings.

Some among us think that Impressionist art is the dead legacy of an alien bourgeois culture. Our critics have developed an entire theory about Impressionism's passivity, individualism, and subjectivism, and especially its aesthetics of the sketch. From all of this they conclude that because from a Marxist point of view Impressionism has so many negative aspects, it cannot be added to the interests of our artistic culture. . . .

The Pissarro exhibition serves as an example of this incorrect assessment of Impressionism. To Pissarro, as well as Millet, goes the credit of having discovered French peasants. And it must be noted that he did not portray them as an individualist or subjectivist. There is a feeling of objective truth and materiality on all his canvases. . . . Was the Impressionist method a hindrance here? Of course not. On the contrary, Pissarro's skillful use of it helped him to *feel* the village more broadly and deeply. . . .

Of course, I don't imagine that Impressionism can be resurrected today in the form in which it existed in the 1880s and 1890s. The idea of imitating Monet and his followers, especially for Soviet artists, who are living in a different culture and have assigned art different tasks, is impossible and absurd. But this great movement has much that our young artists—once they have critically processed it, of course—could learn with considerable benefit to themselves. The most prominent French masters of our day, Henri Matisse and Pierre Bonnard, grew up and evolved on Impressionist soil, although they later moved away from Monet and created their own methods (Post-Impressionism). But they could not do this until they had absorbed Impressionist principles.

Impressionism knew no geographical or national boundaries. Artists from all countries fell under its influence. Let us not forget that our best artists, Surikov and Korovin, are also to a significant degree indebted to Impressionism. . . .

I think that if our other artists had studied Monet, Renoir, and Pissarro instead of Zorn, Kaulbach, and Stuck, we would not have to deal with the academic trends we observe today.

127

Aleksandr Severdenko

"Response to an Impressionist" (1929)

Aleksandr Severdenko (1900–1938) was a painter and activist in OMAKhR (Organization of Youth of the Association of Revolutionary Artists) and RAPKh (Russian Association of Proletarian

Artists) and became a member of the Communist Party in 1924. Along with other former leaders of RAPKh, Severdenko was executed during the Great Terror as a member of the fictitious "Fighting Terrorist Group of Moscow Artists." This article was published in *Iskusstvo v massy* (Art to the Masses) 5–6 (1929).

. . . we must categorically reject the attitude toward the viability of bourgeois ideology proposed by Comrade Niurenberg , author of "The Pissarro Exhibition." . . .

We think it entirely superfluous to present any arguments to prove that Impressionist ideas belong to the overall ideology of the bourgeoisie during its decline and decay, but we cannot understand how Comrade Niurenberg, a member of the Association of *Revolutionary* Artists, could bring himself to maintain that the decadent bourgeoisie's artistic notions are essential for us as well.

Even if he had in mind purely formal aspects, then as well he should have realized that the revolutionary artistic ideas of the proletariat will find appropriate new formal means for their own expression.

Changes in form result from changes in content. . . .

No one intends to diminish the greatness and significance of Impressionist masters such as Monet, Renoir, Pissarro, and others, and no one refuses to use the techniques they discovered, but no one will ever agree to insist on the "viability" of that which is historically destined to die away, and no one will ever agree to channel our development toward a resurrection of Impressionism. . . .

128

Anatolii Lunacharskii

"The Painter of Happiness: On Viewing Renoir's Canvases" (1933)

On September 12, 1929, Lunacharskii was removed from his post as people's commissar of enlightenment. Later he was appointed Soviet ambassador to Spain. He died on December 26, 1933, on the Côte d'Azur. The Renoir exhibition at the Musée de l'Orangerie inspired one of his last essays, which was published in *Sovetskoe iskusstvo* (Soviet Art) on October 2, 1933.

. . . Impressionism gave him a great deal indeed. It drove him out of his dark studio. Impressionism opened his eyes to the immediate and sensual charm of sunlight. It taught him all the hidden luxury of the beauty of brown and gray shadows especially. It brought out before his talented and sensitive eye the flickering of lights and colors on the surface of objects and in the space between them. . . .

The best Impressionist artists . . . were not representatives of the dominant bourgeoisie. Most of them could not stand it: they hated and despised its tastes and the artists who served it. . . .

Unlike the other Impressionists, especially those closest to him, for whom "mood" (the "poetry" of painting) seemed almost more important than the craft itself, Renoir inherently possessed an unusual unity of mood; actually, his mood was always the same, but it was a very rich one. This mood was happiness. . . .

No, Renoir is not a bourgeois artist. But he is also not a revolutionary. He is a man who hungers for happiness and has found a great deal of it. He is a man who has portrayed it a great deal. He is a man who has given a great deal of it to others in a kind of special airy currency that seems counterfeit only to the crudest bumpkins.

. . . There is an entire world in Renoir, but it is much narrower. There are unusually sweet, warm, and amiable women friends—women who, however, for all their charming freshness and irresistible attractiveness, could rarely pass for clever. There is an entire collection of children; they are unforgettable, and if you look at them in a sorrowful moment they can comfort you. There is the free, joyful, festive crowd. There is the beautiful earth beneath the heavens' smile. Many thanks to him for this. We must not forget how much good fate has granted us, or at least how happy we could be.

Ask this of Renoir and he will give it to you. Ask great mastery and he will give it. Ask for the spiritual lucidity of an almost saintly man and he will give it.

Isn't that enough?

XI

THE END OF AN ERA

On April 23, 1932, a resolution by the Central Committee of the Communist Party dissolved all artistic societies and urged the cultural community to unite in professional corporations—"all-Russian unions"—of writers, artists, composers, and so on. Because these unions were controlled by the Party bureaucracy rather than "proletarian" artistic organizations, such as RAPKh (Russian Association of Proletarian Artists), which were scapegoated for usurping the Party's commanding role, the regime was able to get rid of the remnants of intellectual pluralism and simultaneously to produce the impression that cultural life was returning to normal. In 1934, at the First Congress of Soviet Writers, Socialist Realism was proclaimed the keystone of Soviet literature, and a similar aesthetic was instantly extended to the other arts. For a while, Socialist Realism, which was discussed as a "style" in the Wölfflinian sense, stimulated criticism's interest in monumental and decorative art and even led to the publication of several of Matisse's letters in the Soviet press.* Later, though, official theory labeled Socialist Realism a "creative method" in order to hide the derivative nature of its formal language.

On January 28, 1936, *Pravda,* the central Party newspaper, began publishing a series of anonymous articles attacking formalism in the arts. The first two were aimed at the composer Dmitrii Shostakovich. On the first day of March, an article, "On Dauber Artists," leveled a demagogic critique at a number of illustrators of children's books, with Vladimir Lebedev as the main target. Although officially the new campaign was directed against both formalism and naturalism, its chief target was the former, which in effect had always been regarded as the product of Western influence.

This campaign marked the point of no return for artistic discourse: an accusation of "formalism" (i.e., following Western models) became life-threatening and could be followed by the accused's extermination. The KGB files of Nikolai Punin, who was arrested in 1949 and died in the GULAG four years later, reveal that Punin's overt defense of Cézanne and Picasso had been considered a political sin.†

The abolition of the Museum of Modern Western Art during the xenophobic campaign "against adulation of the West" was the definitive end to the extremely productive relationship between Russian and Western art that dated back to the 1890s.

*See letters to Alexander Romm on the painter's work for Barnes, in *Iskusstvo* (Art) 4 (1934); also in *Matisse on Art,* edited by Jack Flam (Berkeley and Los Angeles, 1995), 113–18.

†Leonid Zykov, "Nikolai Punin. Materialy sledstviia i pis'ma iz lageria" (Nikolai Punin. Materials of the Investigation and Letters from [Prison] Camp), *Russkaia mysl'* (Russian Thought) (Paris, July 8–14, 1999): 12.

129

Polikarp Lebedev

"Against Formalism in Soviet Art" (1936)

Polikarp Lebedev (1904–81) was an art critic and a functionary of the Party's Central Committee. In February 1948 he became the head of the Soviet government's Art Committee, and in 1954 director of the State Tretiakov Gallery. This article was published in the Party's theoretical journal, *Pod znamenem marksizma* (Under Marxism's Banner) 6 (1936).

. . . Formalist art develops amid capitalist decline and decay. From the late nineteenth century and through the twentieth, the artistic life of the West has been marked by the creation of a great many trends, one after another: Impressionism, Neo-Impressionism, Symbolism, Fauvism, Dadaism, Cubism, Futurism, and so on and so forth. Their rapid appearance and disappearance is explained by the fact that none of them had any basis in real life.

The beginning of bourgeois art's decline was reflected as early as the 1870s and 1880s, in the worldview and works of the Impressionists. . . . The Impressionists' worldview coincides perfectly with the philosophy of subjective idealism. Art for them is not a means of cognizing and representing the real world and social relations; on the contrary, they value the subjective and incidental. Art is merely the expression of the artist's transitory subjective impressions at a given moment and in a given emotional state.

All their attention is concentrated on color and on presenting on canvas subtle color combinations conveying light, atmosphere, and so on. Lines marking the boundaries of objects disappear, humans are eliminated, and the human figures that do occur in portraits or pictures serve merely as occasions for demonstrating properties of color. The Impressionists maintain that "if a head is illuminated from one side by an orange color and by blue indoor light from the other, green reflections are bound to appear on the nose and the middle of the face," so that contrary to all common sense the Impressionist artist will paint the nose green. . . .

Thus, for the Impressionists, as for the Machists, the real world becomes a "set of sensations," a set of visual sensations expressed in accordance with the artist's emotional state. . . .

Our formalists have been imitators of Western formalism since before the Revolution. In Russia, the Jack of Diamonds, Donkey's Tail, Futurists, Cubo-Futurists, Non-Objectivists, and so on have been far removed from the struggle of the proletariat and the problems of real life. Like their Western brethren, they have ignored the revolutionary struggle of the working class and eliminated real people and their social life from art. Besides admiring the negative aspects of contemporary bourgeois art, all of our formalists, including those of the "left," have typically disregarded our genuine artistic heritage. . . .

At the Seventeenth Party Congress, Comrade Stalin declared, "The Seventeenth Conference of our Party has determined that the basic political tasks of the Second

Five-Year Plan include 'overcoming the survivals of capitalism in people's minds.' This is an absolutely correct thought. But can it be said that we have already overcome all such survivals in economics? No, this cannot be said. It is all the less possible to say that we have overcome the survivals of capitalism in people's minds. This cannot be said not only because people's minds lag in development behind the economic situation, but also because there still exists a capitalist encirclement that is attempting to revive and support the survivals of capitalism in economics and in people's minds in the USSR and against which we Bolsheviks must always keep our powder dry."

The appearance of formalism in Soviet art is a survival of capitalism that is particularly hostile to socialism.

130

Nina Iavorskaia

"An Eyewitness Account of the Closing of the Museum of Modern Western Art" (1988)

The Museum of Modern Western Art became inaccessible after the outbreak of war in 1941. In 1949, during the chauvinistic and isolationist campaign attacking "adulation of the West," the museum was abolished and the collection divided between the Pushkin Museum in Moscow and the Hermitage in Leningrad.

Nina Iavorskaia (1902–92), Boris Ternovets's wife, was deputy director of the Museum of Modern Western Art from 1944 to 1948. This recollection appeared in *Dekorativnoe iskusstvo SSSR* (Decorative Art of the USSR) 7 (1988).

. . . The museum staff attempted to organize public opinion in the museum's defense. True, even then this was very difficult. Everyone was frightened, and many prominent public figures had lost all their authority.

Further events developed as follows.

The Arts Committee issued an order to open the museum exposition immediately (practically overnight). The order was carried out, although large works such as Matisse's *Music* and *Dance* could not be displayed because they were still rolled up after the reevacuation. Two reviewers from the Council of People's Commissars, Kardashev and Abolimov (I'm not exactly sure of the surnames . . .), came to the museum. . . . We spoke with them for five hours, explaining the museum's work thoroughly and familiarizing them with the project for its reorganization. At the end of our conversation I asked their opinion as to the rumors circulating about the museum's possible closure, to which they answered unanimously that their opinion coincided with that of all cultured people.

At this point the museum director returned, and they reiterated their opinion to him, adding that they were moved by the love the staff displayed for its work.

Their conclusion reassured us, and we assumed that it was worth something.

The following day we were visited by M. Khrapchenko,* who headed the Arts Committee, and P. M. Sysoev. After viewing the exhibits they called for me and told me that K. E. Voroshilov would be arriving the next day and that I shouldn't even think of lobbying him. I was very surprised by this remark. I decided that their position must be extremely shaky.

One of the bosses, however, guessed that we were being "clever" and had not shown anything "risqué." . . . Again the telephone rings. A. K. Lebedev† commands that by eleven o'clock the following day (that is, before Voroshilov's arrival) Matisse's *Music* and *Dance* be unrolled and exhibited. I tried under various pretexts to prove why this could not be done: removing the paintings required restorers and there weren't any. But nothing helped. They found some restorers and both of Matisse's panels were laid out on the floor. True, next to them they put Jean-Paul Laurens's "realistic" canvas *The Execution of Maximilian.*‡

Voroshilov arrived with Aleksandr Gerasimov, Sysoev, P. I. Lebedev (Polikarp, who at this time was working in the Central Committee), and A. K. Lebedev. . . .

Everyone was jostling for a place next to Voroshilov. The reviewers I had spoken with earlier literally pushed me closer to him, while Gerasimov pushed me away. He managed to guide Voroshilov to the exhibit not from its beginning, as we had thought to do, but from the end, taking him directly to Matisse. Voroshilov took a look and let out a sound: "Heh, heh, heh," and the whole entourage echoed him: "Heh, heh, heh." Many years have passed, but this chorus of chuckles still rings in my ears. It paralyzed me, but I tried anyway to direct attention to other pictures as well, particularly to Laurence. But one of the visitors said, "Well of course there are also some like that, but they are not the main ones." They went on to Renoir. Voroshilov liked his *Nude,* but someone (perhaps A. K. Lebedev) said as he made a circular motion with his hand near Renoir's picture, "But here is where it begins, it starts here."

I must say that Voroshilov reacted negatively to far from all the works in the museum, but Gerasimov described everything devastatingly. After the viewing I asked Voroshilov what he thought. He didn't answer. . . .

For a while the situation remained unsettled. We did not close the exhibit and showed it to friends of the museum (although officially it was not open). An enormous number of artists and art scholars wanted to visit. . . .

Then the order to liquidate the museum came, signed by Stalin (it was said at the time that Molotov refused to sign, but I cannot vouch for that). A liquidation commission was formed that included me.

The museum section of the Arts Committee intended to scatter the works around various provincial museums and simply destroy some of them. The best would be

*Mikhail Khrapchenko (1904–86), head of the Arts Committee of the Soviet government (1939–48).

†Aleksei Lebedev, art historian, a functionary of the Academy of Fine Arts.

‡Jean-Paul Laurens, *The Last Moments of Maximilian, Emperor of Mexico,* (1882, Hermitage).

transferred to the Museum of Fine Arts and the Hermitage. It is difficult to convey the state we of the museum staff were experiencing.

My greatest desire under these conditions was that all of the works be sent to the Museum of Fine Arts and the Hermitage (rather than to provincial museums). I almost literally prayed to God that I. A. Orbeli,* the director of the Hermitage, would come, knowing that he would not break up the collection. What was my delighted surprise when I stepped into the office of S. D. Merkurov (then the director of the Museum of Fine Arts)† for a meeting of the commission and the first person I saw was Orbeli. I took him aside and begged him to take everything the MFA did not want. He replied that he had received the same instructions from A. N. Izergina (then working in the Hermitage's Western art section),‡ who when she heard about the threat to our museum compelled Orbeli to come to Moscow.

The distribution of the works began. Most active from the MFA were B. R. Vipper and A. D. Chegodaev.** True, owing to the subjective peculiarities of the latter's taste the most pungent of Matisse's pictures and also those of Picasso were rejected by the MFA and consequently ended up in Leningrad. . . .

According to A. I. Leonov's memoirs, Gerasimov once told him, "If anyone dares to exhibit Picasso, I'll have him hanged." These words were uttered by the first president of the Soviet Academy of Arts.

*Iosif Orbeli (1887–1961), director of the Hermitage (1934–51).

†Sergei Merkurov (1881–1952), sculptor, creator of monuments of Lenin and Stalin, director of the Pushkin Museum.

‡Antonina Izergina (1906–69), curator of the Hermitage, Orbeli's common-law wife.

**Boris Wipper (1888–1967) and Andrei Chegodaev (1905–94), art historians.

CHRONOLOGY

In this chronology, major political events are shown in bold, Western cultural events in italics, and Russian artistic events in regular type.

1861
Emancipation of the serfs in Russia.

1870
The Society of Traveling Art Exhibitions (Wanderers) is founded; their first exhibition is in 1871.

1874
First Impressionist exhibition, Paris.

1878
Emile Zola publishes his reviews on the Impressionists in the influential liberal St. Petersburg monthly magazine *Vestnik Evropy* (Messenger of Europe).

1881
March 1: Emperor Alexander II is assassinated, and his son, Alexander III, comes to power (1881–94).

1888
First exhibition of French art in St. Petersburg.

1891
January: "French Industrial and Artistic Exhibition," St. Petersburg (to Moscow in May).

1892
Munich Secession is founded (Vienna and Berlin Secessions are founded in 1897 and 1898, respectively).
August: Pavel Tretiakov, who started collecting in 1856, donates his collection of Russian Realist art and the collection of his brother Sergei, which includes paintings by French Realist artists, to the city of Moscow.

1893
Nikolai Mikhailovskii, "Russian Reflection of French Symbolism," *Russkoe bogatstvo* (Russian Wealth) 2 (1893), considers Russian "decadence" an outcome of Western influence.
May 1: Chicago World's Fair, where Russia has a pavilion, opens.

1894
Nicholas II comes to power (1894–1917).
Alexandre Benois's survey of Russian art is published in the third volume of Richard Muter's *Geschichte der Malerei im XIX. Jahrhundert* (Munich).

1896
A group of Russian artists participates in the Munich Secession. A few young Russian artists study in Munich, among them Vasily Kandinsky, Igor' Grabar', Dmitrii Kardovskii, and, later, Aleksei von Jawlensky and Marianne von Werefkin.
November: French art exhibition in St. Petersburg (to Moscow in December), with paintings from Bernheim-Jeune's collection (Ingres, Corot, Millet, Courbet, et al.); its contemporary section consists of Salon artists and a few works by the Impressionists (Monet, Renoir, Sisley) and Puvis de Chavannes.

1897
March: "Exhibition of English and German Water-Color Painters," organized by Sergei Diaghilev, St. Petersburg.

October: "Scandinavian Exhibition," organized by Diaghilev, St. Petersburg (more than 70 artists). Anders Zorn visits Russia.
November: "First International Exhibition of Artistic Posters" (Steinlen, Forain, Mucha, et al.).

1898

January: "Exhibition of Russian and Finnish Artists," the first exhibition of the World of Art society, St. Petersburg. English art exhibition, St. Petersburg (to Moscow in March).
March: Museum of Alexander III (later, the State Russian Museum) is founded.
May–June: Eighteen Russian and Finnish artists participate in the Munich Secession with 120 paintings; Levitan and Serov are elected members of the Secession.
November: *Mir iskusstva* (World of Art) is founded (publishes until 1904). *Iskusstvo i khudozhestvennaia promyshlennost'* (Art and Artistic Industry) is founded (publishes until 1901); its editor Nikolai Sobko follows Vladimir Stasov's anti-modernist approach. "First Belgian Art Exhibition," organized by the Society for the Encouragement of the Arts, St. Petersburg. Petr and Sergei Shchukin buy their first Impressionist painting from the Durand-Ruel gallery.

1899

January: "French Art and Artistic-Industrial Exhibition," St. Petersburg, presenting mostly Salon art.
January–February: "First International Art Exhibition," organized by Diaghilev, St. Petersburg (45 artists, including 23 Western artists).
November to January 1900: "Austro-Hungarian Art Exhibition" opens in St. Petersburg.

1900

February: "All-German Art Exhibition" opens in Moscow (to St. Petersburg in May) (400 works).
April: World's Fair in Paris. Exhibitions of French art of the nineteenth century and the last ten years.
November–December: Part of the Art Section of the 1900 Paris World's Fair exhibition is shown at the St. Petersburg Society for the Encouragement of the Arts.

1902

February: "Italian Artistic and Industrial Exhibition," St. Petersburg.
June: Alexandre Benois, *History of Russian Painting in the Nineteenth Century,* a major modernist history of the national school, is published.

1903

"Salon d'Automne" is established in Paris.
January: "French Art Exhibition" at the Society for the Encouragement of the Arts, St. Petersburg (includes Bougereau, Carolus-Duran).
December: First exhibition of the Union of Russian Artists, Moscow; the World of Art (reestablished as an independent organization in 1910) merges with it. Sergei Shchukin buys his first paintings by Cézanne (*Fruits,* 1879–80, Hermitage) and Gauguin. Ivan Morozov acquires his first Impressionist painting (Sisley, *Frost in Louveciennes,* Pushkin State Museum of Fine Arts).

1904

Vesy (Scales) is founded in Moscow (publishes until 1909), featuring European Symbolist art (Redon, Moreau, Vogeler, Beardsley, et al.).
January 27, 1904–September 5, 1905: Russo-Japanese War.

1905

The Die Brücke group is founded in Dresden, Germany.
January 9: Government troops shoot workers during demonstrations in St.

Petersburg ("Bloody Sunday"). First Russian Revolution (1905–7) begins.
March–April: Moscow-based *Iskusstvo* (Art), no. 2, publishes 24 reproductions of modern French painters from Sergei Shchukin's collection, including Monet, Cézanne, Gauguin, Van Gogh, Bonnard, Vuillard, and Denis.
October–November: Fauve paintings exhibited at "Salon d'Automne," Paris.
October 17: Nicholas II's manifesto introduces major political change by establishing the State Duma (Russian parliament) and proclaiming civil liberties.

1906

Russian art exhibition at "Salon d'Automne," organized by Diaghilev, covers Russian painting from icons to Symbolist art; many younger Russian participants visit Paris.
Zolotoe runo (Golden Fleece) is founded in Moscow (publishes regularly until 1909; last issue published in April 1910).
Sergei Shchukin buys his first Matisse painting (*Dishes on a Table,* 1900, Hermitage).
October–November: Gauguin retrospective at the "Salon d'Automne."

1907

Cézanne retrospective at the "Salon d'Automne."
Picasso paints Les Demoiselles d'Avignon.
January: Sergei Shchukin bequeaths his collection to the Tretiakov Gallery.
March: Symbolist exhibition, "The Blue Rose," Moscow.
October–November: Ivan Morozov commissions Maurice Denis to paint *The Story of Psyche* cycle for his Moscow home.

1908

Braque's one-man show at Kahnweiler's Gallery, Paris.
Matisse exhibition at the Kassirer Gallery, Berlin.
April–May: "Golden Fleece Salon," Moscow (Pissarro, Cézanne, Van Gogh, Gauguin, Matisse, Derain, Braque, Van Dongen, Metzinger, Le Fauconnier, Rouault, Gleizes, Redon, et al.).
May: Diaghilev's "Russian Week" in Paris. Russian artists (Kandinsky and Konchalovskii among them) participate in the "Salon d'Automne."

1909

Kandinsky organizes New Artists' Association (Neuen Künstlervereinigung) in Munich; founding members include A. Kubin, W. Bekhmeteff, M. von Werefkin, V. Izdebsky, G. Munter, and A. von Jawlensky.
Sergei Shchukin begins to buy works by Picasso (*Woman with a Fan,* 1909, Pushkin State Museum of Fine Arts).
January: Maurice Denis comes to Moscow to install his panels in Morozov's dining room; Morozov commissions four statues from Maillol for the same room.
January–February: Second *Golden Fleece* exhibition (Braque, Matisse, Vlaminck, Derain, Van Dongen, Manguin, Marquet, Le Fauconnier, et al.).
February 20: First Futurist Manifesto is published in Le Figaro.
March: Sergei Shchukin commissions *Dance* and *Music* from Matisse.
March–April: "Munich" exhibition (167 items, 82 artists: Lenbach, Stuck, Leibl, Liebermann, et al.), St. Petersburg.
May–June: First performance by Diaghilev's Ballets Russes in Paris.
October: First issue of *Apollon* (Apollo); publishes to 1917.
November: "Union of Youth" Society of Artists is founded in St. Petersburg by Elena Guro and Mikhail Matiushin (officially registered in February 1910).
December: Third *Golden Fleece* exhibition, Moscow (no foreign participants).
December 1909 to July 1910: "Interna-

tional Exhibition of Paintings, Sculpture, Prints and Drawing" (the so-called Izdebsky Salon), organized by Vladimir Izdebsky, opens in Odessa (to Kiev, February–March; St. Petersburg, April–May; Riga, June–July); foreign participants include Braque, Derain, Denis, Vlaminck, Matisse, Balla, Kandinsky, et al.

1910

Der Sturm *is founded in Berlin by Herwarth Walden.*
Matisse's *Dance* and *Music* poorly received at the "Salon d'Automne."
Morozov commissions a triptych from Bonnard (*On the Mediterranean,* 1911, Hermitage).
February: "Exhibition of Modern French Graphic Art," organized by *Apollon* (Apollo) magazine, St. Petersburg.
March: "Union of Youth" exhibition, St. Petersburg (Burliuk brothers, Mashkov, Exter, Larionov, Goncharova, et al.).
July: Exhibition of Russian painting at the Bernheim-Jeune Gallery, Paris (Leon Bakst, Alexandre Benois, Dobuzhinskii, Roerich, et al.).
October–November: Russian artists (including Kandinsky, Baranoff, Konchalovskii, and Mashkov) participate in the "Salon d'Automne."
November: "First Post-Impressionist Exhibition," London.
December: Matisse's *Dance* and *Music* are installed in Shchukin's house, Moscow.
December to January 1911: First "Jack of Diamonds" exhibition, Moscow (Kandinsky, Le Fauconnier, Gabriele Münter, Gleizes, et al.).

1911

The emerging Cubists exhibit at the "Salon des Indépendants" and "Salon d'Automne."
January: Mikhail Larionov and Natal'ia Goncharova organize a new group, Donkey's Tail, which holds its first exhibit the following spring.
February: In Berlin, Paul Cassirer exhibits works by Burliuk and other Russians.
February–May: "International Exhibition" (the second "Izdebsky Salon") in Odessa, Nikolaev, and Kherson includes new Western and Russian art (54 paintings by Kandinsky), with essays in the catalogue by Kandinsky and Arnold Schönberg.
October 16: First Cubist painting by Picasso is reproduced in the Russian press: *Lady with a Fan* (1908), in *Zerkalo* (Mirror).
October–November: Matisse comes to Moscow to reinstall his paintings in Shchukin's house and visits St. Petersburg.
December: At Second All-Russian Congress of Artists, St. Petersburg, Nikolai Kulbin presents Vasily Kandinsky's *Concerning the Spiritual in Art* (published in the proceedings of the Congress).
December: First exhibition of Der Blaue Reiter, *in Munich.*

1912

January: Kandinsky's Über das Geistige in der Kunst *is published in Munich.*
January: Second "Jack of Diamonds" exhibition, Moscow; Larionov's group does not participate; foreign exhibitors include Gleizes, Van Dongen, Derain, Delaunay, Camoin, Kandinsky, Kirchner, Léger, Matisse, Macke, Müller, Münter, Picasso, Pechstein, Le Fauconnier, Friez, and Heckel. Second *Blaue Reiter* exhibition, with graphics by Goncharova, Larionov, and Malevich.
January–March: "One Hundred Years of French Painting 1812–1912," organized by *Apollon* and the Institut Français de St. Pétersbourg; modern painting is represented by Manet (10 works), Monet (9), Renoir (24), Cézanne (17), Gauguin (21), et al.
February: Futurist exhibition at the Bernheim-Jeune Gallery, Paris.
February 12: Public debates on contemporary art organized by the Jack of

Diamonds at the Moscow Polytechnical Museum; Kulbin and Burliuk lecture on Cubism and other contemporary movements.
April: First issue of the "Union of Youth" Society of Artists miscellany *Soiuz molodezhi* (Union of Youth).
May: Der Blaue Reiter Almanac *is published in Munich.*
June: Second issue of *Union of Youth* is published.
July–August: Waldemar Matveis (Vladimir Markov) travels to Germany and France to study ethnographic museums and collect works for a Museum of Contemporary Art proposed by the Union of Youth.
October: "Second Post-Impressionist Exhibition," London (a Russian section organized by Boris Anrep includes Goncharova and Larionov). Albert Gleizes and Jean Metzinger, Du Cubisme, *is published in Paris.*
November: André Salmon, La jeune peinture française, *is published in Paris.*
November 23: Alexandre Benois publishes his polemical essay "Cubism or Hooliganism," in *Rech'* (Speech).
December: *A Slap in the Face of Public Taste,* the first collective volume by Russian Futurists, is published, along with a leaflet manifesto by the same name.

1913
"Exhibition of Contemporary French Painting," at the Art Salon, Moscow, including works by the Nabis, Fauves, and Cubists.
Collection of articles, *Bubnovyi valet* (Jack of Diamonds) is published in Moscow, including essays by Le Fauconnier and Apollinaire on Léger.
Winter: Guillaume Apollinaire, Les Peintres cubistes, *is published in Paris.*
February: Armory Show opens in New York (later to Chicago and Boston). Third "Jack of Diamonds" exhibition, Moscow; foreign participants include Braque, Derain, Picasso, Henri Rousseau, Signac, Vlaminck, and Le Fauconnier (to St. Petersburg in April with some works added). Last exhibition of the Union of Youth.
March: Exhibition of icons organized by the Moscow Archeological Institute.
"Target" exhibition in Moscow, organized by Larionov (Goncharova, Ledantiu, Malevich, Shevchenko, et al.), where the first Rayonnist works are presented; includes a section of old Russian icon designs and Russian and Oriental folk prints *(lubki).*
Summer: Iakov Tugendkhol'd, *Apollon's* leading Paris correspondent, returns to Moscow from Europe, where he has lived since 1902.
August: Goncharova's one-woman show, Moscow.
October: Karl Ernst Osthaus, director of the Volkwang Museum (Hagen, Germany), visits Shchukin's collection.
December 3 and 5: *Victory over the Sun,* a Futurist opera by Aleksei Kruchenykh and Mikhail Matiushin, with stage design by Malevich, is performed in St. Petersburg.
December 22: Aleksandr Smirnov lectures on Simultaneism and presents *La Prose du transsibérien et la petite Jeanne de France,* by Blaise Cendrars, illustrated by Sonia Delaunay-Terk, at the Stray Dog cabaret, St. Petersburg.

1914
January 1: Iakulov, Livshits, and Lourie publish their manifesto, "We and the West."
January 26–February 17: Marinetti visits Moscow and St. Petersburg.
February: Fourth "Jack of Diamonds" exhibition, Moscow (Braque, Derain, Picasso, La Fauconnier, Vlaminck, et al.). "No. 4" exhibition of Larionov's group (Larionov, Goncharova, Chekrygin, Shevchenko, Exter, Kamenskii, et al.).
February 15: Russian Futurists start a critical polemic and publish an anti-Marinetti letter in *Nov'* (Virgin Soil).

March: Vladimir Tatlin visits Picasso's studio in Paris.
May 1: "Free International Futurist Exhibition" at the Sprovieri Gallery, Rome; the Russian section includes Rozanova, Kulbin, Exter, and Arkhipenko.
June: Larionov and Goncharova exhibition in Paris; Apollinaire writes an essay for the catalogue.
August 1: Russia enters World War I.
November: Kandinsky, Chagall, and other Russian artists return to Russia from Europe.

1915

Julius Meier-Graefe is taken prisoner of war and spends several months in Russia, first near Moscow, later in Siberia (Omsk); Shchukin helps him during his captivity.
Summer: Larionov and Goncharova move to Lausanne, invited by Diaghilev; later they settle in Paris.
December: "The Last Futurist Exhibition of Paintings 0.10," Petrograd (includes Boguslavskaia, Kliun, Puni, Tatlin, and Men'kov; Malevich shows his Suprematist paintings for the first time).

1916

Zurich Dada's Cabaret Voltaire.
Kandinsky exhibition at the Der Sturm gallery, Berlin.

1917

February 27 (March 12, N.S.): Revolution in Russia.
Spring–Autumn: Emigrés familiar with contemporary Western art return to Russia, including art critic Anatolii Lunacharskii, painter David Shterenberg, sculptor Vladimir Izdebsky, and writer Ilya Ehrenburg.
April: "Exhibition of Finnish Art," Petrograd.
October 25–26 (November 7–8, N.S.): Bolshevik Revolution.

1918

January: Department of Visual Arts of the People's Commissariat of Enlightenment is established in St. Petersburg (head, David Shterenberg; members include Nikolai Punin, Natan Al'tman, and Vladimir Mayakovsky); the Moscow branch includes Vladimir Tatlin, Malevich, Kandinsky, Sophia Dymshits-Tolstaia, Rozanova, Udal'tsova, and Shevchenko.
January–February: Armed uprising of the Whites on the Don and in the Kuban (Northern Caucasus), starting the Civil War.
February 14 (February 1, O.S.): Russia adopts the Gregorian calendar.
March 3: Soviet delegation signs peace treaty with Germany and its allies in Brest (Belarus), whereby Russia quits the war.
March: Soviet government moves to Moscow.
August: Sergei Shchukin emigrates to France.
September: First All-Russian Conference of the Organizations of Proletarian Culture (Proletkult).
October 29: The Soviet government nationalizes Shchukin's collection.
Autumn: Ivan Morozov starts to reinstall his collection, which is opened to the public during the autumn and winter. Ludwig Baehr, a German artist and former prisoner of war, returns from Russia, bringing an "Appeal from Progressive Russian Artists to Their German Colleagues," which is published in the German press in early 1919.
November 9: Revolution in Germany, a republic proclaimed.
November 11: Armistice.
December: The Museum of Artistic Culture is founded in Petrograd.
December 19: Ivan Morozov's collection is nationalized.

1919
January: The International Bureau of the Department of Visual Arts of the People's Commissariat of Enlightenment is organized.
Spring: Shchukin's and Morozov's collections constitute the First and Second Museums of Modern Western Art, respectively.
March: The Third International (Communist International, Comintern) is established in Petrograd. The International Bureau works on *The International of Art* magazine (never published).
March 19: The Hungarian Soviet Republic is proclaimed in Budapest (lasts for 133 days).
June 28: A peace treaty is signed in Versailles, France, ending World War I.

1920
February 2: The Soviet-Estonian peace treaty is signed, ending the Soviet Republic's political isolation.
May: First exhibition of the Society of Young Artists (ObMoKhU). The Institute of Artistic Culture (INKhUK) is established in Moscow.
June–August: Dada-Messe, Berlin.
August: "The Realistic Manifesto" is issued for the Naum Gabo and Anton (Antoine) Pevsner exhibition, Moscow.
November: Red Army occupies the Crimea; Civil War ends in European Russia.
November 8: Vladimir Tatlin exhibits his *Monument to the Third International* in Petrograd (to Moscow in December).

1921
January–May: Igor' Grabar' takes part in Polish-Soviet negotiations in Riga, Latvia, as a museum expert and brings recent publications on Western art back to Moscow.
February 21: Lenin visits the VKhUTEMAS student commune and criticizes avant-garde movements.
March 17: Lenin proclaims the New Economic Policy (NEP), a liberalization of the Bolshevik regime.
April: The Department of Painting of the Museum of Painterly Culture opens in Petrograd (exhibition, "From Impressionism to Cubism"); Malevich becomes the director in 1922.
May–June: Second ObMoKhU exhibition.
September: "5 × 5 + 25" exhibition in Moscow (Varvara Stepanova, Aleksandr Vesnin, Liubov' Popova, Aleksandr Rodchenko, Alexandra Exter).
October: Russian (later State) Academy of Artistic Sciences established (RAKhN-GAKhN).
November: INKhUK meeting rejects easel painting in favor of construction and industrial design (Rodchenko, Popova, Brik); a group of easel painters leaves INKhUK (Ivan Kliun, Nadezhda Udal'tsova, Aleksandr Drevin).
December 8: Hungarian émigré art critic Alfred Kemeni (Durus) gives a lecture, "New Trends in Contemporary German and Russian Art," at INKhUK, Moscow.

1922
April: First issue of *Veshch'* (Object), an international review of contemporary art edited by Ilya Ehrenburg and El Lissitsky, is published in Berlin in Russian, German, and French.
April 16: Russian-German treaty signed in Rapallo, Italy, during the Genoa Peace Conference.
May: Association of Artists of Revolutionary Russia (AKhRR) is established.
June 20: Soviet government decides to organize a German art exhibition in Moscow (held in 1924).
June 22–July 12: Third Congress of the Comintern, Moscow and Petrograd; delegates include the artists Sandor Ek and Bela Uitz (Hungary), Peter Alma (Netherlands), and Krum Kuliavkov (Bulgaria).

Summer: George Grosz spends several weeks in Murmansk, Moscow, and Petrograd, traveling with Danish writer Martin Andersen Neksø.
Autumn: Kandinsky moves to Germany, teaches at the Bauhaus.
October 15: "Die Erste Russische Kunstausstellung" at the Galerie Van Diemen, Berlin, the first exhibition of Soviet art abroad (157 artists, 750 items); in 1923 a shorter version of it goes on view in Amsterdam.
October–December: Vladimir Mayakovsky travels to Berlin and Paris (November 19–25) via Tallinn.
December 30: Union of Soviet Socialist Republics is established.

1923

The First and Second Museums of Modern Western Art officially merge as the State Museum of Modern Western Art.
"Exhibition of Contemporary German Books" opens in the Historical Museum, Moscow.
March: *Lef* (Left Front of Arts) is issued (publishes until 1925, later reestablished as *Noyvi* [New] *Lef,* 1927–28).
Spring: State Institute of Artistic Culture (GINKhUK) is established in Petrograd, with Malevich as director. Heinrich Vogeler travels through the Soviet Union with AKhRR's support, and his one-man show takes place in Moscow in March 1924; he remains in Russia until 1926 heading the Art Department of the Communist University of Western Nations in Moscow.

1924

January 21: Vladimir Lenin dies.
February: Great Britain recognizes the Soviet Union.
May–June: "First Discussion Exhibition of the Unions of Active Revolutionary Arts," Moscow.
June: "Fourteenth International Exhibition," Venice, with an extensive Soviet section (97 artists, 492 works).
October: "First All-German Art Exhibition" opens in the Historical Museum, Moscow, organized by the Central Committee of the International Workers' Relief (MezhRabPom) (to Saratov and Leningrad in 1925).
October 28: Diplomatic relations with France are established.
November 15: *Pravda* publishes a propaganda cartoon by Georges Grosz.

1925

"International Exhibition of Modern Industrial and Decorative Art," Paris; Soviet section includes Konstantin Mel'nikov's Constructivist pavilion of the USSR and Rodchenko's Workers' Club.
Society of Easel Painters (OST) is set up (Shterenberg, Deineka, Pimenov, et al.).
June 18: Declaration of the Central Committee of the Communist Party "On Party Policy in Literature," giving approval to stylistic pluralism.
Autumn: "German Art of the Last Fifty Years," taken from the collection of the State Museum of Modern Western Art, Moscow.

1926

Alexandre Benois finally settles in Paris.
May: "Revolutionary Art of the West," Picture Gallery of the Rumiantsev Museum, Moscow, organized by the State Academy of Artistic Sciences (GAKhN) and the All-Union Society for Foreign Cultural Contacts (VOKS).
Summer: AKhRR exhibition, "Life of the Peoples of the USSR," Moscow and Leningrad. Discussion of AKhRR is organized by the Leningrad-based weekly *Zhizn' iskusstva* (Life of Art).
Summer–Autumn: After a severe defamation campaign, GINKhUK in Leningrad is

banned and its collection moved to the State Russian Museum.
August: "Exhibition of Soviet Art," Tokyo (133 works).
September: "Contemporary English Print and Lithography," Museum of Fine Arts, Moscow.
December: Hungarian émigré artist Bela Uitz's one-man show, State Academy of Artistic Sciences, Moscow.
December–January 1927: Walter Benjamin visits Moscow.

1927

March–June: Malevich shows his art in Warsaw and Berlin, visits the Bauhaus, Dessau.
April: "Exhibition of Soviet Art," Tokyo (72 artists, 279 works).
April–September: Exhibition of new acquisitions at the State Museum of Modern Western Art (Vlaminck, Derain, Cocteau, Ozenfant, Modigliani, Picasso, Masereel, et al.).
October–November: A group of foreign artists (Käthe Kollwitz, Diego Rivera, William Gropper, and Louis Lozowick) takes part in the tenth-anniversary celebration of the October Revolution.
November 12: Trotsky is stripped of his positions and expelled from the Party.
December: Alfred H. Barr, Jr., director of the Museum of Modern Art, New York, visits Moscow.

1928

The Association of Artists of Revolutionary Russia (AKhRR) is renamed the Association of Revolutionary Artists (AKhR); the younger generation takes control of the organization.
The collections of the State Museum of Modern Western Arts are merged in the former Morozov mansion.
Le Corbusier visits Russia.
February: "10 Years of the Workers' and Peasants' Red Army," AKhRR's tenth exhibition, Moscow, including major non-AKhRR figurative artists.
March: Declaration of the October group is published in *Sovremennaia arkhitektura* (Contemporary Architecture).
July: Room of contemporary Italian drawing opens at the State Museum of Modern Western Art (de Chirico, Casorati, Tosi, Funi, et al.).
September–October: "Contemporary French Art," State Museum of Modern Western Art, Moscow, organized by the State Academy of Artistic Sciences, State Tretiakov Gallery, and Museum of Modern Western Art.
October: First Five-Year Plan starts.

1929

In 1929–31, according to government policy for rearranging the museums, the Hermitage gives a number of its paintings to the Museum of Fine Arts in Moscow and some of the Museum of Modern Western Art collection is moved to the Hermitage, including works by Cézanne, Gauguin, Monet, Van Gogh, Matisse, Derain, and Picasso; for the first time, a Leningrad public collection is able to show contemporary Western painting.
Le Corbusier visits Russia again.
January 31: Trotsky is deported from the USSR.
February: "Exhibition of Contemporary Art of Soviet Russia," New York (later to Philadelphia, Boston, Detroit).
August 19: Sergei Diaghilev dies in Venice.
September 12: Lunacharskii is removed as people's commissar of enlightenment.
Autumn: Defamation campaign against Boris Pil'niak and Evgenii Zamiatin, the leaders of non-Communist writers' organizations in Moscow and Leningrad, under the pretext that their books had been published abroad. Pil'niak recanted publicly and was allowed to travel to the United States in June 1931. Zamiatin

emigrates to France in October 1931, after writing a letter to Stalin.
October 29: "Black Tuesday," stock market crash, in New York. Great Depression begins in the West.
November 17: Nikolai Bukharin, previously criticized as a leader of the "right opposition," is expelled from the Politburo. Stalin takes full control of the Party and the country.
November 21: Capital punishment is introduced for defectors.
December 27: Stalin proclaims the policy of total collectivization and elimination of the kulaks (wealthy peasants).

1930

International Bureau of Revolutionary Artists is established.
April 14: Vladimir Mayakovsky commits suicide.
April–May: "Exhibition of German Industrial Graphics," Moscow.
May: "Exhibition-Demonstration" of the October group, Moscow (Klutsis, Lissitsky, Rodchenko, Telingater, et al.).
July–November: Belgian artist Frans Masereel's one-man show, State Museum of Modern Western Art, Moscow.
Autumn: Hannes Meyer, director of the Bauhaus (Dessau), is dismissed by the Nazi-dominated city council, settles in the Soviet Union, and seven of his pupils follow him; Meyer moves to Switzerland in 1937. Second Congress of Revolutionary Writers, Kharkov, Ukraine.

1931

Heinrich Vogeler moves to the USSR.
April: John Heartfield visits the Soviet Union.
May: Russian Association of Proletarian Artists (RAPKh) is established.
June–September: Exhibition of the Bauhaus (Dessau), related to Hannes Meyer's emigration, Moscow.
August–September: "Anti-Imperialist Exhibition," Park of Culture and Recreation, Moscow, organized by the Federation of Unions of Soviet Artists (FOSKh) (Kollwitz, Grosz, Dix, Steinlen, Masereel, and Gropper, with a special section devoted to the John Reed Club).
October: Exhibition of contemporary Austrian prints (155 works, 28 artists, including Oscar Kokoschka), Moscow.
November–December: John Heartfield's one-man show, organized by the All-Russian Union of Co-operative Comradeships of Visual Arts Workers (VseKoKhudozhnik), Moscow.

1932

Herwarth Walden emigrates to the Soviet Union and edits *Das Wort* magazine there; in 1941, he is arrested and dies in the Saratov prison.
March: John Reed Club exhibition, State Museum of Modern Western Art, Moscow (Lozowick, Refregier, Ellis, Gropper, David Burliuk, et al.). Heinrich Vogeler exhibition, State Museum of Modern Western Art, Moscow.
April 23: Central Committee of the Communist Party officially dissolves all artistic and literary groups, replacing them with the Union of Soviet Artists.
April–June: "Exhibition of Contemporary Dutch Art," State Museum of Modern Western Art, Moscow (20 artists).
May–June: Käthe Kollwitz retrospective, Moscow (142 prints).
November 13: "RSFSR Artists over the Last Fifteen Years," State Russian Museum, Leningrad (423 artists, including major leaders of the avant-garde); a shortened version of the exhibition moves to Moscow in June 1933.
November to February 1933: "Revolutionary Art in the Capitalist Countries," State Museum of Modern Western Art, Moscow, dedicated to the fifteenth anniversary of the October Revolution (Bela Uitz, George Grosz, Hans Grundig, Otto Dix, Käthe

Kollwitz, Otto Nagel, Max Pechstein, Conrad Felixmüller, a group of French political cartoonists, leftist American artists close to the John Reed Club, et al.).
Fall to early 1933: Famine in Ukraine and southern Russia, resulting from "collectivization."

1933

Maxim Gorky settles in Moscow, having lived in Germany, Czechoslovakia, and Italy since fall 1921, after a series of trips to the Soviet Union.
January 30: Adolf Hitler becomes chancellor of Germany.
April: Fred Ellis's one-man show, State Museum of Modern Western Art, Moscow (135 works).
October–November: Soviet-American diplomatic relations are established; William Bullitt and Aleksandr Troianovskii are appointed ambassadors.
November: "Exhibition of Contemporary Polish Art," State Tretiakov Gallery, Moscow.

1934

May–June: "Exhibition of Contemporary Latvian Art," VseKoKhudozhnik, Moscow (219 works, 38 artists).
August: Albert Marquet visits Moscow, Leningrad, Kharkov, DneproGES, and the Caucasus. Jean Lurçat visits Kharkov, Moscow, and Leningrad as head of the French Society of Friends of the USSR (Association française des amis de l'Union Soviétique).
August 17–September 1: First All-Union Congress of Soviet Writers approves "Socialist Realism" as the official doctrine.
September 18: Soviet Union joins the League of Nations.
November–December: "Exhibition of Finnish Art," Museum of Fine Arts, Moscow.
December 1: Sergei Kirov, Party leader of Leningrad, is assassinated; mass political purges ensue.

1935

March: "Exhibition of Contemporary Estonian Art," VseKoKhudozhnik, Moscow.
April: Frans Masereel visits Moscow; his exhibition is held in May–June at the State Museum of Modern Western Art.
August–September: Jacques Lipchitz visits Moscow and Leningrad.

1936

January 28: *Pravda* publishes an editorial, "Muddle Instead of Music," stigmatizing Dmitrii Shostakovich and launching the crusade against "Formalism."
March 1: *Pravda* publishes an editorial, "On Dauber Artists," against Vladimir Lebedev and contemporary children's book illustration, opening the anti-Formalist campaign in the visual arts.
June–September: Frans Masereel visits Moscow again and travels down the Volga to Transcaucasia.
August 19–24: The Moscow Trials begin with the "Trotskyist-Zinoviev's Terrorist Center" trial ("Trial of 16").
December 5: The Soviet Constitution is officially adopted.

ACRONYMS

AKhR	Association of Revolutionary Artists (1928–32)
AKhRR	Association of Artists of Revolutionary Russia
ARBKD/BRBKD	German Association of Revolutionary Artists/German Alliance of Revolutionary Artists
FOSKh	Federation of Unions of Soviet Artists
GAKhN	State Academy of Artistic Sciences
GINKhUK	State Institute of Artistic Culture
GMII	Pushkin State Museum of Fine Arts
GMNZI	State Museum of Modern Western Art
GTG	State Tretiakov Gallery
INKhUK	Institute of Artistic Culture
IZO	Visual Arts (department of Narkompros)
Lef	Left Front of Arts
Mezhrabpom	International Workers Relief
Narkompros	People's Commissariat of Enlightenment
ObMoKhU	Society of Young Artists
OMAKhR	Society of Youth of the Association of Revolutionary Artists
Opoyaz	Society for the Study of Poetic Language
OST	Society of Easel Painters
Proletkult	Organizations of Proletarian Culture
RANION	Russian Association of Scientific Research Institutes in the Social Sciences
RAPKh	Russian Association of Proletarian Artists
VKhUTEIN	Higher Artistic-Technological Institute
VKhUTEMAS	Higher Art and Technical Studios
VOKS	All-Union Society for Foreign Cultural Contacts
VseKoKhudozhnik	All-Russian Union of Co-Operative Comradeships of Visual Arts Workers

SELECTED BIBLIOGRAPHY

Adkins, Helen. "Erste Russische Kunstausstellung," in *Stationen der Moderne, Die bedeutenden Kunstausstellungen des 20. Jahrhunderts in Deutschland.* Berlin: Berlinische Galerie, Museum für Moderne Kunst, Photographie und Architektur, 1988.

Aleshina, L. S., and Iavorskaia, N. V. *Iz istorii khudozhestvennoi zhizni SSSR: Internatsional'nye sviazi v oblasti izobrazitel'nogo iskusstva, 1917–1940: Materialy i dokumenty* (From the History of the Artistic Life of the USSR: International Relations in the Visual Arts, 1917–1940: Materials and Documents). Moscow: Iskusstvo, 1987.

Antonowa, Irina, and Merkert, Jörn, eds. *Berlin Moskau, 1900–1950 = Moskva Berlin, 1900–1950.* Munich and New York: Prestel, 1995.

Bann, Stephen, and Bowlt, John E., eds. *Russian Formalism: A Collection of Articles and Texts in Translation.* New York: Barnes and Noble, 1973.

Barr, Alfred, Jr. *Matisse: His Art and His Public.* New York: Museum of Modern Art, 1951.

———. "Russian Diary, 1927–28," *October* (Winter 1978): 10–51.

Barron, Stephanie, and Tuchman, Maurice, eds. *The Avant-Garde in Russia, 1910–1930: New Perspectives.* Los Angeles: Los Angeles County Museum of Art, 1980.

Basner, Elena. "Malevich's Painting in the Collection of the Russian Museum (The Matter of the Artist's Creative Evolution)," in *Kazimir Malevich in the Russian Museum.* St. Petersburg: Palace Editions, 2000.

Benjamin, Walter. "Moscow [1927]," in Walter Benjamin, *Reflections: Essays, Aphorisms, Autobiographical Writings,* edited and with an introduction by Peter Demetz. New York: Harcourt Brace Jovanovich, 1978.

———. "Moscow Diary," *October* (Winter 1985).

Benois, Alexandre. *The Russian School of Painting,* introduction by Christian Brinton. New York: Knopf, 1916.

Blakesley, Rosalind P., and Reid, Susane, eds. *Russian Art and the West: A Century of Dialogue in Painting, Architecture, and the Decorative Arts.* De Kalb: Northern Illinois University Press, 2006.

Bowlt, John E. *The Silver Age: Russian Art of the Early Twentieth Century and the "World of Art" Group.* 2nd ed. Newtonville, Mass.: Oriental Research Partners, 1982.

———. "Hungarian Activism and the Russian Avant-Garde," in S. A. Mansbach, *Standing in the Tempest: Painters of Hungarian Avant-Garde,* pp. 143–67. Cambridge, Mass., and London: Santa Barbara Museum of Art and MIT Press, 1991.

———. "The Cow and the Violin: Toward a History of Russian Dada," in *The Eastern Dada Orbit: Russia, Georgia, Ukraine, Central Europe and Japan,* edited by Gerald Janecek and Toshiharu Omuka, pp. 137–63. *Crisis and the Arts: The History of Dada,* vol. 4. New York: G. K. Hall and Prentice Hall International, 1998.

———, ed. *Russian Art of the Avant-Garde: Theory and Criticism, 1902–1934,* translated by John E. Bowlt. New York: Viking, 1976.

Bowlt, John E., and Drutt, Matthew. *Amazons of the Avant-Garde: Alexandra Exter, Natalia Goncharova, Liubov Popova, Olga Rozanova, Varvara Stepanova, and Nadezhda Udaltsova.* New York: Guggenheim Museum; London: Thames and Hudson, 2000.

Bown, Matthew Cullerne. *Socialist Realist Painting.* New Haven: Yale University Press, 1998.
Bullen, J. B. *Post-Impressionists in England.* London: Routledge, 1988.
Dabrowsky, Magdalena. "Tatlin and Cubism," *Source* (Spring–Summer 1992): 39–52.
Dorontchenkov, Ilia. "Picasso in Russia at the Turn of the 1920s: On the History of Perception," *Kulturologia: The Petersburg Journal of Cultural Studies* (St. Petersburg and Petrozavodsk) 3 (1993): 69–80.
———. "Against the Cult of the French: Modern Western Art and Cultural Politics in the Early Stalin Era," *Zimmerli Journal* (Fall 2006): 32–51.
Douglas, Charlotte. "The New Russian Art and Italian Futurism," *Art Journal* (Spring 1975): 229–39.
———. *Swans of the Other Worlds: Kazimir Malevich and the Origins of Abstraction in Russia.* Ann Arbor, Mich.: UMI Research Press, 1976.
Durfee, Thea. "Natalia Goncharova," and Natalia Goncharova, "Letter to the Editor," *Experiment* 1 (1995): 159–63.
Flam, Jack. *Matisse on Art.* Berkeley and Los Angeles: University of California Press, 1995.
———, with Miriam Deutch, eds. *Primitivism and Twentieth-Century Art: A Documented History.* Berkeley: University of California Press, 2003.
Flint, Kate, ed. *Impressionists in England: The Critical Reception.* London and Boston: Routledge & Kegan Paul, 1984.
Gamwell, Lynn. *Cubist Criticism.* Ann Arbor, Mich.: UMI Research Press, 1980.
Garafola, Lynn, and Van Norman Baer, Nancy, eds. *"The Ballets Russes" and Its World.* New Haven and London: Yale University Press, 1999.
Gassner, Hubertus. "Heartfield's Moscow Apprenticeship 1931–32," in *John Heartfield,* edited by Peter Pachnicke and Klaus Honnef, pp. 256–87. New York: Abrams, 1992.
Gassner, Hubertus, and Gillen, Eckhart, eds. *Zwischen Revolutionkunst ind Socialistischem Realismus: Dokumente und Kommentare Kunstdebatten in der Sowjetunion von 1917 bis 1934.* Cologne: Du Mont Buchverlag, [1979].
Gogen: Vzgliad iz Rossii (Gauguin: The View from Russia). Moscow: Sovetskii Khudozhnik, 1990.
Gray, Camilla. *The Russian Experiment in Art, 1863–1922.* Revised and enlarged edition by Marian Burleich-Motley. London: Thames and Hudson, 1990.
The Great Utopia: The Russian and Soviet Avant-Garde, 1915–1932. New York: Guggenheim Museum, 1992.
Grosz, George. *An Autobiography,* translated by Nora Hodges. Foreword by Barbara McCloskey. Berkeley: University of California Press, 1998.
Henderson, Linda Dalrymple. *The Fourth Dimension and Non-Euclidean Geometry in Modern Art.* Princeton: Princeton University Press, 1983.
Hilton, Alison. "The Impressionist Vision in Russia and Eastern Europe," in *World Impressionism, the International Movement, 1860–1920,* edited by Norma Broude. New York: Abrams, 1990.
———. "Holiday in the Kolkhoz: Socialist Realism's Dialogue with Impressionism," in *Russian Art and the West: A Century of Dialogue in Painting, Architecture, and the Decorative Arts,* edited by Rosalind P. Blakesley and Susane Reid, pp. 195–216. De Kalb: Northern Illinois University Press, 2006.
Howard, Jeremy. *The Union of Youth: An Artists' Society of the Russian Avant-Garde.* Manchester and New York: Manchester University Press, 1992.

Ingold, Felix, ed. *Picasso in Russland: Materialien zur Wirkungsgeschichte, 1913–1971.* Zurich: Verlag der Arche, 1973.
Jackson, David. "Western Art and Russian Ethics," *Russian Review* (July 1998): 394–409.
Janecek, Gerald. *The Look of Russian Literature: Avant-Garde Visual Experiments, 1900–1930.* Princeton: Princeton University Press, 1984.
Jensen, Robert. *Marketing Modernism in* Fin-de-Siècle *Europe.* Princeton: Princeton University Press, 1994.
Kandinsky, Wassily. *Complete Writings on Art,* edited by Kenneth C. Lindsay and Peter Vergo. 2 vols. Boston: G. K. Hall, 1982.
———, and Marc, Franz, eds. *The "Blaue Reiter" Almanac,* edited and with an introduction by Klaus Lankheit. New documentary edition. New York: Viking Press, 1974.
Kean, Beverly Whitney. *All the Empty Palaces: The Merchant Patrons of Modern Art in Pre-Revolutionary Russia.* New York: Universe Books, 1983.
Kelly, Catriona, ed. *Utopias: Russian Modernist Texts 1905–1940.* London: Penguin Books, 1999.
Kennedy, Janet. *The "Mir Iskusstva" Group and Russian Art, 1898–1912.* New York: Garland, 1977.
———. "Pride and Prejudice: Serge Diaghilev, the *Ballet Russes,* and the French Public," in *Art, Culture, and National Identity in Fin-de-Siècle Europe,* edited by Michelle Facos and Sharon L. Hirsh, pp. 90–118. Cambridge: Cambridge University Press, 2003.
Kiaer, Christina. "Rodchenko in Paris," *October* (Winter 1996): 3–35.
Klimov, Pavel Y. "Puvis de Chavannes and Russia," in *Toward Modern Art: From Puvis de Chavannes to Matisse and Picasso,* edited by Serge Lemoine, pp. 227–37. New York: Rizzoli, 2002.
Kostenevich, Albert. *French Art Treasures at the Hermitage: Splendid Masterpieces, New Discoveries.* New York: Abrams, 1999.
———. "Moscow's Two Great Collectors: Shchukin and Morozov," in *Russia!: Nine Hundred Years of Masterpieces and Master Collections,* pp. 238–50. New York: Guggenheim Museum; London: Thames and Hudson, 2005.
———. "Russian Clients of Ambroise Vollard," in *Cézanne to Picasso: Ambroise Vollard, Patron of the Avant-Garde,* edited by Rebecca A. Rabinow, pp. 243–56. New York: Metropolitan Museum of Art; New Haven: Yale University Press, 2006.
Kostenevich, Albert, and Semyonova, Natalia. *Collecting Matisse.* Paris: Flammarion, 1993.
Lawton, Anna. *Vadim Shershenevich: From Futurism to Imaginism.* Ann Arbor: Ardis, 1981.
Le Dantiu, Mikhail. "The Painting of Everythingists," *Experiment* 1 (1995).
Lewis, Beth Irwin. *George Grosz: Art and Politics in Weimar Republic.* Princeton: Princeton University Press, 1971.
Lissitzky, El. "The Conquest of Art" (1922), in *El Lissitzky, 1890–1941,* pp. 59–61. Cambridge: Harvard University Art Museum, Busch-Reisinger Museum, 1987.
Lissitzky-Küppers, Sophie. *El Lissitzky: Life, Letters, Texts.* London: Thames and Hudson, 1968.
Lunacharsky, Anatoly. *On Literature and Art,* translated by Avril Pyman and Fainna Glagoleva. 2nd rev. ed. Moscow: Progress, 1973.
Lushchnik, Sergei. "Vladimir Izdebsky's Salons," in *Vladimir Izdebsky: The Return Cycle,* pp. 43–59. St. Petersburg: Palace Editions, 2005.

Malevich, K. S. *Essays on Art, 1915–1933,* edited by Troels Andersen, translated by Xenia Glowacki-Prus and Arnold McMillin. 2 vols. London: Rapp and Whiting; Chester Springs, Pa.: Dufour, 1969.

———. *The World as Non-Objectivity: Unpublished Writings, 1922–25,* edited by Troels Andersen, translated by Xenia Glowacki-Prus and Arnold McMillin. Copenhagen: Borgen, 1976.

———. *The Artist, Infinity, Suprematism. Unpublished Writings 1913–33,* edited by Troels Andersen, translated by Xenia Glowacki-Prus and Arnold McMillin, vol. 4. Copenhagen: Borgen, 1978.

Markov, Vladimir. *Russian Futurism: A History.* Berkeley: University of California Press, 1968.

———. "Russian Expressionism," in *Expressionism as an International Literary Phenomenon,* edited by Ulrich Weisstein. Paris: Didier, 1973.

Markova, Viktoria. "Hollow Laughter," *The Art Newspaper* 40 (1994).

McCloskey, Barbara. *George Grosz and the Communist Party: Art and Radicalism in Crisis, 1918 to 1936.* Princeton: Princeton University Press, 1997.

McCully, Marilyn, ed. *A Picasso Anthology: Documents. Criticism. Reminiscences.* Princeton: Princeton University Press, 1981.

Mickiewicz, Denis, "*Apollo* and Modernist Poetics," *Russian Literature Triquarterly* (Fall 1971).

Milner, John. *Vladimir Tatlin and the Russian Avant-Garde.* New Haven: Yale University Press, 1983.

"Mir iskusstva": On the Centenary of the Exhibition of Russian and Finnish Artists, 1898. St. Petersburg: Palace Editions, 1998.

Monas, Sidney, and Krupala, Jennifer Greene, eds. *The Diaries of Nikolay Punin: 1904–1953,* translated by Jennifer Greene Krupala. Austin: University of Texas Press, 1999.

Morozov, Shchukin: The Collectors: Monet to Picasso: 120 Masterpieces from the Hermitage, St. Petersburg, and the Pushkin Museum, Moscow. Cologne: DuMont, 1993.

Mukhina, T. D. *Russko-skandinavskie khudozhestvennye sviazi kontsa XIX–nachala XX v.* (Russian-Scandinavian Artistic Relations of the Late Nineteenth and Early Twentieth Centuries). Moscow: Moscow University Publishers, 1984.

Nachtigäller, Roland, and Gassner, Hubertus. "3 x 1 = 1. Vešc'. Objet. Gegenstand," in *Vešc'. Objet. Gegenstand. Berlin 1922 Herausgegeben von Il'ja Erenburg, El Lisickij: Komentar und Übertragungen.* Reprint ed. Baden: Verlag Lars Müller, 1994.

Nesterova, Yelena. *The Itinerants: The Masters of Russian Realism, Second Half of the 19th and Early 20th Centuries.* Bournemouth: Parkstone; St. Petersburg: Aurora, 1996.

Origins of the Russian Avant-Garde: Celebrating the 300th Anniversary of St. Petersburg. St. Petersburg: Palace Editions, 2003.

Paris-Moscou, 1900–1930: Arts Plastiques, Arts Appliqués et Objets Utilitaires, Architecture, Urbanisme, Agitprop, Affiche, Théâtre, Ballet, Littérature, Musique, Cinéma, Photo Créative. Paris: Centre Georges Pompidou, Gallimard, 1991.

Parton, Anthony. *Mikhail Larionov and the Russian Avant-Garde.* Princeton: Princeton University Press, 1993.

Plekhanov, G[eorge]. V. *Art and Society,* translated by Paul S. Leitner, Alfred Goldstein, and C. H. Crout, introduction by Granville Hicks. New York: Critics Group, 1936.

———. *Art and Social Life,* translated by A. Fineberg. London: Lawrence & Wishart, 1974.

Pol' Sezann i russkii avangard nachala XX veka (Paul Cézanne and the Russian Avant-Garde of the Early Twentieth Century], edited by A. G. Kostenevich. Exhibition catalogue. St. Petersburg: Slavia, 1998.

Poliakov, Vladimir. *Knigi russkogo kubofuturizma* (Books of Russian Cubo-Futurism). Moscow: Gileia, 1998; 2nd ed., 2007.

Pospelov, Gleb. *Moderne Russische Malerei. Die Künstlergrupps Karo-Bube.* Stuttgart: Kohlhammer, 1985.

Pyman, Avril. *A History of Russian Symbolism.* Cambridge: Cambridge University Press, 1994.

Richardson, John, with Marilyn McCully. *A Life of Picasso,* vols. 1–2. New York: Random House, 1991, 1996.

Richardson, William. Zolotoe Runo *and Russian Modernism: 1905–1910.* Ann Arbor, Mich.: Ardis, 1986.

———. "The Dilemmas of a Communist Artist: Diego Rivera in Moscow, 1927–1928," *Mexican Studies* (Winter 1987): 49–69.

Rizzi, Daniela, "Artisti e literati russi negli scritti di Ardengo Soffici," *Archivio Italo-Russo* (Salerno) 2 (2002): 318–22.

Roman, Gail Harrison, and Marquardt, Virginia Hagelstein, eds. *The Avant-Garde Frontier: Russia Meets the West, 1910–1930.* Gainesville: University Press of Florida, 1992.

Romm, Alexander. *Matisse: A Social Critique,* translated by Jack Chen. New York: Lear, 1947.

Rougle, Charles. "National and International in Mayakovskij," in *Vladimir Mayakovskij: Memoirs and Essays,* edited by Bengt Jangfeldt and N.Å.Nilsson, pp. 184–96. Stockholm: Almqvist & Wiksell International, 1975.

Rusakov, Yurii. "Matisse in Russia in the Autumn of 1911," *Burlington Magazine* (May 1975): 284–91.

Russian Futurism Through Its Manifestos, 1912–1928, translated by Anna Lawton and Herbert Eagle, edited by Anna Lawton, with an introduction by Anna Lawton and an afterword by Herbert Eagle. Ithaca, N.Y.: Cornell University Press, 1988.

Russkii avangard 1910–1920-kh godov i problema ekspressionizma (The Russian Avant-Garde of the 1910–1920s and the Problem of Expressionism), edited by G. F. Kovalenko et al. Moscow: Nauka, 2003.

Russkii avangard 1910–1920-kh godov v evropeiskom kontekste (The Russian Avant-Garde of the 1910–1920s in the European Context), edited by G. F. Kovalenko. Moscow: Nauka, 2000.

Sarabianov, D[mitri]. V. *Russkaia zhivopis' XIX veka sredi evropeiskikh shkol* (Russian Nineteenth-Century Painting among the European Schools). Moscow: Sovetskii Khudozhnik, 1980.

———. "Noveishie techeniia v russkoi zhivopisi predrevoliutsionnogo desiatiletiia (Rossia i Zapad)" (Latest Trends in Russian Painting of the Prerevolutionary Decade [Russia and the West]), *Sovetskoe iskusstvoznanie '80* (Moscow) 1 (1981): 117–60.

———. *Russian Art: From Neoclassicism to the Avant-Garde, 1800–1917: Painting—Sculpture—Architecture.* New York: Abrams, 1990.

———. *Rossiia i zapad: Istoriko-khudozhestvennye sviazi XVIII–nachala XX v.* (Russia and the West: Historical and Artistic Relations from the Eighteenth to Early Twentieth Centuries). Moscow: Iskusstvo XXI Vek, 2003.

Semenova, Natalia. *Zhizn' i kollektsiia Sergeia Shchukina* (Sergei Shchukin's Life and Collection). Moscow: Trilistnik, 2002.

Sharp, Jane Ashton. *Russian Modernism between East and West: Natal'ia Goncharova and the Moscow Avant-Garde.* Cambridge: Cambridge University Press, 2006.

Sokolov, Ippolit. "The Charter of an Expressionist: A Baedecker to Expressionism," *Russian Literature Triquarterly* 13 (Fall 1975): 604–11.

Stasov, Vladimir. "The Poor in Spirit," *Experiment* 7 (August 2001).

Sternin, G. Iu. *Khudozhestvennaia zhizn' Rossii na rubezhe XIX–XX vekov* (Russian Artistic Life at the Turn of the Twentieth Century). Moscow: Iskusstvo, 1970.

———. *Khudozhestvennaia zhizn' Rossii 1900–1910-kh godov* (Russian Artistic Life, 1900–1920). Moscow: Iskusstvo, 1988.

Strigalev, A. "O poezdke Tatlina v Berlin i Parizh" (On Tatlin's Journey to Berlin and Paris), *Iskusstvo* 3 (August 1989).

Taylor, Brandon. "On AKhRR," in *Art of the Soviets: Painting, Sculpture and Architecture in a One-Party State, 1917–1932,* edited by Matthew Cullerne Bown and Brandon Taylor, pp. 51–72. Manchester: Manchester University Press, 1993.

Valkenier, Elizabeth Kridl. *Russian Realist Art: The State and Society: The Peredvizhniki and Their Tradition.* New York: Columbia University Press, 1989.

———. "Opening Up to Europe: The *Peredvizhniki* and the *Miriskusniki* Respond to the West," in *Russian Art and the West: A Century of Dialogue in Painting, Architecture, and the Decorative Arts,* edited by Rosalind P. Blakesley and Susane Reid, pp. 45–60. De Kalb: Northern Illinois University Press, 2006.

Werckmeister, Otto Karl. "The 'International' of Modern Art: From Moscow to Berlin, 1918–1922," in *Künstlerischer Austausch/Artistic Exchange,* edited by Thomas W. Gaehtgens, vol. 3, pp. 553–74. Berlin: Akademie Verlag, 1993.

Williams, Robert C. *Russian Art and American Money, 1900–1940.* Cambridge: Harvard University Press, 1980.

ILLUSTRATIONS

INDEX

Page numbers in italics refer to illustrations.

Text: 10.5/13.5 Adobe Garamond
Display: DIN
Compositor: Integrated Composition Systems
Printer/binder: Thomson-Shore